Literature *& Media* 11

Authors
Neil Andersen
James Barry

NELSON

THOMSON LEARNING

stralia • Canada • Mexico • Singapore • Spain • United Kingdom • United States

NELSON
THOMSON LEARNING

Literature & Media 11

Director of Publishing
David Steele

Publisher
Carol Stokes

Program Manager
Norma Kennedy

Project Manager
Isobel Stevenson

Project/Developmental Editor
David MacDonald

Editorial Assistant
Georgina Tresnak

Senior Managing Editor
Nicola Balfour

Senior Production Editor
Carol Martin

Copyeditors
Maraya Raduha
Glen Herbert

Proofreaders
Dawn Hunter
Rebecca Vogan

Production Manager
Renate McCloy

Production Coordinator
Julie Preston

Permissions Editor and Photo Researcher
Vicki Gould

Art Director
Angela Cluer

Interior Design
Suzanne Peden
Linda Neale

Cover Design
Peter Papayanakis

Composition
Silver Birch Graphics

Printer
Best Book

The publishers gratefully acknowledge the contributions of the following educators:

Contributing Writers
Bill Anderson, ON
Robert Bilan, MB
Sandy Brown, BC
Anne Carrier, ON
Mary Dunnigan, AB
Ian Mills, ON
Donna Nentwig, MB
Dave Normandale, MB

Reviewers
Nancy Alford, NS
Marnie Armstrong, AB
Lynn Ibsen, ON
Gerard Lavelle, ON
Carol Murray, BC
Jack Reid, NF
John Rogers, ON
Jon Terpening, BC

Equity Consultants
Rocky Landon
Zubeda Vahed

National Library of Canada Cataloguing in Publication Data

Main entry under title:
Literature & media 11

(Nelson English)

ISBN 0-17-619709-5 (bound).—
ISBN 0-17-619708-7 (pbk.)

1. Readers (Secondary)
I. Andersen, Neil, 1949- II. Barry, James, 1939- III. Title: Literature and media 11.

PE1121.L58 2001   428.6
C2001-930252-5

TABLE OF CONTENTS

Unit 4: Drama

About Drama: Scribe's Paradox, or The Mechanical Rabbit *Michael Feingold* .. 287

Drama

Unit 5: Media

About Media: Listening to Marshall McLuhan 335

Interviews and Speeches

Reviews

Visuals

Cyberspace

Media Issues

Fine Art and Media Images

People

Individual Identity

The Leaving 63, Alias Grace 131, Man, You're a Great Player! 176, Mother Tongue 188, Voices of the Grandmothers 195, For My Great-Grandmother 238, The Old Man's Lazy 242, Another Story Altogether 245, Hunger Striking 300

Family

The Leaving 63, Wandering 75, The Third Bank of the River 101, Thanks for Not Killing My Son 174, Mother Tongue 188, Voices of the Grandmothers 195, Better or Worse? 203, The Hoop 232, For My Great-Grandmother 238, Another Story Altogether 245, Roller Coaster 248, One Ocean 327, Flight of an Eagle 420, Zits 425

Childhood

Fairy Tales 3, The Dead Child 45, The Leaving 63, A Handful of Dates 96, My Old Newcastle 209, Another Story Altogether 245, One Ocean 327, Kids and TV Violence 405

Teenage Years

Reading, writing … and going to work 147, Teens' Top Homework Tool 151, Makonnen Hannah 154, Thanks for Not Killing My Son 174, Finding Their Own Groove 179, For My Great-Grandmother 238, Did I Miss Anything? 240, Roller Coaster 248, Hunger Striking 300, But I Love Him 354, Zits 425, Platinum Protection 427

Relationships

The Dead Child 45, A Bolt of White Cloth 51, The Leaving 63, A Handful of Dates 96, The Fog Horn 107, Another Story Altogether 245, Common Magic 246, The River-Merchant's Wife 256, On Monsieur's Departure 258, Let me not to the marriage 259, If You Were Coming in the Fall 263, My Song 268, Little Ruth 276, But I Love Him 354, Titanic: Cheers and Jeers 356, Couple on Bridge 416

Heroism

Communities

Outsiders

Places

Home

School

Workplace

Urban Life

Rural Life

Nature

Concepts

Crime and Punishment

Freedom

Rights and Responsibilities

Language

Persuasion and Manipulation

Design

Food

Events

Canadian History

World History

Adventure

Quest

Change

*A writer is, after all, only half the book. The other half is the
reader...*

—P.L. Travers

It was with both writers and readers in mind that the selections in
Literature and Media 11 were chosen. In this anthology, you'll find
writers from a variety of centuries, countries, cultures, and backgrounds, all writing with a distinctive voice about ideas, experiences,
and issues that led them to put pen to paper (or fingers to keyboard).
Specific pieces were chosen for their ability to move, amuse, instruct,
inform, or inspire readers of varying tastes and interests.

Along with texts in a variety of forms and genres, you'll find a full-
colour section of visuals divided into two parts: fine art images and
media images. These visuals illustrate how artists and designers, like
writers, use strategies and techniques to tell a story, accomplish a
purpose, or appeal to an audience.

The units on fiction, poetry, drama, and media begin with an introductory selection that will help you to start thinking about important
issues related to each genre.

Included with each selection are four activities that offer opportunities to consolidate your comprehension; formulate personal
responses; analyze style, structure, and technique; and extend the
meaning of the selection by researching related topics or creating
original work of your own.

The table of contents, organized by genre, is followed by a the-
matic index, which can help you to make links between selections, as
well as locate pieces that deal with topics and themes that interest
you. Biographies of authors and artists provide a context for selections, and often include other titles for further reading. A useful glossary of literary and media terms appears at the back of the book.

Language and Writing 11, the companion volume to this book, provides additional models of the forms and genres represented here,
along with an integrated language skills focus.

Reading is a lifelong journey of discovery. We hope your journey
through this book will be an enriching and enjoyable one.

Fiction

I write to complete the world,
to add an eighth day to creation.

—Antonine Maillet

When you reread a classic, you do not see more in the
book than you did before; you see more in you than there
was before.

—Clifton Fadiman

Fiction comes in many forms: novels, short stories, legends, even fairy tales. It can deal with the real world or with imagined worlds, with types of people we know well, or those we have never met. We read it for enjoyment and also because it can broaden our experience. Fiction expands the boundaries of our world. But fiction can also shine a spotlight into our own world and show us that we are not alone—other people have to deal with the same types of issues that we do. And seeing how they respond to these issues can help us to assess our own options.

Fairy tales and folk tales are among the earliest forms of fiction and were obviously told only to entertain children. Or were they? See what Isaac Asimov has to say on this subject before you plunge into reading the fiction in this unit. You may find that, as with fairy tales, there is a lot going on under the surface.

Fairy Tales

Isaac Asimov

What are "fairy tales"?

The easiest definition is, of course, that they are tales about fairies where a fairy is a kind of imaginary being possessing many supernatural powers.

We most commonly picture fairies, in these Disneyish degenerate times of ours, as being cute little beings with butterfly wings, whose chief amusement is nestling in flowers. That, however, is a foolish narrowing of the notion. Properly, fairies are *any* imaginary beings possessing many supernatural powers. Some are large and grotesque.

Therefore, stories dealing with witches, wizards, giants, ogres, jinn, afrits, baba-yagas, and many of the other creatures of legend may fairly be considered to be "fairy tales." Since the powers of such "fairies" include the granting of wishes, the casting of spells, the conversion of men into other creatures or vice versa, fairy tales are obviously a kind of fantasy, and some might even consider them one of the strands that went into the making of modern science fiction.

Because many fairy tales have unknown authors and were transmitted in oral form for many generations before they were written down by students of such things, and because, as a result, they lack polished literary form, they have been called "folktales." But then some of our most beloved fairy tales have been written by known authors in comparatively modern times (for instance, *Cinderella* and *The Ugly Duckling*), so I think we had better stick to "fairy tales."

Fairy tales have always been considered suitable reading for youngsters. Adults who have forgotten them, or who have never read them in the first place, seem to think of them as charming little stories full of sweetness and light. After all, don't they all end, "And they all lived happily ever after"? So we all say, "Oh, my, wouldn't it be great if our lives were just like a fairy tale?"

And we sing songs that include lines like, "Fairy tales can come true/It can happen to you ..."

That's all nonsense, of course, for, you see, not all "fairies" are benevolent. Some are mischievous, some are spiteful, and some are downright wicked, so that some of the fairy tales are rough going.

This all hit home once, about a quarter of a century ago, when I was even younger than I am now. At that time, I had two young children and I was wondering what I ought to do with them, so I attended some sort of parents/teachers meeting at the local school. At that meeting, a woman rose and said, "Is there some way we can keep children from reading the awful science fiction things they put out these days? They're so frightening. Why can't they read the delightful fairy tales that *we* read when we were young?"

Of course, I wasn't as well known in those days as I am now, so I'm sure she didn't mean it as a personal blow at me, but I reacted very promptly just the same, as you can well imagine.

I got up as though someone had shoved a long pin up through the seat of my chair and began to recite some of the plots of those delightful fairy tales.

How about *Snow White*. She's a nice little girl, whose mother had died and whose father has married a beautiful woman as a second wife. The new stepmother doesn't like Snow White, and the more good and beautiful the girl comes to be, the more her stepmother doesn't like her. So stepmother orders an underling to take Snow White into the woods and *kill* her and, just as a little added attraction, she orders him to cut out her heart (after she is dead, I hope, though the stepmother doesn't specify) and bring it back to her as evidence.

Talk about child abuse!

The wicked stepmother theme is a common one in fairy tales. Cinderella had one also, and two wicked stepsisters to boot, and she was mistreated by them all constantly—ill-fed, ill-dressed, ill-housed—and forced to watch those who abused her swimming in cream while she slaved away for them.

Sure both stories end happily, but how many children are scarred forever by these horribly sadistic passages? How many women, innocent and good, who marry a man with children and are prepared to love and care for those children, are met with undying suspicion and hostility by those children because of the delightful fairy tales they've read?

There are wicked uncles, too. *The Babes in the Wood* is a short, all-time favourite. They are driven into the woods by their wicked uncle and starve to death there. Of course, the robins cover them with leaves, if you want to consider *that* a happy ending.

Wicked uncles were so popularized by fairy tales that they are to be found in formal literature. They make excellent villains in Stevenson's *Kidnapped*, and in Dickens's *Nicholas Nickleby*. If you have read fairy tales and are young, I wonder if you don't view some perfectly pleasant uncle of yours with careful wariness.

Or how about *Little Red Riding Hood*, in which an innocent little girl *and* her grandmother are swallowed by a wolf. Permanently, too, because if you've ever watched a wolf eat a little girl, you know that she gets torn apart. So don't believe that bit about the hunters coming and cutting open the wolf, in order to allow the kid *and* her grandmother to jump out alive. That was made up afterward by people who had watched kids going into convulsions after reading that delightful fairy tale in its original form.

My favourite, though, is *Hansel and Gretel*. Here are two perfectly charming little children who have the misfortune to have a father who is a poor woodcutter. There happens to be a famine and they run out of food. What happens? The children's mother (*not* their stepmother, but their very own mother) suggests they be taken deep into the woods and left there. In that way, there will be two less mouths to feed. Fortunately, they found their way back, to the disappointment and chagrin of their mother. Consequently, when famine struck again, the mother was right on the ball with her insistence that a second attempt be made to get rid of those little pests. This time the device is successful.

Can you imagine how much confidence this instills in any child reading the story? Thereafter, he keeps a sharp eye on the refrigerator and the pantry to see if the food is running short, for he knows who's going to be taken out to the garbage dump and left there in case the family runs short.

But that's not the worst. In the forest, Hansel and Gretel come across a gingerbread house owned by a witch, who promptly imprisons Hansel and starts fattening him up for a feast, with him as main course. Cannibalism—just in case the kid reader didn't get enough kicks out of abandonment and starvation. Of course, it ends happily because the kids get away from the witch (killing her by burning her in an oven, of course) and come home to their loving father. Their mother (hurray, hurray) has died.

Can you imagine mothers wanting their children to read stuff like this, instead of good, wholesome science fiction? Why if we printed stories à la Grimm (grim indeed) in our magazine, we'd be harried out of town by hordes of indignant citizenry.

Think of that when next you feel moved to complain about the "violence" in some of our stories. Why, they're mother's milk compared to the stuff you expect your eight-year-olds to read.

Of course, fairy tales reflect the times in which they were told. Those were hard times. Poor woodcutters were *really* poor and there was no welfare roll they could get onto. Famines were *really* famines. What's more, mothers frequently died in childbirth, and fathers had to marry again to have someone take care of the youngster. Naturally, the new wife promptly had children of her own (or had them already by an earlier husband) and any woman would favour her own children over some stranger. And fathers did die young and leave their property to an infant child and appoint a brother the guardian of both child and property. Naturally, the brother, knowing that once the child grows up and takes over the property in his own right, he himself is out on his ear, is tempted to prevent that dire possibility from coming to pass.

Nowadays with children less likely to be orphaned before they have reached the age of self-care, those plots are passé and seem needlessly sadistic. They were realistic in their own times, however.

Nevertheless, if some of the problems of the past have been ameliorated, others have cropped up. Parents are less likely to die while their children are infants; but are more likely to get divorced.

If wicked uncles are passé, wicked landlords are not. If wolves don't roam the suburbs much anymore, drug pushers do.

Some define science fiction as "today's fairy tales." If so, you have to expect them to deal with the realistic dangers of today.

Isaac Asimov (*born 1920, Russia; died 1992, New York*), author, scientist, professor, moved to the United States with his family in 1923. Extremely prolific, he wrote over 400 books. Best known as an author of science fiction, Asimov also wrote many books on scientific subjects for a general audience. *The Foundation Trilogy* is his most famous science fiction.

Exploring Fiction

Evaluate Techniques: Work with a partner to identify examples of Asimov's use of the following techniques: variety in diction, ironic tone, first-person voice, exaggeration, allusions, anecdotal evidence. In a short personal response, indicate your reasons for enjoying any two of these techniques.

Identify Argument: Identify at least three important ideas about literature in general in this essay. For each, provide two specific pieces of supporting evidence from this selection and two from your other readings in this anthology or elsewhere.

Apply Information: Asimov states that fairy tales reflect the times in which they were told. How might modern fairy tales reflect our society? In a small group, compile a list of modern characters and situations that could be included in "today's fairy tales."

Reflect on Values: In a personal journal, explore your attitude to reading fiction. Consider questions such as: What do you like and not like to read? What value does reading have for you? For others? Share your writing in a small group and ask the other group members to recommend their favourite books.

A Television-Watching Artist

(with apologies to Franz Kafka)

J.J. Steinfeld

On the hundred-and-ninth day of sitting in the window of a Charlottetown department store, Patrick Warlin was nearing a state of total peacefulness. A Hindu mystic, sanctified by deprivation, could hardly have appeared more placid and otherworldly. Sitting under fluorescent lighting, as he watched for the ninth consecutive time a three-minute video replay of himself being interviewed by a local television reporter, Patrick was unaware that it would take an Act of God to shatter his serenity. After all, by the hundred-and-ninth day, Patrick believed that he could go on watching television in the department store window indefinitely.

Patrick was oblivious of the small afternoon crowd that had gathered to watch him watching television. He was concentrating on himself, mesmerized by his own image, his beard then only one week long. He had told the interviewer as she held the microphone near his face that the more he watched television, the less real he became. The expression on the interviewer's face indicated that she wasn't taking Patrick seriously. Those were the days when he still didn't mind speaking, and enjoyed the attention he was receiving. He was once one of the city's most unusual tourist attractions but now he was just part of the scenery. People still stopped and looked at Patrick but it was almost as if he were another mannequin in the window. At first he used to turn periodically from his TV set and gaze through the glass to see who was observing him, picking out friends and relatives, waving at tourists, smiling for the photograph takers. But he had lost interest in the viewers even before he had surpassed his original goal of thirty days. Soon he did not have any desire to stop watching television—ever.

Patrick had gotten the idea for his TV-watching marathon two weeks after he had lost his job. During a late-night party, three of his friends drunkenly attempted to come up with ways to get into the *Guinness Book of World Records*. Patrick was too depressed and preoccupied to offer any suggestions that night. He had worked at one job or another for all of the nine years since the day he turned sixteen, when he had quit high school. To his friends' disbelief, Patrick was upset by the prospect of receiving unemployment insurance. The day after the party, he once again found nothing for himself on the Employment Centre's job board, and struggled to think of something that would keep him occupied and earn some money too. Nothing frightened Patrick more than not having a job.

Then he noticed the department store window with the display of television sets. He had been saving money in order to replace his seven-year-old black-and-white set with a colour one, but losing his job forced him to abandon that plan. Now a window full of TV-watching mannequins seemed to mock his unemployment.

TV SPECTACULAR EXTRAVAGANZA MONTH ... DISCOUNTS
   GALORE ...
MANUFACTURER'S REBATES ... NOW IS THE TIME TO BUY ...
FROM 5 INCHES TO 4 FEET, WE HAVE THE PERFECT MODEL
   FOR YOU ...
WE DEFY ANYONE TO BEAT OUR PRICES ...

The idea struck Patrick like a revelation. He rushed home, and as his old TV blared, he began to compose a letter to the manager of the department store. He offered to attempt entry into the *Guinness Book of World Records* by sitting in a store window and watching TV. Publicity, he emphasized with thick underlining, could have a positive effect on sales during these difficult economic times. Three days later Patrick received a phone call from the department store manager and was asked to stop into the store to discuss his interesting suggestion.

The manager was impressed with Patrick's initiative and imagination. Even the owner, whom the manager had talked with earlier, thought that Patrick's proposal had possibilities.

"The retail business always needs fresh ideas," the manager said, and they settled on a modest thirty dollars a day remuneration and a bonus of any television set other than the model with a four-foot screen, if Patrick made it into the record book. At the time, neither man knew what the record was or if anyone had ever attempted such a feat, but as the manager said with a damp smile, "If Christopher Columbus had never set out, where would we be now?"

The guidelines were quickly worked out: Patrick would have a "home" set up in the ground-floor centre window of the store on Grafton Street, be provided with the finest twenty-six-inch colour television set, good food, and a comfortable reclining chair from the furniture department. Reasonable bathroom breaks were allowed. Patrick, awake or asleep, would be expected to sit in front of the operating television set and watch for a minimum of sixteen continuous hours each day. Cable TV and a video cassette recorder would be provided so that he could record his favourite programs and watch them again. Once he had completed a sixteen-hour viewing day, he could sleep or rest behind a screen that could be drawn around the reclining chair for privacy. An exercise bicycle would be stationed next to the chair so Patrick could maintain his health. Patrick wryly requested that the four mannequins remain in the window display with him, for company. The store would take care of publicity and advertising; all Patrick had to do was watch television.

"If this doesn't increase sales, nothing will," the manager claimed. They agreed to begin in two days. Patrick predicted he could last for a month but the manager said the owner would be satisfied with two weeks. "No need to go overboard," the manager said as he gave Patrick a robust handshake. There were only two weeks left in the TV promotional month, a month that so far was not going well at all.

The first day in the window Patrick felt awkward and uneasy. Although he was friendly and outgoing, he wasn't an exhibitionist by nature. He changed channels frequently with his remote control channel changer and ate nervously. On the second day a TV crew from a local station gave him his first media coverage. The next day the local newspapers ran photographs of him. An AM radio station picked up the story of the TV Watcher on the fifth day and began to issue periodic progress reports. Before the first week was over Patrick felt comfortable, as if he belonged in the department store window watching television.

By the start of the second week a marked upturn in TV set sales was noticed. Other stores in the mall that housed the department store were eager to capitalize on the publicity. Merchants donated a variety of items—from monogrammed pillows to a specially designed pendant—to the determined TV Watcher. The department store set up a rack with a lavish assortment of the latest men's fashions for Patrick to model during his stay in the window, but he insisted on wearing his favourite outfit—patched jeans and an oversized Boston Bruins sweatshirt—day after day. Patrick told the manager to let the mannequins wear the fancy stuff; they were the clothes-conscious ones. Signs, of course, were placed in the window, giving full credit to the generous donors. Employees of the fast-food outlets on the second floor of the mall took turns bringing food down to Patrick, no limit on what and how much he could eat. One civic-minded businessman offered to donate one dollar to charity for each hour that Patrick stayed in the window and challenged the other store owners in the mall to match his pledge. Within a day nearly every store in the mall plus several nearby ones had promised to donate one dollar to charity for each hour of Patrick's unusual enterprise. Before he knew it, Patrick was raising thirty-eight dollars an hour for worthy causes. His publicity increased. Local church leaders commended his effort to help the less fortunate. City fathers wandered by the window and had their photographs taken with the twenty-five-year-old who wasn't allowing the bleak unemployment situation to get the best of him. No one really believed that Patrick would stay in the window longer than two or three weeks.

Yet Patrick watched and watched TV. He watched with the obsession of a man determined to sail solitarily across an ocean, damn the threatening weather and the dreamless critics. On the twenty-fourth day he even made the national CBC news broadcast. The reporter, doing her story from inside the window, asked the TV Watcher at the end of the segment, "What if the great thinkers of history had been forced to watch TV all the time?"

To the multitude of Canadians watching the national news Patrick answered: "I guess other people would have had to become the great thinkers."

The story on Patrick the TV Watcher and fundraiser provided welcome relief from the gloomy economic stories and the usual barrage of worldwide crises. It was near the end of the tourist season and a visit to the Island wasn't complete without seeing *Anne of Green Gables* at the Confederation Centre *and* Patrick Warlin watching TV in the department store window. No one knew how many photographs were taken of him, but the tourists certainly found him as worthy as the dazzling Island landscapes. For the first two weeks Patrick posed obligingly; later he paid no attention and kept his back to the window. Being a celebrity ceased to have an effect on him. As far as he was concerned, he had a job to do and was determined to do it better than anyone could, no matter what.

On the day marking the completion of one month in the window for Patrick, the manager paid his regular daily visit and related the sales figures for the last thirty days. They had outstripped the manager's most optimistic expectations. Two weeks earlier, the manufacturer of the brand featured in the promotional sale had sent a representative to the department store to announce that the sale would be extended for as long as Patrick could hold out.

But Patrick's sales-stimulating magic proved to be finite. On the forty-fifth day the manager, realizing that sales figures had levelled off and were beginning to decrease, suggested to Patrick that he could end his sitting. Surely he was now eligible for enshrinement in the *Guinness Book of World Records*, not to mention the hearts of Islanders and Tourism Department officials. "We could try it again next year," the manager said, standing behind a mannequin and patting it enthusiastically on the back.

"I'd like to go a little longer," Patrick said as he stared at the TV screen, not the manager. The manager offered Patrick a real job as a salesman in the home entertainment department if he was ready to finish his TV-watching.

By the end of the second month TV sales were lower than before the publicity stunt had started and the manager was more insistent that Patrick give up his obsession. The manager wanted to use the strategically located centre window for another display. "Merchandising should be fluid, never allowed to become static or stale," he lectured Patrick. When Patrick refused to respond, the manager argued with an unexpected burst of vehemence that the novelty of the promotional gimmick had completely worn off. "Let's not beat a dead horse," he added in a more reasonable tone. Patrick brought to the manager's attention the blackboard in the window exhibiting the running charity pledge total, then at $57,720. Did the manager want to be responsible for ending that?

A handful of the less prosperous merchants in the mall were getting nervous. One store owner visited Patrick and joked about the financial consequences to his business if the TV-watching went on forever. Patrick merely smiled and claimed that three years would be a more realistic goal—*nothing lasts forever*.

The worried store owner removed a small calculator from his pocket and punched the buttons. "There are exactly 8760 hours in a year," the man said uneasily.

"That's good to know," Patrick responded, as if just informed of a bland weather forecast. Then Patrick instructed him to multiply 8760 hours times thirty-eight dollars times three years....

On the seventieth day the owner of the department store, through the manager, *ordered* Patrick to stop watching television. Patrick refused. "You going to remove me bodily?" Patrick challenged as he watched an entertaining children's program. "Wouldn't that provide excellent publicity for the store," Patrick said with the precise timing of an accomplished television comedian. "We're over $63,000 already—and that's just the beginning." Without a trace of enthusiasm in his voice, Patrick stated that he had calculated that at thirty-eight dollars an hour he could raise a million dollars in a little over three years.

By the seventy-sixth day Patrick had earned $2280 for himself. The manager, acting on the owner's instructions, offered the stubborn TV Watcher another $500 to stop. On the seventy-ninth day the owner raised this to a $750 bonus plus a video cassette recorder of his own, but Patrick said no. It would take force—and perhaps violence—to remove him from the window, he explained.

"I could get a court order removing you," the manager threatened, unable to contain his frustration. Patrick responded without irritation that if the manager got a court order, the department store's name would replace Scrooge's as a synonym for coldheartedness and miserliness.

On the eighty-first day a journalist from Nova Scotia arrived on the Island especially to interview Patrick for an in-depth magazine story. The journalist had already decided to call the story, "What

Makes Patrick Watch?" Patrick had no desire to talk to him. He only wanted to watch TV. The required sixteen hours a day had on Patrick's initiative become seventeen then eighteen then nineteen hours by the end of the first month. It wasn't unusual for Patrick to watch TV for twenty hours or more a day, viewing video replays of his favourite programs when there was nothing interesting to watch. There were a few days when he watched TV for twenty-four hours straight and his record for continuous TV-watching, except for bathroom breaks, stood at forty-three hours.

When the journalist from Nova Scotia commented that Patrick's TV-watching was a form of captivity, a voluntary imprisonment at best, Patrick reacted calmly and said softly, "I feel unbounded, unlimited.... I really feel free in front of this TV.... I can tape a war scene or a love scene or myself on the local news.... I can stop a scene or turn the most powerful world leaders off.... With the video recorder I can keep the Beatles together or Elvis Presley alive forever.... TV allows me to be in command...." Then he refused to answer any more questions.

On the eighty-seventh day, while Patrick was on one of his bathroom breaks (which seemed to be less and less frequent as the days passed), two men entered the window and began to dismantle his TV viewing room. The manager was eager to do a feature display on winter wear before the Island's first snowfall. Patrick arrived back as the two men were starting to lift the sturdy twenty-six-inch set out of the window. Patrick grabbed one of the men, and the other let go of the television set in order to help his startled accomplice. The TV banged to the floor with a thud. An infuriated Patrick, weak from sitting and watching TV for nearly three months, managed to push the intruders out of his home. One of the men attempted to reenter the window display, but Patrick punched him in the stomach with a strength he was astonished to discover he still had. Patrick warned the men that if they came back he would kill them. He hurriedly hooked up the set and resumed watching television.

As the third month ended, weekly TV sales were down to their lowest level in twelve years. Patrick was more content than he could ever remember being. The manager threatened to stop Patrick's food supply and Patrick muttered that an emaciated corpse in the window would be a marvellous testimonial to free enterprise. The truth was that Patrick ate very little anymore. He could live on French fries and blueberry muffins, he believed. If only he had bathroom facilities in the window, then he wouldn't have to leave his TV at all.

When the manager told Patrick he was going to send the documentary material he had been accumulating to the Guinness organization for verification, the TV Watcher was indifferent and uncooperative. Without documentation and verification, the manager complained, the Guinness people would never enter Patrick into the record book. Patrick said that he couldn't care less about the *Guinness Book of World Records*.

Each day the manager continued to beg, plead, bribe, and threaten, but Patrick refused to leave the window or even to discuss the matter with him.

"Don't you know that fluorescent lighting is bad for you?" the manager said, pointing to the rows of overhead lights. "And watching too much colour TV from as close as you sit will do who knows what to your insides," he added with conviction.

Patrick merely grunted in reply. Now he rarely spoke and slept no more than three or four hours a night. He no longer used his exercise bicycle and started to feel lightheaded if he stood too long. Even the French fries and blueberry muffins seemed excessive. He ate only so he would have the strength to watch TV. Untroubled, relaxed, and with a firm sense of purpose, Patrick Warlin was genuinely happy.

On the ninety-sixth day, as he was watching the midnight movie, a rock was hurled through the window, but Patrick was unhurt. He endured a chill draft that night—the first fresh air he had breathed in ninety-six days—and the next morning the broken window was replaced. Two days later a beer bottle was thrown through the window, again at midnight, and Patrick cut himself when he picked up a piece of glass that had fallen near his chair. He bled heavily before he bothered to take a tie from the clothes rack near the TV and wrap it around the deep cut. When the manager arrived in the morning the floor was covered with dried blood, yet Patrick was watching TV unperturbed. The manager insisted that Patrick go to the hospital.

"Bring a doctor here," Patrick replied.

"You're insane, you're insane," the manager screamed at the TV Watcher.

"Perhaps," Patrick whispered. A store staff member with first-aid knowledge was brought to the display window and attended to Patrick's wound as he continued to watch a morning exercise program.

On the hundred-and-ninth day, during the first major snowstorm of the season, there was an Island-wide power blackout. In the downtown area, where the department store was located, the power wasn't restored for an hour and forty-five minutes. Flashlights in hand, the manager and the store's lawyer rushed in and informed Patrick that the terms of the agreement with the department store had been violated: he had failed to watch television continuously during store hours. Patrick was too weak to fight as two men carted off the television set and three more store employees stood guard to make sure the TV Watcher didn't go berserk. Patrick gripped his remote control channel changer and pressed futilely as the manager said, "Thank God it's over, thank God...."

Patrick stood up, feeling faint and dizzy, took a parka off a nearby mannequin, and slowly walked out of the department store. As he stumbled toward his apartment building a few blocks from the store, the lights came back on, as if to salute the conquering hero. Once in his apartment, Patrick's first action was to turn on his old black-and-white television set. Later, when the night's local news came on, the newscaster announced, "It took an Act of God to stop Patrick Warlin, but earlier today the twenty-five-year-old Charlottetown man ended his one-hundred-and-nine-day TV-watching marathon after raising nearly $100,000 for Island charities...." Patrick sat still in front of his television set, fighting not to lose consciousness, intent on continuing his television-watching.

J.J. Steinfeld (*born 1946*) lives in Charlottetown, Prince Edward Island, the setting for many of his stories. His work has appeared in a variety of Canadian literary magazines and anthologies. He has published several books, including a novel and eight collections of short stories.

Activities: A Television-Watching Artist

1. ***Analyze Character:*** Choose one of Patrick's character traits that remains the same from the beginning and one that changes. Support your choices with references to the text. Explain any links between the traits you identify and Patrick's refusal to stop watching TV.

2. ***Look for Clues:*** Did you accurately predict the ending? If yes, identify which clues let you know what was going to happen. If no, explain what you thought was going to happen, and what made you think so.

3. ***Identify Theme:*** What is Steinfeld's message in this story? Is it about TV, or young people today, or modern society at large? Discuss ideas in a small group, list two possible themes, and compare them with another group's.

4. ***Write a Report:*** Write a newspaper report about Patrick that might have appeared the day after the blackout. Find and study models for appropriate structure and style. Ask a classmate to edit your report, and post it in the classroom.

A Matter of Balance

W.D. Valgardson

He was sitting on a cedar log, resting, absentmindedly plucking pieces from its thick layer of moss, when he first saw them. They were standing on the narrow bridge above the waterfall. When they realized he had noticed them, they laughed, looked at each other, then turned their backs. In a moment, the short, dark-haired one turned around to stare at him again. His companion flicked a cigarette into the creek.

Bikers, he thought with a mixture of contempt and fear. He had seen others like them, often a dozen at a time, muscling their way along the road. These two had their hair chopped off just above the shoulders and, from where he sat, it looked greasy for it hung in tangled strands. They both had strips of red cloth tied around their heads. The dark-haired boy, he thought, then corrected himself, man, not boy, for he had to be in his middle twenties, was so short and stocky that he might have been formed from an old-fashioned beer keg. They both wore black leather vests, jeans, and heavy boots.

He was sorry that they were there but he considered their presence only a momentary annoyance. They had probably parked their bikes at the pull-off below the waterfall, walked up for god knows what reason—he could not imagine them being interested in the scenery—and would shortly leave again. He would be happy to see them go. He was still only able to work part time and had carefully arranged his schedule so that his Wednesdays were free. He didn't want anything to interfere with the one day he had completely to himself.

The tall blond man turned, leaned against the railing, and stared up at Harold. He jabbed his companion with his elbow and laughed. Then he raised his right hand, pointed two fingers like he would a pistol, and pretended to shoot.

The action, childish as it was, unsettled Harold and he felt his stomach knot with anxiety. He wished that he had been on the other side of the bridge and could simply have picked up his pack and walked back to his station wagon. The only way across the river, however, was the bridge and he had no desire to try to force his way past them. They reminded him of kids from his public school days who used to block the sidewalk, daring anyone to try to get by. He had been in grade two at the time and had not yet learned about fear. When he had attempted to ignore them and go around, they had shifted with him to the boulevard, then to the road and, finally, to the back lane. As his mother was washing off his scrapes and bruises and trying to get blood off his shirt, he had kept asking her why, why did they do it? Beyond saying that they were bad boys and that she would speak to the principal, she had no answers. Only later, when he was much older, had he understood that their anger was not personal and, so, could not be reasoned with.

Every Wednesday for the last six months, he had hiked to the end of this trail and then used his rope to lower himself to the river bank. Before the winter rains began and flooded the gorge, he wanted to do as much sniping as possible. The previous week, he had discovered a crack in the bedrock that looked promising but, before he had a chance to get out all the gravel, the day had started to fade and he had been forced to leave. The gorge was no place to spend the night. Even at noon, the light was filtered to a pale grey. He dressed warmly, wearing a cotton shirt, then a wool shirt and, finally, a wool jack-shirt; yet, within a few hours he was always shaking with cold. As strenuous as the panning was, it could not keep out the chill. The air was so damp that when he took a handful of rotting cedar and squeezed it, red water ran like blood between his fingers. On the tree trunks, hundreds of mushrooms grew. At first, because of their small size and dark grey colour, he thought they were slugs, but then he pried one loose with his fingernail and discovered its bright yellow gills.

Although he had been nowhere near the bottom of the crack, he had found a few flakes of gold which he meticulously picked out of his pan with tweezers. Panning in the provincial parks was illegal so he always went right to the end of the path, then worked his way along the river for another hundred yards. Recently, he had started taking as much as half-an-ounce of dust and small nuggets out of the river in a day and he wondered if someone had found out, but he immediately dismissed the idea. Only Conklin knew. When they met each Thursday he always showed Conklin his latest find. As far as his friends and colleagues were aware, he spent his days off hiking, getting himself back into shape after having been ill for over a year.

As he studied the two men below, he told himself he was letting his imagination run away with him again and to get it under control. There was no good in borrowing trouble. He stood up, swung his pack onto his shoulders and, being careful not to look like he was running away, resumed his hike.

From this point on, the trail was a series of switchbacks. If the two on the bridge were planning on following him and stealing his equipment or wallet, they would probably give up after a short distance and wait for easier prey. Unless they were in good condition, the steep climb would leave them gasping for breath.

Large cedars pressed close to the path, blocking out the light. Old man's beard hung from the branches. The ground was a tangle of sword fern, salal, and Oregon grape. In a bit of open space, an arbutus twisted toward the sun. Its bark, deep earth-red, hung in shreds. Here and there, the new pale green bark was visible. That was the way he felt, like a snake or an arbutus, shedding his old skin for a new, better one. The previous year, when nothing else had seemed to work, he had taken his pack and hiked from sunrise to sunset, exhausting himself so completely that he could not stay awake. The sniping, looking for gold in cracks, under rocks, among the roots of trees, had come when he had started to feel better.

At the next bend he stopped and hid behind a rotting stump. In a couple of minutes his pursuers—he told himself not to be foolish, not to be paranoid—appeared. They were walking surprisingly fast. If the trail had been even slightly less steep, they would have been running.

He wished there were a cutoff that would allow him to circle back. He could, he realized, use his equipment, if necessary, to lower himself to the river but to do so, he would need to gain enough of a lead to have time to untie and uncoil the rope, to set it around a tree, to climb down, and then to pull his rope down after him so that it could not be taken away or cut. He then would be faced with the problem of finding a route up. He had to be back by seven. It was the agreed upon time. Since their mother had been killed, the children became upset if he were even a few minutes late.

He looked at his watch. It was ten o'clock. It was a two-hour hike to the end of the trail, but he could hike out in an hour and a half. That did not leave him much time. First, he wanted to clean out the crack and, if possible, begin undercutting a large rock that sat in the centre of the river. Undercutting was dangerous. It would require that he move rocks and logs to divert the shallow water to either side of where he was going to work. Then he would need more logs to prop up the rock. He didn't want to get the work partly done and have half a ton of stone roll onto him. The nuggets that might be clustered around the base were worth some risk but there was no sense in taking more chances than necessary.

Ahead, through a gap in the trees, he saw the railway trestle. The two behind him would, he told himself, stop there. Hardly anyone went further. The trestle was an inexplicable focal point. Every weekend dozens of people hiked to it, then dared each other to cross over the gorge. Many, terrified of heights, balked after the first few steps and stood, rigid, unable to force themselves to go any further.

That, he reassured himself, was what those two were coming for. They would cross the trestle and scare each other by roughhousing like a couple of adolescents.

He had hoped, unreasonably, that there would be hikers or a railway crew on the tracks. Normally, it was a relief when there was no one there. Hikers were inclined to talk about their experiences and, in the past, he had been afraid that if he were frequently seen on the same trail his weekly visits might come to the attention of a park warden. To avoid that, he had deliberately arranged to come when the park was empty.

He did not stop but crossed over the tracks and entered the forest on the far side. The path dwindled to a narrow line of crushed ferns. The trees were shagged with wind-blown moss and deadfall was everywhere. It was old forest and, in all the times he had come, he had never seen a bird or animal. As a child he had dreamed of living in the forest. In his dreams, his hunting had always been rewarded with game. The discrepancy between what he had hoped for and reality still astounded him.

While he was able to see the railway tracks he stopped and waited. His legs had begun to tire and cramp. He stretched them, then kneaded his right calf with his thumb and forefinger. Always before he had valued the silence and the isolation. Now, however, as he watched the two bikers look up and down the roadbed then cross to the path, Harold felt the forest close around him like a trap.

He hurried away. Even as he fled he reassured himself that they had done nothing. Anyone was free to hike wherever he wanted. If he just stopped, they would catch up and pass him by without paying any attention to him.

He kept his eyes on the path. He had no intention of tripping over a vine or slipping on a log. His fear, he chided himself, was not rational. If a mountie suddenly appeared and asked him what was the matter, what could he say? That he hadn't liked the way they had looked at him earlier? That they had threatened him? And how was that, sir? He could hear the question. And the answer? The blond one pointed his finger at me. Any mountie would think him mad.

The moss was so thick that his feet made no sound. There was only the creak of his pack, the harsh sound of his breathing. He would, he decided, abandon his plans, and when he got to the end of the granite ridge that ran along on his left, he would double back through the narrow pass on its far side. People don't assault other people without good reason, he told himself, but it did no good. His panic fluttered like dry leaves in a rising wind.

He wished that he had brought a hunting knife. It would have made him feel better to have had a weapon. His mind scurried over the contents of the pack as he tried to determine what he could use in a fight. The only possibility was his rack of chock nuts. It wasn't much. A dozen aluminum wedges, even clipped together on a nylon sling, would not be very effective.

As he came to the end of the ridge he turned abruptly to the left. The pass was nearly level and, unlike the area around it, contained only a few, scattered trees. There were, he remembered, circles of stone where people had made campfires. One day he had poked about and discovered some plastic sandwich bags and four or five beer bottles. A broken beer bottle, he thought, would serve as a weapon. He was just beginning to search for one when he saw a movement at the far end of the pass.

He became absolutely still. He felt so weak that he thought he was going to fall down. He craned his neck for a better look. If there were two of them, he could circle back the other way. In a moment, he realized that there was only one. That meant the other was on the path he had just left. He spun on his heel and ran back to the fork. No more than a quarter of a mile away the path ended. At that point, there was nothing to do but return the way he had come or descend to the river. In either case, he was trapped. His mouth, he realized, was so dry he could not swallow.

Behind him, he heard someone ask a question that sounded like "Where did he go?" and a muffled reply but he could not be sure of the words. The ground was nearly level. He was running when he burst out onto an area where the rock fell from the side of the trail like a frozen set of rapids. There were few places here for trees to root. Leaves and pine needles were swept from the pale green lichen by the winter rains. Rather than continue to what he knew was a dead end, he clambered down the slope. He had not explored this area. In the back of his mind was the hope that the rough rock continued all the way to the river. By the time they found out he was no longer on the path, he could have climbed the other cliff. All at once, he stopped. The rough, black rock turned into sixty feet of smooth slab.

There was no time to go back. He glanced over his shoulder, then at the slab. It was, he realized, deceptive. It angled down toward the river then stopped at a ragged edge. No steeper than a roof at the outset, it curved just enough that every few feet the angle increased. Patches of lichen and the smooth texture of the stone guaranteed that anyone who ventured out on it would be engaged in a test of balance.

There was a chance, because of his friction boots, that he could work his way onto the steepest part of the slope. If the two behind him were not pursuing him, they would pass by and he would never see them again. If they were, for whatever reason, meaning him some harm, they would have great difficulty reaching him.

Quickly, he unzipped the right-hand pocket of his pack and pulled out a section of three-millimetre rope. He tied a figure eight knot in both ends, wrapped the rope around his left hand, then crept down to a small evergreen. Ten feet to the right, in a completely exposed area, there was a gnarled bush. Here and there, stunted trees, their trunks nearly as hard as the rock itself, protruded from cracks.

There was little room for error. If he began to slide, it would be difficult to stop before he went over the edge. At this part of the river, the fall would not be great, but height would not make any difference. Even a twenty-foot fall onto the scattered boulders of the river bed would certainly be fatal. He leaned out, brushed away some dust that had collected on the rock, then took his first step.

Above him someone whistled sharply. It startled him but he kept his eyes fixed on the surface of the rock. He fitted the toe of his boot onto a small nubbin, then his other toe onto a seam of cracked quartz. The greatest danger was that, for even a split second, he would allow himself to be distracted. For his next move, he chose a pebbled area no bigger than a silver dollar. From there, he moved to a depression that was only noticeable because of its slight shadow. He had crossed more difficult areas than this but always with the security of a harness and rope and a belayer he could trust. A fall in those circumstances meant no more than some scraped skin and injured pride.

When he was within two feet of the bush he felt a nearly overwhelming urge to lunge forward. He forced himself to stay where he was. On the rock there could be no impetuous moves.

Patience, above all else, was to be valued. There seemed to be no place for him to put his foot. He scanned the surface. Just below him there was a hairline crack. If he pressed down hard on it, it would hold him long enough for him to step to the side and up and catch hold of the bush.

Slowly, he pirouetted on his left foot, then brought his right foot behind it. He took a deep breath, forced the air out of his lungs, then in one fluid movement, stepped down, up and across. Even as his hand grasped the wooden stem, he felt his feet begin to slide.

While he unwrapped the three-millimetre rope from his arm, he sat with his legs on either side of the stem. He fitted a loop of rope around an exposed root, then slipped the second loop around his wrist. Unless the root gave way, the most he was going to fall was a couple of feet.

Only then did he allow himself to look back. There was still no sign of anyone. The area of tumbled rock ran on for a fair distance and, he realized, would take awhile to search. Realizing this, he cursed himself for not taking a chance and running back the way he had come.

He hooked his pack to the bush, took out the sling with the hardware on it, then eased himself out onto the steepest section of slab he could reach. Here he crouched, with his back to the trail, his hands splayed against the rock.

There was a sharp whistle above him. It was immediately answered from some distance back toward the trestle. With that, he realized that they had split up. One had blocked the trail while the other had done the searching.

He looked back again. Thirty feet behind him was the dark-haired biker. His blond companion was swinging down from the left. Both of them, Harold could see, were tired. He had, he thought with a distant kind of pleasure, given them a good run for their money. If they had been carrying packs, he would have outdistanced them.

They both stopped at the rough edge, some ten feet apart, looked at each other and smirked.

"Did you want something?" he asked. He had meant to make it a casual question, even offhand, as though he had no idea they had followed him, but panic sharpened his voice.

They both laughed as if at a joke.

"What do you want?" He was no longer sure that what he had planned would work. The blond-haired man had a small leather purse attached to his belt. He unsnapped it and took out a bone-handled clasp knife. He pried out a wide blade.

"Are you crazy?" Harold cried. "What's the matter with you? I don't even know you."

They both grinned foolishly and studied their boots. They looked, he thought wildly, like two little boys caught in the middle of a practical joke.

Panic made him feel like he was going to throw up. "Are you nuts?" he shouted. "Are you crazy or something?"

Their answer was to start down the slab, one on each side of him. Their first steps were confident, easy. The surface of the rock was granular and bare at the edge and provided plenty of friction. He could see that neither was experienced. They both came down sideways, leaning into the rock, one hand pressed to the surface. He gripped the nylon sling in his right hand and concentrated on keeping his balance.

The dark-haired one was closest. He was coming down between the tree and the shrub, taking little steps, moving his left foot down, then his right foot, then his left, dangerously pressing all his weight onto the edge of his boot and, even more dangerously, leaning backwards, throwing off his centre of balance. Suddenly, a piece of lichen peeled away and his left foot slid out from under him. Instead of responding by bending out from the rock and pressing down with his toes, he panicked. He was sliding faster and faster. His body was rigid, his face contorted with fear, his eyes, instead of searching for a place he could stop his slide, were desperately fixed on the safe area he had just left behind. He made no sound. When he was finally even with Harold, he reached out his hand as though expecting it to be taken. There was, Harold saw, on the back of the hand, a tattoo of a heart pierced by a knife. A red and blue snake wound up the arm and disappeared beneath the sleeve. It was only by luck that his one foot struck a piece of root and he stopped. He was no more than a foot from the edge.

The blond man had come at an angle, picking his way along by fitting his knife blade into a crack. Just before his companion had lost control, the blond man had started to work his way across an area where there were no cracks. He seemed frozen into place.

"Why?" Harold shouted at him.

The sound seemed to wake the blond man from a stupor. He turned his head slowly to look at Harold. He squinted and formed his mouth into a small circle, then drew his chin down and ran his tongue along his lower lip. For a moment, Harold thought the biker was going to turn and leave.

"Get me out of here," his companion cried. Fear made his voice seem as young as a child's.

The blond man shook his head, then half-snarled, stood up, and tried to walk across the intervening space. It was as though momentum and will held him upright; then Harold swung the nylon sling over his head, lunged forward, and struck his opponent on the upper arm. The blow was not powerful and, normally, it would have been swept aside. But here, as they both teetered on the steep surface, it was enough to knock them both off balance.

As the blond man skidded down the rock, he jabbed at it with his knife, trying to find an opening. Six feet from the edge, he managed to drive the blade into a crack. The knife held. He jammed the tips of his fingers into the crack.

Harold had slipped, fallen, then been caught by the rope around his wrist. He pulled himself back to the shrub and knelt with his knee against the stem.

"Help us up," the dark-haired man begged. He looked like he was on the verge of weeping.

Harold loosened the rope, then untied it. Carefully, giving his entire attention to the task, he retraced his original route. Once at the evergreen, he knew he was safe. His sides were soaked with sweat and he could smell his own fear, bitter as stale tobacco. The two men never stopped watching him.

When Harold reached the top of the slab, the blond man called, in a plaintive voice, "For God's sake, don't leave us here."

Fear had softened their eyes and mouths but he knew it was only temporary. If he drew them to safety, they would return to what they had been.

"Pull us up," the dark-haired man whined. His red headband had come off and was tangled in his hair.

Around them, the forest was silent. Not a bird called, not an animal moved. The moss that covered the rock and soil, the moss that clung thickly to the tree trunks, the moss that hung in long strands from the branches, deadened everything, muted it, until there were no sharp lines, no certainties. The silence pressed upon them. Harold had, for a moment, a mad image of all three of them staying exactly as they were, growing slowly covered in moss and small ferns until they were indistinguishable from the logs and rocks except for their glittering eyes.

"Tell somebody about us," the dark-haired man asked.

The words tugged at him like little black hooks. He looked down. Their faces were bleached white with fear. He could tell someone, a park warden, perhaps, but then what would happen? If he had been certain they would be sent to prison he might have dared tell somebody, but he knew that would not happen. If charges were laid he would have to testify. They would discover his name and address. And, from then on, he would live in fear. Afraid to leave his house. Afraid to go to sleep at night. Afraid for his children. And what if they denied everything, turned it all around? He had the necessary equipment to rescue them and had refused. What if one of them had fallen by the time someone came? He could be charged with manslaughter and the children would be left without mother or father. No matter how he tried to keep Conklin out of it, he would become involved. Harold knew how people thought. His short stay in hospital for depression, his weekly visits to a psychiatrist to siphon off pain and, automatically, he was crazy.

"You bastard," the blond one screamed. "You bastard. Get us out of here." He kept shifting his feet about, trying to find a purchase where there was none. "If you don't, our friends will come. They'll get us out. Then we'll start looking for you. There's thousands of us. We'll find you."

The screaming startled him for a moment but then he thought about how soon the little warmth from the sun would disappear, of how the fog would drift down with the darkness, of how the cold would creep into everything, of how few people came this way.

"No," he said. He wondered if his wife had screamed like that. Six of her fingernails had been broken. *Unto the third generation*, Conklin had said. His children and his grandchildren, should he have any, would feel the effects. Alone on a dark parking lot, desperately fighting for her life, and he had been sitting in his study, reading. "Help never comes when it is most needed."

Then with real regret for the way things were but which couldn't be changed, he hefted his pack so that it settled firmly between his shoulders and returned the way he had come.

W.D. Valgardson (*born 1939, Winnipeg, Manitoba*), author, editor, grew up in Gimli, Manitoba. He has written stories, novels, and radio dramas. A teacher of creative writing at the University of Victoria, Valgardson has received many awards for his writing, including the Ethel Wilson Award for Fiction. He writes for both children and adults. It has been said that his "sparse and rigorously concrete style mirrors both the cold, brittle landscape in which the stories are set and the harsh fates that befall most of the central characters."

Activities: A Matter of Balance

1. **Map the Story:** Make a map or diagram of the setting of the story. Label the important places and, in point form, describe the events that occur at each. Display your visual in the classroom.

2. **Identify Skills:** What skills and attributes enable Harold to function as he does? Discuss with a partner, making specific references to the text. Then write your own detailed character sketch of Harold, using material from your discussion.

3. **Reflect on the Title:** In a small group, discuss how the title is related to the story. Consider other possible titles. Choose the group's two best titles and explain to the class why they are appropriate.

4. **Write Your Own Ending:** The author does not bring the events of the story to a final conclusion. Write your own continuation of the narrative. Share your version in a group and comment on each other's completions in terms of style, content, interest, and fidelity to the tone of the original.

The Wedding Gift

Thomas Raddall

Nova Scotia, in 1794. Winter. Snow on the ground. Two feet of it in the woods, less by the shore, except in drifts against Port Marriott's barns and fences; but enough to set sleigh bells ringing through the town, enough to require a multitude of paths and burrows from doors to streets, to carpet the wharves and the decks of the shipping, and to trim the ships' yards with tippets of ermine. Enough to require fires roaring in the town's chimneys, and blue wood smoke hanging low over the roof tops in the still December air. Enough to squeal underfoot in the trodden places and to muffle the step everywhere else. Enough for the hunters, whose snowshoes now could overtake the floundering moose and caribou. Even enough for the always-complaining loggers, whose ox sleds now could haul their cut from every part of the woods. But not enough, not nearly enough snow for Miss Kezia Barnes, who was going to Bristol Creek to marry Mr. Hathaway.

Kezia did not want to marry Mr. Hathaway. Indeed she had told Mr. and Mrs. Barclay in a tearful voice that she didn't want to marry anybody. But Mr. Barclay had taken snuff and said "Ha! Humph!" in the severe tone he used when he was displeased; and Mrs. Barclay had sniffed and said it was a very good match for her, and revolved the cold blue eyes in her fat moon face, and said Kezia must not be a little fool.

There were two ways of going to Bristol Creek. One was by sea, in one of the fishing sloops. But the preacher objected to that. He was a pallid young man lately sent out from England by Lady Huntingdon's Connexion, and seasick five weeks on the way. He held Mr. Barclay in some awe, for Mr. Barclay had the best pew in the meetinghouse and was the chief pillar of godliness in Port Marriott. But young Mr. Mears was firm on this point. He would go by road, he said, or not at all. Mr. Barclay had retorted "Ha! Humph!" The road was twenty miles of horse path through the woods, now deep in snow. Also the path began at Harper's Farm on the far side of the harbour, and Harper had but one horse.

"I shall walk," declared the preacher calmly, "and the young woman can ride."

Kezia had prayed for snow, storms of snow, to bury the trail and keep anyone from crossing the cape to Bristol Creek. But now they were setting out from Harper's Farm, with Harper's big brown horse, and all Kezia's prayers had gone for naught. Like any anxious lover, busy Mr. Hathaway had sent Black Sam overland on foot to find out what delayed his wedding, and now Sam's day-old tracks marked for Kezia the road to marriage.

She was a meek little thing, as became an orphan brought up as house-help in the Barclay home; but now she looked at the preacher and saw how young and helpless he looked so far from his native Yorkshire, and how ill-clad for this bitter trans-Atlantic weather, and she spoke up.

"You'd better take my shawl, sir. I don't need it. I've got Miss Julia's old riding cloak. And we'll go ride-and-tie."

"Ride and what?" murmured Mr. Mears.

"I'll ride a mile or so, then I'll get down and tie the horse to a tree and walk on. When you come up to the horse, you mount and ride a mile or so, passing me on the way, and you tie him and walk on. Like that. Ride-and-tie, ride-and-tie. The horse gets a rest between."

Young Mr. Mears nodded and took the proffered shawl absently. It was a black thing that matched his sober broadcloth coat and smallclothes, his black woollen stockings, and his round black hat. At Mr. Barclay's suggestion he had borrowed a pair of moose-hide moccasins for the journey. As he walked a prayer-book in his coat-skirts bumped the back of his legs.

At the top of the ridge above Harper's pasture, where the narrow path led off through gloomy hemlock woods, Kezia paused for a last look back across the harbour. In the morning sunlight the white roofs of the little lonely town resembled a tidal wave flung up by the sea and frozen as it broke against the dark pine forest to the west. Kezia sighed, and young Mr. Mears was surprised to see tears in her eyes.

She rode off ahead. The saddle was a man's, of course, awkward to ride modestly, woman-fashion. As soon as she was out of the preacher's sight she rucked her skirts and slid a leg over to the other stirrup. That was better. There was a pleasant sensation of freedom about it, too. For a moment she forgot that she was going to Bristol Creek, in finery second-hand from the Barclay girls, in a new linen shift and drawers that she had sewn herself in the light of the kitchen candles, in white cotton stockings and a bonnet and shoes from Mr. Barclay's store, to marry Mr. Hathaway.

The Barclays had done well for her from the time when, a skinny weeping creature of fourteen, she was taken into the Barclay household and, as Mrs. Barclay so often said, "treated more like one of my own than a bond-girl from the poorhouse." She had first choice of the clothing cast off by Miss Julia and Miss Clara. She was permitted to sit in the same room, and learn what she could, when the schoolmaster came to give private lessons to the Barclay girls. She waited on table, of course, and helped in the kitchen, and made beds, and dusted and scrubbed. But then she had been taught to spin and to sew and to knit. And she was permitted, indeed encouraged, to sit with the Barclays in the meetinghouse, at the convenient end of the pew, where she could worship the Barclays' God and assist with the Barclay wraps at the beginning and end of the service. And now, to complete her rewards, she had been granted the hand of a rejected Barclay suitor.

Mr. Hathaway was Barclay's agent at Bristol Creek, where he sold rum and gunpowder and corn meal and such things to the fishermen and hunters, and bought split cod—fresh, pickled or dry—and ran a small sawmill, and cut and shipped firewood by schooner to Port Marriott, and managed a farm, all for a salary of fifty pounds, Halifax currency, per year. Hathaway was a most capable fellow, Mr. Barclay often acknowledged. But when after fifteen capable years he came seeking a wife, and cast a sheep's eye first at Miss Julia, and then at Miss Clara, Mrs. Barclay observed with a sniff that Hathaway was looking a bit high.

So he was. The older daughter of Port Marriott's most prosperous merchant was even then receiving polite attentions from Mr. Gamage, the new collector of customs, and a connection of the Halifax Gamages, as Mrs. Barclay was fond of pointing out. And Miss Clara was going to Halifax in the spring to learn the gentle art of playing the pianoforte, and incidentally to display her charms to the naval and military young gentlemen who thronged the Halifax drawing-rooms. The dear girls laughed behind their hands whenever long solemn Mr. Hathaway came to town aboard one of the Barclay vessels and called at the big house under the elms. Mrs. Barclay bridled at Hathaway's presumption, but shrewd Mr. Barclay narrowed his little black eyes and took snuff and said "Ha! Humph!"

It was plain to Mr. Barclay that an emergency had arisen. Hathaway was a good man—in his place; and Hathaway must be kept content there, to go on making profit for Mr. Barclay at a cost of only £50 a year. 'Twas a pity Hathaway couldn't satisfy himself with one of the fisherman's girls at the Creek, but there 'twas. If Hathaway had set his mind on a town miss, then a town miss he must have; but she must be the right kind, the sort who would content herself and Hathaway at Bristol Creek and not go nagging the man to remove and try his capabilities elsewhere. At once Mr. Barclay thought of Kezia—dear little Kezzie. A colourless little creature but quiet and well-mannered and pious, and only twenty-two.

Mr. Hathaway was nearly forty and far from handsome, and he had a rather cold, seeking way about him—useful in business of course—that rubbed women the wrong way. Privately Mr. Barclay thought Hathaway lucky to get Kezia. But it was a nice match for the girl, better than anything she could have expected. He impressed that upon her and introduced the suitor from Bristol Creek. Mr. Hathaway spent two or three evenings courting Kezia in the kitchen—Kezia in a quite good gown of Miss Clara's, gazing out at the November moon on the snow, murmuring now and again in the tones of someone in a rather dismal trance, while the kitchen help listened behind one door and the Barclay girls giggled behind another.

The decision, reached mainly by the Barclays, was that Mr. Hathaway should come to Port Marriott aboard the packet schooner on December twenty-third, to be married in the Barclay parlour and then take his bride home for Christmas. But an unforeseen circumstance had changed all this. The circumstance was a ship, "from Mogador in Barbary" as Mr. Barclay wrote afterwards in the salvage claim, driven off her course by gales and wrecked at the very entrance to Bristol Creek. She was a valuable wreck, laden with such queer things as goatskins in pickle, almonds, wormseed, pomegranate skins, and gum arabic, and capable Mr. Hathaway had lost no time in salvage for the benefit of his employer.

As a result he could not come to Port Marriott for a wedding or anything else. A storm might blow up at any time and demolish this fat prize. He dispatched a note by Black Sam, urging Mr. Barclay to send Kezia and the preacher by return. It was not the orthodox note of an impatient sweetheart, but it said that he had moved into his new house by the Creek and found it "extream empty lacking a woman," and it suggested delicately that while his days were full, the nights were dull.

Kezia was no judge of distance. She rode for what she considered a reasonable time and then slid off and tied the brown horse to a maple tree beside the path. She had brought a couple of lamp wicks to tie about her shoes, to keep them from coming off in the snow, and she set out afoot in the big splayed tracks of Black Sam. The soft snow came almost to her knees in places and she lifted her skirts high. The path was no wider than the span of a man's arms, cut out with axes years before. She stumbled over a concealed stump from time to time, and the huckleberry bushes dragged at her cloak, but the effort warmed her. It had been cold, sitting on the horse with the wind blowing up her legs.

After a time the preacher overtook her, riding awkwardly and holding the reins in a nervous grip. The stirrups were too short for his long, black-stockinged legs. He called out cheerfully as he passed, "Are you all right, Miss?" She nodded, standing aside with her back to a tree. When he disappeared ahead, with a last flutter of black shawl tassels in the wind, she picked up her skirts and went on. The path climbed and dropped monotonously over a succession of wooded ridges. Here and there in a hollow she heard water running, and the creak of frosty poles underfoot, and knew she was crossing a small stream, and once the trail ran across a wide swamp on half-rotten corduroy, wind-swept and bare of snow.

She found the horse tethered clumsily not far ahead, and the tracks of the preacher going on. She had to lead the horse to a stump so she could mount, and when she passed Mr. Mears again she called out, "Please, sir, next time leave the horse by a stump or a rock so I can get on." In his quaint old-country accent he murmured, "I'm very sorry," and gazed down at the snow. She forgot she was riding astride until she had passed him, and then she flushed, and gave the indignant horse a cut of the switch. Next time she remembered and swung her right leg back where it should be, and tucked the skirts modestly about her ankles; but young Mr. Mears looked down at the snow anyway, and after that she did not trouble to shift when she overtook him.

The ridges became steeper, and the streams roared under the ice and snow in the swales. They emerged upon the high tableland between Port Marriott and Bristol Creek, a gusty wilderness of young hardwood scrub struggling up amongst the grey snags of an old forest fire, and now that they were out of the gloomy softwoods they could see a stretch of sky. It was blue-grey and forbidding, and the wind whistling up from the invisible sea felt raw on the cheek. At their next meeting Kezia said, "It's going to snow."

She had no knowledge of the trail but she guessed that they were not much more than halfway across the cape. On this high barren the track was no longer straight and clear, it meandered amongst the meagre hardwood clumps where the path-makers had not bothered to cut, and only Black Sam's footprints really marked it for her unaccustomed eyes. The preacher nodded vaguely at her remark. The woods, like everything else about his chosen mission field, were new and very interesting, and he could not understand the alarm in her voice. He looked confidently at Black Sam's tracks.

Kezia tied the horse farther on and began her spell of walking. Her shoes were solid things, the kind of shoes Mr. Barclay invoiced as "a Common Strong sort, for women, Five Shillings"; but the snow worked into them and melted and saturated the leather. Her feet were numb every time she slid down from the horse and it took several minutes of stumbling through the snow to bring back an aching warmth. Beneath her arm she clutched the small bundle which contained all she had in the world—two flannel nightgowns, a shift of linen, three pairs of stout wool stockings—and of course Mr. Barclay's wedding gift for Mr. Hathaway.

Now as she plunged along she felt the first sting of snow on her face and, looking up, saw the stuff borne on the wind in small hard pellets that fell amongst the bare hardwoods and set up a whisper everywhere. When Mr. Mears rode up to her the snow was thick in their faces, like flung salt.

"It's a nor'easter!" she cried up to him. She knew the meaning of snow from the sea. She had been born in a fishing village down the coast.

"Yes," mumbled the preacher, and drew a fold of the shawl about his face. He disappeared. She struggled on, gasping, and after what seemed a tremendous journey came upon him standing alone and bewildered, looking off somewhere to the right.

"The horse!" he shouted. "I got off him, and before I could fasten the reins some snow fell off a branch—startled him, you know—and he ran off, over that way." He gestured with a mittened hand. "I must fetch him back," he added confusedly.

"No!" Kezia cried. "Don't you try. You'd only get lost. So would I. Oh, dear! This is awful. We'll have to go on, the best we can."

He was doubtful. The horse tracks looked very plain. But Kezia was looking at Black Sam's tracks, and tugging his arm. He gave in, and they struggled along for half an hour or so. Then the last trace of the old footprints vanished.

"What shall we do now?" the preacher asked, astonished.

"I don't know," whispered Kezia, and leaned against a dead pine stub in an attitude of weariness and indifference that dismayed him.

"We must keep moving, my dear, mustn't we? I mean, we can't stay here."

"Can't stay here," she echoed.

"Down there—a hollow, I think. I see some hemlock trees, or are they pines?—I'm never quite sure. Shelter, anyway."

"Shelter," muttered Kezia.

He took her by the hand and like a pair of lost children they dragged their steps into the deep snow of the hollow. The trees were tall spruces, a thick bunch in a ravine, where they had escaped the old fire. A stream thundered amongst them somewhere. There was no wind in this place, only the fine snow whirling thickly down between the trees like a sediment from the storm overhead.

"Look!" cried Mr. Mears. A hut loomed out of the whiteness before them, a small structure of moss-chinked logs with a roof of poles and birch-bark. It had an abandoned look. Long streamers of moss hung out between the logs. On the roof shreds of birch-bark wavered gently in the drifting snow. The door stood half open and a thin drift of snow lay along the split-pole floor. Instinctively Kezia went to the stone hearth. There were old ashes sodden with rain down the chimney and now frozen to a cake.

"Have you got flint and steel?" she asked. She saw in his eyes something dazed and forlorn. He shook his head, and she was filled with a sudden anger, not so much at him as at Mr. Barclay and that— Hathaway, and all the rest of mankind. They ruled the world and made such a sorry mess of it. In a small fury she began to rummage about the hut.

There was a crude bed of poles and brushwood by the fireplace— brushwood so old that only a few brown needles clung to the twigs. A rough bench whittled from a pine log, with round birch sticks for legs. A broken earthenware pot in a corner. In another some ash-wood frames such as trappers used for stretching skins. Nothing else. The single window was covered with a stretched moose-bladder, cracked and dry rotten, but it still let in some daylight while keeping out the snow.

She scooped up the snow from the floor with her mittened hands, throwing it outside, and closed the door carefully, dropping the bar into place, as if she could shut out and bar the cold in such a fashion. The air inside was frigid. Their breath hung visible in the dim light from the window. Young Mr. Mears dropped on his wet knees and began to pray in a loud voice. His face was pinched with cold and his teeth rattled as he prayed. He was a pitiable object.

"Prayers won't keep you warm," said Kezia crossly.

He looked up, amazed at the change in her. She had seemed such a meek little thing. Kezia was surprised at herself, and surprisingly she went on, "You'd far better take off those wet moccasins and stockings and shake the snow out of your clothes." She set the example, vigorously shaking out her skirts and Miss Julia's cloak, and she turned her small back on him and took off her own shoes and stockings, and pulled on dry stockings from her bundle. She threw him a pair.

"Put those on."

He looked at them and at his large feet helplessly.

"I'm afraid they wouldn't go on."

She tossed him one of her flannel nightgowns. "Then take off your stockings and wrap your feet and legs in that."

He obeyed, in an embarrassed silence. She rolled her eyes upward, for his modesty's sake, and saw a bundle on one of the low rafters—the late owner's bedding, stowed away from mice. She stood on the bench and pulled down three bearskins, marred with bullet holes. A rank and musty smell arose in the cold. She considered the find gravely.

"You take them," Mr. Mears said gallantly. "I shall be quite all right."

"You'll be dead by morning, and so shall I," she answered vigorously, "if you don't do what I say. We've got to roll up in these."

"Together?" he cried in horror.

"Of course! To keep each other warm. It's the only way."

She spread the skins on the floor, hair uppermost, one overlapping another, and dragged the flustered young man down beside her, clutched him in her arms, and rolled with him, over, and over again, so that they became a single shapeless heap in the corner farthest from the draft between door and chimney.

"Put your arms around me," commanded the new Kezia, and he obeyed.

"Now," she said, "you can pray. God helps those that help themselves."

He prayed aloud for a long time, and privately called upon heaven to witness the purity of his thoughts in this strange and shocking situation. He said "Amen" at last; and "Amen," echoed Kezia, piously.

They lay silent a long time, breathing on each other's necks and hearing their own hearts—poor Mr. Mears' fluttering in an agitated way, Kezia's as steady as a clock. A delicious warmth crept over them. They relaxed in each other's arms. Outside, the storm hissed in the spruce tops and set up an occasional cold moan in the cracked clay chimney. The down-swirling snow brushed softly against the bladder pane.

"I'm warm now," murmured Kezia. "Are you?"

"Yes. How long must we stay here like this?"

"Till the storm's over, of course. Tomorrow, probably. Nor'easters usually blow themselves out in a day and a night, 'specially when they come up sharp, like this one. Are you hungry?"

"No."

"Abigail—that's the black cook at Barclay's—gave me bread and cheese in a handkerchief. I've got it in my bundle. Mr. Barclay thought we ought to reach Bristol Creek by supper time, but Nabby said I must have a bite to eat on the road. She's a good kind thing, old Nabby. Sure you're not hungry?"

"Quite. I feel somewhat fatigued but not hungry."

"Then we'll eat the bread and cheese for breakfast. Have you got a watch?"

"No, I'm sorry. They cost such a lot of money. In Lady Huntingdon's Connexion we—"

"Oh well, it doesn't matter. It must be about four o'clock—the light's getting dim. Of course, the dark comes very quick in a snowstorm."

"Dark," echoed young Mr. Mears drowsily. Kezia's hair, washed last night for the wedding journey, smelled pleasant so close to his face. It reminded him of something. He went to sleep dreaming of his mother, with his face snug in the curve of Kezia's neck and shoulder, and smiling, and muttering words that Kezia could not catch. After a time she kissed his cheek. It seemed a very natural thing to do.

Soon she was dozing herself, and dreaming, too; but her dreams were full of forbidding faces—Mr. Barclay's, Mrs. Barclay's, Mr. Hathaway's; especially Mr. Hathaway's. Out of a confused darkness Mr. Hathaway's hard acquisitive gaze searched her shrinking flesh like a cold wind. Then she was shuddering by the kitchen fire at Barclays', accepting Mr. Hathaway's courtship and wishing she was dead. In the midst of that sickening wooing she wakened sharply.

It was quite dark in the hut. Mr. Mears was breathing quietly against her throat. But there was a sound of heavy steps outside, muffled in the snow and somehow felt rather than heard. She shook the young man and he wakened with a start, clutching her convulsively.

"Sh-h-h!" she warned. "Something's moving outside." She felt him stiffen.

"Bears?" he whispered.

Silly! thought Kezia. People from the old country could think of nothing but bears in the woods. Besides, bears holed up in winter. A caribou, perhaps. More likely a moose. Caribou moved inland before this, to the wide mossy bogs up the river, away from the coastal storms. Again the sound.

"There!" hissed the preacher. Their hearts beat rapidly together.

"The door—you fastened it, didn't you?"

"Yes," she said. Suddenly she knew.

"Unroll! quick!" she cried ... "No, not this way—your way."

They unrolled, ludicrously, and the girl scrambled up and ran across the floor in her stockinged feet, and fumbled with the rotten door-bar. Mr. Mears attempted to follow but he tripped over the nightgown still wound around his feet, and fell with a crash. He was up again in a moment, catching up the clumsy wooden bench for a weapon, his bare feet slapping on the icy floor. He tried to shoulder her aside, crying "Stand back! Leave it to me!" and waving the bench uncertainly in the darkness.

She laughed excitedly. "Silly!" she said. "It's the horse." She flung the door open. In the queer ghostly murk of a night filled with snow they beheld a large dark shape. The shape whinnied softly and thrust a long face into the doorway. Mr. Mears dropped the bench, astonished.

"He got over his fright and followed us here somehow," Kezia said, and laughed again. She put her arms about the snowy head and laid her face against it.

"Good horse! Oh, good, good horse!"

"What are you going to do?" the preacher murmured over her shoulder. After the warmth of their nest in the furs they were shivering in this icy atmosphere.

"Bring him in, of course. We can't leave him out in the storm." She caught the bridle and urged the horse inside with expert clucking sounds. The animal hesitated, but fear of the storm and a desire for shelter and company decided him. In he came, tramping ponderously on the split-pole floor. The preacher closed and barred the door.

"And now?" he asked.

"Back to the furs. Quick! It's awful cold."

Rolled in the furs once more, their arms went about each other instinctively, and the young man's face found the comfortable nook against Kezia's soft throat. But sleep was difficult after that. The horse whinnied gently from time to time, and stamped about the floor. The decayed poles crackled dangerously under his hoofs whenever he moved, and Kezia trembled, thinking he might break through and frighten himself, and flounder about till he tumbled the crazy hut about their heads. She called out to him "Steady, boy! Steady!"

It was a long night. The pole floor made its irregularities felt through the thickness of fur; and because there seemed nowhere to put their arms but about each other the flesh became cramped, and spread its protest along the bones. They were stiff and sore when the first light of morning stained the window. They unrolled and stood up thankfully, and tramped up and down the floor, threshing their arms in an effort to fight off the gripping cold. Kezia undid her bundle in a corner and brought forth Nabby's bread and cheese, and they ate it sitting together on the edge of the brushwood bed with the skins about their shoulders. Outside the snow had ceased.

"We must set off at once," the preacher said. "Mr. Hathaway will be anxious."

Kezia was silent. She did not move, and he looked at her curiously. She appeared very fresh, considering the hardships of the previous day and the night. He passed a hand over his cheeks and thought how unclean he must appear in her eyes with this stubble on his pale face.

"Mr. Hathaway— " he began again.

"I'm not going to Mr. Hathaway," Kezia said quietly.

"But—the wedding!"

"There'll be no wedding. I don't want to marry Mr. Hathaway. 'Twas Mr. Hathaway's idea, and Mr. and Mrs. Barclay's. They wanted me to marry him."

"What will the Barclays say, my dear?"

She shrugged. "I've been their bond-girl ever since I was fourteen, but I'm not a slave like poor black Nabby, to be handed over, body and soul, whenever it suits."

"Your soul belongs to God," said Mr. Mears devoutly.

"And my body belongs to me."

He was a little shocked at this outspokenness but he said gently, "Of course. To give oneself in marriage without true affection would be an offence in the sight of Heaven. But what will Mr. Hathaway say?"

"Well, to begin with, he'll ask where I spent the night, and I'll have to tell the truth. I'll have to say I bundled with you in a hut in the woods."

"Bundled?"

"A custom the people brought with them from Connecticut when they came to settle in Nova Scotia. Poor folk still do it. Sweethearts, I mean. It saves fire and candles when you're courting on a winter evening. It's harmless—they keep their clothes on, you see, like you and me—but Mr. Barclay and the other Methody people are terrible set against it. Mr. Barclay got old Mr. Mings—he's the Methody preacher that died last year—to make a sermon against it. Mr. Mings said bundling was an invention of the devil."

"Then if you go back to Mr. Barclay—"

"He'll ask me the same question and I'll have to give him the same answer. I couldn't tell a lie, could I?" She turned a pair of round blue eyes and met his embarrassed gaze.

"No! No, you mustn't lie. Whatever shall we do?" he murmured in a dazed voice. Again she was silent, looking modestly down her small nose.

"It's so very strange," he floundered. "This country—there are so many things I don't know, so many things to learn. You—I—we shall have to tell the truth, of course. Doubtless I can find a place in the Lord's service somewhere else, but what about you, poor girl?"

"I heard say the people at Scrod Harbour want a preacher."

"But—the tale would follow me, wouldn't it, my dear? This—er—bundling with a young woman?"

"'Twouldn't matter if the young woman was your wife."

"Eh?" His mouth fell open. He was like an astonished child, for all his preacher's clothes and the new beard on his jaws.

"I'm a good girl," Kezia said, inspecting her foot. "I can read and write, and know all the tunes in the psalter. And—and you need someone to look after you."

He considered the truth of that. Then he murmured uncertainly, "We'd be very poor, my dear. The Connexion gives some support, but of course—"

"I've always been poor," Kezia said. She sat very still but her cold fingers writhed in her lap.

He did something then that made her want to cry. He took hold of her hands and bowed his head and kissed them.

"It's strange—I don't even know your name, my dear."

"It's Kezia—Kezia Barnes."

He said quietly, "You're a brave girl, Kezia Barnes, and I shall try to be a good husband to you. Shall we go?"

"Hadn't you better kiss me, first?" Kezia said faintly.

He put his lips awkwardly to hers; and then, as if the taste of her clean mouth itself provided strength and purpose, he kissed her again, and firmly. She threw her arms about his neck.

"Oh, Mr. Mears!"

How little he knew about everything! He hadn't even known enough to wear two or three pairs of stockings inside those roomy moccasins, nor to carry a pair of dry ones. Yesterday's wet stockings were lying like sticks on the frosty floor. She showed him how to knead the hard-frozen moccasins into softness, and while he worked at the stiff leather she tore up one of her wedding bed-shirts and wound the flannel strips about his legs and feet. It looked very queer when she had finished, and they both laughed.

They were chilled to the bone when they set off, Kezia on the horse and the preacher walking ahead, holding the reins. When they regained the slope where they had lost the path, Kezia said, "The sun rises somewhere between east and southeast, this time of year. Keep it on your left shoulder a while. That will take us back towards Port Marriott."

When they came to the green timber she told him to shift the sun to his left eye.

"Have you changed your mind?" he asked cheerfully. The exercise had warmed him.

"No, but the sun moves across the sky."

"Ah! What a wise little head it is!"

They came over a ridge of mixed hemlock and hardwood and looked upon a long swale full of bare hackmatacks.

"Look!" the girl cried. The white slot of the axe path had showed clearly in the trees at the foot of the swale, and again where it entered the dark mass of the pines beyond.

"Praise the Lord!" said Mr. Mears.

When at last they stood in the trail, Kezia slid down from the horse.

"No!" Mr. Mears protested.

"Ride-and-tie," she said firmly. "That's the way we came, and that's the way we'll go. Besides, I want to get warm."

He climbed up clumsily and smiled down at her.

"What shall we do when we get to Port Marriott, my dear?"

"Get the New Light preacher to marry us, and catch the packet for Scrod Harbour."

He nodded and gave a pull at his broad hat brim. She thought of everything. A splendid helpmeet for the world's wilderness. He saw it all very humbly now as a dispensation of Providence.

Kezia watched him out of sight. Then, swiftly, she undid her bundle and took out the thing that had lain there (and on her conscience) through the night—the tinderbox—Mr. Barclay's wedding gift to Mr. Hathaway. She flung it into the woods and walked on, skirts lifted, in the track of the horse, humming a psalm tune to the silent trees and the snow.

Thomas Head Raddall (*born 1903, England; died 1994, Nova Scotia*), author, historian, came to Canada at the age of 10 and left school at 15 when his father was killed in action in World War I. He worked as a wireless operator and bookkeeper and wrote in the evenings until he was able to earn his living as a full-time writer. He wrote short stories, historical novels, nonfiction histories, and radio and TV scripts, in which he "carefully and respectfully interpreted Nova Scotia's past and present to his fellow Nova Scotians and to the world." He twice won the Governor General's Literary Award, in 1943 for *The Pied Piper of Dipper Creek and Other Tales*, and in 1948 for *Halifax: Warden of the North* (nonfiction).

Activities: The Wedding Gift

1. *Note Details of Setting:* List at least five details of the weather and geography that inform the reader of a "hostile" environment. How does Kezia respond to the elements? What do her responses reveal about her?

2. *Examine the Ending:* Why does Kezia throw away the tinderbox? How does the second-last paragraph provide a contrast to the last one? Does Raddall foreshadow the ending? Discuss in a small group and share a summary of your discussion with another group.

3. *Diagram Plot:* Create a plot diagram showing the initiating event, rising action, climax, and denouement. Include at least four specific events for rising action. Compare your diagram with a partner's and discuss differences.

4. *Design a Pamphlet:* Research, write, and design a survival pamphlet appropriate for the weather and geography in your region. Consider how audience, purpose, and situation might influence your writing and design decisions.

The Dead Child

Gabrielle Roy

Why then did the memory of that dead child seek me out in the very midst of the summer that sang?

When till then no intimation of sorrow had come to me through the dazzling revelations of that season.

I had just arrived in a very small village in Manitoba to finish the school year as replacement for a teacher who had fallen ill or simply, for all I know, become discouraged.

The principal of the Normal School[1] had called me to his office toward the end of my year's study. "Well," he said, "there's a school available for the month of June. It's not much but it's an opportunity. When the time comes for you to apply for a permanent position, you'll be able to say you've had experience. Believe me, it's a help."

And so I found myself at the beginning of June in that very poor village—just a few shacks built on sand, with nothing around it but spindly spruce trees. "A month," I asked myself, "will that be long enough for me to become attached to the children or for the children to become attached to me? Will a month be worth the effort?"

Perhaps the same calculation was in the minds of the children who presented themselves at school that first day of June—"Is this teacher going to stay long enough to be worth the effort?"—for I had never seen children's faces so dejected, so apathetic, or perhaps sorrowful. I had had so little experience. I myself was hardly more than a child.

---

1. A Normal School is a college for training teachers.

Nine o'clock came. The room was hot as an oven. Sometimes in Manitoba, especially in the sandy areas, an incredible heat settles in during the first days of June.

Scarcely knowing where or how to begin, I opened the attendance book and called the roll. The names were for the most part very French and today they still return to my memory, like this, for no reason: Madeleine Bérubé, Josephat Brisset, Emilien Dumont, Cécile Lépine....

But most of the children who rose and answered "Present, mamzelle," when their names were called had the slightly narrowed eyes, warm colouring and jet black hair that told of Métis blood.

They were beautiful and exquisitely polite; there was really nothing to reproach them for except the inconceivable distance they maintained between themselves and me. It crushed me. "Is this what children are like then," I asked myself with anguish, "untouchable, barricaded in some region where you can't reach them?"

I came to the name Yolande Chartrand.

No one answered. It was becoming hotter by the minute. I wiped a bit of perspiration from my forehead. I repeated the name and, when there was still no answer, I looked up at faces that seemed to me completely indifferent.

Then from the back of the classroom, above the buzzing of flies, there arose a voice I at first couldn't place. "She's dead, mamzelle. She died last night."

Perhaps even more distressing than the news was the calm level tone of the child's voice. As I must have seemed unconvinced, all the children nodded gravely as if to say, "It's true."

Suddenly a sense of impotence greater than any I can remember weighed upon me.

"Ah," I said, lost for words.

"She's already laid out," said a boy with eyes like coals. "They're going to bury her for good tomorrow."

"Ah," I repeated.

The children seemed a little more relaxed now and willing to talk, in snatches and at long intervals.

A boy in the middle of the room offered, "She got worse the last two months."

We looked at one another in silence for a long time, the children and I. I now understood that the expression in their eyes that I had taken for indifference was a heavy sadness. Much like this stupefying heat. And we were only at the beginning of the day.

"Since Yolande ... has been laid out," I suggested, "and she was your schoolmate ... and would have been my pupil ... would you like ... after school at four o'clock ... for us to go and visit her?"

On the small, much too serious faces there appeared the trace of a smile, wary, still very sad but a sort of smile just the same.

"It's agreed then, we'll go to visit her, her whole class."

From that moment, despite the enervating heat and the sense that haunted us all, I feel sure, that human efforts are all ultimately destined to a sort of failure, the children fixed their attention as much as possible on what I was teaching and I did my best to rouse their interest.

At five past four I found most of them waiting for me at the door, a good twenty children but making no more noise than if they were being kept in after school. Several of them went ahead to show me the way. Others pressed around me so closely I could scarcely move. Five or six of the smaller ones took me by the hand or the shoulder and pulled me forward gently as if they were leading a blind person. They did not talk, merely held me enclosed in their circle.

Together, in this way, we followed a track through the sand. Here and there thin spruce trees formed little clumps. The air was now barely moving. In no time the village was behind us—forgotten, as it were.

We came to a wooden cabin standing in isolation among the little trees. Its door was wide open, so we were able to see the dead child from quite far off. She had been laid out on rough boards suspended between two straight chairs set back to back. There was nothing else in the room. Its usual contents must have been crowded into the only other room of the house for, besides a stove and table and a few pots on the floor, I could see a bed and a mattress piled with clothes. But no chairs. Clearly the two used as supports for the boards on which the dead child lay were the only ones in the house.

The parents had undoubtedly done all they could for their child. They had covered her with a clean sheet. They had given her a room to herself. Her mother, probably, had arranged her hair in the two very tight braids that framed the thin face. But some pressing need had sent them away: perhaps the purchase of a coffin in town or a few more boards to make her one themselves. At any rate, the dead child was alone in the room that had been emptied for her—alone, that is to say, with the flies. A faint odour of death must have attracted them. I saw one with a blue body walk over her forehead. I immediately placed myself near her head and began to move my hand back and forth to drive the flies away.

The child had a delicate little face, very wasted, with the serious expression I had seen on the faces of most of the children here, as if the cares of the adults had crushed them all too early. She might have been ten or eleven years old. If she had lived a little longer, I reminded myself, she would have been one of my pupils. She would have learned something from me. I would have given her something to keep. A bond would have been formed between me and this little stranger—who knows, perhaps even for life.

As I contemplated the dead child, those words "for life"—as if they implied a long existence—seemed to me the most rash and foolish of all the expressions we use so lightly.

In death the child looked as if she were regretting some poor little joy she had never known. I continued at least to prevent the flies from settling upon her. The children were watching me. I realized that they now expected everything from me, though I didn't know much more than they and was just as confused. Still I had a sort of inspiration.

"Don't you think Yolande would like to have someone with her always till the time comes to commit her to the ground?"

The faces of the children told me I had struck the right note.

"We'll take turns then, four or five around her every two hours, until the funeral."

They agreed with a glow in their dark eyes.

"We must be careful not to let the flies touch Yolande's face."

They nodded to show they were in agreement. Standing around me, they now felt a trust in me so complete it terrified me.

In a clearing among the spruce trees a short distance away, I noticed a bright pink stain on the ground whose source I didn't yet know. The sun slanted upon it, making it flame, the one moment in this day that had been touched by a certain grace.

"What sort of girl was she?" I asked.

At first the children didn't understand. Then a boy of about the same age said with tender seriousness, "She was smart, Yolande."

The other children looked as if they agreed.

"And did she do well in school?"

"She didn't come very often this year. She was always being absent."

"Our teacher before last this year said Yolande could have done well."

"How many teachers have you had this year?"

"You're the third, mamzelle. I guess the teachers find it too lonesome here."

"What did Yolande die of?"

"T.B., mamzelle," they replied with a single voice, as if this was the customary way for children to die around here.

They were eager to talk about her now. I had succeeded in opening the poor little doors deep within them that no one perhaps had ever much wanted to see opened. They told me moving facts about her brief life. One day on her way home from school—it was in February; no, said another, in March—she had lost her reader and wept inconsolably for weeks. To study her lesson after that, she had to borrow a book from one of the others—and I saw on the faces of some of them that they'd grudged lending their readers and would always regret this. Not having a dress for her first communion, she entreated till her mother finally made her one from the only curtain in the house: "the one from this room ... a beautiful lace curtain, mamzelle."

"And did Yolande look pretty in her lace curtain dress?" I asked.

They all nodded deeply, in their eyes the memory of a pleasant image.

I studied the silent little face. A child who had loved books, solemnity, and decorous attire. Then I glanced again at the astonishing splash of pink in the melancholy landscape. I realized suddenly that it was a mass of wild roses. In June they open in great sheets all over Manitoba, growing from the poorest soil. I felt some alleviation.

"Let's go and pick some roses for Yolande."

On the children's faces there appeared the same slow smile of gentle sadness I had seen when I suggested visiting the body.

In no time we were gathering roses. The children were not yet cheerful, far from that, but I could hear them at least talking to one another. A sort of rivalry had gripped them. Each vied to see who could pick the most roses or the brightest, those of a deep shade that was almost red.

From time to time one tugged at my sleeve, "Mamzelle, see the lovely one I've found!"

On our return we pulled them gently apart and scattered petals over the dead child. Soon only her face emerged from the pink drift. Then—how could this be?—it looked a little less forlorn.

The children formed a ring around their schoolmate and said of her without the bitter sadness of the morning, "She must have got to heaven by this time."

Or, "She must be happy now."

I listened to them, already consoling themselves as best they could for being alive.

But why, oh why, did the memory of that dead child seek me out today in the very midst of the summer that sang?

Was it brought to me just now by the wind with the scent of roses?

A scent I have not much liked since the long ago June when I went to that poorest of villages—to acquire, as they say, experience.

Gabrielle Roy (*born 1909, St. Boniface, Manitoba; died 1983*), teacher, journalist, writer, was one of 11 children in a French-speaking family. She taught in Manitoba before moving to Europe for two years. She then settled in Quebec where she worked as a writer of articles, short stories, and novels. She was awarded three Governor General's Literary Awards, for *The Tin Flute*, *Children of My Heart*, and *Street of Riches*.

Activities: The Dead Child

1. **Examine Mood:** What mood does Roy establish in this story? Use references to the text to support your answer.

2. **Make Inferences:** With a partner, discuss possible answers to the question in the first line of the story. Why might this memory be significant to the narrator? Record your ideas and share them with another pair of students.

3. **Defend Opinions:** How would you rate the effectiveness of the teacher on her first day? Is there any evidence that she taught the children something of value? Explain your evaluation of her effectiveness and be prepared to defend it to the class.

4. **Investigate the Author:** Find and read another story by Roy. Prepare a summary of the plot, and identify and list examples of specific literary techniques she uses in the story. Share your summary and analysis with a small group.

A Bolt of White Cloth

Leon Rooke

A man came by our road carrying an enormous bolt of white cloth on his back. Said he was from the East. Said whoever partook of this cloth would come to know true happiness. Innocence without heartbreak, he said, if that person proved worthy. My wife fingered his cloth, having in mind something for new curtains. It was good quality, she said. Beautifully woven, of a fine, light texture, and you certainly couldn't argue with the colour.

"How much is it?" she asked.

"Before I tell you that," the man said, "you must tell me truthfully if you've ever suffered."

"Oh, I've suffered," she said. "I've known suffering of some description every day of my natural life."

I was standing over by the toolshed, with a big smile. My wife is a real joker, who likes nothing better than pulling a person's leg. She's known hardships, this and that upheaval, but nothing I would call down-and-out suffering. Mind you, I don't speak for her. I wouldn't pretend to speak for another person.

This man with the bolt of cloth, however, he clearly had no sense of my wife's brand of humour. She didn't get an itch of a smile out of him. He kept the cloth neatly balanced on his shoulder, wincing a little from the weight and from however far he'd had to carry it, staring hard and straight at my wife the whole time she fooled with him, as if he hoped to peer clear through to her soul. His eyes were dark and brooding and hollowed out some. He was like no person either my wife or me had ever seen before.

"Yes," he said, "but suffering of what kind?"

"Worse than I hope forever to carry, I'll tell you that," my wife said. "But why are you asking me these questions? I like your cloth and if the price is right I mean to buy it."

"You can only buy my cloth with love," he said.

We began right then to understand that he was some kind of oddity. He was not like anybody we'd ever seen and he didn't come from around here. He'd come from a place we'd never heard of, and if that was the East, or wherever, then he was welcome to it.

"Love?" she said. "Love? There's *love* and there's *love*, mister. What kind are you talking about?" She hitched a head my way, rolling her eyes, as if to indicate that if it was *passionate* love he was talking about then he'd first have to do something with me. He'd have to get me off my simmer and onto full boil. That's what she was telling him, with this mischief in her eyes.

I put down my pitchfork about here, and strolled nearer. I liked seeing my wife dealing with difficult situations. I didn't want to miss anything. My life with that woman has been packed with the unusual. Unusual circumstances, she calls them. Any time she's ever gone out anywhere without me, whether for a day or an hour or for five minutes, she's come back with whopping good stories about what she's seen and heard and what's happened to her. She's come back with reports on these unusual circumstances, these little adventures in which so many people have done so many extraordinary things or behaved in such fabulous or foolish ways. So what was rare this time, I thought, was that it had come visiting. She hadn't had to go out and find it.

"Hold these," my wife told me. And she put this washtub of clothes in my hands, and went back to hanging wet pieces on the line, which is what she'd been doing when this man with the bolt of cloth ventured up into our yard.

"Love," she told him. "You tell me what kind I need, if I'm to buy that cloth. I got good ears and I'm listening."

The man watched her stick clothespins in her mouth, slap out a good wide sheet, and string it up. He watched her hang two of these, plus a mess of towels, and get her mouth full again before he spoke. He looked about the unhappiest I've ever seen any man look. He didn't have any joy in him. I wondered why he didn't put down that heavy bolt of cloth, and why he didn't step around into a spot of shade. The sun was lick-killing bright in that yard. I was worried he'd faint.

"The ordinary kind," he said. "Your ordinary kind of love will buy this cloth."

My wife flapped her wash and laughed. He was really tickling her. She was having herself a wonderful time.

"What's ordinary?" she said. "I've never known no *ordinary* love."

He jumped right in. He got excited just for a second.

"The kind such as might exist between the closest friends," he said. "The kind such as might exist between a man and his wife or between parents and children or for that matter the love a boy might have for his dog. That kind of love."

"I've got that," she said. "I've had all three. Last year this time I had me a fourth, but it got run over. Up on the road there, by the tall trees, by a man in a car who didn't even stop."

"That would have been your cat," he said. "I don't know much about cats."

I put down the washtub. My wife let her arms drop. We looked at him, wondering how he knew about that cat. Then I laughed, for I figured someone down the road must have told him of my wife's mourning over that cat. She'd dug it a grave under the grapevine and said sweet words over it. She sorely missed that cat.

"What's wrong with loving cats?" she asked him. "Or beasts of the fields? I'm surprised at you."

The man shifted his burden and worked one shoe into the ground. He stared off at the horizon. He looked like he knew he'd said something he shouldn't.

She pushed me out of the way. She wanted to get nearer to him. She had something more to say.

"Now listen to me," she said. "I've loved lots of things in my life. Lots and lots. *Him!*" she said (pointing at me), "*it*" (pointing at our house), "*them!*" (pointing to the flower beds), "*that!*" (pointing to the sky), "*those*" (pointing to the woods), "*this*" (pointing to the ground)—"practically *everything!* There isn't any of it I've hated, and not much I've been indifferent to. Including cats. So put that in your pipe and smoke it."

Then swooping up her arms and laughing hard, making it plain she bore no grudge but wasn't just fooling.

Funny thing was, hearing her say it, I felt the same way. *It, them, that, those*—they were all beautiful. I couldn't deny it was love I was feeling.

The man with the cloth had turned each way she'd pointed. He'd staggered a time or two but he'd kept up. In fact, it struck me that he'd got a little ahead of her. That he knew where her arm was next going. Some trickle of pleasure was showing in his face. And something else was happening, something I'd never seen. He had his face lifted up to this burning sun. It was big and orange, that sun, and scorching-hot, but he was staring smack into it. He wasn't blinking or squinting. His eyes were wide open.

Madness or miracle, I couldn't tell which.

He strode over to a parcel of good grass.

"I believe you mean it," he said. "How much could you use?"

He placed the bolt of white cloth down on the grass and pulled out shiny scissors from his back pocket.

"I bet he's blind," I whispered to my wife. "I bet he's got false eyes."

My wife shushed me. She wasn't listening. She had her excitement hat on; her *unusual circumstances* look. He was offering free cloth for love, ordinary love, and she figured she'd go along with the gag.

How much?

"Oh," she said, "maybe eight yards. Maybe ten. It depends on how many windows I end up doing, plus what hang I want, plus the pleating I'm after."

"You mean to make these curtains yourself?" he asked. He was already down on his knees, smoothing the bolt. Getting set to roll it out.

"Why, sure," she said. "I don't know who else would do it for me. I don't know who else I would ask."

He nodded soberly, not thinking about it. "That's so," he said casually. "Mend your own fences first." He was perspiring in the sun, and dishevelled, as though he'd been on the road a long time. His shoes had big holes in them and you could see the blistered soles of his feet, but he had an air of exhilaration now. His hair fell down over his eyes and he shoved the dark locks back. I got the impression that some days he went a long time between customers; that he didn't find cause to give away this cloth every day.

He got a fair bit unrolled. It certainly did look like prime goods, once you saw it spread out on the grass in that long expanse.

"It's so pretty!" my wife said. "Heaven help me, but I think it is prettier than grass!"

"It's pretty, all right," he said. "It's a wing-dinger. Just tell me when to stop," he said. "Just shout yoo-hoo."

"Hold up a minute," she said. "I don't want to get greedy. I don't want you rolling off more than we can afford."

"You can afford it," he said.

He kept unrolling. He was up past the well house by now, whipping it off fast, though the bolt didn't appear to be getting any smaller. My wife had both hands up over her mouth. Half of her wanted to run into the house and get her purse so she could pay; the other half wanted to stay and watch this man unfurl his beautiful cloth. She whipped around to me, all agitated.

"I believe he means it," she said. "He means us to have this cloth. What do I do?"

I shook my head. This was her territory. It was the kind of adventure constant to her nature and necessary to her well-being.

"Honey," I said, "you deal with it."

The sun was bright over everything. It was whipping-hot. There wasn't much wind but I could hear the clothes flapping on the line. A woodpecker had himself a pole somewhere and I could hear him pecking. The sky was wavy blue. The trees seemed to be swaying.

He was up by the front porch now, still unrolling. It surprised us both that he could move so fast.

"Yoo-hoo," my wife said. It was no more than a peep, the sound you might make if a butterfly lands on your hand.

"Wait," he said. "One thing. One question I meant to ask. All this talk of love, your *it*, your *those* and *them*, it slipped my mind."

"Let's hear it," my wife said. "Ask away." It seemed to me that she spoke out of a trance. That she was as dazzled as I was.

"You two got no children," he said. "Why is that? You're out here on this nice farm, and no children to your name. Why is that?"

We hadn't expected this query from him. It did something to the light in the yard and how we saw it. It was as if some giant dark bird had fluttered between us and the sun. Without knowing it, we sidled closer to each other. We fumbled for the other's hand. We stared off every which way. No one on our road had asked that question in a long, long time; they hadn't asked it in some years.

"We're not able," we said. Both of us spoke at the same time. It seemed to me that it was my wife's voice which carried; mine was some place down in my chest, and dropping, as if it meant to crawl on the ground.

"We're not able," we said. That time it came out pure, without any grief to bind it. It came out the way we long ago learned how to say it.

"Oh," he said. "I see." He mumbled something else. He kicked the ground and took a little walk back and forth. He seemed angry, though not at us. "Wouldn't you know it?" he said. "Wouldn't you know it?"

He swore a time or two. He kicked the ground. He surely didn't like it.

"We're over that now," my wife said. "We're past that caring."

"I bet you are," he said. "You're past that little misfortune."

He took to unrolling his bolt again, working with his back to the sun. Down on his knees, scrambling, smoothing the material. Sweating and huffing. He was past the front porch now, and still going, getting on toward that edge where the high weeds grew.

"About here, do you think?" he asked.

He'd rolled off about fifty yards.

My wife and I slowly shook our heads, not knowing what to think.

"Say the word," he told us. "I can give you more if more is what you want."

"I'd say you were giving us too much," my wife said. "I'd say we don't need nearly that much."

"Never mind that," he said. "I'm feeling generous today."

He nudged the cloth with his fingers and rolled off a few yards more. He would have gone on unwinding his cloth had the weeds not stopped him. He stood and looked back over the great length he had unwound.

"Looks like a long white road, don't it?" he said. "You could walk that road and your feet never get dirty."

My wife clenched my hand; it was what we'd both been thinking.

SnipSnipSnip. He began snipping. His scissors raced over the material. *SnipSnipSnip.* The cloth was sheared clear and clean of his bolt, yet it seemed to me the size of that bolt hadn't lessened any. My wife saw it too.

"He's got cloth for all eternity," she said. "He could unroll that cloth till doomsday."

The man laughed. We were whispering this, but way up by the weeds he heard us. "There's doom and there's doom," he said. "*Which* doomsday?"

I had the notion he'd gone through more than one. That he knew the picture from both sides.

"It is smart as grass," he said. "Smarter. It never needs watering." He chuckled at that, spinning both arms. Dancing a little. "You could make *nighties* out of this," he said. "New bedsheets. Transform your whole bedroom."

My wife made a face. She wasn't too pleased, talking *nighties* with another man.

Innocence without heartbreak, I thought. That's what we're coming to.

He nicely rolled up the cloth he'd sheared off and presented it to my wife. "I hope you like it," he said. "No complaints yet. Maybe you can make yourself a nice dress as well. Maybe two or three. Make him some shirts. I think you'll find there's plenty here."

"Goodness, it's light," she said.

"Not if you've been carrying it long as I have," he said. He pulled a blue bandanna from his pocket and wiped his face and neck. He ran his hand through his hair and slicked it back. He looked up at the sky. His dark eyes seemed to have cleared up some. They looked less broody now. "Gets hot," he said, "working in this sun. But a nice day. I'm glad I found you folks home."

"Oh, we're most always home," my wife said.

I had to laugh at that. My wife almost never is home. She's forever gallivanting over the countryside, checking up on this person and that, taking them her soups and jams and breads.

"We're homebodies, us two."

She kept fingering the cloth and sighing over it. She held it up against her cheek and with her eyes closed rested herself on it. The man hoisted his own bolt back on his shoulder; he seemed ready to be going. I looked at my wife's closed lids, at the soft look she had.

I got trembly, fearful of what might happen if that cloth didn't work out.

"Now look," I said to him, "what's wrong with this cloth? Is it going to rot inside a week? Tomorrow is some *other* stranger going to knock on our door saying we owe him a hundred or five hundred dollars for this cloth? Mister, I don't understand you," I said.

He hadn't bothered with me before; now he looked me dead in the eye. "I can't help being a stranger," he said. "If you never set eyes on me before, I guess that's what I would have to be. Don't you like strangers? Don't you trust them?"

My wife jumped in. Her face was fiery, like she thought I had wounded him. "We like strangers just fine," she said. "We've helped out many a-one. No, I can't say our door has ever been closed to whoever it is comes by. Strangers can sit in our kitchen just the same as our friends."

He smiled at her but kept his stern look for me. "As to your questions," he said, "you're worried about the golden goose, I can see that. Fair enough. No, your cloth will not rot. It will not shred, fade, or tear. Nor will it ever need cleaning, either. This cloth requires no upkeep whatsoever. Though a sound heart helps. A sweet disposition, too. Innocence without heartbreak, as I told you. And your wife, if it's her making the curtains or making herself a dress, she will find it to be an amazingly easy cloth to work with. It will practically do the job itself. No, I don't believe you will ever find you have any reason to complain of the quality of that cloth."

My wife had it up to her face again. She had her face sunk in it.

"Goodness," she said, "it's *soft*! It smells so fresh. It's like someone singing a song to me."

The man laughed. "It is soft," he said. "But it can't sing a note, or has never been known to."

It was my wife singing. She had this little hum under her breath.

"This is the most wonderful cloth in the world," she said.

He nodded. "I can't argue with you on that score," he said. Then he turned again to me. "I believe your wife is satisfied," he said. "But if you have any doubts, if you're worried someone is going to knock on your door tomorrow asking you for a hundred or five hundred dollars, I suppose I could write you up a guarantee. I could give you a PAID IN FULL."

He was making me feel ashamed of myself. They both were. "No, no," I said, "if she's satisfied then I am. And I can see she's tickled pink. No, I beg your pardon. I meant no offence."

"No offence taken," he said.

But his eyes clouded a token. He gazed off at our road and up along the stand of trees and his eyes kept roaming until they snagged the sun. He kept his eyes there, unblinking, open, staring at the sun. I could see the red orbs reflected in his eyes.

"There is one thing," he said.

I caught my breath and felt my wife catch hers. The hitch? A hitch, after all? Coming so late?

We waited.

He shuffled his feet. He brought out his bandanna and wiped his face again. He stared at the ground.

"Should you ever stop loving," he said, "you shall lose this cloth and all else. You shall wake up one morning and it and all else will no longer be where you left it. It will all be gone and you will not know where you are. You will not know what to do with yourself. You will wish you'd never been born."

My wife's eyes went saucer-size.

He had us in some kind of spell.

Hocus-pocus, I thought. He is telling us some kind of hocus-pocus. Yet I felt my skin shudder; I felt the goose bumps rise.

"That's it?" my wife said. "That's the only catch?"

He shrugged. "That's it," he said. "Not much, is it? Not a whisper of menace for a pair such as yourselves."

My wife's eyes were gauzed over; there was a wetness in them.

"Hold on," she said. "Don't you be leaving yet. Hold this, honey."

She put the cloth in my arms. Then she hastened over to the well, pitched the bucket down, and drew it up running over with fresh water.

"Here," she said, coming back with a good dipperful. "Here's a nice drink of cool water. You need it on a day like this."

The man drank. He held the dipper in both hands, with the tips of his fingers, and drained the dipper dry, then wiped his chin with the back of his hand.

"I did indeed," he said. "That's very tasty water. I thank you."

"That's good water," she said. "That well has been here lo a hundred years. You could stay on for supper," she said. "It's getting on toward that time and I have a fine stew on the stove, with plenty to spare."

"That's kind of you," he said back, "and I'm grateful. But I'd best pass on up your road while there's still daylight left, and see who else might have need of this cloth."

My wife is not normally a demonstrative woman, not in public. Certainly not with strangers. You could have knocked me over with a feather when she up and kissed him full on the mouth, with a nice hug to boot.

"There's payment," she said, "if our money's no good."

He blushed, trying to hide his pleasure. It seemed to me she had him wrapped around her little finger ... or the other way around.

"You kiss like a woman," he said. "Like one who knows what kissing is for, and can't hardly stop herself."

It was my wife's turn to blush.

I took hold of her hand and held her down to grass, because it seemed to me another kiss or two and she'd fly right away with him.

He walked across the yard and up by the well house, leaving by the same route he had come. Heading for the road. At the turn, he spun around and waved.

"You could try the Hopkins place!" my wife called. "There's a fat woman down that road got a sea of troubles. She could surely use some of that cloth."

He smiled and again waved. Then we saw his head and his bolt of white cloth bobbing along the weeds as he took the dips and rises in the road. Then he went on out of sight.

"There's that man with some horses down that road!" my wife called. "You be careful of him!"

It seemed we heard some sound come back, but whether it was his we couldn't say.

My wife and I stood a long time in the yard, me holding the dipper and watching her, while she held her own bolt of cloth in her arms, staring off to where he'd last been.

Then she sighed dreamily and went inside.

I went on down to the barn and looked after the animals. Getting my feeding done. I talked a spell to them. Talking to animals is soothing to me, and they like it too. They pretend to stare at the walls or the floor as they're munching their feed down, but I know they listen to me. We had us an *unusual circumstances* chat. "That man with the cloth," I said. "Maybe you can tell me what you make of him."

Thirty minutes later I heard my wife excitedly calling me. She was standing out on the back doorstep, with this incredulous look.

"I've finished," she said. "I've finished the windows. *Nine* windows. It beats me how."

I started up to the house. Her voice was all shaky. Her face flushed, flinging her arms about. Then she got this new look on.

"Wait!" she said. "Stay there! Give me ten minutes!"

And she flung herself back inside, banging the door. I laughed. It always gave me a kick how she ordered me around.

I got the milk pail down under the cow. Before I'd touched and drained all four teats she was calling again.

"Come look, come look, oh come look!"

She was standing in the open doorway, with the kitchen to her back. Behind her, through the windows, I could see the streak of a red sunset and how it lit up the swing of trees. But I wasn't looking there. I was looking at her. Looking and swallowing hard and trying to remember how a body produced human speech. I had never thought of white as a colour she could wear. White, it pales her some. It leaves her undefined and washes out what parts I like best. But she looked beautiful now. In her new dress she struck me down to my bootstraps. She made my chest break.

"Do you like it?" she said.

I went running up to her. I was up against her, hugging her and lifting her before she'd even had a chance to get set. I'd never held on so tightly or been so tightly held back.

Truth is, it was the strangest thing. Like we were both so innocent we hadn't yet shot up out of new ground.

"Come see the curtains," she whispered. "Come see the new sheets. Come see what else I've made. You'll see it all. You'll see how our home has been transformed."

I crept inside. There was something holy about it. About it and about us and about those rooms and the whole wide world. Something radiant. Like you had to put your foot down easy and hold it down or you'd float on up.

"That's it," she said. "That's how I feel too."

That night in bed, trying to figure it out, we wondered how Ella Mae down the road had done. How the people all along our road had made out.

"No worry," my wife said. "He'll have found a bonanza around here. There's heaps of decent people in this neck of the woods."

"Wonder where he is now?" we said.

"Wonder where he goes next?"

"Where he gets that cloth?"

"Who he *is*?"

We couldn't get to sleep, wondering about that.

Leon Rooke (*born 1934, Roanoke Rapids, North Carolina*), short-story writer, novelist, playwright, has taught creative writing at various places in Canada since 1969. Much of his writing is experimental and explores a wide range of unusual characters. Rooke is best known for his novels, which include the Governor General's Literary Award winner *Shakespeare's Dog*.

Activities: A Bolt of White Cloth

1. **Understand Terms:** Define *magic realism*. Reread the story, noting where fantastic elements mesh with realistic events in the narrative. List the unique attributes of the travelling salesman and the magical qualities of the bolt of white cloth.

2. **Examine Symbolism:** What might the bolt of white cloth symbolize? Do you see any other symbols in the story? Discuss your ideas in a small group and report on your conclusions.

3. **Explore Characters:** Characters act as foils when their contrasting traits emphasize character differences. Work with a partner to explain how the husband and wife act as foils to each other.

4. **Represent Theme:** What is the overall theme or message of the story? On one side of a piece of paper, combine images, words, and phrases that are related to the theme. On the back, explain why you used the images and words on the front to express the theme.

The Leaving

Budge Wilson
(Canadian)

She took me with her the day she left. "Where y' goin', Ma?" I asked.
She was standing beside my bed with her coat on.

"Away," said Ma. "And yer comin', too."

I didn't want to go anywhere. It was three o'clock in the morning,
and I was warm in my bed.

"Why me?" I complained.

I was too sleepy to think of any more complicated questions. In
any case, there were no choices and very few questions back then
when we were kids. You went to school and you came home on the
school bus. If your father wanted you to shovel snow or fetch eggs,
he told you, and you did it. He didn't ask. He told. Same with Ma. I
did the dishes and brought in the firewood when it was required. She
just pointed to the sink or to the woodbox, and I would leave
whatever I was doing and start work. But at 3:00 a.m., the situation
seemed unusual enough to permit a question. Therefore I asked
again, "Why me?"

"Because yer the smartest," she said. "And because yer a woman."

I was twelve years old that spring.

Ma was a tall, rangy woman. She had a strong handsome face, with
high cheekbones and a good firm chin line. Her lips were full. Her
teeth were her own, although she smiled so rarely that you seldom
saw them; her mouth tended to be held in a set straight line. She did
not exactly frown; it was more as though she were loosely clenching
her teeth. Her eyes were veiled, as if she had shut herself off from her
surroundings and was thinking either private thoughts or nothing at
all. Oh, she was kind enough and gentle enough when we needed it,
though perhaps we needed it more often than she knew. But when
we had cut knees or tonsillectomies, or when friends broke our
hearts, she would hold us and hug us. Her mouth would lose its hard
tight shape, and her eyes would come alive with concern and love.

Her lovely crisp auburn hair was short and unshaped making her
face look uncompromising and austere. She wore baggy slacks over

her excellent legs, and she owned two shabby grey sweaters and two faded graceless blouses. I did not ask myself why my mother looked this way, or why she had retreated behind her frozen face. One accepts one's parents for a long time, without theory or question. Speculation comes later, with adolescence and all the uncertainty and confusion it brings.

But when she woke me that chilly May morning, I was still a child. I rose and dressed quickly, packing my school bag with my pyjamas and toothbrush, the book I was reading, a package of gum, the string of Woolworth pearls that my grandmother had given me on my tenth birthday, and some paper to write and draw on. I wore jeans, my favourite blue sweater, my winter jacket, and rubber boots. I forgot my hat.

My mother had told me to be quiet, so I slithered down the stairs without a single board creaking. She was waiting at the door, holding a black cardboard suitcase with a strap around it. A shopping bag held sandwiches and some of last fall's bruised apples. She wore a brown car coat over her black slacks, and her hair was hidden under a grey wool kerchief. Her mouth had its tense fixed look, but her eyes were alive. Even at my age and at that hour, I could see that.

We stopped briefly before walking out into the cold night air. The stove in the kitchen was making chugging noises, and from different parts of the small house could be heard a variety of snores and heavy breathing. My four brothers and my father were not going to notice our departure.

For a moment, my mother seemed to hesitate. Her mouth softened, and a line deepened between her eyebrows. Then she straightened her shoulders and opened the door. "Move!" she whispered.

We stepped into the night and started walking down the mountain in the direction of town, six miles away. I did not quarrel with the need for this strange nocturnal journey, but I did question the reason.

"Ma," I said.

She turned and looked at me.

"Ma. Why are we leavin'?"

She didn't answer right away. It crossed my mind that she might not be sure of the reason herself. This was a frightening thought. But apparently she knew.

"I plans t' do some thinkin'," she said.

We walked quickly through the night. North and South Mountains closed off the sky behind us and far ahead, but a full moon made it easy to see our way on the frosty road. The hill country was full of scrub growth, stubby spruce, and sprawling alders, unlike the tidy fields and orchards of the Valley. But the frost lent a silver magic to the bushes and the rough ground, and the moonlight gave a still dignity to the shabby houses. It was cold, and I shivered. "Fergot yer hat," said Ma. "Here." She took the warm wool kerchief from her head and gave it to me. I took it. Parents were invincible, and presumably would not feel the cold. My mother was not a complainer. She was an endurer. It was 1969, and she was forty-five years old.

When we reached Annapolis, we stopped at a small house on the edge of town, and Ma put down her suitcase and dug around in her purse. She took out a key and opened the door. Even my silent mother seemed to think that an explanation was required. "Lida Johnson's in Glace Bay, visitin' her daughter. Said I could use the house while she's gone. Normie's at a 4-H meetin' in Bridgetown. Joseph's truckin'. We'll wait here till th' train goes."

"Ma," I asked, "how long we gonna be gone?"

She bent her head down from its rigid position and looked at the floorboards of the front hall. She touched her mouth briefly with her fist. She closed her eyes for a second and took a deep breath.

"Dunno," she replied. "Till it's time."

We slept in the parlour until we left for the station.

I guess that six-mile walk had shunted me straight from childhood into adolescence, because I did an awful lot of thinking between Annapolis and Halifax. But at first I was too busy to think. I was on a train, and I had never been inside one before. There were things to investigate—the tiny washroom with its little sink, and the funny way to flush the toilet. In the main part of the Dayliner, the seats slid up and down so that people could sleep if they wanted to. I watched the world speed by the windows—men working on the roads; kids playing in schoolyards; cows standing dumbly outside barns in the chilly air, all facing in the same direction; places and towns I had never seen till then. My ma looked over at me and placed a comic book and a bag of peanuts on my lap. "Fer th' trip," she said, and smiled, patting my knee in an unfamiliar gesture. "Mind missin' school?" she added.

"No," I said. But I did. I had a part in the class play, and there was a practice that afternoon. I was the chief fairy, and I had twenty-five lines, all of which I knew by heart already. But this trip was also a pretty special, if alarming, adventure. It had a beginning but no definite end, and we were still speeding toward the middle. What would Halifax be like? We never had enough money to have more than one ride on the Exhibition ferris wheel at Lawrencetown; but here we were buying train tickets and reading comics and eating peanuts and travelling to heaven knows what expensive thrills.

"Maw," I asked, "where'd the money come from?"

She looked at me, troubled.

"Don't ask," she said. "I'll tell you when you're eighteen."

Eighteen! I might as well relax and enjoy myself. But I wondered.

Before long, she fell asleep, and I felt free to think. Until then, it was almost as though I were afraid she would read my thoughts.

Why had we left? How long would we be gone? How would Pa and my brothers cook their dinner? How would they make their beds? Who would they complain to after a hard day? Who would fetch the eggs, the mail, the water, the wood, the groceries? Who would wash their overalls, mend their socks, put bandages on their cuts? It was inconceivable to me that they could survive for long without us.

When we reached Halifax, we went to what I now realize was a cheap and shabby hotel in the South End of the city. But to me it seemed the height of luxury. The bed was made of some kind of shiny yellow wood. The bedspread was an intense pink, with raised nubbles all over it. A stained spittoon sat in the corner. There was actually a sink in the room, with taps that offered both cold and hot water. A toilet that flushed was down the hall. I checked under the bed; there was no chamber pot. But who needed it? There were two pictures on the walls—one of a curly-headed blonde, displaying a lot of bare flesh, and another of three dead ducks hanging upside down from a nail. I spent a lot of time inspecting both of these pictures.

Halifax was a shock to me. How could the buildings be so huge and the stores so grand? Here I was in the province's capital city before I really understood what a capital city could be. I admired the old stone buildings with their carvings around the doors and windows. I stretched my neck to see the tops of the modern apartments, with their glass and concrete reaching up into the clouds. The buses and cars alarmed me as they rushed up and down the long streets, but they excited me, too. The weather changed; it was warm and comforting, and the wind was gentle and caressing. We went down the hill to the harbour, and saw the bridge; rooted in the ground and in the sea bottom, it lifted its enormous metal wings into the sky. I marvelled that a thing so strong could be so graceful, so beautiful. What a lovely way, I thought, to get from one place to another. We walked across the bridge to Dartmouth and watched the ships, far below, headed for Europe, for Africa, for the distant North. My mother, who had started to talk, told me about all these things. It was as though she were trying to tell me something important, but didn't want to say things right out. "They're goin' somewheres," she said. Later on, she took me out to Dalhousie University, and we walked among the granite buildings and beside the playing fields. "If yer as smart as the teacher claims," she said, "maybe you'll come here some day t' learn." I thought this highly unlikely. If we couldn't afford running water, how could we afford such a thing as that? I said so.

"They's ways," she said.

We walked up and down Spring Garden Road and gazed in the big windows. I looked at a candy store with at least five million kinds of candy, shops with dresses so fancy that I could scarcely believe it, shelves full of diamonds and gold and sparkling crystal. "Is there ways for all this, too?" I asked my mother. She hesitated.

"Don't need all that stuff," she concluded.

The weather was dazzling—a sunny Nova Scotia May day. We walked through the huge iron gates into the Public Gardens and ate our sandwiches and apples beside the duck pond. I kicked off my rubber boots and wiggled my toes in the sun as I watched the swans and the yellow ducklings. The Gardens were immense, full of massive and intricate flowerbeds, winding paths, and strange exotic trees. There were statues, a splashing fountain, an elaborate round bandstand, and a little river with a curved bridge over it. Lovers strolled arm in arm, and children shrieked with laughter as they chased the pigeons. I asked Ma why everyone seemed so happy. "Dunno," she said. "Weather does things t' people." She looked around. "And maybe some of them's free," she added.

On the second day, we watched women racing to work in the morning, mini-skirts flipping, heels clicking, faces eager, faces tense. We looked on as shopping women pulled twenty-dollar bills out of their purses as though they were nickels. We saw the drunks sleeping on the pavement outside the mission. We visited the courthouse and looked at the pictures of the stern-faced judges as they watched us from the walls. "They fixes things what aren't right," said Ma. I wondered how. "But not always," she added.

We spent an hour in the public library, looking at the shelves and shelves of books, smelling their wonderful book smells, idly turning the pages. On a book dolly, she picked up a copy of *The Feminine Mystique*. She, who had not to my knowledge read a single book since I was born, said shyly, "I read this book." I was astonished.

"You!" I exclaimed. "How come? When?"

"I kin read!" she retorted, miffed. "Even if y' leaves school in grade five, y' kin read. Y' reads slow, but y' knows how."

"But where'd you get it?" I demanded, amazed.

"Y' remember that day the Salvation Army lady brought us that big box o' clothes?" she asked. "Yer pa was mad and said we didn't need no charity. But I hid the box, and after a time he forgot about it. Well, there was other things in there, too—an eggbeater, some toys what I gave to Lizzie's kids, even a string o' yellow beads and a bracelet that I bin savin' fer you. And some books. There was comic books and that big colourin' book y' got fer Christmas, and them *Popular Mechanics* magazines the boys read, and a coupla others. And this." She placed the palm of her hand on the book. "Seemed like it was for me, special. So I read it. She was real tough goin', but I read every word. Took me near a year. Finished it last Thursday."

I could hardly believe it. My ma didn't even read recipes. She kept them all in her head. I asked, "Was it good?"

She thought for a moment before answering. "She was a real troublin' book. But she was good."

I couldn't understand that. "If it was so troublin', why was it so good?"

She answered that one without hesitation. "Found I weren't alone," she said. She stroked its cover tenderly before putting it back on the dolly. I liked the library, with all the silent people bent over their books, and the librarians moving soundlessly to and fro. I wasn't used to quiet places.

In the afternoon, we climbed the Citadel and went into its museum, walking up and down among the sea things, old things, rich things. Later on, we went to what I thought was a very fancy restaurant. There were bright, shiny chrome tables with place mats of paper lace and green glass ashtrays. I ordered a hot dog and chips, because that was my favourite meal. My mother, her mouth now soft and cheerful, ordered something with a strange name.

"Ain't gonna come all this way and spend all th' hen money jest t' eat what I kin eat at home," she said.

The egg money! So that was it. I let on I didn't notice. But a thrill of fear ran through me. I wondered what Pa would do.

In the evening we returned early to the hotel, and I slept deeply, but with strange and troubled dreams.

On the third day, Ma said, "It's time. T'day we go home." I asked why.

"Because," she said.

"Because why?" I insisted.

She was silent for a moment, and then said again, "It's time." I was pleased. It had been an interesting trip, but it frightened me a little because there were no explanations, no answers to my unspoken questions. Besides, I was afraid that someone else would get to be chief fairy in the school play. "Have you done yer thinkin'?" I asked. She looked at me strangely. There was hope in her look and an odd fierce dignity.

"I has," she said.

We took the bus home instead of the train, and it was late afternoon when we arrived in Annapolis to start the six-mile climb to our farm. The day was damp and cold, and I wore my mother's wool kerchief again. We were very quiet, and I knew she was nervous. Her mouth was back in its taut line, and her eyes were troubled. But even in the wind, her shoulders were straight and firm, and I could feel a difference in her. Fearful though her eyes were, she was fully alert, and you could sense a new dogged strength in the set of her face.

There was no such strength in me, except such as I derived from her. Home is home when you are twelve, and I did not want to live a tourist's life in Halifax forever. But I worried every step of the long journey.

As we turned the bend at Harrison's Corner, we could see the farm in the distance. It was as though I were seeing it for the first time. The house had been white once, but it had needed paint for almost nineteen years. Around the yard was a confusion of junk of all kinds: two discarded cars—lopsided and without wheels—an unpiled jumble of firewood, buckets, a broken hoe, rusty tools, an old oil drum for burning garbage. To the left were the few acres of untidy fields, dotted with spruce trees and the grey skeletons of trees long dead of Dutch elm disease. To the right, close to the henhouse, was the barn—small and unpainted, grey and shabby in the dim afternoon light. We could hear the two cows complaining, waiting for milking time.

When we opened the kitchen door, they were all there. My four big brothers were playing cards at the table, and my father was sitting by the kitchen stove, smoking a cigarette and drinking from a bottle of beer. I had forgotten how darkly handsome he was. But because it was not Sunday, he was unshaven, and his eyes glared out at us from beneath heavy black eyebrows.

Pa rose from his chair and faced us. He was very tall, and his head almost reached the low ceiling. He seemed to fill the entire room. He crushed out his cigarette on the top of the stove.

His voice was low and threatening. "Where you bin, woman?" he said.

She spoke, and I was amazed that she had the courage. Then I realized with a jolt that his words were little different in tone and substance from hundreds I had heard before: "How come my supper's not ready, woman?" "Move smart, woman! I'm pressed fer time!" "Shut up them damn kids, woman!" "Move them buckets, woman! They're in my way!" "This food ain't fit t' eat, woman. Take it away!"

She spoke quietly and with dignity. "You is right to be angry, Lester," she said. "I left a note fer y', but I shoulda tole y' before I left."

"Shut yer mouth, woman, and git my supper!" he shouted, slamming the beer bottle down on the table.

She moved to the centre of the room and faced him. "My name," she began, and faltered. She cleared her throat and ran her tongue over her lower lip. "My name," she repeated, this time more steadily, "is Elizabeth."

He was dumbfounded. My brothers raised their heads from their card game and waited, cards poised in midair.

Pa looked at her. He looked at me. Then he looked at Jem and Daniel and Ira and Bernard, sitting there silent and still like four statues, waiting for his reaction.

Suddenly my father threw back his head and laughed. His ugly laughter filled the little kitchen, and we all listened, frozen, wishing for it to stop.

"'My name is Elizabeth!'" he mocked, between choking guffaws, slapping his thighs and holding his stomach, and then he repeated himself and her, mincingly, "'My ... name ... is ... Elizabeth!'" Then his face changed, and there was silence. "Git over here 'n' make my supper, woman! I'm gonna milk them cows. But my belly is right empty, and y' better be ready when I gits back from th' chores!"

I watched my mother. During the laughter, I could see her retreat for a minute behind her eyes, expressionless, lifeless, beaten. Then she took a deep breath and looked at him directly, squarely, with no fear in her face. Pain, yes, but no fear. My brothers looked down and continued their card game.

"Act smart there, Sylvie," she said to me, as soon as he had left. "I need yer help bad. You clean up, 'n' I'll fix supper." She was already moving swiftly about the kitchen, fetching food, chopping onions, peeling potatoes.

In the sink was a mountainous pile of dirty dishes. Open cans, crusted with stale food, cluttered the counter. I surveyed the scene with distaste.

"Ma," I asked, complaining like the true adolescent that I had now become, "how come they couldna washed the dishes themselves? They goes huntin' and fishin' and has lotsa little vacations in th' winter. We always do their work for them when they're gone. How come we gotta clean up their mess?"

"Listen," she said, cutting the potatoes and dropping them into the hot fat, "the way I sees it is y' kin ask fer kindness or politeness from time t' time. But y' can't expect no miracles. It's my own fault fer raisin' four boys like they was little men. I shoulda put them in front of a dishpan fifteen years ago. Now it's too late. Yer pa's ma did the same thing. She aimed t' raise a boy who was strong and brave, with no soft edges." She wiped her forehead with the back of her hand. "All along I bin blamin' men fer bein' men. But now I see that oftentimes it's the women that makes them that way." It was a long, long speech for my ma. But she went on. "The boys is seventeen, eighteen, nineteen, and twenty years old. Y' can't start makin' 'em over now. They's set." Then she smiled wryly, with a rare show of humour. She bowed formally in the direction of the card game. "I apologizes," she said, "to your future wives."

Then she stopped, and looked from one son's face to the next, and so on, around the table. "I loves you all, regardless," she said softly, "and it's worth a try. Jem"—she spoke to the youngest—"I'd be right grateful if you'd fetch some water for Sylvie. She's real tired after the long walk."

Jem looked at his brothers, and then he looked at her. Water carrying was woman's work, and she knew she was asking a lot of him. He rose silently, took the bucket from her, and went outside to the well.

"And you," she said, addressing Daniel and Ira and Bernard, "one snigger out of you, and yer in bad trouble." I'm sure she knew she was taking an awful chance. You can say a thing like that to little boys, but these were grown men. But no one moved or so much as smiled when Jem returned. "I thank you right kindly," said Ma, thereby delivering a speech as unusual as her other one.

You could say, I suppose, that our leaving made no large difference in my mother's life. She still worked without pay or praise, and was often spoken to as though she were without worth or attraction. Her days were long and thankless. She emptied chamber pots and spittoons, scrubbed overalls and sheets on her own mother's scrub board, and peeled the frozen clothes from the line in winter with aching fingers. But not all things remained the same. She now stood up to my father. Her old paralytic fear was gone, and she was able to speak with remarkable force and dignity. She did not nag. Nagging is like a constant blow with a small blunt instrument. It annoys, but it seldom makes more than a small dent. When she chose to object to Pa's cruel or unfair behaviour, her instrument was a shining steel knife with a polished cutting edge. A weapon like that seemed to make my father realize that if he went too far—if he beat her, or if he scolded too often or too unjustly—she would leave. After all, she had done it once before. And this time, she might not return.

So there were changes. One day, for no apparent reason, he started to call her Elizabeth. She did not let on that this was remarkable, but the tight line of her mouth relaxed, and she made him a lemon pie for supper. She fixed up the attic storeroom as a workroom for herself. The boys lugged up her treadle sewing machine, and she brought in an old wicker chair and a table from the barn. It was a hot room in summer and cold in winter, but it was her own place—her escape. She made curtains from material bought at Frenchy's, and hooked a little rug for the floor. No one was allowed to go there except her. She always emerged from this room softer, gentler, more still.

I never did hear a single word about the missing egg money. Maybe Pa didn't notice, or perhaps Ma attacked the subject with her sharp-edged knife. Possibly it was the egg money that sent me to Dalhousie—that and my scholarship and my summer jobs. I never asked. I didn't really want to know.

When I was home last February during the term break, I stole a look into Ma's attic room. There were library books on the table, material on the sewing machine, paper piled on the floor for her letters to me and to the boys. I respected her privacy and did not go in. But the room, even in that chilly winter attic, looked like an inviting place.

My ma is now fifty-five, and has a lot of life still to live. My pa is fifty-eight. He still shaves once a week, and he has not yet cleared up the yard. But he often speaks to my mother as though she were more of a person and less of a thing. Sometimes he says thank-you. He still has a raging temper, but he is an old dog, and new tricks come hard. He loves my mother and she him, with a kind of love that is difficult for my generation to understand or define. In another time and in another place, the changes could have been more marked. But my mother is a tough and patient woman, and these differences seem to be enough for her. Her hair is worn less severely. Her mouth is not set so straight and cold and firm. She talks more. She has made a pretty yellow blouse to wear with her baggy slacks. She smiles often, and she is teaching her two grandsons how to wash dishes and make cookies.

I often wonder about these things: but when my mind approaches the reasons for all that has happened, my thinking slides away and my vision blurs. Certainly the book and the leaving do not explain everything. Maybe my mother was ready to move into and out of herself anyway; and no one can know exactly what went on in her thoughts before and after she left. Perhaps she was as surprised as I was by the amount of light and warmth she let in when she opened the door to step into the dark and frosty morning. But of that strange three-day departure, I can say, as Ma did of her book, "She was a real troublin' trip. But she was good."

Budge Wilson (*born 1927, Halifax, Nova Scotia*), teacher, commercial artist, photographer, librarian, published her first book at age 50, and has published 18 more since. *The Leaving* was recognized by the American Library Association as one of the best 75 young-adult books of the last 25 years.

Activities: The Leaving

1. **Summarize Events:** Summarize the important events of the story, using a time line, or map. For each event, note any change it produced in the narrator.

2. **Share Insights:** With a partner, discuss Elizabeth's motives for leaving and for taking her daughter with her. In the mother's voice, confide to your diary several years later what you think you achieved. Share your diary entry with other students and comment on each other's ideas and insights.

3. **Write a Monologue:** Working in a group of four, choose one of the following roles, making sure that each is represented: the father, the mother, the daughter, one of the sons. Write an interior monologue about the character's thoughts the night of the return. Share and discuss your monologues.

4. **Define "Love":** Consider the nature of the love that exists between the different characters. Write a definition of "love" that encompasses all these relationships. Post your definition and, as a class, discuss the different ideas.

Wandering

Maureen Hynes

Send one photo, says the form, one photo taken within the last three months, three by five inches, head and shoulders of the patient. Black-and-white or colour. The photo to accompany the application form my sister and I have already filled out.

The form than asks about her middle name (oh, she hates Gertrude so much). Date of Birth: 13/11/13. Height: 5′2″. But she used to be 5′5″. Weight: about 140, my sister and I guess. (And what does *your* mother weigh? I want to write.) Colour of Eyes: grey-hazel. Colour of Hair: brown-grey. Even at 77, still so little grey. Thin Eyebrows or Thick: very thin. Any Scars: many scars; a very old thyroid operation scar at base of throat, recent lumpectomy scar on left breast, recent scar on left hip from surgery for broken hip, scars on left arm from pins for a broken wrist, toenails removed on both big toes. Amputations: no, we shudder. Prostheses: no. False Teeth: yes. Hearing Aid: no. Glasses: yes, on a string around her neck. Tattoos: no, we chuckle. How about a snake entwined around her right forearm? "Mother" surrounded by hearts and flowers? Mother. No, no tattoos. And so many other details: build, precise skin colour and complexion (ruddy, freckled, pock-marked?), hair style (bald, receding, curly, wavy, sideburns, wig, or toupee?), eye defects, moustache, disabilities, birthmarks, any special medications.

And where is the patient likely to wander, the form asks. We print three locations: to the Dominion Store at the Yonge–Eglinton Centre;

Saint Michael's Cathedral, for the 12:15 Mass; 26 St. Hilda's Avenue, her mother's old home.

Send one photo. Today, alone, I look at the eight shiny black-and-white photos I picked up from the camera store. Six of my mother, two of me taken on a warm and brilliant sunny Saturday, a surprise in early March. But the weather scares us now, because the deep cold has kept her in all winter. Now, we think, in the warm weather, she's more likely to go out.

I'll take the pictures on Saturday, I'd told my sister. I trick my mother a bit, to take the photos. I hide in the living room winding a new spool of TMAX 400 black-and-white film into my camera, walk into the kitchen. What a gorgeous day, I say. It's spring, I say. Look, it's so mild. I open the back door, the one off the kitchen. Feel that, I say. Oooh, we both exclaim, our pleasure immediate, welcoming the warmth. Look, I say, I want to finish this roll of film, can I take some pictures. Let's go out on the porch. Just step out on the porch. Just there. She looks nervously at me, at the camera. Okay, she says, just out on the porch. She steps out into the sunshine and looks around the yard. We both take deep breaths and smile at the new warmth. It's lovely, isn't it, I say. I just want to finish this roll, I tell her, lifting the camera to my eyes. *Head and shoulders*, I remind myself, focusing quickly through the viewfinder. Isn't it gorgeous out? I snap a photo. Hey, I laugh, can you manage to look a little bit *friendly*? She breaks into a great smile. I snap another. Oh, the roll's not finished, I say, pretending annoyance. I snap another. That's enough, she tells me. Just one more, I snap another. Here, you take some of me, I say, handing her the camera. Just press *here*, I show her. She snaps one. Take another, I tell her, and quickly advance the film for her, not caring if she focuses or not. Oh, *still* not finished, I say, taking the camera from her. I pretend annoyance again. Let's trade places, I say, you stand over here. The late afternoon light is casting long sharp shadows. I want to bracket the shots; don't want to repeat all this. I take two more. Let's go inside, she says. Okay, Mom, just one more. But she won't allow one more. That's enough, she says. No more, she says. She goes inside with relief, having indulged me. Her anxiety to get back into the kitchen is like a taste I can hold in my mouth. I wonder if we can count on it, her wanting to stay inside the house. Or does she sense my dishonesty, the purpose I am pretending not to have? Oh, it's finished now anyway, I tell her, eight shots into my roll of twenty-four. I rewind the film, open the camera, fish out the roll, and put it in my purse. You want a cup of Nescafé? she asks, the tenth time in an hour.

Send one photo. Almost every day she talks about her mother, about going to see her. She packs a plastic bag with a few things, a towel, some underwear, a sweater, a new pair of pantyhose, a nightgown, and something that looks like it might be a gift, a pair of shiny turquoise plastic earrings in an old blue Birks box, an expensive little bar of soap, or a cheap china figurine. Little things I never knew she had. She ties up the plastic bag tight by its two plastic handles and puts it in a corner of her room. The next day she stashes the bag in the back of her closet and packs a new bag. On her really bad days she comes downstairs with her plastic bag and looks at it in confusion. I was going to take this down to Mom's ... she starts to say, but doesn't finish. Oh, that's okay, we say. We'll do that later. Okay, she says, and lets us take the bag from her hands. When she isn't looking we take it back upstairs and unpack it.

If I haven't been there for a few days, I have to go up to her room and unpack three or four of these bags and put their contents away. We don't like to do this, go through her things, but we have to because fairly often she's packed away all her underwear. Sometimes she comes downstairs for dinner, looks in the dining room, and then looks at me puzzled. Where's Mom? she asks. My mind scrambles. Ahh, I say soothingly, remembering the information sheets from the Alzheimer Society about how to handle these behaviours.

Ahh, you're missing Nan a lot, I say. You're thinking about Nan again, I say. Address the emotion, not the facts, the information sheet says, the sense of loss, the nostalgia for a safer, surer time. Don't tell the patient her mother is dead. You run the risk of tripping off the grieving process again. Don't say she's in Heaven, which she might understand, or she died in 1964, which she won't. You're missing Nan again? Yeah, she says, shaking her head, I haven't seen her in *so long*. I give her a small hug. It's Sunday, I say, remember how she used to come here almost every Sunday night after Devotions at church? And she always brought Maple Walnut ice cream. And I never liked Maple Walnut ice cream. Sometimes Neopolitan, and I didn't like that much either. It was always so soft and melted and, I pause, ersatz. Ersatz? She says blankly, and I remember the precise moment she taught me that word, in the basement of Eaton's Annex, cheap merchandise, she said, ersatz.

I keep going, what I liked was Butterscotch Ripple, but Nan never brought that. But *you* used to buy Butterscotch Ripple for me at Hall's Dairy, I end brightly. We both laugh. I have edged her past the bad moment again. Or is that what she thinks? What does she think? Oh, but I am not always this kind. Sometimes if it's the fourth or fifth time in an hour that she asks about going to her mom's, I get exasperated. Mom! I say sharply. Nan's not there. She's not there and we're not going. She turns and leaves the room and I feel awful.

Send one photo. I am looking at the six shiny black-and-white photos on the desk, lined up in front of the keyboard. There are two really good shots.

I like the one with the great smile the best. But it's a little dark, too. I decide on the one that has the best light. She looks just about to speak. Her forehead is furrowed a bit, and fine wrinkles cushion her skin. Laugh-lines emanate from the corners of her eyes, across her cheeks. Deep folds run from her nose to the corners of her mouth and down her chin; the folds are familiar—I recognize the beginnings of them in my own face. Her throat looks corded but soft, too. Her hair is lifted up in small wisps in the mild afternoon breeze. She's wearing her white cardigan over a green and blue blouse. Of course her glasses are hanging around her neck, as they have for years. Her new glasses that I bought her in a pharmacy, because now she refuses to go to an eye doctor for a checkup.

I'll keep the one with the great smile for myself. It's a little dark, and besides, she won't be wandering around smiling like that.

Yesterday on the way to the doctor's in a taxi, she turns to me in the back seat. She leans over and whispers, so the cabby can't hear, in a voice so urgent and panic-filled that chills ripple across my shoulders, *I don't know where my kids are.* Panicked like she's lost sight of us at a beach. I take her hand. Your kids are fine, I say. We're all grown up now. We're all fine, we're all okay. I'm Maureen, I'm one of your kids, and I very slowly detail where we all are, where we all live. Oh yeah, she says, oh yeah, that's right, and she comes back slowly to the present. For the moment.

Send one photo to the Wandering Patients' Registry at the Alzheimer Society. The Alzheimer Society sent us the form, but they'll forward it to the police. The police will keep it on file. Sometimes inside the subway you see a photo of an older person taped inside the glass ticket taker's booth. Missing, it says above the photo of an old man in his long winter coat, staring flatly out at you. If the patient goes missing, you call the police immediately and tell them she's registered. One day last fall, about five o'clock in the afternoon, my father had a big scare. My mother hadn't come home yet from the noon Mass at St. Michael's Cathedral. He saw a police car on the street and went out to talk to the policeman in it. I'm worried about my wife, he said. He explained that she was in the early stages of Alzheimer's, but still pretty independent and reliable. Is she registered, they asked. When he said no, they said, there's not much we can do about it. When she got back about half an hour later, she was upset. She didn't want to talk much about it, but my father pressed her. I got turned around on the subway, she said. I got on at a new entrance. A man gave me the wrong directions. I went down to Union Station instead. I had to come all the way back. Then she changed the subject. She said that at the cathedral she met a woman who had twins; the woman's husband was away in the Air Force, and she was taking in roomers to pay the mortgage. My father noticed the woman had the same life story as my mother. She hasn't wanted to go out on her own since that September day. But every day she wants to see her mother. Now that the cold weather is ending, we get scared, we ask each other, do you think she'd go out? It would only take a few moments. She's so much worse now, we tell each other.

Send one photo. Grieving in pieces, that's what the social workers are telling us to do. You have to mourn the loss of what your mother was and accept what she still is. You have to grieve the part of her that has wandered away and will never come back.

Maureen Hynes (*born Moncton, New Brunswick*), author, faculty member at George Brown College in Toronto, has trained teachers in China and Cuba. Her published works include *Letters from China* and *Rough Skin*, for which she was awarded the Gerald Lampert Memorial Award in 1995. She has published anthologies of stories as well as literary criticism.

Activities: Wandering

1. **Relate to Prior Knowledge:** Working in a small group, list the mother's behaviours that you recognize as symptoms of Alzheimer's disease. For each behaviour, note any actions taken by the family members in an attempt to compensate.

2. **Analyze Use of Repetition:** What effects does Hynes create through the repetition of "Send one photo"? Why might the idea of a photo be significant in this story? Organize and polish your ideas into a short piece of formal writing.

3. **Interpret the Title:** Authors often use titles that have both a literal and figurative meaning. With reference to the selection, explain the literal and figurative meaning of "Wandering." Think of two other examples of poem, story, novel, or movie titles that have these two levels of meaning.

4. **Write a Letter:** In a small group, discuss Hynes's purpose(s) in writing this story and the audience for which you think it was written. Using ideas from the discussion, write a letter that Hynes might write to a friend explaining why she has written this story.

An Incident at Law

Anton Chekhov

The case occurred at a recent session of the N. district court.

In the dock was Sidor Felonovsky, resident of N., a fellow of about thirty, with restless gypsy features and shifty little eyes. He was accused of burglary, fraud and obtaining a false passport, and coupled with the latter was a further charge of impersonation. The case was being brought by the deputy prosecutor. The name of his tribe is Legion. He's totally devoid of any special features or qualities that might make him popular or bring him huge fees: he's just average. He has a nasal voice, doesn't sound his k's properly, and is forever blowing his nose.

Photograph of Anton Chekhov taken in 1897

Whereas defending was a fantastically celebrated and popular advocate, known throughout the land, whose wonderful speeches are always being quoted, whose name is uttered in tones of awe …

The role that he plays at the end of cheap novels, where the hero is completely vindicated and the public bursts into applause, is not inconsiderable. In such novels he is given a surname derived from thunder, lightning and other equally awe-inspiring forces of nature.

When the deputy prosecutor had succeeded in proving that Felonovsky was guilty and deserved no mercy, when he had finished defining and persuading and said: "The case for the prosecution rests"—then defence counsel rose to his feet. Everyone pricked up their ears. Dead silence reigned. Counsel began his speech ... and in the public gallery their nerves ran riot! Sticking out his swarthy neck and cocking his head to one side, with eyes aflashing and hand upraised, he poured his mellifluous magic into their expectant ears. His words plucked at their nerves as though he were playing the balalaika ... Scarcely had he uttered a couple of sentences than there was a loud sigh and a woman had to be carried out ashen-faced. Only three minutes elapsed before the judge was obliged to reach over for his bell and ring three times for order. The red-nosed clerk of the court swivelled round on his chair and began to glare menacingly at the animated faces of the public. Eyes dilated, cheeks drained of colour, everyone craned forward in an agony of suspense to hear what he would say next ... And need I describe what was happening to the ladies' hearts?!

"Gentlemen of the jury, you and I are human beings! Let us therefore judge as human beings!" said defence counsel *inter alia.* "Before appearing in front of you today, this human being had to endure the agony of six months on remand. For six months his wife has been deprived of the husband she cherishes so fondly, for six months his children's eyes have been wet with tears at the thought that their dear father was no longer beside them. Oh, if only you could see those children! They are starving because there is no one to feed them. They are crying because they are so deeply unhappy ... Yes, look at them, look at them! See how they stretch their tiny arms towards you, imploring you to give them back their father! They are not here in person, but can you not picture them? *(Pause.)* Six months on remand ... Six ... They put him in with thieves and murderers ... a man like this! *(Pause.)* One need only imagine the moral torment of that imprisonment, far from his wife and children, to ... But need I say more?!"

Sobs were heard in the gallery ... A girl with a large brooch on her bosom had burst into tears. Then the little old lady next to her began snivelling.

Defence counsel went on and on ... He tended to ignore the facts, concentrating more on the psychological aspect.

"Shall I tell you what it means to know this man's soul? It means knowing a unique and individual world, a world full of varied impulses. I have made a study of that world, and I tell you frankly that as I did so, I felt I was studying Man for the first time ... I understood what Man is ... And every impulse of my client's soul convinces me that in him I have the honour of observing a perfect human being ..."

The clerk of the court stopped staring so menacingly and fished around in his pocket for a handkerchief. Two more women were carried out. The judge forgot all about the bell and put on his glasses, so that no one would notice the large tear welling up in his right eye. Handkerchiefs appeared on every side. The deputy prosecutor, that rock, that iceberg, that most insensitive of organisms, shifted about in his chair, turned red, and started gazing at the floor ... Tears were glistening behind his glasses.

"Why on earth did I go ahead with the case?" he thought to himself. "How am I ever going to live down a fiasco like this!"

"Just look at his eyes!" defence counsel continued (his chin was trembling, his voice was trembling, and his eyes showed how much his soul was suffering). "Can those meek, tender eyes look upon a crime without flinching? No, I tell you, those are the eyes of a man who weeps! There are sensitive nerves concealed behind those Asiatic cheekbones! And the heart that beats within that coarse, misshapen breast—that heart is as honest as the day is long! Members of the jury, can you dare as human beings to say that this man is guilty?"

At this point the accused himself could bear it no longer. Now it was his turn to start crying. He blinked, burst into tears and began fidgeting restlessly ...

"All right!" he blurted out, interrupting defence counsel. "All right! I *am* guilty! It was me done the burglary and the fraud. Miserable wretch that I am! I took the money from the trunk and got my sister-in-law to hide the fur coat. I confess! Guilty on all counts!"

Accused then made a detailed confession and was convicted.

Anton Chekhov (*born 1860, Russia; died 1904*), dramatist and short-story writer, was studying medicine when he began to write humorous stories for journals. Chiefly known for his plays, which include *Three Sisters* and *The Cherry Orchard*, Chekhov often combines comedy, tragedy, and pathos in his work.

Activities: An Incident at Law

1. ***Identify Rhetorical Devices:*** In a small group, research and write brief explanations of several rhetorical devices. Identify examples of some of these devices in the speech of the defence counsel. Individually, decide which device you would find most persuasive. Discuss your choice with group members.

2. ***Examine Hyperbole:*** Review the meaning of *hyperbole*, and then identify four examples of hyperbole used by the narrator. In a short written response, evaluate the impact of the hyperbole on the reader.

3. ***Identify Sentence Structures:*** Review different types of sentence structures (complex, compound, and so forth), and identify in the selection examples of as many different types of sentence structures as you can find. Organize your examples in a chart.

4. ***Speak Persuasively:*** Work with a partner to develop two different oral presentations of the defence counsel's speech. The two presentations should make use of different vocal techniques and gestures, but be equally persuasive. Share and discuss your presentations with another pair.

Rudolph the Nasally Empowered Reindeer

James Finn Garner

The story of Rudolph is a familiar one to most of the pre-adults in America and other parts of the Western world (not that this fact is an endorsement of Western culture, just an acknowledgment that the publicity and merchandising machines run more efficiently in those areas). While the image of an eager young reindeer cheerfully giving his all for Santa Claus might be useful to department stores and jingle writers, the truth of his story is more complicated.

It's true that from birth Rudolph was a unique individual, that his luminescent olfactory organ made him different from (but not inferior to) the other reindeer in his age category, and that they often maliciously taunted him about his supra-nasal capabilities. Some reindeer caregivers, concerned that his nose had resulted from

radioactive fallout or was somehow contagious, warned their fawns not to play with him.

What is *not* true is that Rudolph was disappointed to be so ostracized. While his parents successfully fought to have him schooled alongside the other young bucks and does, Rudolph always fancied himself an outsider. In fact, he worked to cultivate his image as an "angry young reindeer." He had no interest in the other reindeer and their inane games. He took himself and his fluorescent gift seriously and was convinced he had a higher calling in this life: to improve the fortunes of the working reindeer and overthrow the oppressive tyranny of Santa Claus.

For untold years, the success of Santa's toy-making monopoly depended on the co-option and exploitation of both the reindeer and elf populations. To this end, his most important criteria for the reindeer in his team were strong legs, a ten-point rack, and minimal grey matter. (The fact that he only recruited bucks for his team and excluded the does is cause for more outrage—Santa insisted it was to protect the morale of the enlisted bucks—but unfortunately, in Rudolph's time, the does were still awaiting their liberatrix.)

To Santa, Rudolph was one of the Northland's most dangerous creatures: a reindeer with a brain. He had seen a few during his years at the Pole, but there was something about Rudolph that made him especially nervous. It might have been the deer's standoffish attitude, or the rumours that he was organizing meetings with the other reindeer late at night. Santa also sensed a charisma in Rudolph that, if not kept in proper check, might disrupt his tidy little enterprise.

And so it was that, on that fabled foggy evening, Santa found himself in a bind. Harsh weather conditions left him unable to exploit the aerodynamic talents of his team. He had of course flown them through all sorts of dangerous weather before, with no thought to the deer's physical strain or mental trauma. But on this night the weather was so tempestuous that the bearded slave driver was fearful for his own safety and for the insurance headaches that a crash at his own toy works would certainly create.

Although Santa had known for years about Rudolph's gift for incandescent dissemination, he had not called special attention to it. In due time, Santa selfishly calculated, a use for it would arise, and until then there was no need to tip off how valuable Rudolph's skill might prove to be. That moment had finally arrived. On that foggy night, he sought out Rudolph among the herd and, wearing his humblest and most pleading face, asked him, "Rudolph, with your nose so bright, won't you guide my sleigh tonight?"

The young reindeer looked him over carefully. After a few moments of silence, he said, "No."

Santa blinked a few times and repeated, "No?" The herd could scarcely believe its ears as well.

"No. Not without concessions," replied the creature who happened to be antlered. "The days when we jump every time you whistle are over."

"What are you talking about, concessions?" blustered Santa, who hadn't planned on this twist. "This is your big break, your chance to join the team. This is the life's dream of every young reindeer."

Rudolph laughed. "This is starting to sound like *A Star Is Born*. Next you're going to tell me, 'Kid, you're going out there a nervous young buck, but you're coming back ... a star.'"

The herd all chuckled at this remark. Perhaps such a gung-ho speech was all too familiar to them. Santa reddened, realizing he'd made a tactical error in approaching this young firebrand in public. He said, "It's cold out here. Why don't we talk this over inside my chalet. I have some very good moss and lichens, just picked ..."

"I'll eat what everyone else eats," countered Rudolph, "and whatever you have to say to me, you can say out here." The other reindeer were watching this face-off with great interest. For years, they had treated Rudolph with suspicion for all his bold ideas, but now he was bravely sticking up for them at the expense of his own career. Some shouted encouragement, while the more reactionary deer grumbled about not rocking the kayak.

Santa began to feel some pressure as the minutes ticked away and the fog grew thicker. Finally he asked Rudolph what his demands were.

"You work the reindeer too hard, with no consideration for our families," Rudolph said. "We want a guarantee of no work on holidays."

For the next thirty minutes Santa tried to explain the disadvantages of this idea, the main one being, of course, that the reindeer only worked one night a year anyway, and since that night *always* fell on a holiday, such a change would make their jobs (and his) rather difficult to fulfill. Rudolph eventually agreed to table the issue for the time being.

Checking his watch, Santa was starting to sweat, even in the Arctic cold. "Could we speed this up?" he asked. "Or maybe forge a temporary working agreement that we can make permanent after Christmas?"

Rudolph snorted in his face. "We weren't born yesterday, Claus. No contract, no flight. If Christmas doesn't come this year, who do you think the children will blame? The reindeer? The weather? The Interstate Commerce Commission? No, they'll blame the overfed guy in the red suit."

Santa imagined the public relations headaches this would cause him, and his frame began to sag. Rudolph grilled him on such issues as health care, paternity leave, profit sharing, and joint decision-making councils. As the fog refused to lift and the minutes ticked away, Santa granted more and more of the deer's demands.

In the end, Rudolph and the reindeer rank-and-file could claim a number of victories: The deer would be required to fly only one night a year, and after four hours on the job, they would receive a ninety-minute dinner break and three fifteen-minute breaks. Santa was required to keep four alternate reindeer on standby for the duration of Christmas Eve at full pay and benefits. In addition, the mandatory retirement age was lowered to eight years, after which the reindeer were to receive a full pension and lifetime health care.

After all the terms were finalized, an exhausted but relieved Santa Claus hitched Rudolph up with the rest of the team. The other deer gave Rudolph three cheers for standing up for their rights against "the man," which the nasally empowered reindeer, feeling fulfilled for the first time, gratefully accepted. Using his unique luminescent gift, he led the sleigh through the inhospitable weather and Christmas that year was saved.

Epilogue

Like the fabled prophet in his own land, however, Rudolph found his real influence evaporating soon after that. For weeks he was praised by all the other reindeer, who told him, "You'll go down in history/herstory!" All the attention and admiration, however, began to feel superficial and distracting. Rudolph felt that any lionization of him would take energy away from the continuing fight for the well-being of the working reindeer. In a facile attempt to emulate their new hero, the other young reindeer began to wear bright red coverings on their noses. When Rudolph expressed his displeasure with this, some muttered that he was becoming too humourless and doctrinaire.

To Rudolph, this first agreement with Santa was to be just the beginning. He envisioned the eventual creation of a working reindeer's paradise, a toy-making and distribution collective where the means of production were shared by everyone. Unfortunately, many of the other reindeer began to take their newly won benefits as their inviolable right, bestowed by nature. They grew fat on too much moss and complained that their improved work schedules were still too taxing. Factions began to form among them about the best ways to invest their new pension fund. Rudolph tried to convince the dissident deer that they needed to stand united, but they began to resent his holier-than-thou attitude. Some spread the rumour that he was an agent provocateur, sent by other aeronautically gifted animals seeking to gain Santa's favour and put the deer out of their jobs. While such theories were patently absurd, they served to discredit Rudolph and embolden his detractors. Eventually, he was voted out of the union he had helped establish. After this indignity, Rudolph decided to strike off for Lapland, where he felt the undomesticated reindeer were more in control of their own future.

And so, like other revolutionaries before him, Rudolph the angry young reindeer lived out the rest of his days in exile, bitterly wondering how a movement with such promise could prove to be so fragile in the end.

James Finn Garner (*born Detroit, Michigan*) is a writer, satirist, and improvisational comedian. His first book, *Politically Correct Bedtime Stories*, sold more than 2.5 million copies and was translated into 17 languages. His four books to date have all reached the *New York Times* bestseller list for extended periods. He currently lives in Chicago.

Activities: Rudolph the Nasally Empowered Reindeer

1. **Identify Attitude:** Define the phrase "politically correct," and then identify examples of political correctness in the story. What seems to be the author's attitude toward the practice of political correctness? Explain.

2. **Examine Satire:** With a partner, research and discuss the purpose of satire. Using specific examples, explain what the author is satirizing in this story. Summarize your discussion and organize your ideas using subheadings and point-form notes.

3. **Outline Positions:** Negotiation can be defined as "two opposing positions meeting at a point where both parties agree." Outline the opening positions of Santa and Rudolph, and identify the bargaining tactics used by each.

4. **Write and Perform:** In a small group, collaboratively write and perform for the class a brief skit that satirizes some aspect of modern society. Possibilities include an interview with a popular singing group, an infomercial, or a human-interest story about current teen trends.

The Peacemaker's Journey

Haudenosaunee (Iroquois) Legend

The oral history of the Haudenosaunee (the original five nations of the Iroquois) is traditionally told at five-year intervals, a telling that can last six to nine days. The section retold here by Mohawk chief Jake Swamp (Wolf Clan) describes the quest of the Peacemaker.

The Peacemaker, whose birth had miraculous origins, sets out in a canoe of white stone to unite five warring nations and teach them the ways of peace. He journeys from the area of the Great Lakes to the east, where the most warlike people live, where bodies lie on the ground and streams run red with blood. There he proves himself by surviving a fall from a cliff into a swift river, and the people accept his message of peace. First to do so is the woman Jigonsaseh, and to her the Peacemaker promises that she shall be remembered as the Mother of Nations. But the people are not happy, for they grieve over those they had lost in their warlike days.

The Peacemaker is troubled by this, but does not know how to banish their grief. The answer is provided by Ayonwentha, a man who eventually learned the way of relieving sorrow after losing his own family: Wipe the tears from the grieving one's eyes, brush the dust of death from their ears, give medicine water so that the voice could be returned to their throats, and ask the Great Spirit to let them wake the next morning able to see and hear and speak clearly once again.

And so the Peacemaker and Ayonwentha decided to go back to the village to console the people, because at that time the women seemed as though they were always in pain for the losses that they had felt, the sons they had lost. They were always remembering what had happened to them, and it affected the way they lived. After they gave the condolence ceremony to the people, the Peacemaker and Ayonwentha stayed back and just watched. It wasn't too long before things started to change. The women went back into their gardens and their fields. They started to communicate with one another and their laughter started to come back. The children started to play different games, and the men in the village became energetic once more. And so the people were healed.

The Peacemaker faced Ayonwentha and he said, "It is now time to build a great long house. This long house will extend from the rising sun to the setting sun and all the nations will live in this long house as one people. We must now leave here and approach those people toward the west." They started out and soon they were arriving near the villages of the Oneida. There they confronted the leaders, and they wanted them to give in to the peace also. These leaders had already heard that peace was coming and so it was not too difficult for them to accept, although some of them had misgivings about this peace. But in the end, they, too, accepted.

And so they went on, going toward the west, and there they arrived in the territory of the Onondaga Nation. Now this is where they ran into a problem. This evil man, Tadadaho, lived there. He had snakes mixed in with his hair, representative of all the evil things that he used to do. Even his fingers were all twisted up. His whole being was all crooked. He was not very handsome, for all the things that he had done, those evil things, showed on him, on his very person. When the Peacemaker and Ayonwentha went to their villages, the people started to give in, accepting this peace. Soon they all desired this peace, but in the distance Tadadaho lived, and he kept refusing. Each time they would approach him he would just snarl at them. He had accumulated so much power in his life, and this is the reason why he kept refusing. He didn't want to lose that power. They tried different methods, but nothing could faze his evil mind. They would go to him and sing beautiful songs to him, but he would not give in. They would use nice words to him, but he would not listen. So finally one day they made a decision. They said, "We cannot wait here any longer. We must go on to approach those other nations toward the west. We will come back this way later on and we will deal with him then."

So they went on toward the west, and soon they arrived at the place where the Cayuga people lived. The Peacemaker and Ayonwentha explained the whole plan of peace to them, and soon they agreed to this peace. And then they travelled on and finally they arrived where the Seneca people lived in the big hill country. There they confronted the men, who did not want to give in. Those war leaders did not want to lose their power, but finally one day they all agreed to live in peace as well.

The Peacemaker and Ayonwentha sent some runners all the way back to the rising sun in the east, saying: "You tell them when you arrive that peace is now here. You tell them to come to the centre and everybody will meet there in the territory of the Onondaga Nation."

And so they travelled back toward the centre, and when they arrived at the place, Onondaga, they waited there. Soon the other ones were arriving—the ones from the east, the Oneida, the Mohawk, and the Cayugas—and all their work was cut out for them, for now they all had to work together on the evil mind of Tadadaho. He was the only one holding out on this peace; he was the only one holding out on all these nations to be formed into one heart, one body, one mind. Each time they would try something to take away his evil mind they failed, and it was very frustrating for them. So one day the Peacemaker said, "In the future we are going to put together five nations of people, five nations together into one body, one heart, one mind. And we need a fire, a counsel fire that will burn for all, and we need someone to watch over this fire." They went to Tadadaho and they said, "We want you to watch over the counsel fire for all of the five nations who want to live in peace." Then Tadadaho got excited, for he felt that he would still have control over all of the five nations, and he accepted. But in this manner they really tricked him, for now he had to live in peace. It didn't matter if he felt that he still had control, as long as he was peaceful.

Now the people were so happy that finally peace had arrived. The Peacemaker stood there as the men gathered from all directions, the warriors that used to fight with one another. As he observed them, he noticed they all were carrying weapons, although they had all promised that they were not going to fight anymore. He turned to them and he said, "What would happen in the future if weapons were allowed to exist among you? Isn't it true that an accident might happen in the future, someone would get cut and blood would start to flow? And then you would go back to that condition you just came out of." He looked around and there he saw a tall white pine. Because of its height, it seemed as though it went into the sky. He said, "We'll choose this tree standing here, which can be seen from long distances. We shall uproot this tree, and we challenge you men who used to fight one another to bury your weapons of war beneath it, so that they will be carried away forever by the strong currents underneath the ground."

The men were reluctant at first to do this, but finally one by one they came forward and cast their weapons into the hole. He also instructed them to take their feelings of hatred, greed, and jealousy, and to bury them also in this ground. After this was done they replanted the tree on top of the weapons. Then he turned back to them and said, "From the base of this tree will come four white roots. They will go into the four directions. In the future maybe many nations will come and recognize the tree's purpose. Maybe individuals will see it and they will have to take shelter underneath this tree. And now what we're going to do is place an eagle on the tree as a symbol of the future. Everyone who is living underneath this Tree of Peace will be entrusted with the responsibility that they must always look into the future like the eagle that sees afar. The greenery of this tree will represent the peace you have made between yourselves, that this peace must always stay fresh and green year round, for this tree does not turn colours through the season."

And so, as the men gathered there, they appointed all the leaders, and Jigonsaseh was there at the final day. As the Peacemaker had promised, she was the one who put the emblem of the chieftainship titles, the deer horns, on these leaders' heads. He instructed them to stand in a circle around the Tree of Peace, and he brought an arrow forward. He said, "When you're only one nation like this one arrow, you are easily broken," and he broke it in half. Then he took one arrow from each of the nations and he bound the five arrows together. He passed them out among the strongest men, but no one could break them. And so he said, "This will be the symbol of your union, your unity in the future. You must never, as one nation, pull your arrow out. You must always be together as one. In that way, you will always be strong." And so that was the symbol of their union.

Now he told the leaders to hold hands in a circle, and he made some predictions. He said, "In the future, this is what's going to happen: There will be a people coming from somewhere, and they will not understand the meaning of these roots. They will hack at these roots and try to kill the tree, and the tree will weaken and it will start to fall. What is going to happen in those times is that you, the leaders, will be burdened with its heaviness. As this tree falls, it will land on your joined hands. It will rest there for a period of time on your arms, but you must never lose your grip. You must never let it touch the ground, for if you do, peace will come no more.

"When you are burdened with its heaviness and its weight, near the time when you're about to give up, when you're about ready to lose your grip, there will be children born. And when these children observe the leaders burdened with the heaviness and the weight of this tree, they will come forward. One by one they will notice and they will lend a hand, and they will help to raise this tree again. And after it has risen again, a great calm will come and a great peace will arrive, but it will be for the last time." And that is what was predicted.

Chief Jake Swamp (Tekaronianekon) (*Wolf Clan of the Mohawk Nation*), activist, spiritual leader, and author, is a member of the Grand Council of the Haudenosaunee. He has travelled extensively, planting trees for peace and encouraging environmental education.

Activities: The Peacemaker's Journey

1. **Reflect on Reading:** In a journal entry, reflect on your experience of reading this tale. Did you find it challenging? Did you enjoy it? Do you think it contains wisdom? What reading strategies would you recommend for this tale?

2. **Interpret Information:** Describe the Peacemaker's solution to the problem of Tadadaho. Why was the solution successful? What does the Peacemaker understand about Tadadaho's character and motivations?

3. **Apply Information:** Do you think the Peacemaker's process could work in our world today? Outline his process in general terms, and then explain how you would apply the process to a current situation.

4. **Write a Letter:** Write a formal letter nominating the Peacemaker for the Nobel Peace Prize. Follow the appropriate conventions, and give specific reasons to support your nomination. Ask the class to comment on your letter.

A Handful of Dates

Tayeb Salih

I must have been very young at the time. While I don't remember exactly how old I was, I do remember that when people saw me with my grandfather they would pat me on the head and give my cheek a pinch—things they didn't do to my grandfather. The strange thing was that I never used to go out with my father, rather it was my grandfather who would take me with him wherever he went, except for the mornings, when I would go to the mosque to learn the Koran. The mosque, the river, and the fields—these were the landmarks in our life. While most of the children of my age grumbled at having to go to the mosque to learn the Koran, I used to love it. The reason was, no doubt, that I was quick at learning by heart and the Sheikh always asked me to stand up and recite the Chapter of the Merciful whenever we had visitors, who would pat me on my head and cheek just as people did when they saw me with my grandfather.

Yes, I used to love the mosque, and I loved the river, too. Directly we finished our Koran reading in the morning I would throw down my wooden slate and dart off, quick as a genie, to my mother, hurriedly swallow down my breakfast, and run off for a plunge in the river. When tired of swimming about, I would sit on the bank and gaze at the strip of water that wound away eastwards, and hid behind a thick wood of acacia trees. I loved to give rein to my imagination and picture

to myself a tribe of giants living behind that wood, a people tall and thin with white beards and sharp noses, like my grandfather. Before my grandfather ever replied to my many questions he would rub the tip of his nose with his forefinger; as for his beard, it was soft and luxuriant and as white as cotton wool—never in my life have I seen anything of a purer whiteness or greater beauty. My grandfather must also have been extremely tall, for I never saw anyone in the whole area address him without having to look up at him, nor did I see him enter a house without having to bend so low that I was put in mind of the way the river wound round behind the wood of acacia trees. I loved him and would imagine myself, when I grew to be a man, tall and slender like him, walking along with great strides.

I believe I was his favourite grandchild: no wonder, for my cousins were a stupid bunch and I—so they say—was an intelligent child. I used to know when my grandfather wanted me to laugh, when to be silent; also I would remember the times for his prayers and would bring him his prayer rug and fill the ewer for his ablutions without his having to ask me. When he had nothing else to do he enjoyed listening to me reciting to him from the Koran in a lilting voice, and I could tell from his face that he was moved.

One day I asked him about our neighbour Masood. I said to my grandfather: "I fancy you don't like our neighbour Masood?"

To which he answered, having rubbed the tip of his nose: "He's an indolent man and I don't like such people."

I said to him: "What's an indolent man?"

My grandfather lowered his head for a moment; then, looking across at the wide expanse of field, he said: "Do you see it stretching out from the edge of the desert up to the Nile bank? A hundred *feddans*. Do you see all those date palms? And those trees—*sant*, acacia, and *sayal*? All this fell into Masood's lap, was inherited by him from his father."

Taking advantage of the silence that had descended on my grandfather, I turned my gaze from him to the vast area defined by his words. "I don't care," I told myself, "who owns those date palms, those trees or this black, cracked earth—all I know is that it's the arena for my dreams and my playground."

My grandfather then continued: "Yes, my boy, forty years ago all this belonged to Masood—two-thirds of it is now mine."

This was news to me, for I had imagined that the land had belonged to my grandfather ever since God's Creation.

"I didn't own a single *feddan* when I first set foot in this village. Masood was then the owner of all these riches. The position has changed now, though, and I think that before Allah calls me to Him I shall have bought the remaining third as well."

I do not know why it was I felt fear at my grandfather's words—and pity for our neighbour Masood. How I wished my grandfather wouldn't do what he'd said! I remembered Masood's singing, his beautiful voice and powerful laugh that resembled the gurgling of water. My grandfather never laughed.

I asked my grandfather why Masood had sold his land.

"Women," and from the way my grandfather pronounced the word I felt that "women" was something terrible. "Masood, my boy, was a much-married man. Each time he married he sold me a *feddan* or two." I made the quick calculation that Masood must have married some ninety women. Then I remembered his three wives, his shabby appearance, his lame donkey and its dilapidated saddle, his *galabia* with the torn sleeves. I had all but rid my mind of the thoughts that jostled in it when I saw the man approaching us, and my grandfather and I exchanged glances.

"We'll be harvesting the dates today," said Masood. "Don't you want to be there?"

I felt, though, that he did not really want my grandfather to attend. My grandfather, however, jumped to his feet and I saw that his eyes sparkled momentarily with an intense brightness. He pulled me by the hand and we went off to the harvesting of Masood's dates.

Someone brought my grandfather a stool covered with an oxhide, while I remained standing. There were a vast number of people there, but though I knew them all, I found myself for some reason watching Masood: aloof from that great gathering of people he stood as though it were no concern of his, despite the fact that the date palms to be harvested were his own. Sometimes his attention would be caught by the sound of a huge clump of dates crashing down from on high. Once he shouted up at the boy perched on the very summit of the date palm who had begun hacking at a clump with his long, sharp sickle: "Be careful you don't cut the heart of the palm."

No one paid any attention to what he said and the boy seated at the very summit of the date palm continued, quickly and energetically, to work away at the branch with his sickle till the clump of dates began to drop like something descending from the heavens.

I, however, had begun to think about Masood's phrase "the heart of the palm." I pictured the palm tree as something with feeling, something possessed of a heart that throbbed. I remembered Masood's remark to me when he had once seen me playing with the branch of a young palm tree: "Palm trees, my boy, like humans, experience joy and suffering." And I had felt an inward and unreasoned embarrassment.

When I again looked at the expanse of ground stretching before me I saw my young companions swarming like ants around the trunks of the palm trees, gathering up dates and eating most of them. The dates were collected into high mounds. I saw people coming along and weighing them into measuring bins and pouring them into sacks, of which I counted thirty. The crowd of people broke up, except for Hussein the merchant, Mousa the owner of the field next to ours on the east, and two men I'd never seen before.

I heard a low whistling sound and saw that my grandfather had fallen asleep. Then I noticed that Masood had not changed his stance, except that he had placed a stalk in his mouth and was munching at it like someone sated with food who doesn't know what to do with the mouthful he still has.

Suddenly my grandfather woke up, jumped to his feet, and walked toward the sacks of dates. He was followed by Hussein the merchant, Mousa the owner of the field next to ours, and the two strangers. I glanced at Masood and saw that he was making his way toward us with extreme slowness, like a man who wants to retreat but whose feet insist on going forward. They formed a circle around the sacks of dates and began examining them, some taking a date or two to eat. My grandfather gave me a fistful, which I began munching. I saw Masood filling the palms of both hands with dates and bringing them up close to his nose, then returning them.

Then I saw them dividing up the sacks between them. Hussein the merchant took ten; each of the strangers took five. Mousa the owner of the field next to ours on the eastern side took five, and my grandfather took five. Understanding nothing, I looked at Masood and saw that his eyes were darting to left and right like two mice that have lost their way home.

"You're still fifty pounds in debt to me," said my grandfather to Masood. "We'll talk about it later."

Hussein called his assistants and they brought along donkeys, the two strangers produced camels, and the sacks of dates were loaded onto them. One of the donkeys let out a braying which set the camels frothing at the mouth and complaining noisily. I felt myself drawing close to Masood, felt my hand stretch out toward him as though I wanted to touch the hem of his garment. I heard him make a noise in his throat like the rasping of a lamb being slaughtered. For some unknown reason, I experienced a sharp sensation of pain in my chest.

I ran off into the distance. Hearing my grandfather call after me, I hesitated a little, then continued on my way. I felt at that moment that I hated him. Quickening my pace, it was as though I carried within me a secret I wanted to rid myself of. I reached the riverbank near the bend it made behind the wood of acacia trees. Then, without knowing why, I put my finger into my throat and spewed up the dates I'd eaten.

Tayeb Salih (*born 1929, Sudan*) studied first at Khartoum University, then at British universities. He taught briefly in Sudan, then returned to England to head the British Broadcasting Corporation's Arabic drama program.

Activities: A Handful of Dates

1. *Make Inferences:* With a partner, make inferences to provide answers to the following questions: Why doesn't Masood receive any of the harvest? What might the grandfather later discuss with Masood? What is the secret the narrator feels he carries within himself at the end of the story?

2. *Consider Perspective:* What is the effect of the author's use of first-person perspective? Explain why you agree or disagree that this is an effective perspective to use in this story.

3. *Defend an Opinion:* The story presents a negative view of the grandfather's actions. List reasons that could be used to (a) defend his actions and (b) condemn his actions. State and defend your position on the issue

4. *Write a Monologue:* In the role of Masood, tell your version of the story of how you lost your land. Where necessary, add details not in the story. Present your monologue, using body language and vocal techniques to add interest.

The Third Bank of the River

João Guimarães Rosa

My father was a dutiful, orderly, straightforward man. And according to several reliable people of whom I enquired, he had had these qualities since adolescence or even childhood. By my own recollection, he was neither jollier nor more melancholy than the other men we knew. Maybe a little quieter. It was Mother, not Father, who ruled the house. She scolded us daily—my sister, my brother, and me. But it happened one day that Father ordered a boat.

He was very serious about it. It was to be made specially for him, of mimosa wood. It was to be sturdy enough to last twenty or thirty years and just large enough for one person. Mother carried on plenty about it. Was her husband going to become a fisherman all of a sudden? Or a hunter? Father said nothing. Our house was less than a mile from the river, which around there was deep, quiet, and so wide you couldn't see across it.

I can never forget the day the rowboat was delivered. Father showed no joy or other emotion. He just put on his hat as he always did and said goodbye to us. He took along no food or bundle of any sort. We expected Mother to rant and rave, but she didn't. She looked very pale and bit her lip, but all she said was: "If you go away, stay away. Don't ever come back!"

Father made no reply. He looked gently at me and motioned me to walk along with him. I feared Mother's wrath, yet I eagerly obeyed. We headed toward the river together. I felt bold and exhilarated, so much so that I said: "Father, will you take me with you in your boat?"

He just looked at me, gave me his blessing, and, by a gesture, told me to go back. I made as if to do so but, when his back was turned, I ducked behind some bushes to watch him. Father got into the boat and rowed away. Its shadow slid across the water like a crocodile, long and quiet.

Father did not come back. Nor did he go anywhere, really. He just rowed and floated across and around, out there in the river. Everyone was appalled. What had never happened, what could not possibly happen, was happening. Our relatives, neighbours, and friends came over to discuss the phenomenon.

Mother was ashamed. She said little and conducted herself with great composure. As a consequence, almost everyone thought (though no one said it) that Father had gone insane. A few, however, suggested that Father might be fulfilling a promise he had made to God or to a saint, or that he might have some horrible disease, maybe leprosy, and that he left for the sake of the family, at the same time wishing to remain fairly near them.

Travellers along the river and people living near the bank on one side or the other reported that Father never put foot on land, by day or night. He just moved about on the river, solitary, aimless, like a derelict. Mother and our relatives agreed that the food which he had doubtless hidden in the boat would soon give out and that then he would either leave the river and travel off somewhere (which would be at least a little more respectable) or he would repent and come home.

How far from the truth they were! Father had a secret source of provisions: me. Every day I stole food and brought it to him. The first night after he left, we all lit fires on the shore and prayed and called to him. I was deeply distressed and felt a need to do something more. The following day I went down to the river with a loaf of corn bread, a bunch of bananas, and some bricks of raw brown sugar. I waited impatiently a long, long hour. Then I saw the boat, far off, alone, gliding almost imperceptibly on the smoothness of the river. Father was sitting in the bottom of the boat. He saw me but he did not row toward me or make any gesture. I showed him the food and then I placed it in a hollow rock on the river bank; it was safe there from animals, rain, and dew. I did this day after day, on and on and on. Later I learned, to my surprise, that Mother knew what I was doing and left food around where I could easily steal it. She had a lot of feelings she didn't show.

Mother sent for her brother to come and help on the farm and in business matters. She had the schoolteacher come and tutor us children at home because of the time we had lost. One day, at her request, the priest put on his vestments, went down to the shore, and tried to exorcise the devils that had got into my father. He shouted that Father had a duty to cease his unholy obstinacy. Another day she arranged to have two soldiers come and try to frighten him. All to no avail. My father went by in the distance, sometimes so far away he could barely be seen. He never replied to anyone and no one ever got close to him. When some newspapermen came in a launch to take his picture, Father headed his boat to the other side of the river and into the marshes, which he knew like the palm of his hand but in which other people quickly got lost. There in his private maze, which extended for miles, with heavy foliage overhead and rushes on all sides, he was safe.

We had to get accustomed to the idea of Father's being out on the river. We had to but we couldn't, we never could. I think I was the only one who understood to some degree what our father wanted and what he did not want. The thing I could not understand at all was how he stood the hardship. Day and night, in sun and rain, in heat and in terrible mid-year cold spells, with his old hat on his head and very little other clothing, week after week, month after month, year after year, unheedful of the waste and emptiness in which his life was slipping by. He never set foot on earth or grass, on isle or mainland shore. No doubt he sometimes tied up the boat at a secret place, perhaps at the tip of some island, to get a little sleep. He never lit a fire or even struck a match and he had no flashlight. He took only a small part of the food that I left in the hollow rock—not enough, it seemed to me, for survival. What could his state of health have been? How about the continual drain on his energy, pulling and pushing the oars to control the boat? And how did he survive the annual floods, when the river rose and swept along with it all sorts of dangerous objects—branches of trees, dead bodies of animals—that might suddenly crash against his little boat?

He never talked to a living soul. And we never talked about him. We just thought. No, we could never put our father out of mind. If for a short time we seemed to, it was just a lull from which we would be sharply awakened by the realization of his frightening situation.

My sister got married, but Mother didn't want a wedding party. It would have been a sad affair, for we thought of him every time we ate some especially tasty food. Just as we thought of him in our cosy beds on a cold, stormy night—out there, alone and unprotected, trying to bail out the boat with only his hands and a gourd. Now and then someone would say that I was getting to look more and more like my father. But I knew that by then his hair and beard must have been shaggy and his nails long. I pictured him thin and sickly, black with hair and sunburn, and almost naked despite the articles of clothing I occasionally left for him.

He didn't seem to care about us at all. But I felt affection and respect for him, and, whenever they praised me because I had done something good, I said: "My father taught me to act that way."

It wasn't exactly accurate but it was a truthful sort of lie. As I said, Father didn't seem to care about us. But then why did he stay around there? Why didn't he go up the river or down the river, beyond the possibility of seeing us or being seen by us? He alone knew the answer.

My sister had a baby boy. She insisted on showing Father his grandson. One beautiful day we all went down to the riverbank, my sister in her white wedding dress, and she lifted the baby high. Her husband held a parasol above them. We shouted to Father and waited. He did not appear. My sister cried; we all cried in each other's arms.

My sister and her husband moved far away. My brother went to live in a city. Times changed, with their usual imperceptible rapidity. Mother finally moved too; she was old and went to live with her daughter. I remained behind, a leftover. I could never think of marrying. I just stayed there with the impedimenta of my life. Father, wandering alone and forlorn on the river, needed me. I knew he needed me, although he never even told me why he was doing it. When I put the question to people bluntly and insistently, all they told me was that they heard that Father had explained it to the man who made the boat. But now this man was dead and nobody knew or remembered anything. There was just some foolish talk, when the rains were especially severe and persistent, that my father was wise like Noah and had the boat built in anticipation of a new flood; I dimly remember people saying this. In any case, I would not condemn my father for what he was doing. My hair was beginning to turn grey.

I have only sad things to say. What bad had I done, what was my great guilt? My father always away and his absence always with me. And the river, always the river, perpetually renewing itself. The river, always. I was beginning to suffer from old age, in which life is just a sort of lingering. I had attacks of illness and of anxiety. I had a nagging rheumatism. And he? Why, why was he doing it? He must have been suffering terribly. He was so old. One day, in his failing strength, he might let the boat capsize; or he might let the current carry it downstream, on and on, until it plunged over the waterfall to the boiling turmoil below. It pressed upon my heart. He was out there and I was forever robbed of my peace. I am guilty of I know not what, and my pain is an open wound inside me. Perhaps I would know— if things were different. I began to guess what was wrong.

Out with it! Had I gone crazy? No, in our house that word was never spoken, never through all the years. No one called anybody crazy, for nobody is crazy. Or maybe everybody. All I did was go there and wave a handkerchief so he would be more likely to see me. I was in complete command of myself. I waited. Finally he appeared in the distance, there, then over there, a vague shape sitting in the back of the boat. I called to him several times. And I said what I was so eager to say, to state formally and under oath. I said it as loud as I could:

"Father, you have been out there long enough. You are old…. Come back, you don't have to do it anymore…. Come back and I'll go instead. Right now, if you want. Any time. I'll get into the boat. I'll take your place."

And when I had said this my heart beat more firmly.

He heard me. He stood up. He manoeuvred with his oars and headed the boat toward me. He had accepted my offer. And suddenly I trembled, down deep. For he had raised his arm and waved—the first time in so many, so many years. And I couldn't…. In terror, my hair on end, I ran, I fled madly. For he seemed to come from another world. And I'm begging forgiveness, begging, begging.

I experienced the dreadful sense of cold that comes from deadly fear, and I became ill. Nobody ever saw or heard about him again. Am I a man, after such a failure? I am what never should have been. I am what must be silent. I know it is too late. I must stay in the deserts and unmarked plains of my life, and I fear I shall shorten it.

But when death comes I want them to take me and put me in a little boat in this perpetual water between the long shores; and I, down the river, lost in the river, inside the river... the river....

João Guimarães Rosa (*born 1908, Brazil; died 1967*), short-story writer, diplomat, physician, was one of Brazil's foremost writers of the 20th century. His work shows the influence of the American writers Poe and Hawthorne.

Activities: The Third Bank of the River

1. ***Create a Title:*** Think of a new title for the story and list reasons why you think the title would be appropriate. Share your title and reasons with a partner.

2. ***Discuss Symbolism:*** What objects and actions in the story might be considered symbolic? In a small group, list possible symbols and explain what each might represent. Share your list and explanations with the class.

3. ***Define Literary Terms:*** Research the meaning of the literary term *magic realism*. Write a paragraph to explain why you agree or disagree that this term applies to "The Third Bank of the River." Support your opinion with references to the text.

4. ***Role-Play Characters:*** With a partner, role-play the conversation in which the father explains the reasons for his actions to the man who made the boat. Present your role-play to another pair and compare the reasons given for the father's actions.

The Fog Horn

Ray Bradbury

Out there in the cold water, far from land, we waited every night for the coming of the fog, and it came, and we oiled the brass machinery and lit the fog light up in the stone tower. Feeling like two birds in the grey sky, McDunn and I sent the light touching out, red, then white, then red again, to eye the lonely ships. And if they did not see our light, then there was always our Voice, the great deep cry of our Fog Horn shuddering through the rags of mist to startle the gulls away like decks of scattered cards and make the waves turn high and foam.

"It's a lonely life, but you're used to it now, aren't you?" asked McDunn.

"Yes," I said. "You're a good talker, thank the Lord."

"Well, it's your turn on land tomorrow," he said, smiling, "to dance with ladies and drink gin."

"What do you think, McDunn, when I leave you out here alone?"

"On the mysteries of the sea." McDunn lit his pipe. It was a quarter past seven of a cold November evening, the heat on, the light switching its tail in two hundred directions, the Fog Horn bumbling in the high throat of the tower. There wasn't a town for a hundred miles down the coast, just a road which came lonely through dead country to the sea, with few cars on it, a stretch of two miles of cold water out to our rock, and rare few ships.

"The mysteries of the sea," said McDunn thoughtfully. "You know, the ocean's the biggest damned snowflake ever? It rolls and swells a thousand shapes and colours, no two alike. Strange. One night, years ago, I was here alone, when all of the fish of the sea surfaced out there. Something made them swim in and lie in the bay, sort of trembling and staring up at the tower light going red, white, red, white across them so I could see their funny eyes. I turned cold. They were like a big peacock's tail, moving out there until midnight. Then, without so much as a sound, they slipped away, the million of them was gone. I kind of think maybe, in some sort of way, they came all those miles to worship. Strange. But think how the tower must look to them, standing seventy feet above the water, the God-light flashing out from it, and the tower declaring itself with a monster voice. They never came back, those fish, but don't you think for a while they thought they were in the Presence?"

I shivered. I looked out at the long grey lawn of the sea stretching away into nothing and nowhere.

"Oh, the sea's full." McDunn puffed his pipe nervously, blinking. He had been nervous all day and hadn't said why. "For all our

engines and so-called submarines, it'll be ten thousand centuries before we set foot on the real bottom of the sunken lands, in the fairy kingdoms there, and know *real* terror. Think of it, it's still the year 300,000 Before Christ down under there. While we've paraded around with trumpets, lopping off each other's countries and heads, they have been living beneath the sea twelve miles deep and cold in a time as old as the beard of a comet."

"Yes, it's an old world."

"Come on. I got something special I been saving up to tell you."

We ascended the eighty steps, talking and taking our time. At the top, McDunn switched off the room lights so there'd be no reflection in the plate glass. The great eye of the light was humming, turning easily in its oiled socket. The Fog Horn was blowing steadily, once every fifteen seconds.

"Sounds like an animal, don't it?" McDunn nodded to himself. "A big lonely animal crying in the night. Sitting here on the edge of ten billion years calling out to the Deeps, I'm here, I'm here, I'm here. And the Deeps do answer, yes, they do. You been here now for three months, Johnny, so I better prepare you. About this time of year," he said, studying the murk and fog, "something comes to visit the lighthouse."

"The swarms of fish like you said?"

"No, this is something else. I've put off telling you because you might think I'm daft. But tonight's the latest I can put it off, for if my calendar's marked right from last year, tonight's the night it comes. I won't go into detail, you'll have to see it yourself. Just sit down there. If you want, tomorrow you can pack your duffel and take the motorboat in to land and get your car parked there at the dinghy pier on the cape and drive on back to some little inland town and keep your lights burning nights, I won't question or blame you. It's happened three years now, and this is the only time anyone's been here with me to verify it. You wait and watch."

Half an hour passed with only a few whispers between us. When we grew tired waiting, McDunn began describing some of his ideas to me. He had some theories about the Fog Horn itself.

"One day many years ago a man walked along and stood in the sound of the ocean on a cold sunless shore and said, 'We need a voice to call across the water, to warn ships; I'll make one. I'll make a voice like all of time and all of the fog that ever was; I'll make a voice that is like an empty bed beside you all night long, and like an empty house when you open the door, and like trees in autumn with no leaves. A sound like the birds flying south, crying, and a sound like November wind and the sea on the hard, cold shore. I'll make a sound that's so alone that no one can miss it, that whoever hears it will weep in their souls, and hearths will seem warmer, and being inside will seem better to all who hear it in the distant towns. I'll make me a sound and an apparatus and they'll call it a Fog Horn and whoever hears it will know the sadness of eternity and the briefness of life.'"

The Fog Horn blew.

"I made up that story," said McDunn quietly, "to try to explain why this thing keeps coming back to the lighthouse every year. The Fog Horn calls it, I think, and it comes...."

"But—" I said.

"Sssst!" said McDunn. "There!" He nodded out to the Deeps.

Something was swimming toward the lighthouse tower.

It was a cold night, as I have said; the high tower was cold, the light coming and going, and the Fog Horn calling and calling through the ravelling mist. You couldn't see far and you couldn't see plain, but there was the deep sea moving on its way about the night earth, flat and quiet, the colour of grey mud, and here were the two of us alone in the high tower, and there, far out at first, was a ripple, followed by a wave, a rising, a bubble, a bit of froth. And then, from the surface of the cold sea came a head, a large head, dark-coloured, with immense eyes, and then a neck. And then—not a body—but more neck and more! The head rose a full forty feet above the water on a slender and beautiful dark neck. Only then did the body, like a little island of black coral and shells and crayfish, drip up from the subterranean. There was a flicker of tail. In all, from head to tip of tail, I estimated the monster at ninety or a hundred feet.

I don't know what I said. I said something.

"Steady, boy, steady," whispered McDunn.

"It's impossible!" I said.

"No, Johnny, we're impossible. It's like it always was ten million years ago. It hasn't changed. It's us and the land that've changed, become impossible, Us!"

It swam slowly and with a great dark majesty out in the icy waters, far away. The fog came and went about it, momentarily erasing its shape. One of the monster eyes caught and held and flashed back our immense light, red, white, red, white, like a disk held high and sending a message in primeval code. It was as silent as the fog through which it swam.

"It's a dinosaur of some sort!" I crouched down, holding to the stair rail.

"Yes, one of the tribe."

"But they died out!"

"No, only hid away in the Deeps. Deep, deep down in the deepest Deeps. Isn't *that* a word now, Johnny, a real word, it says so much: the Deeps. There's all the coldness and darkness and deepness in a word like that."

"What'll we do?"

"Do? We got our job, we can't leave. Besides, we're safer here than in any boat trying to get to land. That thing's as big as a destroyer and almost as swift."

"But here, why does it come *here*?"

The next moment I had my answer.

The Fog Horn blew.

And the monster answered.

A cry came across a million years of water and mist. A cry so anguished and alone that it shuddered in my head and my body. The monster cried out at the tower. The Fog Horn blew. The monster roared again. The Fog Horn blew. The monster opened its great toothed mouth and the sound that came from it was the sound of the Fog Horn itself. Lonely and vast and far away. The sound of isolation, a viewless sea, a cold night, apartness. That was the sound.

"Now," whispered McDunn, "do you know why it comes here?"

I nodded.

"All year long, Johnny, that poor monster there lying far out, a thousand miles at sea, and twenty miles deep maybe, biding its time, perhaps it's a million years old, this one creature. Think of it, waiting a million years; could *you* wait that long? Maybe it's the last of its kind. I sort of think that's true. Anyway, here come men on land and build this lighthouse, five years ago. And set up their Fog Horn and sound it and sound it out toward the place where you bury yourself in sleep and sea memories of a world where there were thousands like yourself, but now you're alone, all alone in a world not made for you, a world where you have to hide.

"But the sound of the Fog Horn comes and goes, comes and goes, and you stir from the muddy bottom of the Deeps, and your eyes open like the lenses of two-foot cameras and you move, slow, slow, for you have the ocean sea on your shoulders, heavy. But that Fog Horn comes through a thousand miles of water, faint and familiar, and the furnace in your belly stokes up, and you begin to rise, slow, slow. You feed yourself on great slakes of cod and minnow, on rivers of jellyfish, and you rise slow through the autumn months, through September when the fogs started, through October with more fog and the horn still calling you on, and then, late in November, after pressurizing yourself day by day, a few feet higher every hour, you are near the surface and still alive. You've got to go slow; if you surfaced all at once you'd explode. So it takes you all of three months to surface, and then a number of days to swim through the cold waters to the lighthouse. And there you are, out there, in the night, Johnny, the biggest damn monster in creation. And here's the lighthouse calling to you, with a long neck like your neck sticking way up out of the water, and a body like your body, and, most important of all, a voice like your voice. Do you understand now, Johnny, do you understand?"

The Fog Horn blew.

The monster answered.

I saw it all, I knew it all—the million years of waiting alone, for someone to come back who never came back. The million years of isolation at the bottom of the sea, the insanity of time there, while the skies cleared of reptile-birds, the swamps dried on the continental lands, the sloths and saber-tooths had their day and sank in tar pits, and men ran like white ants upon the hills.

The Fog Horn blew.

"Last year," said McDunn, "that creature swam round and round, round and round, all night. Not coming too near, puzzled, I'd say. Afraid, maybe. And a bit angry after coming all this way. But the next day, unexpectedly, the fog lifted, the sun came out fresh, the sky was as blue as a painting. And the monster swam off away from the heat and the silence and didn't come back. I suppose it's been brooding on it for a year now, thinking it over from every which way."

The monster was only a hundred yards off now, it and the Fog Horn crying at each other. As the lights hit them, the monster's eyes were fire and ice, fire and ice.

"That's life for you," said McDunn. "Someone always waiting for someone who never comes home. Always someone loving some thing more than that thing loves them. And after a while you want to destroy whatever that thing is, so it can't hurt you no more."

The monster was rushing at the lighthouse.

The Fog Horn blew.

"Let's see what happens," said McDunn.

He switched the Fog Horn off.

The ensuing minute of silence was so intense that we could hear our hearts pounding in the glassed area of the tower, could hear the slow greased turn of the light.

The monster stopped and froze. Its great lantern eyes blinked. Its mouth gaped. It gave a sort of rumble, like a volcano. It twitched its head this way and that, as if to seek the sounds now dwindled off into the fog. It peered at the lighthouse. It rumbled again. Then its eyes caught fire. It reared up, threshed the water, and rushed at the tower, its eyes filled with angry torment.

"McDunn!" I cried. "Switch on the horn!"

McDunn fumbled with the switch. But even as he flicked it on, the monster was rearing up. I had a glimpse of its gigantic paws, fishskin glittering in webs between the finger-like projections, clawing at the tower. The huge eye on the right side of its anguished head glittered before me like a cauldron into which I might drop, screaming. The tower shook. The Fog Horn cried; the monster cried. It seized the tower and gnashed at the glass, which shattered in upon us.

McDunn seized my arm. "Downstairs!"

The tower rocked, trembled, and started to give. The Fog Horn and the monster roared. We stumbled and half fell down the stairs. "Quick!"

We reached the bottom as the tower buckled down toward us. We ducked under the stairs into the small stone cellar. There were a thousand concussions as the rocks rained down; the Fog Horn stopped abruptly. The monster crashed upon the tower. The tower fell. We knelt together, McDunn and I, holding tight, while our world exploded.

Then it was over, and there was nothing but darkness and the wash of the sea on the raw stones.

That and the other sound.

"Listen," said McDunn quietly. "Listen."

We waited a moment. And then I began to hear it. First a great vacuumed sucking of air, and then the lament, the bewilderment, the loneliness of the great monster, folded over and upon us, above us, so that the sickening reek of its body filled the air, a stone's thickness away from our cellar. The monster gasped and cried. The tower was gone. The light was gone. The thing that had called to it a million years was gone. And the monster was opening its mouth and sending out great sounds. The sounds of a Fog Horn, again and again. And ships far at sea, not finding the light, not seeing anything, but passing and hearing late that night, must've thought: There it is, the lonely sound, the Lonesome Bay horn. All's well. We've rounded the cape.

And so it went for the rest of that night.

The sun was hot and yellow the next afternoon when the rescuers came out to dig us from our stoned-under cellar.

"It fell apart, is all," said Mr. McDunn gravely. "We had a few bad knocks from the waves and it just crumbled." He pinched my arm.

There was nothing to see. The ocean was calm, the sky blue. The only thing was a great algaic stink from the green matter that covered the fallen tower stones and the shore rocks. Flies buzzed about. The ocean washed empty on the shore.

The next year they built a new lighthouse, but by that time I had a job in the little town and a wife and a good small warm house that glowed yellow on autumn nights, the doors locked, the chimney puffing smoke. As for McDunn, he was master of the new lighthouse, built to his own specifications, out of steel-reinforced concrete. "Just in case," he said.

The new lighthouse was ready in November. I drove down alone one evening late and parked my car and looked across the grey waters and listened to the new horn sounding, once, twice, three, four times a minute far out there, by itself.

The monster?

It never came back.

"It's gone away," said McDunn. "It's gone back to the Deeps. It's learned you can't love anything too much in this world. It's gone into the deepest Deeps to wait another million years. Ah, the poor thing! Waiting out there, and waiting out there, while man comes and goes on this pitiful little planet. Waiting and waiting."

I sat in my car, listening. I couldn't see the lighthouse or the light standing out in Lonesome Bay. I could only hear the Horn, the Horn, the Horn. It sounded like the monster calling.

I sat there wishing there was something I could say.

Ray Bradbury (*born 1920, Waukegan, Illinois*), writer, novelist, playwright, essayist, screenwriter, poet, began writing stories on butcher's paper at age eleven. He is now acknowledged as a leading writer of science fiction. Bradbury adapted many of his stories for the TV series *Ray Bradbury Theater*, and won an Emmy Award for *The Halloween Tree*.

Activities: The Fog Horn

1. *Examine Foreshadowing:* Review the meaning of *foreshadowing*. Select specific passages in the story that foreshadow the monster's final act. Using a chart or graphic organizer, show how these passages function as foreshadowing devices.

2. *Appreciate Mood:* Bradbury creates a mysterious, haunting mood in this story. Choose one passage that helps to establish this mood. Identify the words and phrases that are particularly effective and explain why. Share your passage and ideas with a classmate.

3. *Adapt the Story:* In groups of two or three, use both the description and the dialogue from a scene in the story to write a short one-act play that captures the dramatic tension. Provide stage directions and additional dialogue as required. Prepare your play for an informal class presentation.

4. *Represent Setting:* Represent the setting of the story in a painting, drawing, sculpture, or model. Refer to the story to ensure accuracy. Create a title, and display your work in the classroom with a written description of what you tried to achieve, and how.

Marley's Ghost

(From *A Christmas Carol*)

Charles Dickens

Charles Dickens, 1812–1870

Marley was dead, to begin with. There is no doubt whatever about that. The register of his burial was signed by the clergyman, the clerk, the undertaker, and the chief mourner. Scrooge signed it. And Scrooge's name was good upon 'Change for anything he chose to put his hand to. Old Marley was as dead as a door-nail.

Mind! I don't mean to say that I know, of my own knowledge, what there is particularly dead about a door-nail. I might have been inclined, myself, to regard a coffin-nail as the deadest piece of ironmongery in the trade. But the wisdom of our ancestors is in the simile; and my unhallowed hands shall not disturb it, or the Country's done for. You will therefore permit me to repeat, emphatically, that Marley was as dead as a door-nail.

Scrooge knew he was dead? Of course he did. How could it be otherwise? Scrooge and he were partners for I don't know how many years. Scrooge was his sole executor, his sole administrator, his sole assign, his sole residuary legatee, his sole friend and sole mourner. And even Scrooge was not so dreadfully cut up by the sad event, but that he was an excellent man of business on the very day of the funeral, and solemnized it with an undoubted bargain.

Scrooge never painted out old Marley's name. There it stood, years afterwards, above the warehouse door: Scrooge and Marley. The firm was known as Scrooge and Marley. Sometimes people new to the business called Scrooge Scrooge, and sometimes Marley, but he answered to both names. It was all the same to him.

Oh! But he was a tight-fisted hand at the grindstone, Scrooge! a squeezing, wrenching, grasping, scraping, clutching, covetous old sinner! Hard and sharp as flint, from which no steel had ever struck out generous fire; secret, and self-contained, and solitary as an oyster. The cold within him froze his old features, nipped his pointed nose, shrivelled his cheek, stiffened his gait; made his eyes red, his thin lips blue and spoke out shrewdly in his grating voice. A frosty rime was on his head, and on his eyebrows, and his wiry chin. He carried his own low temperature always about with him; he iced his office in the dogdays; and didn't thaw it one degree at Christmas.

External heat and cold had little influence on Scrooge. No warmth could warm, no wintry weather chill him. No wind that blew was bitterer than he, no falling snow was more intent upon its purpose, no pelting rain less open to entreaty. Foul weather didn't know where to have him. The heaviest rain, and snow, and hail, and sleet, could boast of the advantage over him in only one respect. They often "came down" handsomely, and Scrooge never did.

Nobody ever stopped him in the street to say, with gladsome looks, "My dear Scrooge, how are you? When will you come to see me?" No beggars implored him to bestow a trifle, no children asked him what it was o'clock, no man or woman ever once in all his life inquired the way to such and such a place, of Scrooge. Even the blind men's dogs appeared to know him; and when they saw him coming on, would tug their owners into doorways and up courts; and then would wag their tails as though they said, "No eye at all is better than an evil eye, dark master!"

But what did Scrooge care? It was the very thing he liked. To edge his way along the crowded paths of life, warning all human sympathy to keep its distance, was what the knowing ones call "nuts" to Scrooge.

Once upon a time—of all the good days in the year, on Christmas Eve—old Scrooge sat busy in his counting house. It was cold, bleak, biting weather: foggy withal: and he could hear the people in the court outside go wheezing up and down, beating their hands upon their breasts, and stamping their feet upon the pavement stones to warm them. The city clocks had only just gone three, but it was quite dark already—it had not been light all day: and candles were flaring in the windows of the neighbouring offices, like ruddy smears upon the palpable brown air. The fog came pouring in at every chink and keyhole, and was so dense without, that although the court was of the narrowest, the houses opposite were mere phantoms. To see the dingy cloud come drooping down, obscuring everything, one might have thought that Nature lived hard by, and was brewing on a large scale.

The door of Scrooge's counting house was open that he might keep his eye upon his clerk, who in a dismal little cell beyond, a sort of tank, was copying letters. Scrooge had a very small fire, but the clerk's fire was so very much smaller that it looked like one coal. But he couldn't replenish it, for Scrooge kept the coal-box in his own room; and so surely as the clerk came in with the shovel, the master predicted that it would be necessary for them to part. Wherefore the clerk put on his white comforter, and tried to warm himself at the candle; in which effort, not being a man of a strong imagination, he failed.

"A merry Christmas, uncle! God save you!" cried a cheerful voice. It was the voice of Scrooge's nephew, who came upon him so quickly that this was the first intimation he had of his approach.

"Bah!" said Scrooge, "Humbug!"

He had so heated himself with rapid walking in the fog and frost, this nephew of Scrooge's, that he was all in a glow; his face was ruddy and handsome; his eyes sparkled, and his breath smoked again.

"Christmas a humbug, uncle!" said Scrooge's nephew. "You don't mean that, I am sure."

"I do," said Scrooge. "Merry Christmas! What right have you to be merry? What reason have you to be merry? You're poor enough."

"Come, then," returned the nephew gaily. "What right have you to be dismal? What reason have you to be morose? You're rich enough."

Scrooge having no better answer ready on the spur of the moment said "Bah!" again; and followed it up with "Humbug."

"Don't be cross, uncle!" said the nephew.

"What else can I be," returned the uncle, "when I live in such a world of fools as this? Merry Christmas! Out upon merry Christmas! What's Christmas time to you but a time for paying bills without money; a time for finding yourself a year older, but not an hour richer; a time for balancing your books and having every item in 'em through a round dozen of months presented dead against you? If I could work my will," said Scrooge indignantly, "every idiot who goes about with 'Merry Christmas' on his lips, should be boiled with his own pudding, and buried with a stake of holly through his heart. He should!"

"Uncle!" pleaded the nephew.

"Nephew!" returned the uncle, sternly, "keep Christmas in your own way, and let me keep it in mine."

"Keep it!" repeated Scrooge's nephew. "But you don't keep it."

"Let me leave it alone, then," said Scrooge. "Much good may it do you! Much good it has ever done you!"

"There are many things from which I might have derived good, by which I have not profited, I dare say," returned the nephew. "Christmas among the rest. But I am sure I have always thought of Christmas time, when it has come round—apart from the veneration due to its sacred name and origin, if anything belonging to it can be apart from that—as a good time: a kind, forgiving, charitable, pleasant time: the only time I know of, in the long calendar of the year, when men and women seem by one consent to open their shut-up hearts freely, and to think of people below them as if they really were fellow-passengers to the grave, and not another race of creatures bound on other journeys. And therefore, uncle, though it has never put a scrap of gold or silver in my pocket, I believe that it *has* done me good, and *will* do me good; and I say, God bless it!"

The clerk in the tank involuntarily applauded. Becoming immediately sensible of the impropriety, he poked the fire, and extinguished the last frail spark forever.

"Let me hear another sound from *you*," said Scrooge, "and you'll keep your Christmas by losing your situation. You're quite a powerful speaker, sir," he added, turning to his nephew. "I wonder you don't go into Parliament."

"Don't be angry, uncle. Come! Dine with us tomorrow."

Scrooge said that he would see him—yes, indeed he did. He went the whole length of the expression, and said that he would see him in that extremity first.

"But why?" cried Scrooge's nephew. "Why?"

"Why did you get married?" said Scrooge.

"Because I fell in love."

"Because you fell in love!" growled Scrooge, as if that were the only one thing in the world more ridiculous than a merry Christmas. "Good afternoon!"

"Nay, uncle, but you never came to see me before that happened. Why give it as a reason for not coming now?"

"Good afternoon," said Scrooge.

"I want nothing from you; I ask nothing of you; why cannot we be friends?"

"Good afternoon," said Scrooge.

"I am sorry, with all my heart, to find you so resolute. We have never had any quarrel, to which I have been a party. But I have made the trial in homage to Christmas, and I'll keep my Christmas humour to the last. So a merry Christmas, uncle!"

"Good afternoon," said Scrooge.

"And a happy New Year!"

"Good afternoon!" said Scrooge.

His nephew left the room without an angry word, notwithstanding. He stopped at the outer door to bestow the greetings of the season on the clerk, who cold as he was, was warmer than Scrooge; for he returned them cordially.

"There's another fellow," muttered Scrooge; who overheard him: "my clerk, with fifteen shillings a week, and a wife and family, talking about a merry Christmas. I'll retire to Bedlam."

This lunatic, in letting Scrooge's nephew out, had let two other people in. They were portly gentlemen, pleasant to behold, and now stood, with their hats off, in Scrooge's office. They had books and papers in their hands, and bowed to him.

"Scrooge and Marley's, I believe," said one of the gentlemen, referring to his list. "Have I the pleasure of addressing Mr. Scrooge, or Mr. Marley?"

"Mr. Marley has been dead these seven years," Scrooge replied. "He died seven years ago, this very night."

"We have no doubt his liberality is well represented by his surviving partner," said the gentleman, presenting his credentials.

It certainly was; for they had been two kindred spirits. At the ominous word "liberality," Scrooge frowned, and shook his head, and handed the credentials back.

"At this festive season of the year, Mr. Scrooge," said the gentleman, taking up a pen, "it is more than usually desirable that we should make some slight provision for the Poor and Destitute, who suffer greatly at the present time. Many thousands are in want of common necessaries; hundreds of thousands are in want of common comforts, sir."

"Are there no prisons?" asked Scrooge.

"Plenty of prisons," said the gentleman, laying down the pen again.

"And the Union workhouses?" demanded Scrooge. "Are they still in operation?"

"They are. Still," returned the gentleman, "I wish I could say they were not."

"The Treadmill and the Poor Law are in full vigour, then?" said Scrooge.

"Both very busy, sir."

"Oh! I was afraid, from what you said at first, that something had occurred to stop them in their useful course," said Scrooge. "I'm very glad to hear it."

"Under the impression that they scarcely furnish Christian cheer of mind or body to the multitude," returned the gentleman, "a few of us are endeavouring to raise a fund to buy the Poor some meat and drink and means of warmth. We choose this time, because it is a time, of all others, when Want is keenly felt, and Abundance rejoices. What shall I put you down for?"

"Nothing!" Scrooge replied.

"You wish to be anonymous?"

"I wish to be left alone," said Scrooge. "Since you ask me what I wish, gentlemen, that is my answer. I don't make merry myself at Christmas and I can't afford to make idle people merry. I help to support the establishments I have mentioned—they cost enough; and those who are badly off must go there."

"Many can't go there; and many would rather die."

"If they would rather die," said Scrooge, "they had better do it, and decrease the surplus population. Besides—excuse me—I don't know that."

"But you might know it," observed the gentleman.

"It's not my business," Scrooge resumed. "It's enough for a man to understand his own business, and not to interfere with other people's. Mine occupies me constantly. Good afternoon, gentlemen!"

Seeing clearly that it would be useless to pursue their point, the gentlemen withdrew. Scrooge resumed his labours with an improved opinion of himself, and in a more facetious temper than was usual with him....

At length the hour of shutting up the counting house arrived. With an ill-will Scrooge dismounted from his stool, and tacitly admitted the fact to the expectant clerk in the Tank, who instantly snuffed his candle out, and put on his hat.

"You'll want all day tomorrow, I suppose?" said Scrooge.

"If quite convenient, sir."

"It's not convenient," said Scrooge, "and it's not fair. If I was to stop half-a-crown for it, you'd think yourself ill-used, I'll be bound?"

The clerk smiled faintly.

"And yet," said Scrooge, "you don't think me ill-used, when I pay a day's wages for no work."

The clerk observed that it was only once a year.

"A poor excuse for picking a man's pocket every twenty-fifth of December!" said Scrooge, buttoning his great-coat to the chin. "But I suppose you must have the whole day. Be here all the earlier next morning."

The clerk promised that he would; and Scrooge walked out with a growl. The office was closed in a twinkling, and the clerk, with the long ends of his white comforter dangling below his waist (for he boasted no great-coat), went down a slide on Cornhill, at the end of a lane of boys, twenty times, in honour of its being Christmas Eve, and then ran home to Camden Town as hard as he could pelt, to play at blindman's-buff.

Scrooge took his melancholy dinner in his usual melancholy tavern; and having read all the newspapers, and beguiled the rest of the evening with his banker's-book, went home to bed. He lived in chambers which had once belonged to his deceased partner. They were a gloomy suite of rooms, in a lowering pile of building up a yard, where it had so little business to be, that one could scarcely help fancying it must have run there when it was a young house, playing at hide-and-seek with other houses, and forgotten the way out again.

It was old enough now, and dreary enough, for nobody lived in it but Scrooge, the other rooms being all let out as offices. The yard was so dark that even Scrooge, who knew its every stone, was fain to grope with his hands. The fog and frost so hung about the black old gateway of the house, that it seemed as if the Genius of the Weather sat in mournful meditation on the threshold.

Now, it is a fact, that there was nothing at all particular about the knocker on the door, except that it was very large. It is also a fact, that Scrooge had seen it, night and morning, during his whole residence in that place; also that Scrooge had as little of what is called fancy about him as any man in the city of London, even including—which is a bold word—the corporation, aldermen, and livery. Let it also be borne in mind that Scrooge had not bestowed one thought on Marley, since his last mention of his seven years' dead partner that afternoon. And then let any man explain to me, if he can, how it happened that Scrooge, having his key in the lock of the door, saw in the knocker, without its undergoing any intermediate process of change—not a knocker, but Marley's face.

Marley's face. It was not in impenetrable shadow as the other objects in the yard were, but had a dismal light about it, like a bad lobster in a dark cellar. It was not angry or ferocious, but looked at Scrooge as Marley used to look: with ghostly spectacles turned up on its ghostly forehead. The hair was curiously stirred, as if by breath or hot air; and, though the eyes were wide open, they were perfectly motionless. That, and its livid colour, made it horrible; but its horror seemed to be in spite of the face and beyond its control, rather than a part of its own expression.

As Scrooge looked fixedly at this phenomenon, it was a knocker again.

To say that he was not startled, or that his blood was not conscious of a terrible sensation to which it had been a stranger from infancy, would be untrue. But he put his hand upon the key he had relinquished, turned it sturdily, walked in, and lighted his candle.

He did pause, with a moment's irresolution, before he shut the door; and he *did* look cautiously behind it first, as if he half expected to be terrified with the sight of Marley's pigtail sticking out into the hall. But there was nothing on the back of the door, except the screws and nuts that held the knocker on, so he said "Pooh, pooh!" and closed it with a bang.

The sound resounded through the house like thunder. Every room above, and every cask in the wine-merchant's cellars below, appeared to have a separate peal of echoes of its own. Scrooge was not a man to be frightened by echoes. He fastened the door, and walked across the hall, and up the stairs, slowly too, trimming his candle as he went.

Up Scrooge went, not caring a button for that. Darkness is cheap, and Scrooge liked it. But before he shut his heavy door, he walked through his rooms to see that all was right. He had just enough recollection of the face to desire to do that.

Sitting-room, bedroom, lumber-room. All as they should be. Nobody under the table, nobody under the sofa; a small fire in the grate; spoon and basin ready; and the little saucepan of gruel (Scrooge had a cold in his head) upon the hob. Nobody under the bed; nobody in the closet; nobody in his dressing-gown, which was hanging up in a suspicious attitude against the wall. Lumber-room as usual. Old fire-guards, old shoes, two fish-baskets, washing-stand on three legs, and a poker.

Quite satisfied, he closed his door, and locked himself in; double-locked himself in, which was not his custom. Thus secured against surprise, he took off his cravat; put on his dressing-gown and slippers, and his nightcap; and sat down before the fire to take his gruel.

His glance happened to rest upon a bell, a disused bell, that hung in the room, and communicated for some purpose now forgotten with a chamber in the highest story of the building. It was with great astonishment, and with a strange, inexplicable dread, that as he looked, he saw this bell begin to swing. It swung so softly in the outset that it scarcely made a sound; but soon it rang out loudly, and so did every bell in the house.

This might have lasted half a minute, or a minute, but it seemed an hour. The bells ceased as they had begun, together. They were succeeded by a clanking noise, deep down below, as if some person were dragging a heavy chain over the casks in the wine merchant's cellar. Scrooge then remembered to have heard that ghosts in haunted houses were described as dragging chains.

The cellar-door flew open with a booming sound, and then he heard the noise much louder, on the floors below; then coming up the stairs; then coming straight toward his door.

"It's humbug still!" said Scrooge. "I won't believe it."

His colour changed though, when, without a pause, it came on through the heavy door, and passed into the room before his eyes. Upon its coming in, the dying flame leaped up, as though it cried, "I know him; Marley's Ghost!" and fell again.

The same face, the very same. Marley in his pigtail, usual waistcoat, tights and boots; the tassels on the latter bristling like his pigtail, and his coat-skirts, and the hair upon his head. The chain he drew was clasped about his middle. It was long, and wound about him like a tail; and it was made (for Scrooge observed it closely) of cash-boxes, keys, padlocks, ledgers, deeds, and heavy purses wrought in steel. His body was transparent, so that Scrooge, observing him, and looking through his waistcoat, could see the two buttons on his coat behind.

Scrooge had often heard it said that Marley had no bowels, but he had never believed it until now.

No, nor did he believe it even now. Though he looked the phantom through and through, and saw it standing before him; though he felt the chilling influence of its death-cold eyes; and marked the very texture of the folded kerchief bound about its head and chin, which wrapper he had not observed before: he was still incredulous, and fought against his senses.

"How now!" said Scrooge, caustic and cold as ever. "What do you want with me?"

"Much!"—Marley's voice, no doubt about it.

"Who are you?"

"Ask me who I *was*."

"Who *were* you then?" said Scrooge, raising his voice. "You're particular, for a shade." He was going to say "*to* a shade," but substituted this, as more appropriate.

"In life I was your partner, Jacob Marley."

"Can you—can you sit down?" asked Scrooge, looking doubtfully at him.

"I can."

"Do it then."

Scrooge asked the question, because he didn't know whether a ghost so transparent might find himself in a condition to take a chair; and felt that in the event of its being impossible, it might involve the necessity of an embarrassing explanation. But the ghost sat down on the opposite side of the fireplace, as if he were quite used to it.

"You don't believe in me," observed the Ghost.

"I don't," said Scrooge.

"What evidence would you have of my reality, beyond that of your senses?"

"I don't know," said Scrooge.

"Why do you doubt your senses?"

"Because," said Scrooge, "a little thing affects them. A slight disorder of the stomach makes them cheats. You may be an undigested bit of beef, a blot of mustard, a crumb of cheese, a fragment of an underdone potato. There's more of gravy than of grave about you, whatever you are!"

Scrooge was not much in the habit of cracking jokes, nor did he feel, in his heart, by any means waggish then. The truth is, that he tried to be smart, as a means of distracting his own attention, and keeping down his terror, for the spectre's voice disturbed the very marrow in his bones.

To sit staring at those fixed glazed eyes in silence, for a moment, would play, Scrooge felt, the very deuce with him. There was something very awful, too, in the spectre's being provided with an infernal atmosphere of its own. Scrooge could not feel it himself, but this was clearly the case; for though the Ghost sat perfectly motionless, its hair, and skirts, and tassels, were still agitated as by the hot vapour from an oven.

"You see this toothpick?" said Scrooge, returning quickly to the charge, for the reason just assigned; and wishing, though it were only for a second, to divert the vision's stony gaze from himself.

"I do," replied the Ghost.

"You are not looking at it," said Scrooge.

"But I see it," said the Ghost, "notwithstanding."

"Well!" returned Scrooge, "I have but to swallow this, and be for the rest of my days persecuted by a legion of goblins, all of my own creation. Humbug, I tell you—humbug!"

At this the spirit raised a frightful cry, and shook its chain with such a dismal and appalling noise, that Scrooge held on tight to his chair, to save himself from falling in a swoon. But how much greater was his horror, when the phantom taking off the bandage round its head, as if it were too warm to wear indoors, its lower jaw dropped down upon its breast!

Scrooge fell upon his knees, and clasped his hands before his face.

"Mercy!" he said. "Dreadful apparition, why do you trouble me?"

"Man of the worldly mind!" replied the Ghost, "do you believe in me or not?"

"I do," said Scrooge. "I must. But why do spirits walk the earth, and why do they come to me?"

"It is required of every man," the Ghost returned, "that the spirit within him should walk abroad among his fellowmen, and travel far and wide; and if that spirit goes not forth in life, it is condemned to do so after death. It is doomed to wander through the world—oh, woe is me!—and witness what it cannot share, but might have shared on earth, and turned to happiness!"

Again the spectre raised a cry, and shook its chain and wrung its shadowy hands.

"You are fettered," said Scrooge, trembling. "Tell me why?"

"I wear the chain I forged in life," replied the Ghost. "I made it link by link, and yard by yard; I girded it on of my own free will, and of my own free will I wore it. Is its pattern strange to *you*?"

Scrooge trembled more and more.

"Or would you know," pursued the Ghost, "the weight and length of the strong coil you bear yourself? It was full as heavy and as long as this, seven Christmas Eves ago. You have laboured on it, since. It is a ponderous chain!"

Scrooge glanced about him on the floor, in the expectation of finding himself surrounded by some fifty or sixty fathoms of iron cable; but he could see nothing.

"Jacob," he said, imploringly. "Old Jacob Marley, tell me more. Speak comfort to me, Jacob!"

"I have none to give," the Ghost replied. "It comes from other regions, Ebenezer Scrooge, and is conveyed by other ministers, to other kinds of men. Nor can I tell you what I would. A very little more is all permitted to me. I cannot rest, I cannot stay, I cannot linger anywhere. My spirit never walked beyond our counting house— mark me!—in life my spirit never roved beyond the narrow limits of our money-changing hole; and weary journeys lie before me!"

It was a habit with Scrooge, whenever he became thoughtful, to put his hands in his breeches pockets. Pondering on what the Ghost had said, he did so now, but without lifting up his eyes, or getting off his knees.

"You must have been very slow about it, Jacob," Scrooge observed, in a business-like manner, though with humility and deference.

"Slow!" the Ghost repeated.

"Seven years dead," mused Scrooge. "And travelling all the time!"

"The whole time," said the Ghost. "No rest, no peace. Incessant torture of remorse."

"You travel fast?" said Scrooge.

"On the wings of the wind," replied the Ghost.

"You might have got over a great quantity of ground in seven years," said Scrooge.

The Ghost, on hearing this, set up another cry, and clanked its chain so hideously in the dead silence of the night, that the Ward would have been justified in indicting it for a nuisance.

"Oh! captive, bound, and double-ironed," cried the phantom, "not to know that … any spirit working kindly in its little sphere, whatever it may be, will find its mortal life too short for its vast means of usefulness! Not to know that no space of regret can make amends for one life's opportunity misused! Yet such was I! Oh! such was I!"

"But you were always a good man of business, Jacob," faltered Scrooge, who now began to apply this to himself.

"Business!" cried the Ghost, wringing its hands again. "Mankind was my business. The common welfare was my business; charity, mercy, forbearance, and benevolence were all my business. The dealings of my trade were but a drop of water in the comprehensive ocean of my business!"

It held up its chain at arm's length, as if that were the cause of all its unavailing grief, and flung it heavily upon the ground again.

"At this time of the rolling year," the spectre said, "I suffer most. Why did I walk through crowds of fellow beings with my eyes turned down, and never raise them to that blessed Star which led the Wise Men to a poor abode! Were there no poor homes to which its light would have conducted *me*!"

Scrooge was very much dismayed to hear the spectre going on at this rate, and began to quake exceedingly.

"Hear me!" cried the Ghost. "My time is nearly gone."

"I will," said Scrooge. "But don't be hard upon me! Don't be flowery, Jacob! Pray!"

"How it is that I appear before you in a shape that you can see, I may not tell. I have sat invisible beside you many and many a day."

It was not an agreeable idea. Scrooge shivered, and wiped the perspiration from his brow.

"That is no light part of my penance," pursued the Ghost. "I am here tonight to warn you, that you have yet a chance and hope of escaping my fate. A chance and hope of my procuring, Ebenezer."

"You were always a good friend to me," said Scrooge. "Thank 'ee!"

"You will be haunted," resumed the Ghost, "by Three Spirits."

Scrooge's countenance fell almost as low as the Ghost's had done.

"Is that the chance and hope you mentioned, Jacob?" he demanded, in a faltering voice.

"It is."

"I—I think I'd rather not," said Scrooge.

"Without their visits," said the Ghost, "you cannot hope to shun the path I tread. Expect the first tomorrow, when the bell tolls one."

"Couldn't I take 'em all at once, and have it over, Jacob?" hinted Scrooge.

"Expect the second on the next night at the same hour. The third upon the next night when the last stroke of twelve has ceased to vibrate. Look to see me no more; and look that, for your own sake, you remember what has passed between us!"

When it had said these words, the spectre took its wrapper from the table, and bound it round its head, as before. Scrooge knew this, by the smart sound its teeth made, when the jaws were brought together by the bandage. He ventured to raise his eyes again, and found his supernatural visitor confronting him in an erect attitude, with its chain wound over and about its arm.

The apparition walked backward from him; and at every step it took, the window raised itself a little, so that when the spectre reached it, it was wide open. It beckoned Scrooge to approach, which he did.... He became sensible of confused noises in the air; incoherent sounds of lamentation and regret; wailings inexpressibly sorrowful and self-accusatory. The spectre, after listening for a moment, joined in the mournful dirge; and floated out upon the bleak night.

The air was filled with phantoms moaning as they went. Every one of them wore chains like Marley's Ghost. The misery with them all was, clearly, that they sought to interfere, for good, in human matters, and had lost the power forever.

Scrooge closed the window, and examined the door by which the Ghost had entered. It was double-locked, as he had locked it with his own hands, and the bolts were undisturbed. He tried to say "Humbug!" but stopped at the first syllable. And being, from the emotion he had undergone, or the fatigues of the day, or his glimpse of the Invisible World, or the dull conversation of the Ghost, or the lateness of the hour, much in need of repose, went straight to bed, without undressing, and fell asleep upon the instant.

Charles Dickens (*born 1812, England; died 1870*), reporter, editor, novelist, public performer, is still widely read. Characters from *Oliver Twist*, *Great Expectations*, and *A Tale of Two Cities* are recognized everywhere, often from stage, movie, and television adaptations. Dickens championed the cause of the less fortunate in society.

Activities: Marley's Ghost

1. **Explore Style:** Dickens's style involves the piling up of details and the rephrasing of an idea in a variety of ways. Working in a small group, make notes on the way Dickens describes the following elements in the selection: the fact of Marley's being dead, the joys of Christmas, Scrooge's meanness, Marley's ghost.

2. **Analyze Use of Pathetic Fallacy:** Working with a partner, note details of the description of Scrooge and of his home. In a short formal essay, show how Dickens presents Scrooge's home as an extension of his personality. Edit and proofread each other's essays before producing a final copy.

3. **Identify the Message:** In spite of the humorous features of the selection, Dickens is making some serious comments about human nature and society. With a small group, identify four points that you think Dickens is making in this excerpt.

4. **Read Dramatically:** Dickens gained great fame performing dramatic readings from his novels. Prepare and present a dramatic reading of an extract from the selection. Adopt different voices for each character, and use volume, pace, tone, and other oral devices to enhance the impact of your reading. Invite feedback from the audience.

From Alias Grace

Margaret Atwood

Alias Grace is based on the true story of Grace Marks, sentenced to life in prison at the age of 16 for her part in the 1843 murder of house-keeper Nancy Montgomery and her employer, Thomas Kinnear. In this extract, Grace sits in the home of the prison governor, awaiting the arrival of a young American doctor who wants to meet her because he is interested in insanity. He also wants to find out whether she is guilty of the murder for which she has already spent more than 15 years in prison.

1859.

I am sitting on the purple velvet settee in the Governor's parlour, the Governor's wife's parlour; it has always been the Governor's wife's parlour although it is not always the same wife, as they change them around according to the politics. I have my hands folded in my lap the proper way although I have no gloves. The gloves I would wish to have would be smooth and white, and would fit without a wrinkle.

I am often in this parlour, clearing away the tea things and dusting the small tables and the long mirror with the frame of grapes and leaves around it, and the pianoforte; and the tall clock that came from Europe, with the orange-gold sun and the silver

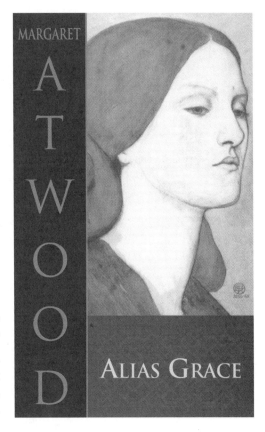

moon, that go in and out according to the time of day and the week of the month. I like the clock best of anything in the parlour, although it measures time and I have too much of that on my hands already.

But I have never sat down on the settee before, as it is for the guests. Mrs. Alderman Parkinson said a lady must never sit in a chair a gentleman has just vacated, though she would not say why; but Mary Whitney said, Because, you silly goose, it's still warm from his bum; which was a coarse thing to say. So I cannot sit here without thinking of the ladylike bums that have sat on this very settee, all delicate and white, like wobbly soft-boiled eggs.

The visitors wear afternoon dresses with rows of buttons up their fronts, and stiff wire crinolines beneath. It's a wonder they can sit down at all, and when they walk, nothing touches their legs under the billowing skirts, except their shifts and stockings. They are like swans, drifting along on unseen feet; or else like the jellyfish in the waters of the rocky harbour near our house, when I was little, before I ever made the long sad journey across the ocean. They were bell-shaped and ruffled, gracefully waving and lovely under the sea; but if they washed up on the beach and dried out in the sun there was nothing left of them. And that is what the ladies are like: mostly water.

There were no wire crinolines when I was first brought here. They were horsehair then, as the wire ones were not thought of. I have looked at them hanging in the wardrobes, when I go in to tidy and empty the slops. They are like birdcages; but what is being caged in? Legs, the legs of ladies; legs penned in so they cannot get out and go rubbing up against the gentlemen's trousers. The Governor's wife never says legs, although the newspapers said legs when they were talking about Nancy, with her dead legs sticking out from under the washtub.

It isn't only the jellyfish ladies that come. On Tuesdays we have the Woman Question, and the emancipation of this or that, with reform-minded persons of both sexes; and on Thursdays the Spiritualist Circle, for tea and conversing with the dead, which is a comfort to the Governor's wife because of her departed infant son. But mainly it is the ladies. They sit sipping from the thin cups, and the Governor's wife rings a little china bell. She does not like being the Governor's wife, she would prefer the Governor to be the governor of something other than a prison. The Governor had good-enough friends to get him made the Governor, but not for anything else.

So here she is, and she must make the most of her social position and accomplishments, and although an object of fear, like a spider, and of charity as well, I am also one of the accomplishments. I come into the room and curtsy and move about, mouth straight, head bent, and I pick up the cups or set them down, depending; and they stare without appearing to, out from under their bonnets.

The reason they want to see me is that I am a celebrated murderess. Or that is what has been written down. When I first saw it I was surprised, because they say Celebrated Singer and Celebrated Poetess and Celebrated Spiritualist and Celebrated Actress, but what is there to celebrate about murder? All the same, *Murderess* is a strong word to have attached to you. It has a smell to it, that word—musky and oppressive, like dead flowers in a vase. Sometimes at night I whisper it over to myself: *Murderess, Murderess*. It rustles, like a taffeta skirt across the floor.

Murderer is merely brutal. It's like a hammer, or a lump of metal. I would rather be a murderess than a murderer, if those are the only choices.

Sometimes when I am dusting the mirror with the grapes I look at myself in it, although I know it is vanity. In the afternoon light of the parlour my skin is a pale mauve, like a faded bruise, and my teeth are greenish. I think of all the things that have been written about me— that I am an inhuman female demon, that I am an innocent victim of a blackguard forced against my will and in danger of my own life, that I was too ignorant to know how to act and that to hang me would be judicial murder, that I am fond of animals, that I am very handsome with a brilliant complexion, that I have blue eyes, that I have green eyes, that I have auburn and also brown hair, that I am tall and also not above the average height, that I am well and decently dressed, that I robbed a dead woman to appear so, that I am brisk and smart about my work, that I am of a sullen disposition with a quarrelsome temper, that I have the appearance of a person rather above my humble station, that I am a good girl with a pliable nature and no harm is told of me, that I am cunning and devious, that I am soft in the head and little better than an idiot. And I wonder, how can I be all of these different things at once?

It was my own lawyer, Mr. Kenneth MacKenzie, Esq., who told them I was next door to an idiot. I was angry with him over that, but he said it was by far my best chance and I should not appear to be too intelligent. He said he would plead my case to the utmost of his ability, because whatever the truth of the matter I was little more than a child at the time, and he supposed it came down to free will and whether or not one held with it. He was a kind gentleman although I could not make head nor tail of much of what he said, but it must have been good pleading. The newspapers wrote that he performed heroically against overwhelming odds. Though I don't know why they called it pleading, as he was not pleading but trying to make all of the witnesses appear immoral or malicious, or else mistaken.

I wonder if he ever believed a word I said.

When I have gone out of the room with the tray, the ladies look at the Governor's wife's scrapbook. Oh imagine, I feel quite faint, they say, and You let that woman walk around loose in your house, you must have nerves of iron, my own would never stand it. Oh well one must get used to such things in our situation, we are virtually prisoners ourselves you know, although one must feel pity for these poor benighted creatures, and after all she was trained as a servant, and it's as well to keep them employed, she is a wonderful seamstress, quite deft and accomplished, she is a great help in that way especially with the girls' frocks, she has an eye for trimmings, and under happier circumstances she could have made an excellent milliner's assistant.

Although naturally she can be here only during the day, I would not have her in the house at night. You are aware that she has spent time in the Lunatic Asylum in Toronto, seven or eight years ago it was, and although she appears to be perfectly recovered you never know when they may get carried away again, sometimes she talks to herself and sings out loud in a most peculiar manner. One cannot take chances, the keepers conduct her back in the evenings and lock her up properly, otherwise I wouldn't be able to sleep a wink. Oh I don't blame you, there is only so far one can go in Christian charity, a leopard cannot change its spots and no one could say you have not done your duty and shown a proper feeling.

The Governor's wife's scrapbook is kept on the round table with the silk shawl covering it, branches like vines intertwined, with flowers and red fruit and blue birds, it is really one large tree and if you stare at it long enough the vines begin to twist as if a wind is blowing them. It was sent from India by her eldest daughter who is married to a missionary, which is not a thing I would care to do myself. You would be sure to die early, if not from the rioting natives as at Cawnpore with horrid outrages committed on the persons of respectable gentlewomen, and a mercy they were all slaughtered and put out of their misery, for only think of the shame; then from the malaria, which turns you entirely yellow, and you expire in raving fits; in any case before you could turn around, there you would be, buried under a palm tree in a foreign clime. I have seen pictures of them in the book of Eastern engravings the Governor's wife takes out when she wishes to shed a tear.

On the same round table is the stack of Godey's Ladies' Books with the fashions that come up from the States, and also the Keepsake Albums of the two younger daughters. Miss Lydia tells me I am a romantic figure; but then, the two of them are so young they hardly know what they are saying. Sometimes they pry and tease; they say, Grace, why don't you ever smile or laugh, we never see you smiling, and I say I suppose Miss I have gotten out of the way of it, my face won't bend in that direction any more. But if I laughed out loud I might not be able to stop; and also it would spoil their romantic notion of me. Romantic people are not supposed to laugh, I know that much from looking at the pictures.

The daughters put all kinds of things into their albums, little scraps of cloth from their dresses, little snippets of ribbon, pictures cut from magazines—the Ruins of Ancient Rome, the Picturesque Monasteries of the French Alps, Old London Bridge, Niagara Falls in summer and in winter, which is a thing I would like to see as all say it is very impressive, and portraits of Lady This and Lord That from England. And their friends write things in their graceful handwriting, *To Dearest Lydia from your Eternal Friend, Clara Richards; To Dearest Marianne In Memory of Our Splendid Picnic on the Shores of Bluest Lake Ontario.* And also poems:

As round about the sturdy Oak
Entwines the loving Ivy Vine,
My Faith so true, I pledge to You,
'Twill evermore be none but Thine, Your Faithful Laura.

Or else:

Although from you I far must roam,
Do not be broken hearted,
We two who in the Soul are One
Are never truly parted. Your Lucy.

This young lady was shortly afterwards drowned in the Lake when her ship went down in a gale, and nothing was ever found but her box with her initials done in silver nails; it was still locked, so although damp, nothing spilt out, and Miss Lydia was given a scarf out of it as a keepsake.

When I am dead and in my grave
And all my bones are rotten,
When this you see, remember me,
Lest I should be forgotten.

That one is signed, *I will always be with you in Spirit, Your loving "Nancy," Hannah Edmonds,* and I must say the first time I saw that, it gave me a fright, although of course it was a different Nancy. Still, the rotten bones. They would be, by now. Her face was all black by the time they found her, there must have been a dreadful smell. It was so hot then, it was July, still she went off surprisingly soon, you'd think she would have kept longer in the dairy, it is usually cool down there. I am certainly glad I was not present, as it would have been very distressing.

I don't know why they are all so eager to be remembered. What good will it do them? There are some things that should be forgotten by everyone, and never spoken of again.

The Governor's wife's scrapbook is quite different. Of course she is a grown woman and not a young girl, so although she is just as fond of remembering, what she wants to remember is not violets or a picnic. No Dearest and Love and Beauty, no Eternal Friends, none of those things for her; what it has instead is all the famous criminals in it—the ones that have been hanged, or else brought here to be penitent, because this is a Penitentiary and you are supposed to repent while in it, and you will do better if you say you have done so, whether you have anything to repent or not.

The Governor's wife cuts these crimes out of the newspapers and pastes them in; she will even write away for old newspapers with crimes that were done before her time. It is her collection, she is a lady and they are all collecting things these days, and so she must collect something, and she does this instead of pulling up ferns or pressing flowers, and in any case she likes to horrify her acquaintances.

So I have read what they put in about me. She showed the scrapbook to me herself, I suppose she wanted to see what I would do; but I've learnt to keep my face still, I made my eyes wide and flat, like an owl's in torchlight, and I said I had repented in bitter tears, and was now a changed person, and would she wish me to remove the tea things now; but I've looked in there since, many times, when I've been in the parlour by myself.

A lot of it is lies. They said in the newspaper that I was illiterate, but I could read some even then. I was taught early by my mother, before she got too tired for it, and I did my sampler with leftover thread, A is for Apple, B is for Bee; and also Mary Whitney used to read with me, at Mrs. Alderman Parkinson's, when we were doing the mending; and I've learnt a lot more since being here, as they teach you on purpose. They want you to be able to read the Bible, and also tracts, as religion and thrashing are the only remedies for a depraved nature and our immortal souls must be considered. It is shocking how many crimes the Bible contains. The Governor's wife should cut them all out and paste them into her scrapbook.

They did say some true things. They said I had a good character; and that was so, because nobody had ever taken advantage of me, although they tried. But they called James McDermott my paramour. They wrote it down, right in the newspaper. I think it is disgusting to write such things down.

That is what really interests them—the gentlemen and the ladies both. They don't care if I killed anyone, I could have cut dozens of throats, it's only what they admire in a soldier, they'd scarcely blink.

No: was I really a paramour, is their chief concern, and they don't even know themselves whether they want the answer to be no or yes.

I'm not looking at the scrapbook now, because they may come in at any moment. I sit with my rough hands folded, eyes down, staring at the flowers in the Turkey carpet. Or they are supposed to be flowers. They have petals the shape of the diamonds on a playing card; like the cards spread out on the table at Mr. Kinnear's, after the gentlemen had been playing the night before. Hard and angular. But red, a deep thick red. Thick strangled tongues.

It's not the ladies expected today, it's a doctor. He's writing a book; the Governor's wife likes to know people who are writing books, books with forward-looking aims, it shows that she is a liberal-minded person with advanced views, and science is making such progress, and what with modern inventions and the Crystal Palace and world knowledge assembled, who knows where we will all be in a hundred years.

Where there's a doctor it's always a bad sign. Even when they are not doing the killing themselves it means a death is close, and in that way they are like ravens or crows. But this doctor will not hurt me, the Governor's wife promised it. All he wants is to measure my head. He is measuring the heads of all the criminals in the Penitentiary, to see if he can tell from the bumps on their skulls what sort of criminals they are, whether they are pickpockets or swindlers or embezzlers or criminal lunatics or murderers, she did not say Like you, Grace. And then they could lock those people up before they had a chance to commit any crimes, and think how that would improve the world.

After James McDermott was hanged they made a plaster cast of his head. I read that in the scrapbook too. I suppose that's what they wanted it for—to improve the world.

Also his body was dissected. When I first read that I did not know what *dissected* was, but I found it out soon enough. It was done by the doctors. They cut him into pieces like a pig to be salted down, he might as well have been bacon as far as they were concerned. His body that I listened to breathing, and the heart beating, the knife slicing through it—I can't bear to think of it.

I wonder what they did with his shirt. Was it one of the four sold to him by Jeremiah the peddler? It should have been three, or else five, as odd numbers are luckier. Jeremiah always wished me luck, but he did not wish any to James McDermott.

I did not see the hanging. They hanged him in front of the jail in Toronto, and You should have been there Grace, say the keepers, it would have been a lesson to you. I've pictured it many times, poor James standing with his hands tied and his neck bare, while they put the hood over his head like a kitten to be drowned. At least he had a priest with him, he was not all alone. If it had not been for Grace Marks, he told them, none of it would have happened.

It was raining, and a huge crowd standing in the mud, some of them come from miles away. If my own death sentence had not been commuted at the last minute, they would have watched me hang with the same greedy pleasure. There were many women and ladies there; everyone wanted to stare, they wanted to breathe death in like fine perfume, and when I read of it I thought, If this is a lesson to me, what is it I am supposed to be learning?

Margaret Atwood (*born 1939, Ottawa, Ontario*), poet, novelist, critic, is one of Canada's foremost authors. Known for her craftsmanship and precise use of language, she often explores contemporary issues of politics, society, and gender in her work. Atwood's many awards include two Governor General's Literary Awards, as well as a Booker Prize for *The Blind Assassin*.

Activities: Alias Grace

1. ***Explore Characters:*** Work with a partner to note and discuss the various ways in which Grace is described in this excerpt. Why are there so many differing notions of who Grace is? Discuss your conclusion with another pair.

2. ***Examine Words:*** Reread Grace's thoughts on the differences between the words *murderer* and *murderess*. Agree or disagree with her explanation of the connotations of these words. Identify another pair of words (e.g., actor/actress) that may have the same denotation but different connotations. Explain the connotations.

3. ***Interpret Text:*** Do research to discover what is meant by the term *romantic figure*. Then explain how, if Grace is indeed a murderess, people can have a romantic notion of her. Write your thoughts in your journal.

4. ***Research the Author:*** Find out more about Margaret Atwood and her work. Create a one-page profile of her and use an appropriate format to organize your ideas. Ask a classmate to edit your profile.

Nonfiction

He is educated who knows where to
find out what he doesn't know.

—Georg Simmel

Read, not to contradict and confute, nor to believe and
take for granted, nor to find talk and discourse, but to
weigh and consider.

—Francis Bacon

About Nonfiction

The range of nonfiction is broad, including any prose writing that is not based on imaginary characters and events. While many people associate nonfiction with facts, it also encompasses writing about opinions (in editorials), feelings (in journals and personal essays), and experiences (in autobiographies and travel books). Most likely, you read some form of nonfiction every day.

When reading nonfiction, consider the author's purpose. What did the author want to achieve by writing the piece? Is he or she trying to convince you to believe or do something, or is the purpose to explain ideas, processes, events, or facts? Sometimes there is more than one purpose, as in a humorous essay that tries to inform and entertain readers at the same time.

The way in which the author tries to fulfill the purpose is often influenced by the characteristics of the intended audience. Important characteristics might include anything from age and gender to socioeconomic status and existing beliefs and opinions. In persuasive texts, such as political speeches and advertisements, audience characteristics are especially important. Writers will carefully weigh the impact of each word, phrase, and argument in order to determine how the audience will respond.

It is also useful to notice how the author has chosen to organize information. When explaining a process or series of events, writers will often present information in sequential order. Other organizational strategies include comparing and contrasting different points of view or, piece by piece, building an argument based on logic.

As you read the selections in this unit, take note of any topics, forms, or authors that interest and intrigue you. Use these as a starting point for your own exploration of the world of nonfiction.

Nonfiction

Canadian English

English is a living language, rich, varied, always changing. It is the first language of at least 400 million people around the world, and the second language of at least 450 million more.

Yet the beginnings of English are less grand. In the 5th century A.D., the precursor of modern English began to evolve in the small island now known as Great Britain. The disintegration of the Roman Empire brought invaders from the Continent—Angles, Saxons, Jutes, and Frisians. These tribes spoke Germanic dialects that replaced Celtic languages and Latin, tongues of earlier invaders. Until the 11th century the blended language that resulted, Old English, also called Anglo-Saxon, was only an insignificant part of the huge Indo-European language family that sprawled across Europe and into Iran, the Indian subcontinent, and other parts of Asia.

If our modern ears could hear it, Old English would be incomprehensible. Middle English, however, the language of the great poet Geoffrey Chaucer, would sound much more familiar to us. Chaucer wrote in the 14th century, and his language was the product of the single greatest revolution in the history of English, the Norman Invasion of 1066 under William the Conqueror. Norman French, with its own stock of words derived from Greek and Latin, soon dominated the business of government and the courts, both legal and regal. Then, as Old English merged with Norman French, its vocabulary became vastly amplified, with many features of Old Germanic grammar disappearing.

But Old English did not die. We stand on its bedrock every day by using two hundred or so extremely common articles, prepositions, conjunctions, pronouns, nouns, and verbs—"the little words of house and home." All the words in that phrase are of Old English origin, as is much of our everyday vocabulary. Nearly 85 percent of our thousand most frequently used words derive from Old English.

At the end of the 15th century, the development of the English language entered a new phase. Gradually, England became an imperial power, competing against the rival empires of Spain, Portugal, the Netherlands, and France and founding colonies that evolved distinctive forms of English now spoken and written in such far-flung corners of the world as Canada, the United States, Australia, New Zealand, South Africa, India, Nigeria, Guyana, and Jamaica. One can now speak not only of English, but of Englishes.

Like that of other nations once part of the British Empire, the English word stock in Canada was initially enriched by heavy borrowing from indigenous languages for the naming of tools, flora and fauna, articles of clothing, foods and drinks, and means of getting about. With these terms came numerous occupational and industrial words and usages; the fur trade, cod fishing, lumbering, wheat farming, cattle raising, and mining each in turn added to the English spoken here. At the same time, a political, legal, and governmental vocabulary arose, directly derived from British institutions.

Immigration and patterns of settlement have had a significant effect on the development of English in Canada, accounting for regional differences in vocabulary, usage, and pronunciation. For example, Newfoundland was claimed by England in 1497. Most of the first permanent settlers there came from southwest England and then, much later, others arrived from Ireland. This combination yielded a mix of diction, syntax, and pronunciation of great linguistic interest. In the 18th century, Nova Scotia received immigrant Germans in Lunenburg, people from Yorkshire in the central and western parts, and Scots Highlanders in both the northern peninsula and Cape Breton. The proximity of New England also had its effect. Each group imparted a distinctive culture to Atlantic Canada and a special character to the English spoken.

The second half of the 18th century substantially altered all of what would become Canada. The American Revolution sent a northward flood of refugees loyal to the British Crown. The first Loyalists came from coastal New England and remained in the Maritimes, especially in New Brunswick, with some families migrating to Lower and Upper Canada. Another wave of Loyalists, chiefly from the states of Vermont, New York, New Jersey, and Pennsylvania, fled to the Eastern Townships of Quebec and the north shore of Lake Ontario. Both groups were primarily of English, Scots, or Scots-Irish origin, though the influx included the Black Loyalists, of African descent, who settled in Nova Scotia. Around the same time, Mennonite refugees found a new home in what is now southern Ontario. Some of these settlers and their descendants maintained their pioneering spirit and took advantage of newly opened lands in the Canadian West, in many cases displacing Aboriginal and Métis hunters and trappers.

The first half of the 19th century brought more immigrants lured by promises of a prosperous life, these arriving directly from England, Scotland, and Ireland. In the late 19th and early 20th centuries, such traditionally English-speaking immigrants were joined by people from northern, southern, and eastern Europe, and even further afield. The Chinese helped to build the transcontinental railway, and Finns came to Ontario's Lakehead, Icelanders and Ukrainians to the Prairies, Greeks and Italians to Montreal and Toronto, Germans to southwestern Ontario, and Japanese to British Columbia. These are just some examples, and the diversification of Canada's population continues to this day. Especially since the end of World War II in 1945, Canada has received people from every part of the world, and our urban areas in particular are increasingly cosmopolitan. Canadian English is being enriched by borrowings from the other languages and dialects that can now be heard within Canadian bounds.

This is the long heritage of our Canadian English. But what are some of the specifics of our pronunciation, spelling, and usage? Though Canadian English has distinctively regional pronunciations, especially in Atlantic Canada, most of us speak more or less like our American neighbours, especially those in border states. There are frequent exceptions, however. Many of these stem from the British influence in our history, such as the tendency to say "zed" rather than "zee" for the letter *z* and "leftenant" instead of "lootenant" for *lieutenant*. On occasion, our pronunciations differ from both American and British ones; for many Canadians, *vase* rhymes with *phase*, whereas in the United States we might hear it rhyming with *place*, and in England rhyming with *spas*. And the way many Canadians pronounce words like "out and about" may sound like "oot and aboot" to an American ear, a phenomenon known as Canadian raising by linguists and the reason some Americans comment on a Scottish flavour in our accent.

If to the British and Europeans we often sound like Americans, to Americans we often spell like the British. The spelling preferences of many Canadians for *-our*, as in colour, and *-re*, as in centre, and for doubling of the *l* in words like *traveller* and *counsellor*, point to the British influence. We usually write *catalogue* rather than *catalog* and *paycheque* rather than *paycheck*. And we rush to get to skating *practice* on time so that we have plenty of time to *practise*. We're anything but consistent, though. We fly in an *airplane* (rather than the British *aeroplane*), and while driving may incur a flat *tire* (rather than the British *tyre*). French, too, has had an effect: many Canadians prefer to pluralize words such as *beau* and *bureau* as *beaux* and *bureaux*, adding an *x* rather than an *s*.

Our history is reflected not only in our pronunciation habits and spelling practices, but also in the words that originated here or that Canadians use in a special way. Think, for example, of all the words that come to English from Aboriginal languages or that relate to Aboriginal cultures, words such as *caribou, igloo, lobstick, pemmican, potlatch, sweetgrass, wapiti*, and *wendigo*. Or consider the words that tell the long story of settlement: *liveyere, coureur de bois, Métis, Hudson's Bay blanket, Loyalist, sodbuster, Klondiker*, and the *last spike*. We have colourful words and terms familiar to particular regions, such as *crunnicks, barachois, beavertail, ghost car, skookum, flipper pie*, and *utilidor*. Other terms, meanwhile, are well known across the land. The language of hockey (*deke, one-time, penalty killer*) is so familiar, it is sometimes used outside the rink (the minister *stickhandled* the controversial bill through Parliament). Of course, no discussion of our Canadian English would be complete without a few examples relating to our *nordicity*, words such as *wind-chill factor, Sheila's Brush, toboggan, frost boil, glitter, pingo*, and *Ski-Doo*.

English, wherever it is spoken, continues to make room for new vocabulary. Many terms are generated by science and technology, from fields such as nuclear physics, biology, space travel, and computer science. Until recently, we did not have words and phrases such as *hypertext, Canadarm, photo radar, e-mail, voice mail,* and *World Wide Web.* We also sometimes give an old word a new twist. For instance, *surfing* and *net* have acquired additional meanings, and a *server* is no longer just a person but also a computer that supports a network of other computers. Medicine is yet another fountainhead of coinages (*Ebola virus, AIDS, chronic fatigue syndrome*) with which we contend.

Then there are changes in society itself that come to be mirrored in language, for example, the replacement of gender-laden terms like *fireman* and *chairman* with *firefighter* and *chair.* Popular culture produces a rapid succession of styles, each of which has its own label (*hip-hop, grunge, bhangra*) and its own jargon (*dis, mosh*). The cosmopolitanism of our cities is another source of new vocabulary. Today Canadians of all backgrounds can enjoy *perogie, jerk chicken, pad Thai, souvlaki, roti, falafel, sushi,* and *dim sum.*

Our intent in this brief introduction has been to show the kinds of changes that occur in a living language such as English, and the reasons behind those changes. We have also sought to show how the development of our own variety of English, Canadian English, mirrors our development as a nation.

Activities: Canadian English

1. ***Respond to Information:*** Identify the two most interesting facts you learned from this essay. For each example, explain in a brief paragraph why you found it interesting.

2. ***Examine Technique:*** The authors develop the essay by using the techniques of classification and cause-and-effect. For each of these techniques, list three examples from the selection. Explain why both of these techniques are appropriate for the topic.

3. ***Add Visual Interest:*** With a partner, think of three different techniques for adding visual interest to the essay. Show or explain how you would use each technique. Share your ideas with the class.

4. ***Explore Study Strategies:*** Imagine that you are to be tested on the information in this essay. What study strategies would you use? List two strategies you would find helpful and share them in a small group. During the group discussion, make notes about any new strategies you might try in the future.

Reading, writing ... and going to work

Bruce Owen

Three-quarters of Manitoba's teens out earning cash

You won't find Julie Biluk aimlessly hanging out at the mall; she's too busy working in it.

The 17-year-old Garden City Collegiate student is one of about 48 000 teens in Manitoba who have part-time jobs. In fact, according to a study just released by the Vanier Institute of the Family, 75 percent of young people aged 15 to 19 in Manitoba are working, the second-highest rate of teen employment in Canada next to Prince Edward Island at 76.3 percent.

The Canadian average youth employment rate is 61.2 percent.

Biluk says her job at Lotions and Potions keeps her out of trouble and gives her something to do.

"I work for the money," said Biluk, a clerk at Lotions and Potions at Garden City Shopping Centre. "It keeps me out of trouble and gives me something to do."

Biluk said she puts in about 23 hours a week at her $5.50-an-hour job. She uses what she earns to buy clothes and pay for entertainment, and save for university.

"Most of my friends work," she said. "They work for spending money and so they can make car payments."

Perception of kids wrong, study shows

Robert Glossop, executive director of programming for the Vanier Institute, said that the national think-tank's report shows parents aren't the only breadwinners in many Manitoba families—and that the perception most kids are lazy is incorrect.

"The nature of teenage employment has changed over the last 25 years," Glossop said. "At one time teenagers earned extra money through babysitting or cutting grass, but now they're earning paycheques. They are part of the overall economy."

Typically, the average annual income for an employed youth is $3346, he said. This group of workers accounts for $2 billion a year in Canada's economy.

"This represents a big consumer market," Glossop said. "Many companies aim their advertising towards this group and to take advantage of these opportunities, these kids have to go out and earn some money."

The vast majority of the jobs filled by teens are in the service industry—fast-food restaurants, shopping-mall stores, movie theatres, and grocery stores, he said.

Most also still live at home with their parents, but they don't hand over their paycheques to contribute to the household finances. What they do earn, however, supplements their parents' income.

"If they want new shoes, their parents might pay half," Glossop said. "So it does represent a reduced drain on the parents. Many kids buy their own essentials and pay their own way."

Such as Carly Krall, a 19-year-old clerk at HMV Canada at Garden City Shopping Centre. For the most part, Krall puts gas in her car, pays her Autopac, and buys her own clothes. Her parents help out when she's strapped for cash.

"I try to do as much as I can, but my parents do help me out," she said.

Krall also represents a new trend in many Manitoba schools. She got her job at the music store through a work-experience program offered by West Kildonan Collegiate.

She earned credits toward her graduation by working at the store.

"It's how I got this job," she said. "It's probably one of the best things that ever happened to me. I love this job. I really lucked out."

HMV store manager Terry McIvor said many schools offer work-experience programs. And although students involved don't get paid, they gain experience for their résumés.

"It's an excellent opportunity to get hired," he said. "More so than someone just walking in."

Glossop said working teens also get a leg up on better, full-time jobs by learning good work habits.

ANOTHER DAY, ANOTHER DOLLAR

Number of teens with employment income in 1993

Canada – 1 033 000

Nfld. – 19 700	P.E.I. – 7 100
N.S. – 36 000	N.B. – 28 900
Que. – 223 900	Ont. – 374 300
Man. – 48 100	Sask. – 39 900
Alta. – 109 900	B.C. – 129 500

Percentage of teens with employment income in 1993

Canada – 61.2%

Nfld. – 44.1%	P.E.I. – 76.3%
N.S. – 62.0%	N.B. – 58.9%
Que. – 52.2%	Ont. – 62.0%
Man. – 74.6%	Sask. – 64.1%
Alta. – 68.6%	B.C. – 72.0%

Young workers facts

• Youths aged 15–19 make up 6.8 percent of the Canadian population, approximately 1.9 million people. Seventy-seven percent of all workers aged 15–19 were employed in a sales, service, or clerical occupation.

• Young women are more likely than their male counterparts to work part time. In 1992, 75 percent of employed females aged 15–19, versus 66 percent of comparable males, worked part time.

• Youths aged 15–19 have the highest unemployment rate of any age group in Canada. In 1992, 184 000 15–19-year-olds, 19.7 percent of all labour force participants in this age range, were unemployed, compared to 16.6 percent for those aged 20–24 and 9.9 percent among those aged 25 and over.

Sources: The Vanier Institute of the Family; Statistics Canada

"They're getting important skills and getting involved in the adult world," he said. "They're learning to show up on time and be responsible."

However, kids still in high school who work more than 20 hours a week tend to do more poorly in school or they drop out, he said.

"It's a very fine balancing act," he said.

"If they're working late and have to go to school the next morning, they burn out and their grades start to suffer."

Terry McLean, principal of Elmwood High School, said many of the students attending classes are working part time. In fact, many older students work to support themselves because they've already left home.

Bruce Owen is a staff reporter with the *Winnipeg Free Press*.

Activities: Reading, writing ... and going to work

1. *Evaluate Opinions:* In a small group, reread the article and list the advantages and disadvantages of part-time work for teenagers at school. Evaluate the validity of each argument, then add new ideas based on the experiences of the group members.

2. *Judge Effectiveness:* Write a short note stating and explaining your opinion on the effectiveness of each of the following elements: headline, lead, photo and caption, subheading for statistics. For each element, come up with an alternative that you think would be more effective.

3. *Examine Statistics:* Examine the statistics in the boxed area and complete the following:
   a) Briefly explain how the first two sets of numbers complement each other.
   b) Make two statements of your own based on an interpretation of the statistics. Share your findings in a small group.

4. *Use Graphics:* Select two pieces of statistical information from the boxed area. Present each in an interesting and eye-catching graphic format. Ask two classmates to evaluate your graphics in terms of clarity and interest. Display the finished graphics in the classroom.

Teens' Top Homework Tool

Bonnie Sherman

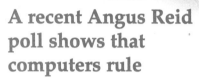

A recent Angus Reid poll shows that computers rule

In a recent poll commissioned by Intel Corp., participants in the Angus Reid Group's Internet Advisory Panel were surveyed in order to better understand the role that the Internet and the World Wide Web play in the educational process. The Internet Advisory Panel consists of 6000 representative, Internet-enabled households across Canada who respond to our surveys using e-mail and the World Wide Web.

Results of this survey show that teens spend an average of 2.1 hours per week (which translates into about nine hours per month) on their computer at home doing homework and 3.2 hours per month on the Net gathering information for school assignments. Teens' favourite Web site for research assignment information is Yahoo!, at 27%. No

Teens' favourite Web site for research assignments is Yahoo!, at 27%. No other site got more than 3%.

For the Intel survey, households that have teens aged 12 to 17 years old were selected. In total, 508 parents and 508 teens were interviewed online. The survey was conducted during March and April of 1998.

other site received more than 3% of the vote.

For those people who are decrying the alienating effects of computers on relationships, there is now some evidence to dispute this

Teens' most important learning tool for doing their homework

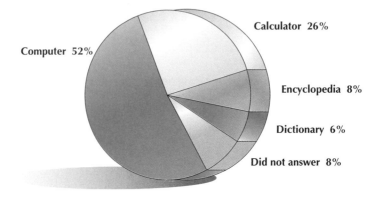

Computer 52%

Calculator 26%

Encyclopedia 8%

Dictionary 6%

Did not answer 8%

worry. Apparently, parents and teens are spending quite a bit of time together on their computer:

- 14% of the households we surveyed indicated that the parent and teen spend up to 1 hour per month together on the computer;
- 11% spend 1 to 2 hours together;
- 16% spend 2 to 5 hours together;
- 8% spend 5 to 10 hours together;
- and 19% spend over 11 hours per month together on the computer.

This is good news in terms of parents and teens spending "quality time" together learning and playing. As well, parents and teens both feel that having a computer at home has had a positive impact on the teen's ability to learn. Eighty percent of parents agree that the computer has had a positive impact on their teen's learning, and 69% of teens agree.

Teen respondents also indicated that the computer is their most important learning tool when it comes to doing homework. As the pie chart (above) shows, over half of teens believe that the computer is their most important learning tool (52%). This is far higher than the 26% of respondents naming the calculator, 8% naming the encyclopedia, and 6% naming the dictionary (8% did not state an answer).

Overall, 81% of respondents agree that computers and technology are having a positive impact on the education of Canadian children. Although computers and the Internet are changing the face of homework in Canadian society, some things never change. Whereas 50% of teen respondents indicated that they have too much homework, only 7% of parents agreed.

Bonnie Sherman is vice-president of panel and database applications at the Angus Reid Group.

Activities: Teens' Top Homework Tool

1. **Conduct a Survey:** Conduct an informal oral survey of 20 students to discover their most important homework tool. Create a pie chart to show your findings. Compare your chart with Bonnie Sherman's. List possible explanations for any differences.

2. **Explain Findings:** Fifty percent of students think they have too much homework, but only 7 percent of parents agree. List five possible reasons to explain this difference of opinion. Share your list with two other students, agree on the top three reasons, and present your choices to the class.

3. **Speak Persuasively:** Using at least three of this article's findings, compose a five- to six-sentence statement to persuade a parent that a computer or an Internet connection is a sound investment. Present your statement to a small group. Ask for feedback on the persuasiveness of your message and delivery.

4. **Explore Graphics:** Consult books, periodicals, and other resources to find examples of at least three different ways of visually representing statistical information. Share your examples with classmates, and develop a class list of techniques for adding visual appeal to statistical graphics.

Makonnen Hannah, 14, is preparing Jamaica for the Digital Age

John Turner

Makonnen Hannah hangs up the phone and brushes the dreadlocks from his pubescent face, exposing a freshly grown line of hair that acts as a moustache. "She won't come over unless we pay for a cab," he informs his friend Leon, his eyes intently scanning his Sharp personal digital assistant (PDA) for a fresh number. Leon nods distractedly; right now he's more preoccupied with installing Windows 98 on his computer than setting up a late-night rendezvous with girls. In the corner of the room, a boombox blasts the latest rhythms from Irie FM, the world's premier reggae station. The sounds blaze as hot as Jamaica's sweltering November heat, but the boys, clad in long khakis, oversized white shirts, and hip sneakers, are paying little attention to either.

The den in Leon's home is their digital clubhouse, but unlike most kids their age, they aren't just toying around with technology.

When the talk turns to video games, it's not about how to play them but how to design them. This is serious business, especially for Hannah, who is developing a prototype of his own multilevel game with two friends, both under 18. Frustrated by Leon's slow-moving computer, Hannah rhymes off his own machine's specs in an act of techno-dissing. His computer is his digital hot rod and he speaks of it with the pride and precision of someone discussing a Porsche engine.

At first, the scene inside Leon's small townhouse apartment on the edges of Kingston's downtown core seems out of place in Jamaica. Extolled as a tropical oasis in tourism commercials, the island isn't exactly known as a hotbed of high-tech activity. Still, Jamaica is looking for a profile upgrade, and the NO FEAR sticker affixed to the back of Hannah's PDA seems a fitting slogan for the task the country has set for itself—to ensure that its entry into the new millennium is accompanied not by the sounds of drug-related gun fights and politically drawn turf wars, but by the ringing of cell phones and the clacking of keyboards.

It's an ambitious goal for a nation burdened with grim economic problems. One-third of the population lives in poverty and the disparity between the haves and have-nots is one of the most pronounced in the world. Half the children graduating from primary school can't read. In fact, a recent report by USAID, an American economic development agency, suggests that unless disadvantaged Jamaican youth are better supported, the country is "unlikely to make a successful transition into the 21st century." The authors conclude that hope for the future rests on making information technology widely available, especially to the new generation. So far, however, only two percent of the population—a mere 40 000 people—have Internet access.

Philip Paulwell, Jamaica's 36-year-old minister of commerce and technology, is hoping to change all that. To help him, he has surprised the world and titillated the media by making Makonnen Hannah, a 14-year-old tech prodigy, his cyber-guru. Like most teens, Hannah is obsessed with pop culture and girls, but also instinctively attuned to the workings of computers and how best to use them. His appointment has already ignited the kind of excitement that Jamaica usually reserves for reggae singers and cricket heroes. It has also invited some pesky questions: Are children really equipped to formulate strategies for high-tech development? For that matter, is it fair to ask them to? And, most contentious of all, is Jamaica's young techno messiah for real, or is he merely a product of media hype, marketing, and parental ambition?

Makonnen Hannah was born at a time of intense struggle for his mother, Barbara. She lived in a house that had no running water when, at age 45, she had her first and only child. As a journalist, however, she was computer-literate and recognized technology's

Is Jamaica's young techno messiah for real, or is he merely a product of media hype, marketing, and parental ambition?

potential to expose her son to a different world. By age three, Hannah was operating his mother's desktop computer on his own. Home-schooled, his education comprised an unorthodox combination of educational software, The Discovery Channel, and *National Geographic*. He was an avid student, learning from any source available to him, even interrogating the technicians who occasionally came around to fix the family computer.

By 11, Hannah was using his mother's PC to do things she didn't understand, such as running his own electronic bulletin board, which quickly became the most popular BBS on the island. Seeking new challenges, Hannah began looking for ways to break into a friend's BBS system. "Sometimes when we have nothing to do, we say, 'OK, let's bring down Colin's board,'" says Hannah. "We just love the underground mentality of it all." (Today, in exchange for lending his security expertise, Hannah gets unlimited access to his friend's system.)

When Barbara realized that Makonnen and his friends were eager to learn more about technology, she established a structured educational environment by founding TechSchool 2000, Jamaica's first summer program for children with an aptitude for computers. Local businesses donated everything from desks to printer paper to the most vital tool for surviving a Jamaican summer—an air-conditioner—and Microsoft pitched in some software. In the end, twelve young people attended that first TechSchool semester. The program lasted only a month, but thanks to new investment, plans are underway to open a school where students will do their learning online.

It was during her work on this project that Barbara brought her son to Philip Paulwell's attention. "He recognized that as part of his IT strategy he needed to target young people," she says. "I told him about what Makonnen was doing and he suggested they meet. Little did I know it would lead to all this media attention."

Officially tagged as youth technology consultant, Hannah's appointment initially met with resistance from people not keen on assigning an important government post to a teenager. Foreign skeptics labelled it a publicity stunt by a country desperately trying to gain media attention in order to lure high-tech dollars. Meanwhile, the support that has emerged places the appointment in a wider context. United Nations representatives and academics from MIT's Media Lab and Harvard University have hailed Jamaica's move as visionary and forward-thinking. They argue that young people have something to say about the world they live in, and may even have sound ideas for shaping its future. Children, with their open-minded curiosity, are naturally predisposed to exploring new digital technology, advocates point out. It's the same reason that kids are the first ones to learn how to program the family VCR or locate the power switch on the computer.

With all the attention on his government appointment and the adult world he has entered, it's easy to forget that Hannah is a kid with a curfew. And on this balmy night, his mission is to break it. As he dials up yet another friend who attends an all-girls school, he boasts that he's the most sought-after date there. Eventually, after making numerous calls, he gives up, frustrated that no girl will come over unless he and Leon fork over change for cab fare.

His social plans aborted, Hannah turns his attention to his plans for a wired Jamaica. "The first thing we need to do," he says, "is privatize the monopoly that [British telco giant] Cable & Wireless has on telecommunications in the Caribbean. We need more competition because that will raise people's awareness [of technology]. C&W isn't doing that good a job—we can't even get AOL down here." Resting his new blue Tommy Hilfiger shoes on the edge of Leon's bed, Hannah brushes the waist-length dreads from his sweaty forehead and continues. "I just want Jamaica to grow in IT. If I wanted to start a company, I could start one right now. It would be a computer security company that would keep hackers out. But I'll do all that after my mission with the ministry is done."

He utters the statement with an almost messianic *gravitas*, which makes it clear that even if his appointment is a publicity stunt, Hannah doesn't think of it that way. He is determined to be a major player in the reinvention of his country—no small vision for someone who's not yet eligible to vote. Though it may seem slightly incongruous, this bright, energetic kid is styling himself as a kind of IT Rasta prophet for Jamaica's largely illiterate and unskilled young population.

Hannah is already full of ideas for using technology to reshape Jamaican culture, such as participating in a UN-funded program that provides computers for community development. His way to make technology appealing to non-techies: gaming. More specifically, a multi-player gaming competition that would pit Kingston's two main ghettos against each other—groups that frequently engage in election violence. By using the game *FIFA: Road to the World Cup 98*, he intends to cloak the technology lesson by appealing to youth's fanaticism for the sport. He's convinced the project would succeed. "This will really boost awareness of computers, because when you go and talk about them, people don't always show up," he says enthusiastically. "But everyone knows what a game is and ultimately they will figure out how to use computer controls to become masters of it. When 70 percent of the population knows how to use a computer, then I'll know that I've done something."

> Hannah is determined to be a major player in the reinvention of his country—no small vision for someone who's not yet eligible to vote.

Located in New Kingston, Jamaica's business district, the office of the Ministry of Commerce and Technology is surrounded by the Blue Mountains on one side and expensive hotels on the other, which shield it from the city. The building is a run-down, semi-air-conditioned concrete structure. Only on the ministry's floor does the cool air come rushing forward to provide relief from the heat.

Hannah has arrived for his regular meeting with the minister, and his attire is relaxed as usual—khakis, Adidas shoes, and a yellow Adidas shirt. As soon as he enters, he is put to work. One of Paulwell's assistants can't seem to get her ICQ network up, her frustration giving way to slight panic. "Can you fix this?" she pleads with Hannah. "Yeah, mon," he says, and quickly attends to the problem.

When Hannah was first brought in as a consultant, the government department barely had a skeleton of a computer network. The minister didn't have his machine hooked up to a printer, and the entire office setup was in disarray. Technicians were called in to install a network in the office, but by the time they arrived, Hannah had done the majority of the work. He also convinced Paulwell to replace his slow machine with a brand-new Pentium, and created a Web site

that the public could access. Paulwell proudly points out that his is the only ministry in all of the Caribbean that has a Web site on which people can dial up a company registry and access information about starting their own businesses. "And everyone," he boasts, "from the driver right up to me, has e-mail."

Each Monday, Hannah meets with the minister to keep him abreast of events in the high-tech world. They discuss everything from computer magazine articles to new software programs. They also keep in touch throughout the week via e-mail and fax. In the spirit of the ministry's new strategy, Paulwell has given Hannah the task of making the office paperless, and has invited him and some of his friends to help draft the IT policy. But most importantly, says Paulwell, "Makonnen will be going on the road to talk to youngsters about IT." He pauses, then notes, "It's funny, but people stop me on the road to say that because of Makonnen they want their children to be consultants as well."

Paulwell's biggest project at the moment is wiring all 800 post offices in the country so that ordinary Jamaicans will be able to send and receive e-mail messages. He's convinced that this, coupled with his other plans, will ensure that

60 percent of Jamaicans will be wired by 2010. Paulwell is also spearheading the new Caribbean Institute of Technology, which will train 5000 programmers over a 10-year period. Upon graduation, they will be guaranteed jobs in Jamaica and salaries on par with their U.S. peers. It's a bit of a crap shoot—the project could backfire if there isn't enough interest—but Paulwell is game for the risk. "It's a calculated gamble," he acknowledges, "but it's the only way we are going to make Jamaica a world power in something other than tourism or reggae music."

After the hustle of downtown Kingston, the Lords Road neighbourhood where the Hannahs live feels like an oasis. The setting sun brings much needed respite from the pounding heat. Like most homes in the city, the house is protected by a large white gate. A palm tree towering over the property sways gently in the front yard. But inside the sparsely furnished bungalow, it's a different story. The atmosphere is frenzied, because this is the first time since summer that Hannah and his friends from the TechSchool have had a chance to hang out together and tinker with PCs. The house is filled with Jamaica's brightest young computer minds, but the bustle of activity makes it feel more like a birthday party.

Signs of Hannah's achievements are everywhere. Above Barbara's computer in the living room hangs a large corkboard covered with newspaper clippings from as far away as Scandinavia. (The machine only has an eight-megabyte hard drive, and Makonnen informs his mother she'd be better off dropping it from a "very high building.") Around the corner, in Makonnen's room, 10 kids are sitting on the floor and on his bed, which serves as the chair for his computer station. The host is seated beside the only girl from the TechSchool, Swabi-Ann Fender, a 14-year-old HTML programmer who helped Hannah redesign his Web page. His PC sits atop a desk constructed of three cardboard boxes. A big television is hooked up to a Sony PlayStation. Strewn about the floor are copies of *Details*, *Premiere*, and Hannah's favourite tech magazine, *EGM*[2]. They are freebies from a family friend who imports them to Jamaica.

To feed the hungry masses assembled in her home, Barbara orders KFC and rushes from room to room to make sure everyone is behaving. In the living room, Hannah's friend Steven Madden has used a screwdriver to expose the guts of a computer hard drive. He is tinkering with the machine and giving it a much needed checkup. Madden started one of the first BBSs in Jamaica and eventually created one for Hannah to run on his own. "When I first heard of Makonnen's appointment, I laughed," says the shy 16-year-old. "But he deserves it."

In the middle of this teenage fun, Hannah is reluctant to pause and talk about his future. "Ten years from today?" he muses. "I might be working at an extremely high-paying job in computers doing network security or game developing. But maybe I'll be playing soccer. Who knows?" He is thinking about university, something that would likely take him away from the island, although he claims his departure would not be permanent. It's hard to tell whether the wish for a higher education is his or his mother's, but he's intrigued by the prospect of travel. "Maybe I'll go to MIT or UCLA. I haven't been there. But I just like the whole *idea* of Los Angeles."

It's still too early to tell what role Hannah will play in Jamaica's long-term technological evolution. The country will need more than high-speed Internet hook-ups and skilled programmers to make the transition from a tourist refuge to a Caribbean Silicon Valley. Hannah's appointment has at least got the country talking about technology, and that is an achievement in itself.

He himself readily admits that his status as the country's best hope for high-tech development doesn't mean that his skills are unique. "I'm good," he says with a sly smile. "I know what I know. But I have a lot of friends who are just like me." He is hinting at the real source of Jamaica's salvation: not one bright, techno-savvy kid, but many.

> Hannah's appointment has at least got the country talking about technology, and that is an achievement in itself.

John Turner is a Toronto-based writer, editor, producer, and commentator. He has worked in Canada and the United States for *The Nation*, *Vibe*, *Gear*, and *Shift*. He is currently the Web content producer for U8TV.com.

Activities: Makonnen Hannah

1. **Explain Technique:** This article tells two stories: one about a teenager, the other about a country. Summarize each story and explain how the author has linked the two.

2. **Chart Information:** Complete a two-column chart that compares Hannah, the typical teenager, with Hannah, the not-so-typical teen. Compare your chart with a partner's.

3. **Write an Article/Editorial:** Write either (a) a newspaper article announcing Hannah's appointment, or (b) an editorial commenting on the appointment. Use newspaper articles or editorials as models for appropriate style.

4. **Create a TV Profile:** Work in a small group to create a one-minute profile on Hannah for television broadcast. Write the script and describe the video clips that would play during each part of the script. Videotape your profile, with group members portraying the real people, and present it to the class.

A World Free of Poverty

New World Bank Report Urges Broader Approach to Reducing Poverty

WASHINGTON, September 12, 2000—Major reductions in poverty are possible but achieving these will require a more comprehensive approach that directly addresses the needs of poor people in three important areas: opportunity, empowerment, and security, according to the World Bank's latest _World Development Report 2000/2001: Attacking Poverty_.

The new study—the World Bank's most detailed-ever investigation of global poverty—adds that economic growth is crucial but often not sufficient to create conditions in which the world's poorest people can improve their lives.

"This report seeks to expand the understanding of poverty and its causes and sets out actions to create a world free of poverty in all its dimensions," **World Bank President James D. Wolfensohn** writes in the foreword to the report. _"It both builds on our past thinking and strategy and substantially broadens and deepens what we think is necessary to meet the challenge of reducing poverty."_

More than two years in the making, the _World Development Report 2000/2001_ draws on a large volume of research, including a background study, _Voices of the Poor_, which systematically sought the personal accounts of more than 60 000 men and women living in poverty in 60 countries. In addition, the report's authors conducted extensive research and consultation with a wide array of governments, non-governmental organizations, civil society groups, universities, development think-tanks, private business groups, and others around the world. An online discussion of an early draft of the report produced hundreds of responses from 44 countries.

The experiences of poor people, described in their own words, underpin the three main themes:

- *"At first I was afraid of everyone and everything: my husband, the village sarpanch, the police. Today I fear no one. I have my own bank account, I am the leader of my village's savings group ... I tell my sisters about our movement. And we have a 40 000-strong union in the district."*—**From a discussion group of poor men and women, India, 1997**

- *"Poverty is humiliation, the sense of being dependent on them, and of being forced to accept rudeness, insults, and indifference when we seek help."*—**A woman in Latvia, 1998**

- *"We face a calamity when my husband falls ill. Our life comes to a halt until he recovers and goes back to work."*—**A woman in Egypt, 1999**

The report builds on the view that poverty means not only low incomes and low consumption but also lack of education and poor nutrition and health. Based on the testimony of poor people themselves, and changes in thinking about poverty, the report goes further and expands the definition of poverty to include powerlessness, "voicelessness," vulnerability, and fear.

"These different dimensions of poverty interact in important ways," says **World Bank Chief Economist and Senior Vice President, Nicholas Stern.** *"We know that economic growth is crucial to sustained poverty reduction. But we also recognize the fundamental role of institutional and social change to the strength of development processes and the inclusion of poor people."*

The report recommends that developing country governments at all levels, donor countries, international agencies, NGOs, civil society, and local communities mobilize behind three priority areas:

- **Opportunity:** Expanding economic opportunity for poor people by stimulating economic growth, making markets work better for poor people, and working for their inclusion, particularly by building up their assets, such as land and education.

- **Empowerment:** Strengthening the ability of poor people to shape decisions that affect their lives and removing discrimination based on gender, race, ethnicity, and social status.

- **Security:** Reducing poor people's vulnerability to sickness, economic shocks, crop failure, unemployment, natural disasters, and violence, and helping them cope when such misfortunes occur.

"Advances in these areas are complementary. Each is important in its own right, and each enhances the others," says **Nora Lustig, Director of the World Development Report 2000/2001.** *"We hope that this framework will be helpful to countries in developing their own poverty-reduction strategies according to their own circumstances. There is no universal blueprint."*

According to Lustig, these priorities can allow the poor to have greater independence and security in their day-to-day lives. For example, empowering women and other socially disadvantaged groups expands their range of economic opportunities. Furthermore, strengthening poor people's organizations and their involvement in decision-making processes enables them to press for improved services and for policy choices that respond to their needs. Finally, making poor people less vulnerable makes it easier for them to take advantage of potential market opportunities.

Poverty in a world of plenty

At a time of unprecedented wealth for many countries, 2.8 billion people—almost half the world's population—live on less than $2 a day. The report says that of these people, 1.2 billion live on the very

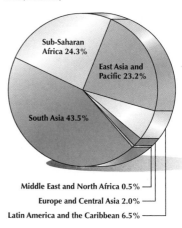

Where the developing world's poor live

Distribution of population living on less than $1 a day, 1988 (1.2 billion)

Sub-Saharan Africa 24.3%

East Asia and Pacific 23.2%

South Asia 43.5%

Middle East and North Africa 0.5%
Europe and Central Asia 2.0%
Latin America and the Caribbean 6.5%

Source: World Bank 2000s.

margins of life, on less than $1 a day. In high-income countries, fewer than one child in 100 dies before reaching five years of age, while in the poorest countries, the number is five times higher. In well-off countries, fewer than 5 percent of children under the age of five are malnourished; in poorer countries, as many as 50 percent of the children suffer from eating too little food.

"This destitution persists even though human conditions have improved more in the past century than in the rest of history," the report notes. *"Global wealth, global connections, and technological capabilities have never been greater."*

But the distribution of these gains is extraordinarily unequal. The average income in the richest 20 countries is 37 times the average in the poorest 20—a gap that has doubled in the past 40 years.

Progress in poverty reduction has varied widely across regions. In East Asia the number of people living on less than $1 a day fell from around 420 million in 1987 to around 280 million in 1998. But in Sub-Saharan Africa, South Asia, and Latin America, the numbers of poor people have been rising steadily. In the countries of Eastern Europe and Central Asia in transition to market economies, the number of people living in poverty has risen 20-fold.

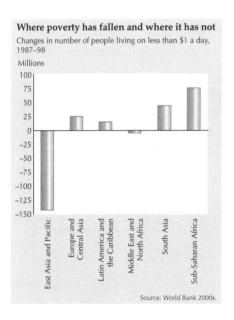

Where poverty has fallen and where it has not

Changes in number of people living on less than $1 a day, 1987–98

Source: World Bank 2000s.

Within countries, too, poverty rates often vary enormously. In some African countries, infant mortality rates are much lower among politically powerful ethnic groups. In Latin America, indigenous groups have far less schooling than non-indigenous groups. In South Asia, women have only about half as many years of education as men, and middle school enrollment rates for girls are only two-thirds those of boys.

The report's three main sections on *opportunity, empowerment, and security* include examples of successful initiatives that address these and other problems afflicting poor people. These include such diverse examples as a Moroccan project called the "Virtual Souk," which allows poor traders and artisans to sell their goods around the world on the Internet; a new approach to land reform in Brazil; "affirmative action" against caste-based discrimination in India; a stronger female voice in policymaking through women's budget initiatives in southern Africa; providing a social safety net and other emergency protections for people at times of crisis in South Korea; and social pensions in Chile and Namibia.

Global initiatives to reduce poverty

Action at national and local levels will often not be enough for rapid poverty reduction. There are many areas that require international action—especially by high-income countries—to improve the prospects for poor countries and their people. An increased focus on debt relief and making development aid more effective are part of the story.

Equally important are actions in other areas, such as expanding the access to developed country markets, promoting the production of public goods that benefit poor people, such as vaccines for tropical diseases and agricultural research, combating HIV/AIDS, enhancing global financial stability, closing of the digital and knowledge divides, enabling the participation of poor countries in international discussions, and fostering global peace.

"I expect the deeper understanding of poverty in this report will lead to new areas of action and new policies," says **Chief Economist Stern**. *"Expanding economic opportunities overall—that is, promoting growth that directly benefits the poor—remains central. Market-oriented reforms, institutional development and investments in health, education and infrastructure are crucial to its delivery. But we must go further and act directly to increase empowerment and security if we are to accelerate the benefits of growth for the poor."*

In conclusion, Stern says if the developing world and the international community work together to combine these insights with real resources—both financial and those embodied in people and institutions—the 21st century will see rapid progress in the fight to end poverty.

Activities: A World Free of Poverty

1. *Make Inferences:* The report expands the definition of poverty to include "powerlessness, voicelessness, vulnerability, and fear." In a small group, discuss why you think the definition was expanded in this way. How is each element related to poverty? Report the main points of your discussion to the class.

2. *Examine Purpose:* In what ways could this press release be considered a persuasive document? What does the report try to persuade people to believe? What does it try to persuade them to do? With a partner, identify the persuasive techniques and examples of each.

3. *Explain Graphic Elements:* Explain the purpose and evaluate the effectiveness of each of the following graphic elements: (a) boldface type, (b) italic type, (c) bullets, and (d) graphs.

4. *Research Organizations:* Research and write a brief report on an organization that helps to combat poverty. The organization could be local, national, or international. Include information about the organization's goals and recent initiatives. Use subheadings to organize information.

The Great Cheese-Off

Robin Harvey and David Graham duke it out over the virtues and vices of Kraft Dinner.

Kraft Dinner makes us fat and alienated

Robin Harvey

With every glutinous orange glob we gobble, Kraft Dinner epitomizes everything that's gone wrong with the millennial mealtime.

It may be the opinion of just one frenzied working mom, but the beginning of the end of family dining started in 1937, when this mushy mixture was introduced as "a meal for four in nine minutes."

And as our love affair with such quick cuisine has grown, so has our collective girth—leaving more than half of us overweight and overfed, largely on such preprocessed packaged cuisine.

First let's sock it to KD (as it has become known in pop culture) for its obvious nutritional deficiencies. (All figures apply to the mixture prepared with the requisite 2 percent milk and butter.)

It's high in salt, containing 198 milligrams per serving. But without the salt and sodium phosphates for preservatives, how to impart flavour and a near-eternal shelf life to "modified milk ingredients"?

If you are wondering how the pasty pasta gets its cheesy golden glow, check out the last line in the ingredients: "contains tartrazine." That's the food colouring linked to rashes and other reactions among sensitive types.

Next look at the fat content. At a time when researchers are finding kids getting flabbier on diets floating in fat, with arteries clogged before they reach 12, one measly serving of KD may have about 15 percent of their recommended daily fat intake. Kids who want second helpings may get almost a third of their daily fat intake.

Which brings us to KD's more sinister side: the makers' bid to gloss over with marketing the product's value as near Number One in the nutritional wasteland—with most of this marketing aimed at kids.

Besides the games, Web sites, contests, toys, and prizes, Kraft offers Pokémon KD, DC Super Heroes KD, Bugs Bunny & Friends KD, and Rugrats KD. The idea is to sneak the grainy gruel into the kitchen cupboard under the guise of ease and convenience, while grabbing unsuspecting youngsters with the hard sell in commercials and off-the-box gimmicks. As an ad executive once opined, if you can get 'em before age five, they're consumers for life!

This sliminess hit home this week when I was astounded to learn my own six-year-old daughter entered a Web site contest linked to KD.

By guessing the answer to a riddle about a hit kids' TV show, she proudly informed me, she may be the happy winner of a year's worth of KD. I bet the folks at KD think that means at least 365 boxes. (Footnote: one older brother supervising her online time has been chastised. We hereby disqualify our household.)

KD is quick, it's easy—it almost makes itself, the ads scream. But do we really need a product like this when fewer than two-thirds of Canadian households with children report they have a main meal together on weekdays? This perpetuates the disposable lifestyle: families sitting glazed in front of the TV, scarfing down a dinner dish of KD, nary a word of conversation or wholesome family debate.

In fact, in this woman's opinion, the soul of KD is revealed in the latest commercial for the microwavable "even faster" version. For those who have missed it, it features a newly dumped boyfriend who apparently whips up a batch of Kraft Dinner in seconds in the dirty dog bowl.

I am sick and tired of fighting the battle against KD and that other kid-friendly competitor's product (rhymes with macaroni, starts with beef).

Sadly, as case after case gets sold and child after child (mine included) clamours for more, I fear I am on the losing side.

Kraft Dinner solaces a victim of big bad world

David Graham

I agree with The Barenaked Ladies.

Even if I had a million dollars, I'd still dive into a dish of Kraft Dinner, the delicious meal-in-a-box you can make-in-a-minute.

My mother and father both worked when I was a kid. And though I had four teenage brothers and sisters, they were never at home. So at age 9, Kraft Dinner was something I was trusted to make without adult supervision.

It was simple. Bring water to boil. Pour in noodles. Cook. Drain. Add incredibly tasty cheese-flavoured mix.

By 11, my culinary talents were solid enough to stray from the directions. I learned that by discarding a fistful of the macaroni noodles before adding the magic powder, both the colour and flavour became more intense, the brilliant orange of an Hermès gift box and a taste so intoxicatingly cheesy it seemed better than natural.

It had always been a mistake in my opinion to add milk or butter to the recipe. They only served to bevel the meal's sharp, acidic edges and nuclear hue.

It was also a mistake when the execs at Kraft began marketing new and improved versions of their world famous dish. "It's creamier and cheesier," they cooed. They didn't stop there. Over the years they've introduced oddly shaped noodles and an assortment of additional flavours. Now there are Pokémon pasta, "white" cheese-flavoured dinners, and microwavable versions.

I'm sure they fly off the supermarket shelf and new generations of kids love them. But for purists, they are pure folly.

Other food companies have capitalized on the popularity of Kraft Dinner by manufacturing their own generic interpretations of the classic instant meal. President's Choice Deluxe White Cheddar Macaroni and Cheese Dinner? Give me a break.

Only the original Kraft Dinner is the object of my affection. Even now a steaming pot of Kraft Dinner is a kind of regression therapy. It has the power to lure me back in time, to a less complicated place when the world was kinder and gentler.

Unfortunately, as to its healthful qualities, I'm at a loss. The best I can offer is that it appears to be a fine source of energy, protein and carbohydrates. It says so on the box.

But Kraft Dinner should not be reduced to the sum of its nutritional contents.

Instead, it fits into a fifth food group that includes the much-maligned Kentucky Fried Chicken, Tang, Wonder Bread, Hamburger Helper, Spam and Cheez Whiz, those kitschy foods that well-meaning nutritionists and faint-hearted, modern-minded parents love to ridicule.

These are the foods we turn to in times of trouble. They are as soft and familiar as a mother's breast and just as comforting.

They are foods that speak to something deep in our psyche.

So in times of trouble, just follow the simple instructions.

Relax with the knowledge that when the cold, hard world turns against you, solace may be just a few minutes away, eight or nine as the directions indicate, "or to desired tenderness."

Activities: The Great Cheese-Off

1. **Examine Structure:** Robin Harvey builds her argument against Kraft Dinner around several main points. Identify these issues by creating headings for the article. Place the headings appropriately. Compare your headings and their placement with a partner's work.

2. **Analyze Technique:** Persuasive writing often makes use of facts, logic, and emotion to persuade readers. To what degree does each writer make use of each of these elements? Support your opinion with examples from the text. Then offer to each writer one suggestion for making a more persuasive argument.

3. **Conduct a Survey:** Work in a small group to conduct a survey to compare adults' and teenagers' attitudes to Kraft Dinner. Make sure your questions are free of bias. Give the survey to 20 adults and 20 teens. Calculate, graph, and interpret the results. Deliver an oral report on your survey to the class, using graphs as visual aids.

4. **Design Packaging:** Create a new design for the front and back of a package of Kraft Dinner. Your design should reflect the viewpoint of either Graham or Harvey. Display your design and, as a class, discuss effective techniques and strategies used during the design process.

Thanks for Not Killing My Son

Rita Schindler

I hope you will print my letter of gratitude to the strangers who have affected our lives.

Sometime between 1:30 p.m., Dec. 8, and 1 a.m., Dec. 9, a young man was viciously attacked—beaten and kicked unconscious for no apparent reason other than walking by you on a public sidewalk.

He was left lying in a pool of blood from an open head wound—in the Victoria Park–Terraview area. He was found around 1 a.m. and taken to Scarborough General Hospital where ironically his mother spent 48 hours in labour before giving him birth, 23 years earlier.

His mother is angry, of course, but thankful for the following reasons.

First of all—his eye socket was shattered and hemorrhaging, but his eyesight will not be affected. Thank you.

His ear canal was lacerated internally from a tremendous blow to the side of his head. The cut could not be stitched and the bleeding was difficult to stop. But his eardrum seems to be undamaged—thank you.

He required numerous stitches to his forehead, temple, and face but your boots didn't knock one tooth out—thank you. His head was swollen to almost twice its size—but Mom knew that his brain was intact—for he held her hand for six hours as he lay on a gurney, by the nurses' station, IV in his arm—his head covered and crusted with dried blood—waiting for X-ray results and the surgeon to stitch him up.

So, thank you for his eyesight, his hearing, and his hands which you could have easily crushed.

His hands—human hands—the most intricately beautiful and complex instruments of incredible mechanism—the result of billions of years of evolution—and you people used yours to beat another human being. Five guys and two girls to beat one person. Who do I thank? Did you know he was a talented young musician with a budding career—and that playing his keyboards and piano mean more to him than my words can say.

And when his friends were talking about revenge, I heard him say, "No, I don't want someone else's mother to go through what mine has." That's who you were kicking in the head. And so—I thank you for not causing the most horrible and devastating thing that can happen to any parent—that is—the untimely tragic loss of a child—at any age.

You could have kicked him to death but you only left him to die, thank you. A person found him and called for help.

I am his mother—and I have been given a second chance—thanks to you.

I hope that someday you'll have children and love them as much as I love mine—but I wouldn't wish on your child what you did to mine.

Rita Schindler was living in Scarborough, Ontario, when she wrote this letter to the editor.

Activities: Thanks for Not Killing My Son

1. **Write a Personal Response:** In your journal, write about your reaction to this letter. What thoughts and feelings did it evoke? Why? Share your response with a partner.

2. **Examine Technique:** What techniques does Schindler use to make her letter effective? What is the effect of each technique? Record your ideas and then share them in a small group. Make a group list of techniques and effects and share it with the class.

3. **Conduct an Interview:** Work with a partner to role-play an interview between a news reporter and Rita Schindler. Write five questions that will elicit information of interest to your audience. Use what you learn about Rita Schindler from her letter to craft responses that she might give. Present your interview to the class.

4. **Research a Topic:** Choose a topic related to violence in today's society, such as violence in schools, TV violence, or spousal abuse. Narrow your topic to a manageable size, research it, and write a brief report on your findings. Include a list of resources you used and footnotes for specific quotations.

Man, You're a Great Player!

Gary Lautens

"It wasn't easy," he confided. "It took practice and encouragement. You know, something like spearing doesn't come naturally. It has to be developed."

"I'm not inclined to flattery but, in my book, you've got it made. You're a dirty player."

"Stop kidding."

"No, no," I insisted. "I'm not trying to butter you up. I mean it. When you broke in there were flashes of dirty play—but you weren't consistent. That's the difference between a dirty player and merely a colourful one."

"I wish my father were alive to hear you say that," he said quietly. "He would have been proud."

"Well, it's true. There isn't a player in the league who knows as many obscene gestures."

"I admit I have been given a few increases in pay in recent years. Management seems to be treating me with new respect."

"You're selling tickets," I said. "You're a gate attraction now—not some bum who only can skate and shoot and the rest of it. Your profanity is beautiful."

"C'mon."

Occasionally I run into sports figures at cocktail parties, on the street, or on their way to the bank.

"Nice game the other night," I said to an old hockey-player pal.

"Think so?" he replied.

"You've come a long way since I knew you as a junior."

"How's that?"

"Well, you high-stick better for one thing—and I think the way you clutch sweaters is really superb. You may be the best in the league."

He blushed modestly.

"For a time," I confessed, "I never thought you'd get the hang of it."

"No, I'm serious. I don't think anyone in the league can incite a riot the way you can."

"I've had a lot of help along the way. You can't make it alone," he stated generously.

"No one does," I said.

"Take that play where I skate up to the referee and stand nose-to-nose with my face turning red. It was my old junior coach who taught me that. He was the one who used to toss all the sticks on the ice and throw his hat into the stands and pound his fist on the boards."

"You were lucky to get that sort of training. A lot of players never learn the fundamentals."

"I think there are a few boys in the league who can spit better than me."

"Farther, perhaps, but not more accurately," I corrected.

"Well, thanks anyway. I've always considered it one of my weaknesses."

"That last brawl of yours was perfectly executed. Your sweater was torn off, you taunted the crowd, you smashed your stick across the goalposts. Really a picture Donnybrook."

"The papers gave me a break. The coverage was outstanding."

"Do you ever look back to the days when you couldn't cut a forehead or puff a lip or insult an official?"

"Everyone gets nostalgic," he confessed. "It's a good thing I got away from home by the time I was 15. I might never have been any more than a ham-and-egger, you know, a 20-goal man who drifts through life unnoticed."

"What was the turning point?"

"I had heard prominent sportsmen say that nice guys finish last, and that you have to beat them in the alley if you hope to beat them in the rink. But it didn't sink in."

"Nobody learns overnight."

"I wasted a few years learning to play my wing and to check without using the butt of the stick. But I noticed I was being passed by. I skated summers to keep in shape, exercised, kept curfew."

"Don't tell me. They said you were dull."

"Worse than that. They said I was clean. It's tough to live down that sort of reputation."

I nodded.

"Anyway, during a game in the sticks, I was skating off the ice—we had won five-one and I had scored three goals. The home crowd was pretty listless and there was some booing. Then it happened."

"What?"

"My big break. My mother was in the stands and she shouted to me. I turned to wave at her with my hockey stick and I accidentally caught the referee across the face.

He bled a lot—took 10 stitches later."

"Is that all?"

"Well, someone pushed me and I lost my balance and fell on the poor man. A real brawl started. Luckily, I got credit for the whole thing—went to jail overnight, got a suspension. And, talk about fate! A big league scout was in the arena. He offered me a contract right away."

"It's quite a success story," I said.

"You've got to get the breaks," he replied, humbly.

Gary Lautens (*born 1928, Fort William, Ontario; died 1992*), sports writer and humour columnist, graduated from McMaster University in 1950. He began his career with *The Hamilton Spectator* and then moved to *The Toronto Star* in 1962. He is best known for his columns with the *Star*. His work twice won the Leacock Medal for Humour.

Activities: Man, You're a Great Player!

1. ***Examine Dialogue:*** Skim the article to note words that are not part of the dialogue. What function do these words serve? What effect does the author create by writing the column almost entirely in dialogue?

2. ***Investigate Irony:*** Work in a small group to identify five specific examples of irony. Explain the irony in each example. Discuss and present to the class your group's views on how irony contributes to the humorous tone in the article.

3. ***Identify the Message:*** In one sentence, state the author's message. In another sentence, state the column's purpose. Give reasons to support both of your responses.

4. ***Develop Skills:*** Read some sports editorials to note the style and tone. Write an editorial to express your opinion on violence in a particular sport or sports in general. Ask a classmate for feedback on how to improve your editorial.

Finding Their Own Groove

San Grewal

Young people are drawn to music without agendas

The sound never stops. Two hundred beats per minute slip, one by one, through the darkness, into bodies glazed with skin white as ice.

On a chilly November night, young people have retreated underground, beneath a King Street building, to Area 51, where silver light paints their faces. The bar attracts a crowd quite distinct from the upscale nightclub across the street, where fashionable 20- and 30-somethings enter for $20 a head.

Patrons at Area 51 have no such expectations. They come not so much to hear electronic music—characterized sound—as to feel it. To feel it vibrate through the darkness, pulsing at punishing velocity through absently placed couches and the shapes of young human bodies.

At upwards of 230 beats per minute, impossible decibels of pounding drum and bass and synthesized, staccato sounds become a felt experience, entering like a jackhammer through the skin, into the mind.

There are no lyrical messages nor attempts to float romantic relationships. These youths find much of pop culture irrelevant.

"A lot of people feel techno is all about escaping or disengaging from the more real, substantial world," says Raymond Sumner, 22. "But I don't think I need music or TV or someone's agenda to tell me what I should want, what I should be doing or buying, or artists telling me how I should feel or react emotionally. We want to figure out all of that for ourselves now.

"Older generations don't realize we don't have the limitations they had," he says. His head sways like a pendulum between rays of synchronized light to the rhythm of trance music that melts from the sound system.

Just as hypertext takes us away from the authors and Web sites, and online chat rooms take us away from TV, music without interpretation draws youth who are tired of being spoken to.

And while techno may lack the narrative force that once created intense personal relationships between artist and fan (Bob Dylan will probably not help these youth understand romance gone wrong with songs like "Boots of Spanish Leather," nor will Leonard Cohen inform them about the complexities of "Suzanne"), these electronic sounds do have their own emotional resonance.

"It's like we interpret the music aesthetically," says Amy Valdron, 21, whose languid body has for the past two hours resembled a marionette held by one thin string from her bobbing head.

"How it feels is physical in a way, but there's a mood that's created. I mean just the music can put you in the same state of comfort that listening to Neil Young or Sarah McLachlan can do for other people," she says. She's finally speaking after being enveloped by trance most of the night.

Valdron talks about a social environment free from the pressures of a popular culture that has polarized men and women, a predatory romantic marketplace that takes its cues from shows like *Seinfeld*.

"There's just so much of that crap to deal with. It's so much easier to come to a place like this where you can feed off the natural physical energy of people, knowing that no one's got other agendas."

The scene is a suspension between a childlike state and a complicated, often vexing, adult life.

These youths push against what they see as the childish appeal of mainstream popular culture, with its Britney observations on the meaning of life, and the torpor of adulthood, with its empty corporate pursuits and fallen marriages.

"Our society and culture is becoming very instant and oriented to self-gratification," says a hyper Tim Gross, 26, who's just walking out of Turbo, a three-storey techno club on Adelaide Street West.

"People aren't listening to lyrics any more. The music doesn't have lyrics, it's all instrumental. It seems to play to the physical need of the audience."

And the increasingly popular sound of techno, in its various forms—Detroit, house, acid, trance—with its pulsing, hypnotic vibe, suggests a broad audience finds an appeal in the music.

"Music is a release, especially punk or techno," says Chris Grimwood, 24. "The music is a chance to vent, to release frustration or get lost from the frustration present outside the music. It's almost cathartic for kids. But I don't think lyrics or the lived life of the musician are that important to most people my age any more.

"My brother's younger, 16, and he and his friends just seem to listen to music as background sound. They almost listen to music as a social function, to define what group they belong to, but not to understand who they are personally. I don't think the techno scene's about understanding yourself personally either, but at least it doesn't pretend to connect to audiences in that way."

The music allows listeners to filter the sounds through their own moods, whether they want to affect melancholy, hysteria or to completely lose themselves.

Grimwood enjoys other, more mainstream forms of music, groups such as Radiohead and the less well-known punk band Strung Out, but is wary of the empty appeal that overtly radio-friendly music has.

"My friend went to Edgefest last summer. When 3 Doors Down came on they played 'Kryptonite' (a Top 10 hit), and as soon as the song ended almost the entire crowd left. The band played out the rest of the set in front of a few dozen people who stuck around.

"I mean I'm not saying techno is any more authentic, but yeah, maybe it just is, maybe it's more purely about the experience of the music and it attracts people who are into it first and foremost for the feel of the music."

So if, as Marshall McLuhan suggested, popular culture serves as an organizing mechanism, a way for people to define their identity, how do these youths see themselves?

"I don't buy that," says Kimberly Stalk, 23. The harmonious rhythm of blue and white light warps off the braids of her hair, as she sinks into a couch with her back turned to Turbo's second-level dance floor.

Her face is hidden by the darkness, only revealed periodically by elliptic snatches of light moving to the DJ's acid house riffs. "I think the day's coming when people at my age realize the music you listen to doesn't define you. I used to think that way. I thought if you listen to hip-hop, you drive sports cars.

"But I think that's what the marketing of pop culture does. It tries to make kids think that to fit in they have to be categorized and defined.

"I guess maybe that's what defines us, people who come for the sensation of the music, no labels, no baggage, no expectations. Just the music."

San Grewal is one of the creators of *Diverge*, an alternative magazine published by Loon's Cry Press in Winnipeg. He also writes for the "Life" section of *The Toronto Star*.

Activities: Finding Their Own Groove

1. ***Identify Audience:*** Identify the target audience of this article and use specific references to the text to support your opinion.

2. ***Compare Elements:*** Work with a partner to create a chart to compare and contrast this human-interest story with a news report of your choice. Consider content, structure, diction, and any other elements you think are important. Share your chart with another pair of classmates.

3. ***Write a Letter:*** The author quotes comments by Chris Grimwood. Discuss these comments in a small group. Individually, write a letter to the editor in which you express your opinions and reactions to Grimwood's comments. Define the purpose of your letter and identify strategies that will help you to achieve this purpose.

4. ***Design a Logo:*** Create a new logo and slogan for your favourite radio station. Both the logo and the slogan should reflect something about the type of music heard on the station or about the station's audience. Display your logo in the classroom, along with a list of five performers or groups frequently played on the station.

Back to the Future

Jill Lawless

Two red-cheeked girls on horseback were thundering at us across the desert, laughing. A stream of horses flowed along in their wake. The pair slowed to a trot as they reached their patch of stony gravel in the ocean of stony gravel that is the Gobi, their homestead with its wisps of midsummer grass, its nearby well, its *ger* battened down with ropes tied to rocks against the unrelenting desert wind.

They jumped down, tied up their mounts to a rope that stretched like a clothesline between two posts, left the other horses to wander. A clump of camel calves sprawled in the shelter of the *ger*, mewling.

"Oh, hello," said the girls, still breathless and giggling. "Excuse us. We were just rounding up the horses."

The horses stayed close to the *ger*. The wind really was fierce, whipping the animals' tails and manes up into gestures of alarm, pelting us with fine grains of sand. The two girls—sisters, I could see—wore sturdy leather boots, dusty *dels*, scarves on their heads to keep off the sun.

"We stopped," I said, "because we were curious about *that*." I pointed just to the left of the *ger* at a concave silver dish, with a small mast in the middle, poking up at the blue desert sky.

"You mean the satellite dish?" said the younger, plumper, more effusive girl as her sister looked away and giggled into her hand. "Oh, it's great. We get 16 or 17 channels—CNN and everything. My favourite is *Star Sports*—I love to watch the motorbike racing."

She said her name was Surenjav. She was 19, and her sister, Byambajav, was 22. They lived in the *ger* with their parents. They were nomads, moving their *ger* twice a year to summer and winter pastures. They'd also make frequent shorter moves in summer to find fresh grass for the animals; the cover in the desert was so sparse the livestock would chew it clean. It didn't take long to dismantle a *ger*; it could be done in an hour.

In addition to the dish, there was a battered red Russian Planeta motorbike sitting in the shade of the tent—a sign of wealth among herders, a lifetime of mobility in the desert.

"Do you want to see?" asked Surenjav. She took us over to the dish. In black letters on its shiny surface was the name of the company that supplied it: Malchin. Herders. On the other side of the *ger*, a wind turbine whirled.

"We bought it about four years ago from a trader who travels around the area," Surenjav explained. "It was 800 000 tugrug for the whole package: the dish, the wind generator, and a colour television."

Eight hundred dollars. Big money.

"It's really good, because you can learn about the outside world, see how other people live. This life can be a bit lonely. The nearest neighbour is a kilometre away, and it's 70 kilometres to Dalanzadgad, the provincial capital."

It was odd; that was the first time I'd heard a Mongol speak of loneliness. I always thought herding must be a terribly solitary life.

"Well, we weren't always herders, you know," said Surenjav, with a hint of pride. "We used to live in the city. I've been to high school!"

"In Ulaanbaatar?" I asked.

"No—in Choir. I miss that life sometimes."

Choir was a desolate desert town on the Trans-Mongolian rail line, a former Soviet military base, where people lived in the hulks of

Russian army buildings or in *gers* pitched amid the rubble. It was one of the grimmest places I'd ever seen.

"Why did you leave?" I asked.

"The economy in the city is not so good. My mother will be home soon. She can tell you all about it. Come inside."

She led us inside the *ger*, sat us down around the stove. Byambajav prepared a pot of salty milk tea in silence, but Surenjav was keen to chat to strangers.

"We subscribe to four newspapers," she said proudly. "And sometimes we take the motorbike to Dalanzadgad to buy books and magazines.

"Don't misunderstand me. This is a good life. We've done well— we have more than 500 animals. It's a better life than in the city, because we don't have to worry about food, and we can make some money from selling animals, sheepskins, cashmere, and camel wool.

"But it's a hard life. We sleep for six hours, and the rest of the time it's all work. We have to get up at sunrise to milk the camels and water the animals; then we take the herds out to pasture, and later we bring them in again. Sometimes we miss our city life, especially when the weather is bad. It's a more interesting life because you have your friends. Here your neighbours are so far away."

Did she have any friends her own age?

"There aren't too many young people around. But I have a boyfriend," she said, turning ever so slightly redder.

"What does he do?" I asked.

"He's a herder." Duh. "He lives 30 kilometres away. We see each other once a week. He'll come over here and watch TV, or sometimes I go to his *ger*. He has a TV as well."

The door's spring hinges gave a creak, and a woman in her forties entered. She was dressed in a clean maroon *del*, a compact, tidy woman with smooth, sandblasted skin, neatly cropped black hair, and silver earrings glinting above fine, high cheekbones. Surenjav told her, in a rush, who we were, why we'd stopped. She went to the stove, refilled our bowls of tea, then perched on the edge of a bed and looked at us levelly. Her movements were neat, efficient, authoritative. Her name, she said, was Odmaa.

"I was born in this country, the Gobi," she said, "but after school I trained to become a doctor, and I went to work in the city. I lived there for 15 years. I worked in the hospital, and my husband was a driver, and we raised a family. But I missed my home country.

"When the transition came," she continued, using the word, *transition*, that Mongols and development workers alike always employed to refer to the decade after the collapse of communism—a word so much more orderly and reasonable than revolution, or cataclysm, or any of the others I could think of. "When the transition came, it became a lot easier to move around. You could go where you liked.

"And, at the same time, life in the city became much harder. The factories closed, the price of everything went up—even if you had a job, it was hard to survive. So we decided to come back here and teach our children how to raise animals. From an economic standpoint, it's much easier to have animals than to live in town. My colleagues in the city earn $40 a month. If you have to buy your meat and milk from the market, you can't live on that."

Thousands of other Mongolian families had done the same thing. They had gone back to their roots, back to the land. Amid the economic chaos of the 1990s, livestock were the one stable thing in a world turned upside down. Animals were wealth and life itself—they were meat and milk and money.

As the 20th century ended, Mongolia was one of the few countries in the world experiencing mass migration from the city to the country. For many, rural life was an existence just as precarious as remaining in the city would have been. Odmaa had grown up herding, but many of the city-raised Mongols going back to the land hadn't the faintest idea how to begin, how to find rich pasture in summer and a sheltered camp in winter. One unusually harsh winter could wipe out a whole herd.

I didn't worry for Odmaa, though. She was in control, capable, I could tell. But I thought I could detect a hint, just the slightest ripple, of wistfulness in her voice.

"Our standard of living has improved here," she said in a measured, decisive tone. "I want my children to be herders, because even if you have a university degree these days the pay is not so high. But maybe for my grandchildren it would be better to get some education and live in town. Now we are working to give our grandchildren opportunities. My children have animals—they have assets."

We thanked her for the tea and got up to go. Surenjav showed us to the door and followed us out to the jeep.

"My mother thinks it's a shame that we lost our close ties with Russia," she said. "My parents firmly believe that the socialist time was much better than this. They remember it fondly. They say things like, 'All for one, and one for all.' Now you have to rely completely on yourself."

Jill Lawless (*born Canada*), journalist, gave up her job as a theatre critic to edit an independent newspaper in Mongolia. She has written articles about Mongolia for the CBC and various international media outlets. Lawless is the author of *Wild East: Travels in the New Mongolia*.

Activities: Back to the Future

1. **Examine Character:** Using information in the selection, write a short character sketch of the mother. What qualities do her words and actions reveal? Compare your character sketch with a partner's.

2. **Explain the Title:** Explain in one or two paragraphs the meaning of the title of the selection and why you think it is or is not an effective title. Exchange your writing with a partner and ask for constructive feedback. Revise and polish your writing, editing for correct grammar, punctuation, and spelling.

3. **Research History:** Work in a small group to find out more about the recent history of Mongolia, including the "transition." Think of creative ways to present your findings to the class. Possibilities include an illustrated time line, role-plays, or a multimedia presentation.

4. **Reflect on Technology:** Surenjav says that learning about "the outside world" is one of the benefits of the satellite dish. How does access to communications technology affect your life? List pros and cons for each of the following: TV, the Web, telephone. Choose the technology you would least like to live without and explain your reasons in a journal entry.

Mother Tongue

Amy Tan

I am not a scholar of English or literature. I cannot give you much more than personal opinions on the English language and its variations in this country or others.

I am a writer. And by that definition, I am someone who has always loved language. I am fascinated by language in daily life. I spend a great deal of my time thinking about the power of language—the way it can evoke an emotion, a visual image, a complex idea, or a simple truth. Language is the tool of my trade. And I use them all—all the Englishes I grew up with.

Recently, I was made keenly aware of the different Englishes I do use. I was giving a talk to a large group of people, the same talk I had already given to half a dozen other groups. The nature of the talk was about my writing, my life, and my book, *The Joy Luck Club*. The talk was going along well enough, until I remembered one major difference that made the whole talk sound wrong. My mother was in the room. And it was perhaps the first time she had heard me give a lengthy speech, using the kind of English I have never used with her.

I was saying things like, "The intersection of memory upon imagination" and "There is an aspect of my fiction that relates to thus-and-thus"—a speech filled with carefully wrought grammatical phrases, burdened, it suddenly seemed to me, with nominalized forms, past perfect tenses, conditional phrases, all the forms of standard English that I had learned in school and through books, the forms of English I did not use at home with my mother.

Just last week, I was walking down the street with my mother, and I again found myself conscious of the English I was using, the English I do use with her. We were talking about the price of new and used furniture and I heard myself saying this: "Not waste money that way." My husband was with us as well, and he didn't notice any switch in my English. And then I realized why. It's because over the 20 years we've been together I've often used the same kind of English with him, and sometimes he even uses it with me. It has become our language of intimacy, a different sort of English that relates to family talk, the language I grew up with.

So you'll have some idea of what this family talk I heard sounds like, I'll quote what my mother said during a recent conversation which I videotaped and then transcribed. During this conversation, my mother was talking about a political gangster in Shanghai who had the same last name as her family's, Du, and how the gangster in his early years wanted to be adopted by her family, which was rich by comparison. Later, the gangster became more powerful, far richer than my mother's family, and one day showed up at my mother's wedding to pay his respects. Here's what she said in part:

"Du Yusong having business like fruit stand. Like off the street kind. He is Du like Du Zong—but not Tsung-ming Island people. The local people call putong, the river east side, he belong to that side local people. That man want to ask Du Zong father take him in like become own family. Du Zong father wasn't look down on him, but didn't take seriously, until that man big like become a mafia. Now important person, very hard to inviting him. Chinese way, came only to show respect, don't stay for dinner. Respect for making big celebration, he shows up. Mean gives lots of respect. Chinese custom. Chinese social life that way. If too important won't have to stay too long. He come to my wedding. I didn't see, I heard it. I gone to boy's side, they have YMCA dinner. Chinese age I was nineteen."

You should know that my mother's expressive command of English belies how much she actually understands. She reads the *Forbes* report, listens to *Wall Street Week*, converses daily with her stockbroker, reads all of Shirley MacLaine's books with ease—all kinds of things I can't begin to understand. Yet some of my friends tell me they understand 50 percent of what my mother says. Some say they understand 80 to 90 percent. Some say they understand none of it, as if she were speaking pure Chinese. But to me, my mother's English is perfectly clear, perfectly natural. It's my mother tongue. Her language, as I hear it, is vivid, direct, full of observation and imagery. That was the language that helped shape the way I saw things, expressed things, made sense of the world.

Lately, I've been giving more thought to the kind of English my mother speaks. Like others, I have described it to people as "broken" or "fractured" English. But I wince when I say that. It has always bothered me that I can think of no way to describe it other than "broken," as if it were damaged and needed to be fixed, as if it lacked a certain wholeness and soundness. I've heard other terms used, "limited English," for example. But they seem just as bad, as if everything is limited, including people's perceptions of the limited English speaker.

I know this for a fact, because when I was growing up, my mother's "limited" English limited *my* perception of her. I was ashamed of her English. I believed that her English reflected the quality of what she had to say. That is, because she expressed them imperfectly her thoughts were imperfect. And I had plenty of empirical evidence to support me: the fact that people in department stores, at banks, and at restaurants did not take her seriously, did not give her good service, pretended not to understand her, or even acted as if they did not hear her.

My mother has long realized the limitations of her English as well. When I was 15, she used to have me call people on the phone to pretend I was she. In this guise, I was forced to ask for information or even to complain and yell at people who had been rude to her. One time it was a call to her stockbroker in New York. She had cashed out her small portfolio and it just so happened we were going to New York the next week, our very first trip outside California. I had to get on the phone and say in an adolescent voice that was not very convincing, "This is Mrs. Tan."

And my mother was standing in the back whispering loudly, "Why he don't send me cheque, already two weeks late. So mad he lie to me, losing me money."

And then I said in perfect English, "Yes. I'm getting rather concerned. You had agreed to send the cheque two weeks ago, but it hasn't arrived."

Then she began to talk more loudly. "What he want, I come to New York tell him front of his boss, you cheating me?" And I was trying to calm her down, make her be quiet, while telling the stockbroker, "I can't tolerate any more excuses. If I don't receive the cheque immediately, I am going to have to speak to your manager when I'm in New York next week." And sure enough, the following week there we were in front of this astonished stockbroker, and I was sitting there red-faced and quiet, and my mother, the real Mrs. Tan, was shouting at his boss in her impeccable broken English.

We used a similar routine just five days ago, for a situation that was far less humorous. My mother had gone to the hospital for an appointment, to find out about a benign brain tumour a CAT scan had revealed a month ago. She said she had spoken very good English, her best English, no mistakes. Still, she said, the hospital did not apologize when they said they had lost the CAT scan and she had come for nothing. She said they did not seem to have any sympathy when she told them she was anxious to know the exact diagnosis, since her husband and son had both died of brain tumours. She said they would not give her any more information until the next time and she would have to make another appointment for that. So she said she would not leave until the doctor called her daughter. She wouldn't budge. And when the doctor finally called her daughter, me, who spoke in perfect English—lo and behold—we had assurances the CAT scan would be found, promises that a conference call on Monday would be held, and apologies for any suffering my mother had gone through for a most regrettable mistake.

I think my mother's English almost had an effect on limiting my possibilities in life as well. Sociologists and linguists probably will tell you that a person's developing language skills are more influenced by peers. But I do think that the language spoken in the family, especially in immigrant families which are more insular, plays a large role in shaping the language of the child. And I believe that it affected my results on achievement tests, IQ tests, and the SAT. While my English skills were never judged as poor, compared to math, English could not be considered my strong suit. In grade school I did moderately well, getting perhaps B's, sometimes B-pluses, in English and scoring perhaps in the sixtieth or seventieth percentile on achievement tests. But those scores were not good enough to override the opinion that my true abilities lay in math and science, because in those areas I achieved A's and scored in the ninetieth percentile or higher.

This was understandable. Math is precise; there is only one correct answer. Whereas, for me at least, the answers on English tests were always a judgement call, a matter of opinion and personal experience. Those tests were constructed around items like fill-in-the-blank sentence completion, such as, "Even though Tom was_____, Mary thought he was _____." And the correct answer always seemed to be the most bland combinations of thoughts; for example, "Even though Tom was shy, Mary thought he was charming," with the grammatical structure "even though" limiting the correct answer to some sort of semantic opposites, so you wouldn't get answers like, "Even though Tom was foolish, Mary thought he was ridiculous." Well, according to my mother, there were very few limitations as to what Tom could have been and what Mary might have thought of him. So I never did well on tests like that.

The same was true with word analogies, pairs of words in which you were supposed to find some sort of logical, semantic relationship—for example, "*Sunset* is to *nightfall* as _____ is to _____." And here you would be presented with a list of four possible pairs, one of which showed the same kind of relationship: *red* is to *stoplight, bus* is to *arrival, chills* is to *fever, yawn* is to *boring.* Well, I could never think that way. I knew what the tests were asking, but I could not block out of my mind the images already created by the first pair, "*sunset* is to *nightfall*"—and I would see a burst of colours against a darkening sky, the moon rising, the lowering of a curtain of stars. And all the other pairs of words—red, bus, stoplight, boring—just threw up a mass of confusing images, making it impossible for me to sort out something as logical as saying "A sunset precedes nightfall" is the same as "a chill precedes a fever." The only way I would have gotten that answer right would have been to imagine an associative situation, for example, my being disobedient and staying out past sunset, catching a chill at night, which turns into feverish pneumonia as punishment, which indeed did happen to me.

I have been thinking about all this lately, about my mother's English, about achievement tests. Because lately I've been asked, as a writer, why there are not more Asian Americans represented in American literature. Why are there few Asian Americans enrolled in creative writing programs? Why do so many Chinese students go into engineering? Well, these are broad sociological questions I can't begin to answer. But I have noticed in surveys—in fact, just last week—that Asian students, as a whole, always do significantly better on math achievement tests than in English. And this makes me think that there are other Asian-American students whose English spoken in the home might also be described as "broken" or "limited." And perhaps they also have teachers who are steering them away from writing and into math and science, which is what happened to me.

Fortunately, I happen to be rebellious in nature and enjoy the challenge of disproving assumptions made about me. I became an English major my first year in college, after being enrolled as pre-med. I started writing nonfiction as a freelancer the week after I was told by my former boss that writing was my worst skill and I should hone my talents toward account management.

But it wasn't until 1985 that I finally began to write fiction. And at first I wrote using what I thought to be wittily crafted sentences, sentences that would finally prove I had mastery over the English language. Here's an example from the first draft of a story that later made its way into *The Joy Luck Club*, but without this line: "That was my mental quandary in its nascent state." A terrible line, which I can barely pronounce.

Fortunately, for reasons I won't get into today, I later decided I should envision a reader for the stories I would write. And the reader I decided upon was my mother, because these were stories about mothers. So with this reader in mind—and in fact she did read my early drafts—I began to write stories using all the Englishes I grew up with: the English I spoke to my mother, which for lack of a better term might be described as "simple"; the English she used with me, which for lack of a better term might be described as "broken"; my translation of her Chinese, which could certainly be described as "watered-down"; and what I imagined to be her translation of her Chinese if she could speak in perfect English, her internal language, and for that I sought to preserve the essence, but neither an English nor a Chinese structure. I wanted to capture what language ability tests can never reveal: her intent, her passion, her imagery, the rhythms of her speech and the nature of her thoughts.

Apart from what any critic had to say about my writing, I knew I had succeeded where it counted when my mother finished reading my book and gave me her verdict: "So easy to read."

Amy Tan (*born 1952, California*), novelist, children's author, often writes about the tension between mothers and daughters and the experiences of Chinese immigrants in the United States. Her first novel, *The Joy Luck Club,* won a National Book Award and was made into a successful film. She has also published *The Kitchen God's Wife* and *The Bonesetter's Daughter.*

Activities: Mother Tongue

1. ***Interpret Text:*** Explain the ways in which Amy Tan's life was affected by her mother's "limited" English. Would you say that, overall, the effect was positive or negative? Give reasons for your answer.

2. ***Explain the Message:*** State the message or main idea of this essay in one sentence. In a small group, compare responses and discuss any differences. After the discussion, revise your sentence if your ideas have changed.

3. ***Define Terms:*** Define the following grammatical terms from the essay: *nominalized forms, past perfect tenses, conditional phrases.* Include in each definition two sentences of your own that show examples of the term discussed.

4. ***Investigate Language:*** Make a list of slang words and phrases popular among your peer group. Write a paragraph using as many of these words and phrases as possible, and then rewrite it using standard English. Explain what, if anything, was lost in the translation.

Voices of the Grandmothers: Reclaiming a Métis Heritage

Christine Welsh

This is the story of my search for the voices of my grandmothers. It is not a story which presumes to speak for all Native people, for we come from many nations and we have many different stories, many different voices. I can only tell my own story, in my own voice. Leslie Marmon Silko, the Laguna poet and storyteller, puts it this way:

> As with any generation
> the oral tradition depends upon each person
> listening and remembering a portion
> and it is together—
> all of us remembering what we have heard together—
> that creates the whole story
> the long story of the people.
>
> I remember only a small part,
> But this is what I remember.

I grew up in Saskatchewan, the great-granddaughter of Métis people who, in the late 1860s, migrated west from Red River in pursuit of the last great buffalo herds and eventually settled in the Qu'Appelle Valley of southern Saskatchewan. My great-grandparents were among the first Métis families to set up camp down on the Flats beside Mission Lake where the village of Lebret now stands. As long as the buffalo were plentiful they continued to live from the hunt, wintering in the Cypress Hills and returning to Lebret each summer to sell their buffalo robes, meat, and pemmican at the Hudson's Bay Company post at Fort Qu'Appelle. With the disappearance of the buffalo they no longer wintered out on the plains, choosing to remain at Lebret and earn their living by trading, freighting, farming, and ranching. They are buried there beside the lake among their kinfolk, and the names on the headstones in that little cemetery—Blondeau, Delorme, Desjarlais, Ouellette, Pelletier, Welsh, and many more— bear silent witness to the diaspora of the Red River Métis.

I don't know when I first realized that among the ghostly relatives there was Indian blood. It was something that just seemed to seep into my consciousness through my pores. I remember my bewilderment when the other children in my predominantly white, middle-class school began to call me "nichi" on the playground. I had never heard the word before and was blissfully ignorant of its meaning, but it wasn't long before I understood that to them it meant "dirty Indian."

By the time I was in high school I had invented an exotic ethnicity to explain my black hair and brown skin and I successfully masqueraded as French or even Hawaiian, depending on who asked. But I still lived in mortal terror that the truth would get out. In 1969, when the province of Saskatchewan dedicated a monument to Louis Riel, all the other girls in my class took advantage of a perfect autumn day and skipped classes to attend the ceremonies. I decided not to go with them and afterward, much to my horror, was commended by the teacher in front of the whole class for behaviour which he deemed to be exemplary—given the fact, he said, that I was the only one who could claim a legitimate right to attend such an observance by virtue of my ancestry. This oblique reference went right over the heads of most of my classmates, but my cheeks still burned with the knowledge that I had been found out. It was no use: no matter how hard I tried to hide it, my Native background seemed to be written all over me.

The 1960s gave rise to a new pride in Native identity among Native people across Canada, and even though I had no contact with other Native people, I was swept up by the spirit of the times and began to feel that it was no longer necessary to try to hide who I was. But who was I? By the time I reached university in the early 1970s, denial of my Native ancestry had given way to a burning need to know. My curiosity was fuelled by the discovery of a much-worn volume entitled *The Last Buffalo Hunter*, a biography of my great-grandfather, Norbert Welsh, which had been written in the 1930s and rescued by my mother from a second-hand bookshop. I revelled in the references to Norbert's Indian mother and his part-Indian wife, but I didn't really understand that I was reading about a distinctly Métis experience which was separate from that of the Indians—or that it was, in fact, one of the few existing memoirs to be left by a Red River Métis.

Though I was clearly interested in tearing away the shroud of mystery that seemed to surround our Native ancestors, my attempts were largely futile. Whenever I tried to raise the subject, strenuous attempts were made, especially by my grandmother, to diminish and deny any connection we might have to Native people. She actively discouraged my burgeoning interest in and involvement with "things Indian": "we" were very different from "them," she implied, and such associations would only bring me grief.

Despite my grandmother's dire predictions, I was increasingly drawn to Indian people by my desperate need to find out who I was and where I belonged. Though I made every effort to fit into Indian society I was continually made aware that here, too, I was an outsider—this time because I was too "white." Nevertheless, I spent much of the next 15 years in "Indian country," travelling to Indian communities across Canada and making documentary films on issues of concern to Native people, and eventually the pieces of my identity began to fall into place.

This experience recording Native oral history was largely responsible for rekindling my relationship with my own grandmother. This happened quite unexpectedly, because in most of the Indian communities we visited it was the men who were put forward as being the tribal historians, and as a consequence we spent most of our time interviewing men. Yet often, when my husband and I had finished interviewing an old man, his wife would manage to manoeuvre me out to the kitchen so that she could speak to me alone. Over cups of strong tea, these women told me the stories of their lives—their experience of marriage and childbirth, their hopes and fears for their children, the work they did, the things that gave them pleasure, and the intricate workings of the communities in which they lived—all freely given, and deliberately so, well after the tape recorder had been turned off and well out of earshot of the men in the next room. For the most part these women were reluctant to be "interviewed" in any formal sense, insisting that they knew nothing about history and that nobody would be interested in what they had to say. But I began to realize that, without their story, an "Indian history of Canada" would be shamefully incomplete, and so I painstakingly went about overcoming their reluctance to speak. In the process I was forced yet again to re-examine my conventional notions of what was historically important and to recognize that the everyday lives of women—the unique patterns and rhythms of female experience—are history, too. In the end, it was this revelation—and the sense of kinship I felt to the Native women who shared their life stories with me—that finally led me back to my own grandmother.

I had seen very little of my grandmother during the years I spent in "Indian country." I was living in Toronto, she was in Regina, and our contact consisted of occasional letters and brief visits once or twice a year. But the passage of time and my own changing perceptions of the value of Native women's experience gradually led me to see her in a whole new light. Whereas in my youth I had felt nothing but contempt for the values that had led her to deny her Native heritage, I now began to feel a genuine bond of compassion and respect for this formidable old lady who seemed to shrink visibly and grow more fragile with each passing season. I was acutely aware that just as we were getting to know each other we would soon be separated for good. She was my only living connection with the past, my only hope of finding out who I really was so, despite her reluctance to talk about the past, I kept on asking my questions. And while she continued to maintain steadfastly the distinctions between our family and other Native people, she must have had some sense of how important this was for me because she began to try to give me some answers. We spent hours poring over old family photographs, putting names and faces to those ghostly ancestors who had haunted my childhood. And then, quite suddenly, she died.

My grandmother had very few possessions, but care was taken to distribute what little she had among her children and grandchildren. I received a child's sampler, embroidered by my grandmother's mother in 1890 when she was still a schoolgirl. There, woven into the cloth amongst the crucifixes and barnyard animals, was my great-grandmother's name: Maggie Hogue. Ironically, my grandmother had bequeathed to me that which she had found so difficult to give me while she was alive—the key to unlocking the mystery of who I was.

We had finished our fieldwork for the "Indian History of Canada," so I decided to pursue my deepening interest in Native women's history by studying the work done by Sylvia Van Kirk on the role of Native women in the North American fur trade. I learned that, initially, very few white women were permitted to brave the perils of the "Indian country" so most fur traders took Indian and mixed-blood women as "country wives." These "marriages à la façon du pays" were socially sanctioned unions, even though they were not formalized according to the laws of church or state. But with the establishment of the Red River settlement white women began to go west, and it soon became fashionable for the traders to legally marry white women and to try to sever their ties with their Native country wives.

In the forefront of this trend was Sir George Simpson, Governor of Rupert's Land and, by all accounts, the most important personage in the Canadian fur trade, who had taken as his country wife a mixed-blood woman named Margaret Taylor. Though she bore him two sons, Margaret Taylor was abandoned by Simpson when he married his English cousin, a move which signalled the widespread rejection of Native women as marriage partners by "men of station" in fur-trade society and reflected the increasing racial and social prejudice against Native women throughout pre-Confederation Canada. Clearly, Margaret Taylor's story epitomized a crucial chapter in the history of Native women in Canada, but I was equally intrigued by its epilogue—her hastily

Sir George Simpson, 1787–1860

arranged marriage to a French-Canadian voyageur whose name was startlingly familiar: Amable Hogue.

On the basis of my great-grandmother's faded sampler and a rather incidental footnote in a history book, I began a search that eventually verified my connection to my great-great-great-grandmother, Margaret Taylor. For me it was the beginning of a journey of self-discovery—of unravelling the thick web of denial, shame, bitterness, and silence that had obscured my past, and picking up the fragile threads that extended back across time, connecting me to the grandmothers I had never known and to a larger collective experience that is uniquely and undeniably Métis.

My search for my grandmothers was hampered both by the inadequacies of traditional historical sources with respect to women and by the code of silence that existed in my own family with respect to our Native heritage. But, after venturing down a couple of blind alleys, I finally called my great-aunt Jeanne, who is my grandmother's youngest sister and the only surviving female relative on that side of my family. When I called Grandma Jeanne I hadn't seen or spoken to her in more than 20 years, yet she was surprised and touched that I remembered her and seemed eager to help me in any way she could. Grandma Jeanne knew about Margaret Taylor, and knew that she had some connection to George Simpson, but said that this had never been discussed because, in the words of Jeanne's mother, it had brought shame on the family. Nonetheless, Grandma Jeanne was able to tell me the names of Margaret Taylor's daughters and granddaughters, and in the act of naming them I finally had the sense of reaching back and grasping hands with all my grandmothers and great-grandmothers—right back to Margaret Taylor.

My great-great-great-grandmother was just 21 years old when she became the "country wife" of the Governor of Rupert's Land. Though George Simpson was notorious for indulging in short-lived liaisons with young Native women, his relationship with Margaret Taylor appeared to be different. He relied on her companionship to an unusual degree, insisting that she accompany him on his historic cross-continental canoe journey from Hudson Bay to the Pacific in 1828. Not only did Simpson recognize and assume responsibility for their two sons, but he also provided financial support for Margaret's mother and referred to Thomas Taylor as his brother-in-law, thus giving Margaret and the rest of fur-trade society every reason to believe that their relationship constituted a legitimate "country marriage." Nevertheless, while on furlough in England in 1830—and with Margaret and their two sons anxiously awaiting his return at Fort Alexander—Simpson married his English cousin, Frances Simpson.

It is not hard to imagine Margaret's shock when she learned that the Governor was returning with a new wife. No doubt she and her children were kept well out of sight when Simpson and his new bride stopped at Fort Alexander during their triumphant journey from Lachine to Red River. Once the Simpsons were installed at Red River the Governor lost no time in arranging for Margaret's "disposal." A few months later she was married to Amable Hogue.

Amable Hogue, who had been among Simpson's elite crew of voyageurs, was hired as a stonemason on the construction of Simpson's new headquarters at Lower Fort Garry. From her vantage point in the Métis labourers' camp just outside the walls, Margaret would have been able to watch the Governor and his bride take up residence in their magnificent new home. For his service, the Hudson's Bay Company gave Hogue a riverfront lot on the Assiniboine River just west of the Forks, and it was there on the banks of the Assiniboine River that Margaret Taylor and her daughters and granddaughters spent most of the rest of their lives, raising their families and working beside their men-folk on the buffalo hunts and riverfront farms that were the mainstay of the Red River Métis.

It is impossible to know when the process of denial and assimilation began in my own family, but I feel in my heart that it goes right back to what happened to Margaret Taylor. Here, I believe, are the roots of our denial—denial of that fact of blood that was the cause of so much pain and suffering and uncertainty about the future. Is it such a surprise that, many years later, Margaret's own son would choose to describe his mother as "a sturdy Scotswoman" rather than the half-breed that she really was? Perhaps Margaret herself perpetrated this myth, if not for her son's sake then certainly for her daughters', to try to spare them a fate similar to her own and that of her mother. I'll never know. But I do know that the denial of our Native heritage, which has been passed on from generation to generation of my family, is explicable in light of those events that took place so long ago, and I am finally able to see it not as a betrayal but as the survival mechanism that it most certainly was. For we *did* survive—even though, for a time, we were cut off from our past and our people—and we did so largely because of the resourcefulness, adaptability, and courage of my grandmothers.

Christine Welsh (*born Saskatchewan*), film director, writer, has a deep interest in the historical and contemporary experiences of First Nations and Métis women. Her documentary films include *Keepers of the Fire* and *The Story of the Coast Salish Knitters*.

Activities: Voices of the Grandmothers

1. *Understand Text:* What clue led to Christine Welsh's discovery of her grandmother's identity? Explain how Welsh used this clue to piece together her grandmother's history.

2. *Explain Relevance:* The essay begins with a quotation from Leslie Silko. With a partner, discuss the relationship of this quotation to the story Welsh tells, and present your conclusions to the class.

3. *Write a Diary Entry:* Choose one of the following: (a) In the role of Margaret Taylor, write an entry about your reaction when you discover that George Simpson has taken an English wife; (b) In the role of George Simpson, write an entry that expresses your thoughts, feelings, and concerns as you return to Canada with your new wife.

4. *Explore Issues:* Welsh realized that without the input of Aboriginal women, an "Indian History of Canada" would be incomplete. In a small group, discuss why the voice of women has often been ignored by historians and how this voice can help to expand our understanding of history. Summarize your discussion.

Better or Worse?

David Macfarlane

My grandfather's opposition to Confederation, and the fact that I was the first issue of a marriage that began not in Newfoundland, where by custom it should have, but in Ontario—a wedding that was almost precisely coincidental with the island's union with Canada—has made me feel a little uneasy all my life. I was born and raised in Southern Ontario, the wealthiest part of the country. Newfoundland is the poorest: its unemployment rate is still twice the national average, and its fishery is, after centuries of crises, in its worst crisis ever. The island's dreams of offshore oil remain unfulfilled with each passing, inconclusive year. And its most recent government-sponsored industrial venture—a vast and fantastically expensive indoor cucumber farm whose special lights and transparent ceilings didn't do much for cucumbers but lit up the St. John's night like a landed UFO—was as unlikely and as doomed an enterprise as anything either Joey Smallwood or my great-uncle Roland ever dreamed of. When Newfoundlanders resent the rest of Canada, they zero their resentment on exactly the part of Canada from which I come. Up-Along, they call it. And strangers, like me, are called Come from Aways.

My uneasiness has never prevented me from feeling proud of my Newfoundland connection, however, and in the fall of 1963, at the age of eleven, I departed from the traditional topic of my relentlessly annual social studies projects. It wasn't a complete revolution, but it had a certain originality. My mother regarded it as a step in the right direction.

In a blue three-ringed binder I drew maps, traced charts, underlined headings with red pencil-crayon, and composed "Hamilton and Newfoundland: A Comparison." It was difficult to say which place came out on top. Hamilton had 273 991 people; Newfoundland had 438 000 but was, by my estimate, almost a thousand times as big and had more annual precipitation. Hamilton had two major steel foundries and dozens of subsidiary industries; Newfoundland had two paper mills, one international airport, and a seal hunt. In Newfoundland, 60 percent of the population lived in rural areas, whereas in Hamilton no one did. Hamilton had no rivers; Newfoundland, no air pollution. Anecdotal evidence seemed to suggest that Hamilton had fewer ghosts; Newfoundland, fewer industrial-related ophthalmological emergencies. Hamilton had no fishing industry to speak of, but it had less fog and fewer shipwrecks. In a paragraph entitled "Recreation," Hamilton was credited with having the YMCA and an exceptional football team, while Newfoundland had the Atlantic Ocean. The paragraph included a brief description of the time my grandfather took me cod-jigging. Hamilton, by my count, had eight movie theatres; Newfoundland, by my mother's, had just as many.

The social studies project was a great success. I received an A, and was even asked to read it over the PA system to a riveted schoolful of young social studies enthusiasts. I did so with quivering voice and considerable pride, but even as I stood at the silver microphone in the principal's office with the sheaves of foolscap trembling in my hand, I was aware that my report had a serious flaw. I knew that it made no mention of the most profound difference between Hamilton and Newfoundland. Nobody noticed my omission, but it was crucial. In fact, I could feel the difference struggling inside me.

Hamilton, I knew, had its legendary silences. Whereas in Newfoundland—as my mother still makes clear at every opportunity—they talk. They talk, as a matter of fact, like no one else ever talks. They never stop.

The humidity of Southern Ontario settled on my Newfoundland relatives like a weight of warm, sodden tissue when they came to visit us in Hamilton in the summer. I'm not really sure why they came, they all hated the weather so much. But they did come from time to time—my mother's sisters and her brother, her uncles, her aunts, and her parents—and when they showed up, with their huge, strapped suitcases and their summer hats, their pouches of tobacco and *Family Herald* magazines and the red bag of Purity biscuits with the yellow caribou on the front that they brought as a treat for me, they sat on my parents' front veranda and talked. They talked and they talked—about the First World War and the Bonavista North forest fire, German submarines and tidal waves, about business problems and sealing disasters, politics and ghosts. They talked about waiting at the airport to see Merle Oberon and about the time Frank Sinatra, when he was young and skinny and the girls were just starting to scream, played at Fort Pepperell, the American base in St. John's. Or about how, when it was overcast on the Straight Shore, you could sometimes hear Dr. Banting's plane—the twin-engine Hudson in which the co-discoverer of insulin was killed in a crash in February 1941—pass overhead. They talked about the family company and the roads it built—from nowhere to nowhere, it always seemed to me—and the strikes in the lumber woods, and berry-picking parties, and about the time my grandfather called Harry Dowding back from the dead.

My grandfather and two of his brothers were partners in a construction firm called J. Goodyear and Sons. The family was also involved in lumber contracting and in operating a number of dry-goods and grocery stores throughout the island. But in the 1950s, the Goodyears' principal occupation was building roads, and Harry Dowding was the foreman on the job they had between Botwood and Leading Tickle. Harry was a good man and a hard worker, and one day, standing on the road's gravel shoulder in his boots and hunting-cap and quilted vest, he waved abruptly to the Caterpillar operator, took a few strange, faltering steps, and keeled over. He'd suffered a massive stroke.

He was rushed to the hospital in Botwood. My grandfather was called at the Goodyear office and told that all hope was lost. He drove to Botwood from Grand Falls. He was wearing his floppy fedora when he arrived at the hospital, and he made his lumbering way to the ward. He stood at the side of Dowding's bed. Then he did an odd thing. He shouted: "Harry!" He waited for a few seconds. He called out "Harry!"—more loudly the second time. "Harry!" he finally bellowed, so loudly a nurse dropped a dinner tray in the corridor. And, like Lazarus, Harry Dowding stirred from his stillness and blinked open his eyes. "Well, Skipper Joe," he said. "You were the last man I was just thinking of."

It was as if Newfoundland contained all the best stories in the world. Just when I thought they'd go on telling them forever, my Newfoundland relatives, briefly interrupting themselves, decided that, although it was too hot and sticky to sleep, it was probably time to go to bed.

What I liked best was that they talked in great, looping circles. I was used to people who spoke in straight lines, darting from subject to subject like foxes looking for winter cover. But my Newfoundland relatives set their stories going and then let them roll from one tale to the next until I—sitting on the steps of the veranda—was certain they had no idea where they had begun. Their plots and jokes and family legends possessed the same broad, meandering curlicues as their accents. Stories that began conversations were left unfinished—just as, in my grandfather's stories of the dreadful Bonavista North forest fire of 1961, the word "fire" was spoken, ominous and uncontainable, without its final consonant. Tales were abandoned in the telling in favour of other tales, but one story led seamlessly to another, spiralling like drifting pipe-smoke, farther and farther away from the conversation's beginnings. Yet somehow, without so much as where-were-we, the stories found their way back, hours later, to where they had started: to the warm fresh bread served on a coastal steamer called the *Glencoe* that stopped in at places with names like Twillingate and Fogo when the Goodyears went to Carmanville for the summer, for there was no road to the Straight Shore until their construction company built it in 1958; or to the flyer who came back after the Second World War with the terrible burns that everyone pretended not to notice; or to the time my grandfather tried to buy his own car, an apple-green Chrysler New Yorker, because, having driven it over every stretch of gravel and mud on Bonavista—going salmon-fishing, going to oversee a road job, going fox-trapping, going to Musgrave Harbour for a glass of the fresh cow's milk he loved so much—he didn't recognize it once it had been washed; or to the night in 1943 when Pop Irish, who lived next to the Goodyears in Grand Falls, awoke to an exploding cellarful of home brew and shouted for his wife to fetch his Home Guard uniform, so certain was he that the Germans had landed and were storming Junction Road.

Or the stories found their way back to my mother, thirty years ago, on those hot, humid summer nights, sitting on our front veranda, passing the bowl of sweet, deep-red Niagara cherries, smiling indulgently at her silent, outnumbered husband and son, and telling her visitors—all of whom were capable of talking the devil's ear off, given half a chance—that whenever she opened her mouth in Hamilton she might as well be talking to herself.

Or they find their way back to me, in Toronto, remembering all this. Remembering how, years ago, I stood with my parents on the deck of a CN ferry called the *William Carson* and watched the bald green bluffs of Port aux Basques disappear from view as we chugged away from Newfoundland. We were steering the course which, on the map in my school atlas, was a dotted red line, linking Newfoundland to Canada. We were on our way home. I was 10 years old, and school would be starting soon. Our summer holiday was over, and the little pale frame houses disappeared behind us, then the green, then the contours of the headland. Soon Newfoundland was just a dark shape against the sky.

My mother was crying. She wore slacks and a beige windbreaker. My father tried to comfort her. He wore desert boots and the hunting-shirt he wore on summer holidays. I was sure my mother's tears had to do with departure and, marked on the ragged grey sea by our wake, with the increasing distance between the ferry and the island and the family we'd left behind. Later I learned this wasn't the case at all; my mother was crying because it had rained every day of our holiday. She was afraid her children would hate Newfoundland. Still, for better or worse, the image has stayed with me. It returns at odd moments and seems to come from far away: the memory of my father holding my mother on the deck of a ship, and the taste of salt that may have been only the spray.

David Macfarlane (*born Hamilton, Ontario*), author, journalist, is a national columnist for *The Globe and Mail*. He has won a National Newspaper Award and numerous National Magazine Awards. Macfarlane's books include a novel, *Summer Gone*, which was shortlisted for the Governor General's Literary Awards, and *The Danger Tree*, a memoir of Newfoundland.

Activities: Better or Worse?

1. ***Determine Purpose:*** What is Macfarlane's purpose in this essay? How well does he achieve his purpose? Write a paragraph to explain and support your opinions. Revise your first draft to improve organization and clarity.

2. ***Examine Tone:*** Define the term *tone* as applied to writing. Decide what tone Macfarlane establishes in this essay and list examples that contribute to the tone. Share your ideas with a partner.

3. ***Apply Research Skills:*** If you were to move to a different province, which province would you choose? Research the province of your choice and then create a chart to compare that province with your current province. Consult at least one of each of the following sources: an Internet site, an encyclopedia, a book.

4. ***Create a Flag:*** Research the symbolism of your province's flag and then design a new provincial flag. Present your design to the class, explaining the design decisions you made. Prepare point-form speaking notes to use during your presentation.

My Old Newcastle

David Adams Richards

In Newcastle, N.B., which I call home, we all played on the ice floes in the spring, spearing tommy-cod with stolen forks tied to sticks. More than one of us almost met our end slipping off the ice.

All night the trains rumbled or shunted their loads off to Halifax or Montreal, and men moved and worked. To this day I find the sound of trains more comforting than lonesome. It was somehow thrilling to know of people up and about in those hours, and wondrous events taking place. Always somehow with the faint, worn smell of gas and steel.

The Miramichi is a great working river.

There was always the presence of working men and women, from the mines or mills or woods; the more than constant sound of machinery; and the ore covered in tarps at the side of the wharf.

But as children, sitting in our snowsuits and hats and heavy boots on Saturday afternoons, we all saw movies that had almost nothing to do with us. That never mentioned us as a country or a place. That never seemed to know what our fathers and mothers did—that we went to wars or had a flag or even a great passion for life.

As far as the movies were concerned, we were in a lost, dark country, it seemed. And perhaps this is one reason I write. Leaving the theatre on a January afternoon, the smell of worn seats and heat and chip bags gave way to a muted cold and scent of snow no movie ever showed us. And night came against the tin roofs of the sheds behind our white houses, as the long spires of our churches rose over the town.

Our river was frozen so blue then that trucks could travel from one town to the other across the ice, and bonfires were lit by kids skating; sparks rose upon the shore under the stars as mothers called children home at 9 o'clock.

All winter long the sky was tinted blue on the horizon, the schools we sat in too warm; privileged boys and girls sat beside those who lived in hunger and constant worry. One went on to be a Rhodes scholar, another was a derelict at 17 and dead at 20. To this day I could not tell you which held more promise.

Spring came with the smell of mud and grass burning in the fields above us. Road hockey gave way to cricket and then baseball. The sun warmed, the ice shifted, and the river was free. Salmon and sea trout moved up a dozen of our tributaries to spawn.

In the summer the ships came in, from all ports to ours, to carry ore and paper away. Sailors smoked black tobacco cigarettes, staring down at us from their decks; blackflies spoiled in the fields beyond town, and the sky was large all evening. Cars filled with children too excited to sleep passed along our great avenues lined with overhanging trees. All down to the store to get ice cream in the dark.

Adolescent blueberry crops and sunken barns dotted the fields near the bay, where the air had the taste of salt and tar, and small spruce trees seemed constantly filled with wind; where, by August, the water shimmered and even the small white lobster boats smelled of autumn, as did the ripples that moved them.

In the autumn the leaves were red, of course, and the earth, by Thanksgiving, became hard as a dull turnip. Ice formed in the ditches and shallow streams. The fields became yellow and stiff. The sounds of rifle shots from men hunting deer echoed faintly away, while women walked in kerchiefs and coats to 7 o'clock mass, and the air felt heavy and leaden. Winter coming on again.

Now the town is three times as large, and fast-food franchises and malls dot the roadside where there were once fields and lumberyards. There is a new process at the mill, and much of the wood is clear-cut so that huge acres lie empty and desolate, a redundancy of broken and muted earth. The river is opened all winter by an ice-breaker, so no trucks travel across the ice, and the trains, of course, are gone. For the most part the station is empty, the tracks fiercely alone in the winter sun.

The theatre is gone now, too. And those thousands of movies showing us, as children filled with happy laughter someplace in Canada, what we were not, are gone as well. They have given way to videos and satellite dishes and a community that is growing slowly farther and farther away from its centre. Neither bad nor good, I suppose—but away from what it was.

David Adams Richards (*born 1950, Newcastle, New Brunswick*), author of novels, poetry, short stories, and screenplays, explores universal truths through his writings about Maritime communities. Titles in his Miramichi trilogy have won the Governor General's Literary Award, the Canadian Authors' Association Award, and the Thomas Raddall award. Two of his screenplays have captured Geminis.

Activities: My Old Newcastle

1. **Note Organization:** What pattern does Adams Richards use to organize his memories of Newcastle? Explain why this pattern is effective in this essay.

2. **Examine Technique:** Work with a partner to identify four examples of concrete diction in the essay. How does the use of concrete diction affect the reader? Identify and find examples of two other techniques that Adams Richards uses to enhance his writing.

3. **Discuss Tone:** Define the term *nostalgia*. Do you agree or disagree that the tone of the essay is nostalgic? Cite three passages to support your conclusion. Discuss your ideas in a small group.

4. **Apply Technique:** Write a short personal essay about your own childhood or the place where you grew up. Use at least two of the techniques Adams Richards uses in the essay. Ask a classmate to give you feedback on the first draft, and then revise it.

The Vikings Are Coming ... Again!

What follows are extracts from an Internet journal of a voyage from Greenland to Newfoundland in Snorri, *an authentic replica of a Viking knarr. The aim was to replicate Leif Eriksson's historic voyage 1000 years ago.*

Date: June 29, 1998
Author: Terry Moore
Lat/Lon: 64.30 N, 52.07 W
Location: At anchor north
    of Nuuk

Course: At anchor
Speed: At anchor
Weather: Sunny and warm. 62°F
Sightings: Jagged snowy peaks
    to the south

Hard to believe that it is nearly time to go to bed once more. For not actually going anywhere today, I feel very satisfied and pleasantly tired. We are anchored on the edge of the Norde Lob, tucked into the only spot I could find that is shallow enough for our anchor to hit anything once we tossed it over. Which is pretty much the norm around here.

The charts of Greenland—and Baffin Island and Labrador for that matter—have next to no depths marked on them. Only the routes frequently used by commercial traffic have soundings marked, and we spend much of our time in places where there is no commercial traffic. When looking for a suitable place to anchor, we poke in carefully, sounding with our lead line the whole way, although the water is usually very clear so we can see the bottom long before we need to worry about hitting it. That is, if there is any bottom to worry about hitting.

The rocky shoreline is so bold we often can't find a bottom even if we are within spitting distance of the shore. Which is a bit of a drag. Most anchors are designed to grab when pulled on horizontally, not vertically, so we need to let out much more anchor line than the water is deep, which is hard to do if the water is deeper than you have line. Rats.

The other night we were rowing into a bit of a headwind among some islands, when I spelled out our anchorage options to the gang. Option number one was "nearby but uninspiring," and option number two was "a bit farther but potentially spectacular."

Now when someone describes something as "a bit farther" while you are rowing a 25-ton boat, you should immediately become suspicious, but being the Viking wanna-be's that we are, and feeling our oats at the beginning of this journey, we of course opted for the "potentially spectacular" anchorage.

Imagine my chagrin as the bottom began to show itself long before we got to the head of this bombproof little hole. I was right, it was spectacular, but it was also too shallow. Once the tide left us, we would have been planted firmly in the mud. Certainly a new experience for Greenland. But tonight, like last night, we are back to business as usual. Had our first anchor watch last night even.

We are pretty exposed to the south, with a slightly tenuous hold on this rock bottom, so we all take turns throughout the night keeping an eye on our position, the weather....

Anchor watch is something no one in their right mind would volunteer for, although I would grudgingly admit that I enjoy the time that the boat is my own. But last night, I felt like a very lucky man in the silence of the night after the wind died, looking out over the snow-covered rock spires in the sub-arctic twilight.

Silence is a relative term, I suppose, as my thoughts turn to bed again. Seems the only true prerequisite to participation in this adventure is the ability to snore like a banshee. Everybody on the boat claims that I would snore, too, if I could ever get to sleep. Right now John Gardner is sounding like a kazoo on both the inhale and the exhale. Unbelievable.

Date: Sunday, August 16, 1998   Location: False Bay, Labrador!
Author: John Abbott   Weather: 40°F and
                                  overcast, no wind
Lat/Lon: 59.47 N, 64.03 W   Sightings: Murres, pilot whales &
                                  polar bear!

A pair of ringed seals, a gaggle of diving murres, and an overly inquisitive polar bear (swimming toward us with purpose) bore witness to our arrival back in North America earlier this evening. While technically Baffin Island is part of the North American continent, Rob Stevens deftly observed that, having landed in Labrador, we could hitchhike back to New England now, should anything go afoul with *Snorri*.

Having sailed for 36 hours, covering close to 150 miles since leaving the Kane Channel on Baffin Island yesterday morning, *Snorri* seems no worse for the wear. The rudder seems to be functioning well and has withstood consistent—and erratic—swell vectors during our meeting with the tidal rush into Hudson Bay last night.

Loathed by seafarers for centuries, the mouth of the Hudson presents tidal flows near 7 knots, and rough navigating when travelling with oppositional winds. While we were tossed a good bit, this tidal flow helped speed us along on our southerly course.

The mood onboard this afternoon was celebratory, as the sun appeared at intervals to light the black-lichened buttresses and massifs of the Northern Labrador coastal mountain range towering over our soon-to-be anchorage in False Bay. The Tourngat Mountains are characterized by smooth and rolling peaks worn by past glacial advances, some peaks rising to nearly 6000 feet above the sea. Down their steep flanks run deeply gouged runnels peppered with blocky granite. Fields of scree and moraine empty finally to the sea and valleys below. Slide paths from avalanches resulting from deep winter's snow are evident everywhere.

As with Baffin Island, this inhospitable appearance is both vexing and attractive to the eye and the imagination. Save for the encouraging populations of walrus, seal, and polar bear that roam these waters, these barren scapes look plainly mysterious. Haunting, clouded peaks stand like defiant ancients until warmed by rays of scattered sun ... or the brilliant orange/rosy skies that fade to indigos and greens upon setting.

In a few of the leeward valleys, grasses fight to grow. These were not encouraging signs for Vikings in search of timber and farmland.

The crew was discussing the number of milestones we've reached over the past two days as we've crossed into the 50-degree parallel of latitude for the first time since our departure from Brattahlid last July.

Hodding believes we are likely the first Viking ship to have visited the shores of Baffin Island in the past 800 years.

The quiet that exists here in the Canadian Arctic is remarkable, and brings with it a calmness that welcomes us to each bay and inlet we explore. Rob spoke this afternoon of the Labrador Sea in its heyday during the 17th century, when the Basque whalers would roam these waters each summer for bowhead and right whales, thousands of miles from their homes in Portugal; 1400 whaling ships would converge in a single season in these waters, hoping to reap the harvest of riches: oil, ambergris, and baleen.

Tonight, all is quiet. The northern lights have shimmered and faded. I've got to wake up Homer for anchor watch and happily report that our bear friends are sleeping on shore as deeply as I will be.

Date: Saturday, September 12   Weather: Rainy and windy
Author: John Abbott   Sightings: Hunters, purple vetch 3
Lat/Lon: 54.32 N, 57.112 W

The engines are revved and the finish line is in sight. Tomorrow the north winds arrive to again deliver us southward, on to L'Anse aux Meadows. How can this be true, we wonder, after months of sitting idly at anchorages waiting out contrary winds and rowing hundreds of miles (yes, we have the calluses to prove it ...)? How can we be sure that our saga is reaching a finale? Only because this evening, Hodding, the parsimonious voice of food consumption conscience, green-flagged an extra can of vegetables to accompany our wild rice! John Gardner and I spun up nonstop meals today, recovery food after our two days under sail. Even though we all assured Hodding we'd have plenty of food should our arrival be delayed, say, until the third week in November. All we've been reading about Franklin, Melville, and the other sailing giants of English polar exploration convinced Hodding that we should have preparations for a fine Thanksgiving meal. Replete with pudding, it's good for crew morale after all.

In all seriousness, our thoughts and imaginings are actually turned to the end of our amazing expedition together. While we are at once excited and then wondrous of what our experience together looks like and means, as a crew we are committing to savouring all it has been as we approach our arrival. I feel this will be an ongoing process of integrating the magnificence of where we've travelled with the meaning that the arctic landscapes, waters, wildlife, people, and light have given to each of us. As it stands this foggy evening in Dark Water Tickle, Viking Voyage 1000 has become such a rich brew of experience, it is impossible to get my arms around it while still in the moment. Only time, memory, and oh, those great storytelling sessions, will help sort it out, as will the context of returning home to all that is familiar.

Evening dew beads on this intrusive glowing screen, water lapping rhythmically against the hull of *Snorri* and the snoring cacophony of the crew keep me anchored in the here and now. The skeletal remains of Native hunting and fishing camps watch from shore, harbouring their own secrets of adventures past. Each anchorage we've slipped into, each adventure we've stumbled onto, and each smelly sleeping bag will tell a story of its own.

We are at the threshold of Groswater Bay and Rigolet, the initial staging site of the Americans Leonidas Hubbard and Dillon Wallace's ill-fated expedition to the Labrador interior in 1903. Dean Plager introduced us to the recounting of this tale in Wallace's *Lure of the Labrador Wild*, an incredible account of their attempt to follow the Naskapi River (or so they thought) to its headwater at Lake Michikamau and visit the Naskapi Indians during the fall hunt of the migrating caribou herds (some here still estimated to be in the tens of thousands according to locals we talked with in Nain), before paddling the George R. north to Ungava Bay on the heels of winter. While their goal was to take home a good story, Hubbard and Wallace couldn't have bargained for a greater tale of determination and lessons learned at the hand of their Native guide.

We all agree the misfortune that eventually befell them (getting lost and slowly running out of food) was painful and tragic to the extreme. Through our reading (we've all gobbled it up and for a time daily relived episodes), endless conversations, and sharing of impressions, we further agree that eating mouldy flour, caribou bone marrow soup, and raw ptarmigan, while losing your expedition leader to starvation, is a terrible way to go. No need to worry here, Hodding proudly eats more than any of us.

This story of their travels and the awesome skill and passion of their Labradorian Scot/Cree guide George Elson have defined some of my more romantic impressions of the rugged and often harsh beauty of the Labrador interior and the people who love, live, and roamed this land earlier this century. Experiencing a modern understanding, firsthand, will have to await my next visit.

Tomorrow we are up early to head downcoast toward the Wonderstrand, a 30-mile stretch of pristine white sand beach, and onward to Battle Harbour. If we can continue our recent fortunes of NW winds and sail through the night, we may just get there.... Hope from aboard *Snorri*, where the only place you can predictably arrive each night is in your sleeping bag. Mine is a-callin'.

Theron (Terry) Moore (*born 1962, Virginia*), captain of *Snorri*, has been an environmental education instructor for the Chesapeake Bay Foundation and a sailing instructor for Outward Bound. Moore has sailed from Turkey through the Mediterranean, down the coast of Africa, and across the Atlantic to the British Virgin Islands.

John Abbott (*born 1966*) is the Outdoor Programs specialist at the University of Vermont. He was the expedition's wilderness expert. He enjoys backcountry skiing in northern Quebec and lives on a horse and llama farm in Hanksville, Vermont.

Activities: The Vikings Are Coming ... Again!

1. *Use Context:* Work with a partner to list words and phrases that are unfamiliar to you. Use context and prior knowledge to predict the meaning of these. Consult appropriate resources to verify your predictions.

2. *Compare Styles:* Create a chart to compare Moore's and Abbott's writing styles. Consider level of language, diction, sentence structure, and other aspects of the entries. Considering the audience, purpose, and medium, whose writing style do you think is more appropriate? Explain why.

3. *Represent the Route:* The *Snorri* sailed from Greenland to Newfoundland, following the route used by Eriksson and other early Vikings. Create an accurate map of this route, using labels and/or symbols to indicate noteworthy locations, including places where they stopped. Indicate on the map which locations were sites of original Viking camps. Post your map in the classroom.

4. *Brainstorm Criteria:* In a small group, brainstorm the criteria you would use to select crew members for a voyage such as that of the *Snorri*. Rank your criteria and present your top three to the class. Explain the reasoning behind your ranking.

Turned on to Sound

Beverly Biderman

An inner-ear implant was allowing me to hear after being deaf for three decades. But I couldn't make any sense of the noises. Surely my husband's conversation shouldn't be filled with the sound of whistles.

One hot summer day, after 30 years of profound deafness, I was able to hear again. My audiologist turned on a cochlear implant in my ear and my world went from quiet to a cacophony of buzzes and whistles I never knew existed. I thought I would never make sense of them.

I had been warned that voices at first would sound like those of Mickey Mouse and Donald Duck, but this was worse. My audiologist, David, anxious that "our" procedure be successful, sounded like he was blowing whistles and horns to communicate. "How does it sound?" he whistled and buzzed. "Awful," I said, and he must have seen from the look on my face that I was terribly disappointed. After a few more words, he asked plaintively, "Does it sound better now?" It didn't.

Because I had been deaf for so long, I was told to keep my expectations low and be patient. My cochlear implant, an electronic device implanted within the inner ear, wouldn't perform miracles, wouldn't restore hearing. It would simply help me perceive sounds that in time I could learn to make sense of. In spite of this preparation, I was dismayed, and overwhelmed by the loud, unfamiliar sounds that were everywhere.

When I got home from the clinic, I trudged up the stairs with heavy feet. "Listen," I said to my husband Bob, as I swayed back and forth, "there's something the matter with the implant. When I rock from side to side it whistles."

"Oh, that," he said. "Those are the floorboards creaking." I had never heard them before.

But wait, why was Bob's speech filled with whistles? Did he have an odd way of talking? Or was it me? It was only after I realized the whistles came at the end of plural nouns that I understood I was hearing the letter s. This was a sound I had no memory of.

As time passed, the weird noises began to make more sense, and I found they gave me a joyful sense of connectedness with the world. When I threw a stone into a river, I heard a satisfying plunk. I learned that plastic bags make a high-pitched sound when they are being folded (I had thought they rustled softly). I learned that carrots squealed when I chopped them. I heard the soft splashing sound of coffee grounds when they're dropped into filter paper (how could such light little things make a noise, I wondered). And I discovered that birds were singing their songs in every tree.

I remember the first time I listened with my electronic hearing to the Beatles' "She's Leaving Home." I couldn't understand the words without lyric sheets, but I could follow along and I could pick up the playful melody and Paul's sweet, sarcastic voice. I had tried hard to hear that song many years before as a teenager. I found myself weeping uncontrollably at how much I had missed in growing up deaf. I never knew how deaf I was until I became more hearing.

Still, even after a few months, I couldn't understand speech unless I saw it on people's lips. I was lip reading the way I had since I was a toddler, when my family realized that with my chin pressed against my chest and looking down, I understood nothing of what they said. Hearing carrots squeal and birds sing was all very nice, but I wanted to be able to phone Bob and tell him I'd be late for dinner. The harder I tried to understand speech without lip reading, the more frustrated I became. I couldn't go back to my quiet world now that I had tasted the sweet pleasures of hearing, but I couldn't move ahead either. I was stuck in sound.

It was only after I resigned myself to never understanding speech without lip reading that I started to improve. I began to pluck words and phrases out of the air without seeing them on people's lips. The first time I realized I could understand words without watching lips was in a store. "Have a nice day," I heard a clerk say, while I was looking down at my purse. Those words, banal perhaps, warmed my heart. I caught kindness in them, and the world became a less hostile place.

Things started to fall in place. I began to speak for myself on the phone and understand people who called me up to talk, something I hadn't been able to do since the age of 12.

It has now been four years since my cochlear implant was turned on. The horns and whistles I hear now seem like normal sounds. I cannot imagine giving up the freedom I have to call up friends and just talk.

I am still learning to hear and I still discover new sounds. Just last month, in my house, I stopped and listened: For the first time, I heard the soft patter of rain on the roof.

Beverly Biderman is an adaptive technology consultant and planning analyst in Toronto. She is the author of *Wired for Sound: A Journey into Hearing*, which was named a *Globe and Mail* Notable Book and an American Library Association Outstanding Title.

Activities: Turned on to Sound

1. **Explain Ideas:** When she began to understand speech without lip reading, Biderman found the world "a less hostile place." Explain why she might have found the world to be hostile before her implant.

2. **Evaluate Technique:** Reread the opening paragraph and decide whether you think it is an effective lead. If you think it is effective, explain why. If you don't think it is effective, write a lead that is more effective. Share your ideas in a small group.

3. **Write Descriptions:** Biderman creates effective descriptions of sounds that are new to her. Choose five sounds, recreate them, and then describe each one as if you were hearing it for the first time. Share your descriptions with a partner.

4. **Create a Brochure:** Research an organization that helps people with a specific disability. Create a brochure outlining the goals, services, and activities of the organization. Decide how you can use text, visuals, and typography to capture attention, organize information, and create visual interest.

Poetry

How beautifully useless / how deliciously
defiant / a poem is!

—Raymond Souster

I throw out the poem like a net and pull things together
with thin threads of language that need mending, that
need new patterns to catch the light.

—Lorna Crozier

Poetry is both ancient and modern. Ancient, because some of the earliest writings discovered are poetry; modern, because new styles and forms are constantly emerging. Poetry is very flexible: it can be used to tell stories, inspire others, convey ideas, protest injustice, or reflect on experiences. Poets choose the forms and techniques that suit them and their purpose.

Just as poets have individual preferences for specific forms, so you, as a reader, will be drawn to some poems more than others. This unit gives you an opportunity to explore poems written in a variety of forms, periods, and cultures and to decide which appeal to you. Some poems you will respond to immediately; others may grow in appeal as you spend time with them.

If you are one of those who is intimidated by the very notion of "poetry," the introductory essay on "How to Read a Poem" may help you overcome your fears and encourage you to be open to what the poets in this collection have to share with you.

How to Read a Poem
Edward Hirsch

Read a poem to yourself in the middle of the night. Turn on a lamp and read it while you're alone or while someone sleeps next to you. Read it when you're wide awake in the early morning, fully alert. Say it over to yourself in a place where silence reigns and the din of the culture—the constant buzzing noise that surrounds us—has momentarily stopped. This poem has come from a great distance to find you.

The great poets Osip Mandelstam and Paul Celan compared the experience of reading a poem to finding a message in a bottle. Imagine that you have gone down to the shore and there, amidst the debris—the seaweed and rotten wood, the crushed cans and dead fish—you find an unlikely looking bottle from the past. You bring it home and discover a special kind of communiqué. It speaks out of a solitude to a solitude; it begins and ends in silence. Now you must decipher it; what is it saying?

A certain kind of poem teaches you how to read it. Poems communicate before they are understood, so don't be anxious if you feel as if you don't understand everything right away. Let the poem work in you as a human experience. Listen to the words and pay attention to the feelings they evoke.

Here is a poem that I have returned to again and again because I have found it instructive and emblematic. It combines deep feeling with a powerful organizing structure.

One Art

Elizabeth Bishop

The art of losing isn't hard to master;
so many things seem filled with the intent
to be lost that their loss is no disaster.

Lose something every day. Accept the fluster
of lost door keys, the hour badly spent.
The art of losing isn't hard to master.

Then practice losing farther, losing faster:
places, and names, and where it was you meant
to travel. None of these will bring disaster.

I lost my mother's watch. And look! my last, or
next-to-last, of three loved houses went.
The art of losing isn't hard to master.

I lost two cities, lovely ones. And, vaster,
some realms I owned, two rivers, a continent.
I miss them, but it wasn't a disaster.

—Even losing you (the joking voice, a gesture
I love) I shan't have lied. It's evident
the art of losing's not too hard to master
though it may look like (*Write it!*) like disaster.

"One Art" is a villanelle, a French form whose structure is rooted in Italian folk song; it came into American poetry late in the 19th century. Bishop's poem sounds natural and is deceptively informal, given its formal structure: 19 lines divided into 6 stanzas, turning on two rhymes and built around two refrains. The first and third lines rhyme throughout, as do the middle lines of each stanza. Bishop modifies the traditional form, since the first refrain—"The art of losing isn't hard to master"—repeats exactly throughout the poem, whereas the second refrain modulates around the word *disaster*. As it turns and returns, Bishop's verse becomes a model of stability and change, repetition and variation, circularity and progressive movement forward.

Do you have to know it's a villanelle to appreciate "One Art" as poetry? No. But knowing what kind of poetic animal you're dealing with can give you a clue about how to read it.

"One Art" is a poem about loss; Bishop starts small and continually enlarges the losses she experiences, beginning with inconsequential things—the door keys, the wasted hour—and moving up from there. But even as the speaker acknowledges that the losses are cutting deeper and deeper, she insists that they aren't disastrous. Loss itself is the emotional truth in this poem, which intellect, through its various gyrations, struggles in vain to escape and deny.

In its final stanza, in an extraordinary turn, the villanelle becomes a love poem. By the poem's structural logic, the loss of the beloved must necessarily be the greatest loss of all. The conclusion is the first acknowledgment that this final loss actually feels like, looks like, a disaster.

By forcing herself to write it down—"(*Write it!*)"—the author forces herself to face her loss. The activity of writing mirrors the psychological process of recognition, and the process of recognition becomes the emotional discovery of this poem. The reader overhears what the poet is making herself acknowledge. Rather than the villanelle's being a container into which a poet pours previously worked out thoughts and feelings, the form itself becomes a way for the writer to unearth those feelings.

Poems can be accessible in different ways. Some may carry meaning that seems readily apparent at first but that deepens the more you attend to them. But even poems that seem initially resistant, even inscrutable, will reveal their secrets after study and reflection.

I say that one should turn on a lamp and read a poem in the middle of the night because poetry is a solitary, intimate, and passionately private communication from a soul to another soul. Remember that poems demand an attentiveness to language and values that requires concentration. But if you invest something of yourself in the daily reading of poetry, you will find this simple act rewarding, even necessary.

Ralph Waldo Emerson once said that poetry is "what will and must be spoken." It is a secret that can no longer be kept secret, a way of knowing. Whenever a poem enacts what it is about, it creates a way for itself to live dramatically inside the reader. The great poem is the message salvaged from a wreck and sealed in the bottle. Take the time to go down to the dunes and search for that bottle. When you find it, bring it home, because it is now yours. This haunted and haunting message was meant for you.

Edward Hirsch (*born 1950, Chicago*), poet, is the author of five books of poetry. He has won numerous awards for his work, including the National Book Critics Circle Award and the Lila Wallace–Reader's Digest Writer's Award. He teaches at the University of Houston.

Exploring Poetry

Identify the Message: The author has several pieces of advice embedded within this article. By referring specifically to the text, identify *three* of these. Overall, what is the author's message?

Examine Structure: What is the traditional structure of a villanelle? How did Bishop modify it? What does Hirsch think of Bishop's changing the traditional structure? Do you believe it is acceptable for poets to modify and manipulate traditional poetic structures? Explain your perspective.

Read a Poem: Select a poem and read it, following Hirsch's suggestions: Listen to the words and pay attention to the feeling they evoke. Identify the vocabulary and images that are powerful. Describe the feelings this poem evokes. Write a journal entry on how this poem speaks to you personally.

Winter Uplands

Archibald Lampman

The Magpie,
Claude Monet, 1869

The frost that stings like fire upon my cheek,
The loneliness of this forsaken ground,
The long white drift upon whose powdered peak
I sit in the great silence as one bound;
The rippled sheet of snow where the wind blew
Across the open fields for miles ahead;
The far-off city towered and roofed in blue
A tender line upon the western red;
The stars that singly, then in flocks appear,
Like jets of silver from the violet dome,
So wonderful, so many and so near,
And then the golden moon to light me home—
The crunching snowshoes and the stinging air,
And silence, frost, and beauty everywhere.

Archibald Lampman (*born 1861, Morpeth, Ontario; died 1899*), poet and member of the Royal Society of Canada, was a graduate of the University of Toronto. His poetry, influenced by the English Romantics and celebrating the beauty of the Canadian landscape, is considered the finest of 19th-century Canada.

Confessions of a Woman Who Burnt Down a Town

Afua Cooper

In June 1734, Marie Joseph Angelique, a Black slave woman, was hanged in Montreal for burning down much of that town in April 1734. Her last days provide the inspiration for this poem.

I buried the twins that evening
they died of smallpox
were only 8 months old
Madame came too to the funeral
and said to me by way of consolation
"c'est la vie,
I too have lost my own."
I went back to work
went back to work in Madame's house
that same evening and at supper she yelled at me
and box me full in the face because
I overturned the gravy bowl in her lap

I remember my journey from my island to this island
From Rhode Island to Montreal
Lived in Rhode Island all my life 'till
Monsieur came from Montreal on one of his business trips
he bought me because he said I looked like a healthy wench.
Monsieur died soon after and Madame never forgave me
but I had nothing to do with it, he died of consumption

The twins died too.
After we buried them that evening
my heart changed position in my chest
and I was seized with one desire and one desire only
and that was to leave the prison of this island
But where could I go
because throughout the whole world
in all the continents people who look like me

were bound
But still, all I could see was
my feet running, no chains, no rope, no shackles
free

Madame talking to her best friend
and confessor Father Labadie
"I'm going to sell that negress, she's getting too much
for me, she's getting too uppity
And furthermore since François died I just can't seem to manage
    too well,
perhaps the church is interested?"
I bring in the food and pretend like ah neva hear
and I serve the food good and proper
was on my best behaviour
roll back mi lip and skin mi teeth
roll back my yai and show the white
den I went back to mi room in the cellar
and mek mi plan

Smoke, smoke, too much smoke
only intend fi one house fi burn
fire, fire, too much fire
but it done go so already
and I running
my feet unshackled, unbound,
free
running pass di city limits
while behind me di fire rage
and my raging heart change back into its rightful position

He was running too
an apprentice, from France
I gave him all my food to take me or show me
the way to New England but he tek the food
and leave me while I was sleeping
an the constables caught me

I don't utter a word as I sit here in the jailhouse
Father Labadie come to confess me

but I refuse
their god is not my god
"Arson is one of the worst crime in New France Marie,"
he say to me, "confess now and save your soul."
But I don't hear him
outside, the mob want to rip me from limb to limb
but I not afraid, a strange calm fill my body
and I at peace, peace, perfect peace

Guilty, the judge pronounce
and the sentence: to be tortured, my hands cut off
my body burned and the ashes scattered
to the four corners of the earth
I break down, my body crumple in a heap
and before my eyes I see the twins
and they look so alive as if they waiting
for me to come nurse them
The sentence is reduced
Now I am to be hanged only and my body burned
Father Labadie come back for di confession
And I confess
is I Marie who set the fire
I say yes
I start it in Madame's house by the river
50 building destroy
the hospital, the cathedral
I confess
is I Marie who burn this city
so write that down Father Labadie
write down my story so it can be known in history
with my heart burning I take the sacrament
and accept the final rites
outside the guard is waiting
to take me to the hangman's noose
Soon I will be free from the prison of this island
and I will fly and fly and fly

Afua Cooper (*born 1958, Jamaica*), poet, writer, has published three collections of poetry and has also written short stories. Co-author of *Essays in African-Canadian Women's History*, Cooper is working on her doctorate in history.

Activities, p. 251

Newfoundland Sealing Disaster

Michael Crummey

Sent to the ice after white coats,
rough outfit slung on coiled rope belts,
they stooped to the slaughter: gaffed pups,
slit them free of their spotless pelts.

The storm came on unexpected.
Stripped clean of bearings, the watch struck
for the waiting ship and missed it.
Hovelled in darkness two nights then,

bent blindly to the sleet's raw work,
bodies muffled close for shelter,
stepping in circles like blinkered mules.
The wind jerking like a halter.

Minds turned by the cold, lured by small
comforts their stubborn hearts rehearsed,
men walked off ice floes to the arms
of phantom children, wives; of fires

laid in imaginary hearths.
Some surrendered movement and fell,
moulting warmth flensed from their faces
as the night and bitter wind doled out

their final, pitiful wages.

Michael Crummey (*born Buchans, Newfoundland*), poet, short-story writer, grew up in Newfoundland and Labrador. He studied at Memorial University in St. John's and at Queen's in Kingston, and has held a variety of jobs. In 1994, he won the Bronwen Wallace Award for Poetry.

Activities, p. 251

The Hoop

Elizabeth Brewster

To have grown up the youngest child
of middle-aged parents
meant always to be aware of the past,
to touch their childhoods
like inherited china figurines:

Father at three years old
chased by a turkey gobbler
twice his size

Mother, dressed in her Sunday best,
at a Baptist prayer meeting,
or visiting (against her mother's orders)
old Mary Ellen, the witch
who smoked a pipe
and told fortunes in the tea leaves
if you crossed her palm;
even my brothers and sisters,
remembering all those Christmases
before I was born,
the box of soldiers and the glass fire engine,
and Christmas trees with wax candles,
and lantern slides of someone's trip to Palestine.

Oh, it was past, not present,
that was most real to all of them.
And I, even when I liked the Now
(the iridescent lights
in soap bubbles
or the pink tongue of the kitten
rasping like warm sandpaper
against my fingers)
wanted time to move back, not forward.

Cheated, I always felt cheated
that I never saw Mother sitting
on her long sable hair
before it was ever cut,
before it was fanned with white;

or saw Grandfather the day
he came back from prospecting,
tossing gold nuggets
carelessly
on the kitchen table,
pretending he had lots more of them.

And I wanted to go back in time
further and further
to my Great-Grandfather Solomon
who played the fiddle at dances
and his twin brother David
who left and made his fortune
down in the States,
and the two young girls
they married on New Year's Day
back in 1852.

I wanted to see the river
before anybody had cut the trees

and before that the refugees
coming up from New England
and emigrants crossing the ocean—
I wanted to know what their journeys were like
and where the blue plate came from
I still bring out
sometimes for company

and back to Lincolnshire
the fens
and the hilly cathedral city
and long, long ago
maybe marauding Vikings
with blue eyes like my father's
or homesick Roman soldiers
camping in Britain

and time unreeling and unreeling
to ancient caves and pyramids
the Golden Age or Eden
primeval chaos
exploding lights
like the lights that will explode (maybe)
at the end of time

when Alpha and Omega meet
and time begins again
circular as the child's hoop
my father played with
made for him by his father.

Elizabeth Brewster (*born 1922, Chipman, New Brunswick*), librarian, poet, professor, has published 16 books, most of them poetry collections, and has received several awards and honours for her work. Her poetry has been described as understated but "valuable for its documentary accuracy as well as its elegance and grace."

Activities, p. 252

*L*ament for the Dorsets

Al Purdy

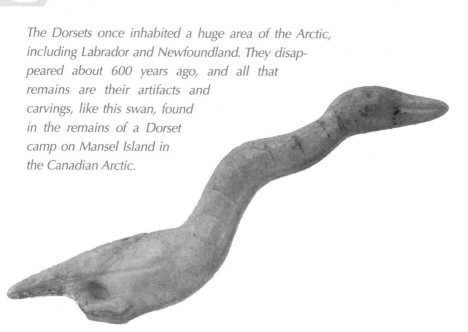

The Dorsets once inhabited a huge area of the Arctic, including Labrador and Newfoundland. They disappeared about 600 years ago, and all that remains are their artifacts and carvings, like this swan, found in the remains of a Dorset camp on Mansel Island in the Canadian Arctic.

Animal bones and some mossy tent rings
scrapers and spearheads   carved ivory swans
all that remains of the Dorset giants
who drove the Vikings back to their long ships
talked to spirits of earth and water
—a picture of terrifying old men
so large they broke the backs of bears
so small they lurk behind bone rafters
in the brain of modern hunters
among good thoughts and warm things
and come out at night
to spit on the stars

The big men with clever fingers
who had no dogs and hauled their sleds
over the frozen northern oceans
awkward giants
                    killers of seal
they couldn't compete with little men
who came from the west with dogs
Or else in a warm climatic cycle
the seals went back to cold waters
and the puzzled Dorsets scratched their heads
with hair thumbs around 1350 A.D.
—couldn't figure it out
went around saying to each other
plaintively
                "What's wrong? What happened?
                Where are the seals gone?"
And died

Twentieth-century people
apartment dwellers
executives of neon death
warmakers with things that explode
—they have never imagined us in their future
how could we imagine them in the past
squatting among the moving glaciers
six hundred years ago
with glowing lamps?
As remote or nearly
as the trilobites and swamps
when coal became
or the last great reptile hissed
at a mammal the size of a mouse
that squeaked and fled

Did they ever realize at all
what was happening to them?
Some old hunter with one lame leg
a bear had chewed
sitting in a caribou-skin tent
—the last Dorset?
Let's say his name was Kudluk
and watch him sitting there
carving 2-inch ivory swans
for a dead grand-daughter
taking them out of his mind
the places in his mind
where pictures are
He selects a sharp stone tool
to gouge a parallel pattern of lines
on both sides of the swan
holding it with his left hand
bearing down and transmitting
his body's weight
from brain to arm and right hand
and one of his thoughts
turns to ivory
The carving is laid aside
in beginning darkness
at the end of hunger
and after a while wind
blows down the tent and snow
begins to cover him

After 600 years
the ivory thought
is still warm

Al Purdy (*born 1918, Wooler, Ontario; died 2000*), poet, travel writer, editor, "rode the rods" to Vancouver during the Depression, and then served in the Royal Canadian Air Force in World War II. He received the Governor General's Literary Award in 1965 for *The Cariboo Horses.*

For My Great-Grandmother

Danielle Lagah

Old Mahnji Chinti, always seemly
your tattoos
were a childhood riddle
Deep blue ink absorbed
by your tissue skin, the pictures
long ago feathered with age
The first time I saw them
I was eight, kneeling on the kitchen stool
elbows on the gold-flecked melamine
of your sink counter. You pushed
up the white sleeves of your cardigan
and I glimpsed the strange dye
before your arms were plunged
into dish soap bubbles. For years after
I waited for you to push up your sleeves

At eleven I had a vision
you as a girl
standing in an Indian temple
held down by priests
who drew symbols of your new womanhood
with cobalt needles and chanted
in Hindi, your
eyes squeezed tight and tears
greyed by *surma* staining
your gold-thread sari

When I was sixteen
I watched at Pargan's *bhangra*
while you danced
bare arms over your head
the blue ink peeking out
from between bouncing bangles
in the dance floor light
hands twisting like swan heads

Two years later
I had enough courage
a grown woman, finally
to ask
while you lay in the hospital
healing from a broken rib
I touched them
your blue tattoos
and I asked

I was a young woman, you said
and every dry season in Jasomajara
the carnival would come
I went with my best girls and we all
got tattoos

the man that did mine was handsome
and I giggled so my arms shook
while he worked
I was always punished after—
my mother would smack my face
But every dry season
I would go again
and get another

You smiled an unseemly smile
and ran your skinny finger over
each cerulean story

This is a flower
This is a peacock
This is my name

Danielle Lagah (*born 1977, Victoria, British Columbia*), student, writer, was studying at Malaspina College, Nanaimo, British Columbia, majoring in Creative Writing, when she wrote this poem. At that time she was living with her parents on 200 acres in Nanoose Bay.

Activities, p. 253

Did I Miss Anything?

Tom Wayman

*Question frequently asked by
students after missing a class*

Nothing. When we realized you weren't here
we sat with our hands folded on our desks
in silence, for the full two hours

Everything. I gave an exam worth
40 per cent of the grade for this term
and assigned some reading due today
on which I'm about to hand out a quiz
worth 50 per cent.

Nothing. None of the content of this course
has value or meaning
Take as many days off as you like:
any activities we undertake as a class
I assure you will not matter either to you or me
and are without purpose

    Everything. A few minutes after we began last time
    a shaft of light descended and an angel
    or other heavenly being appeared
    and revealed to us what each woman or man must do
    to attain divine wisdom in this life and
    the hereafter
    This is the last time the class will meet
    before we disperse to bring this good news to all people
        on earth

Nothing. When you are not present
how could something significant occur?

    Everything. Contained in this classroom
    is a microcosm of human existence
    assembled for you to query and examine and ponder
    This is not the only place such an opportunity has been
        gathered

but it was one place

And you weren't here

Tom Wayman (*born 1945, Hawkesbury, Ontario*), poet, teacher, moved to British Columbia when he was seven. He has worked in the United States and Canada at a variety of jobs and has been writer-in-residence at universities across Canada. He is the author of 13 volumes of poetry including *Did I Miss Anything?* and *The Astonishing Weight of the Dead*.

Activities, p. 253   *Did I Miss Anything?*

The Old Man's Lazy

Peter Blue Cloud

The old man's lazy,
I heard the Indian Agent say,
has no pride, no get up
and go. Well, he came out
here and walked around my
place, that agent. Steps
all thru the milkweed and
curing wormwood; tells me
my place is overgrown
and should be made use
of.
    The old split cedar
fence stands at many
angles, and much of it
lies on the ground like
a curving sentence of
stick writing. An old
language, too, black with
age, with different
shades of green of moss
and lichen.
        He always
says he understands us
Indians,
          and why don't
I fix the fence at least:
so I took some fine
hawk feathers fixed
to a miniature woven
shield
        and hung this
from an upright post
near the house.

        He
came by last week
and looked all around
again, eyed the feathers
for a long time.
        He didn't
say anything, and he didn't
smile even, or look within
himself for the hawk.

    Maybe sometime I'll
tell him that the fence
isn't mine to begin with,
but was put up by
the white guy who used
to live next door.
        It was
years ago. He built a cabin,
then put up the fence. He
only looked at me once,
after his fence was up,
he nodded at me as if
to show that he knew I
was here, I guess.
        It was
a pretty fence, enclosing
that guy, and I felt lucky
to be on the outside
of it.
    Well, that guy
dug holes all over his
place, looking for gold
and I guess
        he never
found any. I watched
him grow old for over
twenty years, and bitter,
I could feel his anger
all over the place.

          And
that's when I took to
leaving my place to do
a lot of visiting.
          Then
one time I came home
and knew he was gone
for good.
          My children would
always ask me why I
didn't move to town
and be closer to them.
          Now, they
tell me I'm lucky to be
living way out here.
          And
they bring their children
and come out and visit me,
and I can feel that they
want to live out here
too, but can't
for some reason, do it.

          Each day
a different story is
told me by the fence:
the rain and wind and snow;
the sun and moon shadows,
this wonderful earth,
          this Creation.
I tell my grandchildren
many of these stories,
          perhaps
this too is one of them.

Peter Blue Cloud (**Aroniawenrate**) *(born 1935, Kahnawake, Quebec)*, poet, carpenter, woodcarver, drum maker, editor, and author of short stories, has also written under the alias of Coyote 2. He is considered one of the Elders of Aboriginal poetry.

Activities, p. 253

Another Story Altogether

Anne Le Dressay

Not my story, but the other one
that was there all along, tangled with mine
and utterly separate, breathing at night
in the bed across the room, while I lived
my own story. My own. Small, centred,
mine, that talked my words and saw
through my eyes.

This other story sees it through her eyes,
and they are 3 years younger and a different
colour. It's not the same family and not the same
traumas. The family is 3 years older when she
starts remembering, and there are more people in it.

Two stories, two worlds barely touching,
the light hitting the same things at such
different angles they are not the same things
at all. To her, I am part of the world outside of
her, in which she must find or make a place.
To me, she is outside.

You'd think it would be the same house at least,
the same bedroom. But she was afraid of the dark
and I wasn't. We had a fair and equal arrangement:
one night, the door closed tightly for me, the next
night, left open a crack for her.

Only now does it occur to me to wonder
if, every second night when the door was closed
to spare me the small distraction of that
shaft of light, she lay awake, facing alone
the terrors of the dark,
while I slept.

Anne Le Dressay (*born Manitoba*), poet and teacher of English and Creative Writing, lives in Edmonton, Alberta. Educated at the universities of Winnipeg, Carleton, and Ottawa, she has published works including *This Body That I Live In* and, in 1997, *Sleep Is a Country*.

Activities, p. 254

Common Magic

Bronwen Wallace

Your best friend falls in love
and her brain turns to water.
You can watch her lips move,
making the customary sounds,
but you can see they're merely
words, flimsy as bubbles rising
from some golden sea where she
swims sleek and exotic as a mermaid.

It's always like that.
You stop for lunch in a crowded
restaurant and the waitress floats
toward you. You can tell she doesn't care
whether you have the baked or the french-fried
and you wonder if your voice comes
in bubbles too.

It's not just women either. Or love
for that matter. The old man
across from you on the bus holds
a young child on his knee; he is singing
to her and his voice is a small boy
turning somersaults in the green
country of his blood.
It's only when the driver calls his stop
that he emerges into this puzzle
of brick and tiny hedges. Only then
you notice his shaking hands, his need
of the child to guide him home.

All over the city
you move in your own seasons
through the seasons of others: old women, faces

clawed by weather you can't feel
clack dry tongues at passersby
while adolescents seethe
in their glassy atmospheres of anger.

In parks, the children
are alien life-forms, rooted
in the galaxies they've grown through
to get here. Their games weave
the interface and their laughter
tickles that part of your brain where smells
are hidden and the nuzzling textures of things.

It's a wonder that anything gets done
at all: a mechanic flails
at the muffler of your car
through whatever storm he's trapped inside
and the mailman stares at numbers
from the haze of a distant summer.

Yet somehow letters arrive and buses
remember their routes. Banks balance.
Mangoes ripen on the supermarket shelves.
Everyone manages. You gulp the thin air
of this planet as if it were the only
one you knew. Even the earth you're
standing on seems solid enough.
It's always the chance word, unthinking
gesture that unlocks the face before you.
Reveals the intricate countries
deep within the eyes. The hidden
lives, like sudden miracles,
that breathe there.

Bronwen Wallace (*born 1945, Kingston, Ontario; died 1989*), poet, essayist, political activist, wrote several award-winning volumes of poetry. Her poetry was influenced by Al Purdy and reflects the magic and love she found in everyday things. Among her collections are *The Stubborn Particulars of Grace* and *Common Magic*.

Activities, p. 254

Roller Coaster

My father laughed and it was
the first and only time so far
I've heard him do it; a real
laugh deep from inside
climbing like an artillery shell
up his throat and pushing out of
his Edvard Munch mouth.
We were commuters aimed at heaven,
riding a steep, open train toward
the sun-god at the end
of the line, padded straps
reefing our shoulders against
plastic seats. This was
the last place I wanted to be,
locked in like an astronaut,
someone else driving,
lunch rising in my chest.
My eyes were open to
the whine of pulleys as we
ascended a slope snow wouldn't

hold to if snow fell through the
ridiculous summer air. There was
a moment as we reached
the first peak and crested
when I smiled too at weightlessness,
the feeling as you float
from a swell in a fast highway until
most of me dropped. I felt
my stomach's desire
to stay behind up there where it could see
halfway to Saskatchewan and
to bail out again at
the bottom as we were
caught like eggs by a
giant hand and sent up again
over a short rise only to
plunge face-first at the ground
continuing as we rolled
through a giant loop, swooped
with the energy of descent and
twisted through a series
of corkscrew turns, our
brains in startled mobius,
my father wide with giddy terror.
Somewhere along the way he
reached over and squeezed my hand
and our astounded spirits
or some other part of us
that it seemed we could do without
for a while raced behind
like afterimages as we rolled on
through the inverted morning,
clutching each other,
wearing death-masks of happiness.

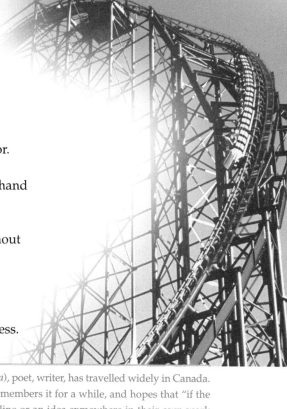

Jay Ruzesky (*born 1965, Edmonton, Alberta*), poet, writer, has travelled widely in Canada.
He considers a poem good if a reader remembers it for a while, and hopes that "if the
reader is also a writer they may echo a line or an idea somewhere in their own work
so that some essence of the poem gets passed along like a baton in a relay."

Activities, p. 255

A Kite Is a Victim

Leonard Cohen

A kite is a victim you are sure of.
You love it because it pulls
gentle enough to call you master,
strong enough to call you fool;
because it lives
like a desperate trained falcon
in the high sweet air,
and you can always haul it down
to tame it in your drawer.

A kite is a fish you have already caught
in a pool where no fish come,
so you play him carefully and long,
and hope he won't give up,
or the wind die down.

A kite is the last poem you've written
so you give it to the wind,
but you don't let it go
until someone finds you
something else to do.

A kite is a contract of glory
that must be made with the sun,
so you make friends with the field
the river and the wind,
then you pray the whole cold night before,
under the travelling cordless moon,
to make you worthy and lyric and pure.

Leonard Cohen (*born 1934, Montreal, Quebec*), poet, novelist, songwriter, was extremely popular and influential in the 1960s and went on to establish an international reputation. He declined a Governor General's Award in 1968. In 1993, he was awarded a Governor General's Performing Arts Award.

Activities, p. 255

Activities: Winter Uplands

1. **Study Form:** Working with a partner, analyze the structure of the sonnet "Winter Uplands." Then compare and contrast the structure with another sonnet. In a short note, outline the essential and optional characteristics of the sonnet form.

2. **Identify Sensory Appeal:** Identify references to sight, sound, and sensation in the poem. In a personal response, examine the extent to which Lampman's experience of winter matches your own, and note any sensory elements that you feel are absent in "Winter Uplands."

3. **Adapt the Poem:** Using either prose or poetry, rewrite Lampman's positive emotional response to the winter scene, changing the reaction to a negative one. Share your rewrite in a group, and provide constructive criticism on each other's versions.

4. **Create a Poster:** Find a poem, Canadian if possible, for each of the four seasons and create a poster displaying the poems and illustrations appropriate to each. Use colour, text, images, space, texture, captions, and so forth to enhance the poster's impact. Display the poster in the classroom.

Activities: Confessions of a Woman Who Burnt Down a Town

1. **Consider Purpose:** What do you think was Cooper's purpose in writing this poem? Is her choice of the first-person perspective related to her purpose? From your point of view, does Cooper achieve this purpose? Record your opinions, supporting them with evidence from the text.

2. **Write in Character:** Why does Marie want her story to be "known in history"? Take on the role of Marie and write a journal entry explaining why you want your story to be known and what effect you hope it will have.

3. **Prepare an Oral Reading:** Work in a group of four to divide the poem into four sections. Each group member should prepare and deliver a dramatic reading of one section. After the reading, comment on how you tried to make your delivery effective.

4. **Make a Storyboard:** Adapt the poem into a storyboard with eight frames. Provide a caption for each frame, using either words from the poem or your own words. Compare your storyboard with a partner's and discuss the differences.

Activities: Newfoundland Sealing Disaster

1. **Research Context:** Use the Internet or print resources to research the Newfoundland Sealing Disaster. How effectively does this poem convey the tragedy of the event? Write your opinion, using references to both the poem and your research.

2. **Consider Diction:** Research the meaning of the following words: *hovelled, muffled, blinkered, flensed, doled.* For each word, write a sentence that clearly and concisely explains how the word helps to evoke the men's situation and condition.

3. **Examine Irony:** With a partner, find definitions of different types of irony. Discuss how the situation in the poem could be considered ironic. Classify the type of irony. Make a point-form list of your discussion ideas.

4. **Use Various Sources:** Use the Internet and materials from support and protest groups to research the present-day Newfoundland seal hunt. Define your personal stand on the issue and communicate it in a persuasive text, such as a poster, TV or radio ad, T-shirt, or other form.

Activities: The Hoop

1. **Discuss Questions:** Write three questions you have about specific passages or the poem as a whole. Meet with a small group to discuss the questions. After the discussion, write a note in your journal about whether or not you find this strategy useful, and give reasons for your opinion.

2. **Explain the Title:** Why do you think Brewster chose the title she did? What significance does the hoop have in the poem? Support your explanations with specific references to the text.

3. **Examine Chronology:** Using clues from the poem and your own inferences, create a time line for the events mentioned. Compare your time line with a partner's and explain to each other the inferences you made.

4. **Design Layout:** Imagine you are an editor and you have four pages for an illustrated version of this poem. Create a layout and sketches of your proposed illustrations. Explain your design decisions to the class.

Activities: Lament for the Dorsets

1. **Discover Links:** List the concrete objects that remain as reminders of the Dorsets. Then, in a few sentences, describe (a) the intangible links that connect the Dorsets with modern day people, and (b) the factors that make the two groups mutually incomprehensible.

2. **Respond to Symbols:** In a small group discuss the ways in which the poet uses the ivory swan as a symbol. In a short written response, evaluate the symbol's effectiveness as a bridge between the poet's mind and your own.

3. **Conduct Research:** Use a variety of sources to find out more about the Dorsets. Present your most interesting findings in an illustrated fact sheet, and display it in the classroom.

4. **Represent an Era:** Select an object that you think accurately represents our society. Imagine that you are an archaeologist in the 27th century and write a report of the discovery of the artifact and your interpretation of its significance. Present the object and the report to the class.

Activities: For My Great-Grandmother

1. *Use Context:* Use context clues to predict the meaning of the following words: *surma, bhangra, cobalt, cerulean.* Check your predictions. What resources could you use for the non-English words?
2. *Consider Theme:* In what ways is this a poem about identity? How are we presented with a changing picture of both characters' identities? Discuss in a small group, and write a statement about the role of identity in the poem.
3. *Determine Significance:* In a small group, decide on the meaning and significance of the following:
   - "your tattoos / were a childhood riddle"
   - "You smiled an unseemly smile"
   - "This is my name"
4. *Write about Identity:* Many teens are preoccupied with issues of identity and experiment with different identities. Why do you think this is so? Should it be discouraged? Should there be limits? Write an opinion piece on this topic.

Activities: Did I Miss Anything?

1. *Identify Emotions:* Working with a partner, for each of the speaker's responses, identify the dominant emotion and support your opinion with reference to the text. Use a specific noun to denote the emotion: regret, resignation, and so on. Share and compare your ideas with another pair.
2. *Infer Attitude:* Which of the responses do you think reflects the speaker's real opinion? Why? Characterize the attitude shown in the other responses using a specific noun to identify the emotion (e.g., humour, regret).
3. *Prepare an Oral Reading:* Read the poem aloud to a small group. Use inflection, tone, volume, and facial expression to convey meaning. Comment on differences in interpretation and technique, and what was most effective.
4. *Write a Poem:* Using this poem as a model, write a poem in which you reveal various responses to a question such as one of the following: Did I keep you waiting long? Why did you miss my class? Do you like my new haircut?

Activities: The Old Man's Lazy

1. *Examine Conflict:* With which individuals does the old man find himself at odds? Write a paragraph that explains how each individual does not share the old man's view of things.
2. *Discuss Symbols:* In what ways can the fence be considered a symbol? Work with a partner to create a web to organize your ideas and supporting details.

3. **Write a Monologue:** The Indian Agent claims to understand the Native people. What evidence is there in the poem to suggest that this is not the case? Write a dramatic monologue in which the Indian Agent reveals his lack of understanding.

4. **Conduct Research:** Research and write a brief oral report about a situation in which Native Canadians fought for their rights. Organize your information effectively, and ask for feedback after your presentation.

Activities: Another Story Altogether

1. **Understand Implication:** In a small group, discuss why the poet might choose to refer to her sister as "this other story." Write a personal evaluation of the poem indicating whether her choice of words is derogatory, and then speculate about how you would react to being referred to in this way.

2. **Evaluate Opinions:** With specific references to the poem, write a short analysis of the irony contained in the phrase "fair and equal arrangement." Compare your perceptions with a partner's.

3. **Assemble Evidence:** List all the factors that would lead to differences in perception between "my story" and "the other one." In a small group, share your lists and exchange anecdotes about personal experiences arising from similar situations.

4. **Write Parallel Accounts:** Write two accounts of a family event, real or imaginary, from the point of view of siblings several years apart in age. Share the accounts in a small group and note any areas of similarity or difference.

Activities: Common Magic

1. **Evaluate the Title:** With a partner, brainstorm four alternate titles for the poem. Decide whether any of your ideas makes for a better title than the original. Present to the class your choice for "best title" and the reasons for your choice.

2. **Explore Diction:** Select two stanzas and closely examine them for examples of interesting and effective diction. In an informal piece of writing, show how the words complement each other and develop the ideas in the stanza. Work with a partner to comment on and develop each other's ideas.

3. **Relate to Experience:** In a small group, list the ways the poet shows "magic" entering everyday life. Add to the list at least five more situations in which "common magic" is present. Post the list in the classroom.

4. **Adopt a Voice:** Select one of the people mentioned in the poem and assume his or her identity. Write about what you are thinking as the poet observes you. Try to convey the sense of "magic" in the mundane world.

Activities: Roller Coaster

1. **Explore Contrast:** Make a list of images the author uses to convey the conflicting feelings of the poem's narrator, then decide which of these images is the most effective. Be prepared to explain your choice to the class.
2. **Research Allusions:** Locate pictures and information to explain the allusions to "Edvard Munch," "the sun-god," and a "mobius." Explain how the visual images suggested by the allusions reinforce the mood the author creates.
3. **Analyze Style:** Identify and explain four examples of effective stylistic elements in the poem, such as line breaks, sentence length, imagery, and diction.
4. **Write a Poem:** Write a poem about an experience in which you felt conflicting emotions, such as dread and joy, or solemnity and humour. Create descriptions that are as vivid as Ruzesky's. Ask a partner for constructive feedback.

Activities: A Kite Is a Victim

1. **Write a Response:** In your journal, write a personal response to the poem. Comment on each stanza in a brief paragraph, noting specific words and images you find particularly striking.
2. **Discuss Metaphor:** In a small group, discuss the metaphor in the first line of each stanza and note how Cohen develops each metaphor. Is this poem really about a kite or is it about something else? List and share your group's ideas.
3. **Research Poets:** Find and read poems by three other Governor General's Award-winning poets. Choose a favourite short poem and prepare an oral reading of it for the class. Experiment with vocal techniques to create an effective reading.
4. **Create a Mime:** In a group of four, take turns creating a pantomime for each stanza. Have one person read the stanza while another acts it out. Present your mime to the class.

The River-Merchant's Wife: A Letter

Li Po

I would play, plucking flowers by the gate;
My hair scarcely covered my forehead, then.
You would come, riding on your bamboo horse,
And loiter about the bench with green plums for toys.
So we both dwelt in Chang-kan town,
We were two children, suspecting nothing.

At fourteen I became your wife,
And so bashful that I could never bare my face,
But hung my head, and turned to the dark wall;
You would call me a thousand times,
But I could not look back even once.

At fifteen I was able to compose my eyebrows,
And beg you to love me till we were dust and ashes.
You always kept the faith of Wei-sheng,
Who waited under the bridge, unafraid of death,
I never knew I was to climb the Hill of Wang-fu
And watch for you these many days.

I was sixteen when you went on a long journey,
Travelling beyond the Keu-Tang Gorge,
Where the giant rocks heap up the swift river,
And the rapids are not passable in May.
Did you hear the monkeys wailing
Up on the skyey height of the crags?
Do you know your foot-marks by our gate are old,
And each and every one is filled up with green moss?

The mosses are too deep for me to sweep away;
And already in the autumn wind the leaves are falling.
The yellow butterflies of October
Flutter in pairs over the grass of the west garden.
My heart aches at seeing them …
I sit sorrowing alone, and alas!
The vermilion of my face is fading.

Some day when you return down the river,
If you will write me a letter beforehand,
I will come to meet you—the way is not long—
I will come as far as the Long Wind Beach instantly.

Li Po (*born ca. 701, China; died 762*) is one of China's most famous poets. He is said to
have written twenty thousand poems, many of which are still widely read both in
Chinese and in translations. Much of his life is shrouded in legend and mystery, but he
seems to have lived with exuberance—drinking, loving, writing, fighting, and playing
music.

Activities, p. 280   *The River-Merchant's Wife*

On Monsieur's Departure

Elizabeth I

Portrait of Elizabeth I

I grieve and dare not show my discontent,
I love and yet am forced to seem to hate,
I do, yet dare not say I ever meant,
I seem stark mute but inwardly do prate.
I am and not, I freeze and yet am burned,
Since from myself another self I turned.
My care is like my shadow in the sun,
Follows me flying, flies when I pursue it,
Stands and lies by me, doth what I have done.
His too familiar care doth make me rue it.
No means I find to rid him from my breast,
Till by the end of things it be supprest.
Some gentler passion slide into my mind,
For I am soft and made of melting snow;
Or be more cruel, love, and so be kind.
Let me or float or sink, be high or low.
Or let me live with some more sweet content,
Or die and so forget what love ere meant.

Elizabeth I (*born 1533, England; died 1603*), Queen of England, was the daughter of Henry VIII and Anne Boleyn, who was beheaded when Elizabeth was three years old. Elizabeth narrowly escaped the same fate during the reign of her sister, Mary Tudor. She was fluent in Greek, Latin, French, and Italian, and was noted as an orator.

Activities, p. 280

Sonnet CXVI: Let me not to the marriage of true minds ...

William Shakespeare

Let me not to the marriage of true minds
Admit impediments. Love is not love
Which alters when it alteration finds,
Or bends with the remover to remove.
O no! it is an ever-fixed mark
That looks on tempests and is never shaken;
It is the star to every wand'ring bark,
Whose worth's unknown, although his height be taken.
Love's not Time's fool, though rosy lips and cheeks
Within his bending sickle's compass come;
Love alters not with his brief hours and weeks,
But bears it out even to the edge of doom.
If this be error and upon me prov'd,
I never writ, nor no man ever lov'd.

William Shakespeare (*born 1564, England; died 1616*) grew up in Stratford-on-Avon. He later moved to London, working first as an actor and later as a playwright. Shakespeare wrote 154 sonnets, 5 long poems, and 37 plays.

Activities, p. 280

A Satirical Elegy on the Death of a Late Famous General

Jonathan Swift

JOHN
Duke of Marlborough.

The "famous general" was John Churchill, the Duke of Marlborough, who was commander-in-chief of the British army in the War of the Spanish Succession. Swift accused him of prolonging the war in order to make money. These accusations led to the Duke being dismissed from his post in 1711. When he died in 1722, Swift wrote this elegy.

His Grace! impossible! what dead!
Of old age, too, and in his bed!
And could that Mighty Warrior fall?
And so inglorious, after all!
Well, since he's gone, no matter how,
The last loud trump must wake him now:
And, trust me, as the noise grows stronger,
He'd wish to sleep a little longer.
And could he be indeed so old
As by the news-papers we're told?
Threescore, I think, is pretty high;
'Twas time in conscience he should die.
This world he cumber'd long enough;
He burnt his candle to the snuff;
And that's the reason, some folks think,
He left behind so great a stink.
Behold his funeral appears,
Nor widow's sighs, nor orphan's tears,
Wont at such times each heart to pierce,
Attend the progress of his hearse.
But what of that, his friends may say,
He had those honours in his day.
True to his profit and his pride,
He made them weep before he dy'd.
Come hither, all ye empty things,
Ye bubbles rais'd by breath of Kings;
Who float upon the tide of state,
Come hither, and behold your fate.
Let pride be taught by this rebuke,
How very mean a thing's a Duke;
From all his ill-got honours flung,
Turn'd to that dirt from whence he sprung.

Jonathan Swift (*born 1667, Ireland; died 1745*), author, poet, clergyman, fought against cruelty, imperialism, and war. Swift is best known for the satirical *Gulliver's Travels*, which caused much controversy when it first appeared.

Ozymandias

Percy Bysshe Shelley

I met a traveller from an antique land
Who said: "Two vast and trunkless legs of stone
Stand in the desert. Near them, on the sand,
Half sunk, a shattered visage lies, whose frown,
And wrinkled lip, and sneer of cold command,
Tell that its sculptor well those passions read
Which yet survive, stamped on these lifeless things,
The hand that mocked them and the heart that fed.
And on the pedestal these words appear—
'My name is Ozymandias, king of kings:
Look on my works, ye Mighty, and despair!'
Nothing beside remains. Round the decay
Of that colossal wreck, boundless and bare
The lone and level sands stretch far away."

Percy Bysshe Shelley (*born 1792, Sussex, England; died 1822, Italy*) is ranked as one of the great English poets of the Romantic period. Much of his poetry reflects his belief in the power of love and reason and his faith in the progress of humankind. His best-known works include "To a Skylark" and "Adonais," written in memory of John Keats.

Activities, p. 281

If You Were Coming in the Fall

Emily Dickinson

If you were coming in the fall,
I'd brush the summer by
With half a smile and half a spurn,
As housewives do a fly.

If I could see you in a year,
I'd wind the months in balls,
And put them each in separate drawers,
Until their time befalls.

If only centuries delayed,
I'd count them on my hand,
Subtracting till my fingers dropped
Into Van Diemen's land.

If certain, when this life was out,
That yours and mine should be,
I'd toss it yonder like a rind,
And taste eternity.

But now, all ignorant of the length
Of time's uncertain wing,
It goads me, like the goblin bee,
That will not state its sting.

Emily Dickinson (*born 1830, Amherst, Massachusetts; died 1886*) wrote numerous poems, but only seven were published during her lifetime. For much of her adult life, Dickinson lived as a virtual recluse in her father's house, although she did correspond with many friends.

Activities, p. 282

The Wild Swans at Coole

William Butler Yeats

The trees are in their autumn beauty,
The woodland paths are dry,
Under the October twilight the water
Mirrors a still sky;
Upon the brimming water among the stones
Are nine and fifty swans.

The nineteenth Autumn has come upon me
Since I first made my count;
I saw, before I had well finished,
All suddenly mount
And scatter wheeling in great broken rings
Upon their clamorous wings.

I have looked upon those brilliant creatures,
And now my heart is sore.
All's changed since I, hearing at twilight,
The first time on this shore,
The bell-beat of their wings above my head,
Trod with a lighter tread.

Unwearied still, lover by lover,
They paddle in the cold,
Companionable streams or climb the air;
Their hearts have not grown old;
Passion or conquest, wander where they will,
Attend upon them still.

But now they drift on the still water
Mysterious, beautiful;
Among what rushes will they build,
By what lake's edge or pool
Delight men's eyes when I awake some day
To find they have flown away?

William Butler Yeats (*born 1865, Ireland; died 1939*), Nobel Prize-winning poet and playwright, was greatly influenced by the Celtic Revival in Ireland, his unrequited love for the Irish revolutionary Maud Gonne, and the war clouds he saw gathering over Europe.

Activities, p. 282

Birches

Robert Frost

When I see birches bend to left and right
Across the lines of straighter darker trees,
I like to think some boy's been swinging them.
But swinging doesn't bend them down to stay.
Ice-storms do that. Often you must have seen them
Loaded with ice a sunny winter morning
After a rain. They click upon themselves
As the breeze rises, and turn many-colored
As the stir cracks and crazes their enamel.
Soon the sun's warmth makes them shed crystal shells
Shattering and avalanching on the snow-crust—
Such heaps of broken glass to sweep away
You'd think the inner dome of heaven had fallen.
They are dragged to the withered bracken by the load,
And they seem not to break; though once they are bowed
So low for long, they never right themselves:
You may see their trunks arching in the woods
Years afterwards, trailing their leaves on the ground
Like girls on hands and knees that throw their hair
Before them over their heads to dry in the sun.
But I was going to say when Truth broke in
With all her matter-of-fact about the ice-storm,
(Now am I free to be poetical?)
I should prefer to have some boy bend them
As he went out and in to fetch the cows—
Some boy too far from town to learn baseball,
Whose only play was what he found himself,
Summer or winter, and could play alone.
One by one he subdued his father's trees
By riding them down over and over again
Until he took the stiffness out of them,
And not one but hung limp, not one was left

For him to conquer. He learned all there was
To learn about not launching out too soon
And so not carrying the tree away
Clear to the ground. He always kept his poise
To the top branches, climbing carefully
With the same pains you use to fill a cup
Up to the brim, and even above the brim.
Then he flung outward, feet first, with a swish,
Kicking his way down through the air to the ground.
So was I once myself a swinger of birches.
And so I dream of going back to be.
It's when I'm weary of considerations,
And life is too much like a pathless wood
Where your face burns and tickles with the cobwebs
Broken across it, and one eye is weeping
From a twig's having lashed across it open.
I'd like to get away from earth awhile
And then come back to it and begin over.
May no fate willfully misunderstand me
And half grant what I wish and snatch me away
Not to return. Earth's the right place for love:
I don't know where it's likely to go better.
I'd like to go by climbing a birch tree,
And climb black branches up a snow-white trunk
Toward heaven, till the tree could bear no more,
But dipped its top and set me down again.
That would be good both going and coming back.
One could do worse than be a swinger of birches.

Robert Frost (*born 1874, San Francisco; died 1963*), poet, teacher, lecturer, goodwill emissary to South America and the Soviet Union, is among the most popular of 20th-century American poets. His poems often echo the life and colloquialisms of rural New England.

My Song

Rabindranath Tagore

This song of mine will wind its music around you,
   my child, like the fond arms of love.

This song of mine will touch your forehead
   like a kiss of blessing.

When you are alone it will sit by your side and
   whisper in your ear, when you are in the crowd
      it will fence you about with aloofness.

My song will be like a pair of wings to your dreams,
   it will transport your heart to the verge of the unknown.

It will be like the faithful star overhead
   when dark night is over your road.

My song will sit in the pupils of your eyes,
   and will carry your sight into the heart of things.

And when my voice is silenced in death,
   my song will speak in your living heart.

Rabindranath Tagore (*born 1861, India; died 1941*), poet, songwriter, novelist, dramatist, educator, painter, received the Nobel Prize for Literature in 1913. The author of both the Indian and the Bangladeshi national anthems, he was a prolific writer who translated his own works into English.

Where Are Those Songs?

Micere Githae Mugo

Where are those songs
my mother and yours
always sang
fitting rhythms
to the whole
vast span of life?

What was it again
they sang
       harvesting maize, threshing millet, storing the grain …

What did they sing
bathing us, rocking us to sleep …
and the one they sang
stirring the pot
(swallowed in parts by choking smoke)?

What was it
the woods echoed
as in long file
my mother and yours and all the women on our ridge
beat out the rhythms
trudging gaily
as they carried
piles of wood
through those forests
miles from home
What song was it?

And the row of bending women
hoeing our fields
to what beat
did they
break the stubborn ground
as they weeded
our *shambas*?

What did they sing
at the ceremonies
      child-birth
      child-naming
      second birth
      initiation ...?
how did they trill the *ngemi?*
What was
the warriors' song?
how did the wedding song go?
sing me
the funeral song.
What do you remember?

Sing
      I have forgotten
      my mother's song
      my children
      will never know.
This I remember:
Mother always said
      sing child sing
      make a song
      and sing
      beat out your own rhythms
      and rhythms of your life
      but make the song soulful
      and make life
      sing

Sing daughter sing
around you are
unaccountable tunes
some sung
others unsung
sing them
to your rhythms
observe
listen
absorb
soak yourself
bathe
in the stream of life
    and then sing
    sing
    simple songs
    for the people
    for all to hear
    and learn
    and sing
    with you

Micere Githae Mugo (*born 1942, Kenya*), poet, playwright, professor, studied at the University of Makere in Uganda and the University of Toronto. She has taught at universities in Zimbabwe, Canada, and the United States. Her first book of poetry was *Daughter of My People, Sing!* Her plays include *The Trial of Dedan Kimachi*.

Activities, p. 283

Colombe

Kamau Brathwaite

C

olumbus from his after-
deck watched stars, absorbed in water,
melt in liquid amber drifting

through my summer air
Now with morning shadows lifting
beaches stretched before him cold & clear

Birds circled flapping flag & mizzen
mast. birds harshly hawking. without fear
Discovery he sailed for. was so near

C

olumbus from his after-
deck watched heights he hoped for
rocks he dreamed. rise solid from my simple water

Parrots screamed. Soon he would touch
our land. his charted mind's desire
The blue sky blessed the morning with its fire

But did his vision
fashion as he watched the shore
the slaughter that his soldiers

furthered here? Pike
point & musket butt
hot splintered courage. bones

cracked with bullet shot
tippled black boot in my belly. the
whips uncurled desire?

C

olumbus from his after-
deck saw bearded fig trees. yellow pouis
blazed like pollen & thin

waterfalls suspended in the green
as his eyes climbed towards the highest ridges
where our farms were hidden

Now he was sure
he heard soft voices mocking in the leaves
What did this journey mean. this

new world mean. dis
covery? or a return to terrors
he had sailed from. known before?

I watched him pause

Then he was splashing silence
Crabs snapped their claws
and scattered as he walked towards our shore

Kamau Brathwaite (*born 1930, Barbados*), poet, historian, and essayist, won the Neustadt International Prize for Literature in 1994. His poetry explores the Caribbean identity and the Black experience in Britain. He has taught Social and Cultural History at the University of the West Indies and Comparative Literature at New York University.

The Prison Cell

Mahmoud Darwish

It is possible ...
It is possible at least sometimes ...
It is possible especially now
To ride a horse
Inside a prison cell
And run away ...

It is possible for prison walls
To disappear
For the cell to become a distant land
Without frontiers:

—What did you do with the walls?
—I gave them back to the rocks.
—And what did you do with the ceiling?
—I turned it into a saddle.
—And your chain?
—I turned it into a pencil.

The prison guard got angry:
He put an end to the dialogue.
He said he didn't care for poetry,
And bolted the door of my cell.

He came back to see me
In the morning;
He shouted at me:

—Where did all this water come from?
—I brought it from the Nile.
—And the trees?
—From the orchards of Damascus.
—And the music?
—From my heartbeat.

The prison guard got mad;
He put an end to the dialogue.
He said he didn't like poetry,
And bolted the door of my cell.

But he returned in the evening:

—Where did this moon come from?
—From the nights of Bagdad.
—And the wine?
—From the vineyards of Algiers.
—And this freedom?
—From the chain you tied me with last night.

The prison guard grew so sad ...
He begged me to give him back
His freedom.

Mahmoud Darwish (*born 1942, Palestine*), poet, editor, has published several volumes of poetry. His family fled to Lebanon in 1947 and returned to Israel in 1948 to find their village in ruins. He was awarded the Lenin Peace Prize in 1983.

Activities, p. 284

*L*ittle Ruth

Yehuda Amichai

Sometimes I remember you, little Ruth,
We were separated in our distant childhood and they burned you
    in the camps.
If you were alive now, you would be a woman of sixty-five,
A woman on the verge of old age. At twenty you were burned
And I don't know what happened to you in your short life
Since we separated. What did you achieve, what insignia
Did they put on your shoulders, your sleeves, your
Brave soul, what shining stars
Did they pin on you, what decorations for valor, what
Medals for love hung around your neck,
What peace upon you, *peace unto you.*
And what happened to the unused years of your life?
Are they still packed away in pretty bundles,

Were they added to my life? Did you turn me
Into your bank of love like the banks in Switzerland
Where assets are preserved even after their owners are dead?
Will I leave all this to my children
Whom you never saw?

You gave your life to me, like a wine dealer
Who remains sober himself.
You sober in death, lucid in the dark
For me, drunk on life, wallowing in my forgetfulness.
Now and then, I remember you in times
Unbelievable. And in places not made for memory
But for the transient, the passing that does not remain.
As in an airport, when the arriving travellers
Stand tired at the revolving conveyor belt
That brings their suitcases and packages,
And they identify theirs with cries of joy
As at a resurrection and go out into their lives;
And there is one suitcase that returns and disappears again
And returns again, ever so slowly, in the empty hall,
Again and again it passes.
This is how your quiet figure passes by me,
This is how I remember you until
The conveyor belt stands still. *And they stood still. Amen.*

Yehuda Amichai (*born 1924, Germany; died 2000*), poet, playwright, short-story writer, fled to Israel with his parents at age 12 to escape the Nazis. He is known as "the national poet of Israel," and his works have been translated into 29 languages.

The End and the Beginning

Wislawa Szymborska

After every war
someone has to tidy up
Things won't pick
themselves up, after all.

Someone has to shove
the rubble to the roadsides
so the carts loaded with corpses
can get by.

Someone has to trudge
through sludge and ashes,
through the sofa springs,
the shards of glass,
the bloody rags.

Someone has to lug the post
to prop the wall,
someone has to glaze the window,
set the door in its frame.

No sound bites, no photo opportunities,
and it takes years.
All the cameras have gone
to other wars.

The bridges need to be rebuilt,
the railroad stations, too.
Shirtsleeves will be rolled
to shreds.

Someone, broom in hand,
still remembers how it was.
Someone else listens, nodding
his unshattered head.
But others are bound to be bustling nearby
who'll find all that
a little boring.

From time to time someone still must
dig up a rusted argument
from underneath a bush
and haul it off to the dump.

Those who knew
what this was all about
must make way for those
who know little.
And less than that.
And at last nothing less than nothing.

Someone's got to lie there
in the grass that covers up
the causes and effects
with a cornstalk in his teeth,
gawking at clouds.

Wislawa Szymborska (*born 1923, Poland*) gained international attention in 1996 after receiving the Nobel Prize for Literature. Her first volume of poetry, *Dlatego Zyjemy* (*That's Why We Are Still Alive*), appeared in 1952, and she has published more than a dozen collections since. Her work has been translated into many languages.

Activities, p. 285   *The End and the Beginning*

Activities: The River-Merchant's Wife: A Letter

1. ***Research Context:*** In a small group, make a list of questions that require answering before you can fully understand the poem. Use electronic, print, and human resources to find the answers, and keep notes of your research. Share your information with other groups so that the references in the selection are clear to all in the class.

2. ***Interpret Detail:*** Identify the emotions experienced by the river-merchant's wife at the different stages of her life. In a few sentences, explain how Li Po uses concrete details to convey the wife's feelings.

3. ***Write a Reply:*** Write a similar poem containing the river-merchant's reply to the letter. Include the history of the relationship and indicate your present feelings. Provide an appropriate illustration and explain the reason for your choice.

4. ***Compare Poems:*** Find a contemporary poem or song in which the speaker misses his or her beloved. Create a chart to compare similarities and differences in content and technique. Work with a partner to see whether you can add ideas to each other's chart.

Activities: On Monsieur's Departure

1. ***Examine Structure:*** In a small group, analyze the structure of the poem, paying attention to Elizabeth's use of rhyme. Then examine the use of contrasts and seeming contradictions in the poem. Have a spokesperson present your group's ideas along with supporting details from the poem.

2. ***Examine Rhythm:*** With a partner, examine Elizabeth's use of rhythm, noting which words in each line are stressed. Then compare lines to note how the pattern of stressed words changes. Collaboratively write a paragraph commenting on the use and effect of rhythm in the poem.

3. ***Reflect on Theme:*** In a journal entry, reflect on one of the following statements: (a) The experience of love is full of contradictory feelings; or (b) Love is so powerful that it can make you feel helpless, like a victim.

4. ***Research Information:*** Brainstorm five questions that you would like answered about Elizabeth and her times. Use Internet sources to try to find answers. Create and display a poster of interesting facts about her life and her period in history. Display your poster in the classroom.

Activities: Sonnet CXVI: Let me not to the marriage of true minds . . .

1. ***Understand Vocabulary:*** In a small group, identify words you find difficult to understand. Use context to deduce the meaning of these words and use a dictionary to verify your answer. Then write a definition, in your own words, for each one. Share your group's results with the class.

2. **Identify Theme:** Choose the part of the poem that you think best expresses the theme. Cite the passage and explain its meaning. Using poetry or prose, express your own ideas about this concept.

3. **Explore Language:** Choose one of the three quatrains and rewrite it as prose, using modern language and style. Edit your passage for clarity, effectiveness, spelling, grammar, and punctuation.

4. **Prepare a Reading:** Prepare an oral reading of another Shakespeare sonnet. Work with a partner to exchange suggestions about how to use tone of voice, pauses, and tempo effectively. Present your reading to the class or a small group.

Activities: A Satirical Elegy on the Death of a Late Famous General

1. **Discuss Strategies:** In a small group, discuss any difficulties you encountered in reading and understanding this poem. Describe strategies you used that were helpful. After the discussion, record at least two strategies you might find helpful in the future.

2. **Define Terms:** Define the literary terms *satire* and *elegy*. Using examples, explain how each term applies to this poem.

3. **Consider Purpose:** Why do you think Swift wrote this poem? Use examples from the text to support your opinion. Compare your opinion with a partner's.

4. **Explain a Satire:** View a talk show, television series, or movie that makes use of satire. Explain what is being satirized and how it is satirized. Write one or two sentences summarizing the point you think the satire tried to make.

Activities: Ozymandias

1. **Analyze Diction:** The transitive verb "survive" in line seven has two direct objects, "hand" and "heart." What do "hand" and "heart" refer to? Give possible reasons for the poet's choice of diction here.

2. **Consider Significance:** Some believe that the actual inscription on the statue was "I am Ozymandias, king of kings; if anyone wishes to know what I am and where I lie, let him surpass me in some of my exploits." Explain whether the poet has changed the meaning and why he might have made this change.

3. **Express the Theme:** How does Shelley use visual images to express the poem's theme? Create your own image to express a similar theme.

4. **Write a Poem:** Find a famous painting, statue, or sculpture you like. What qualities of the work make it meaningful for you? Write a poem to describe how the work of art makes you feel and, possibly, what it makes you think about.

Activities: If You Were Coming in the Fall

1. **Discuss the Title:** In a small group, discuss other possible titles for the poem. Debate the merits of various suggestions and choose one to represent your group. Present it to the class and explain your choice.

2. **Respond to Grammar:** Make a list of all the pronouns in the poem. Together with a partner, come to an agreement about the antecedent of each one. Discuss whether this strategy helps your understanding of the poem.

3. **Examine Diction:** Using examples from the poem, write a paragraph discussing the following statement about Dickinson's diction: "Her vocabulary is ordinary but it is wide and she uses usual words in unusual ways."

4. **Consider Music:** Which popular singer or group would you choose to record a musical version of the poem? What instruments would be effective? Explain your choice to a small group. If possible, play a short section of an appropriate song by the artist of your choice.

Activities: The Wild Swans at Coole

1. **Read Closely:** Examine each stanza for any information you learn or can infer about the speaker. Organize the information into two categories: (a) information stated in the poem and (b) information implied by the poem.

2. **Support Opinions:** Does the speaker identify with the scene he observes, or does he feel apart from it? Use examples from the poem to support your opinion.

3. **Discuss Theme:** In a small group, decide what message you think Yeats is trying to communicate in this poem. Identify lines that support your opinion. Share your ideas with another group.

4. **Classify Poems:** Find two other poems in which the speaker observes a natural scene. Share your poems in a small group. Find at least three different ways to classify the group's poems.

Activities: Birches

1. **Examine Text:** Identify four examples of Frost's accurate observation of everyday life and of the natural world. Share your examples with a partner. What effect do these observations have on the reader?

2. **Write a Response Journal:** In a journal entry, record your reactions to Frost's poem and write about the things you liked about the poem *and* those you disliked.

3. **Examine Imagery:** Identify five images in the poem that you found particularly effective. For any three, explain your choice and evaluate the effectiveness of the images. Share your evaluations with a partner and compare your reactions to the images.

4. ***Write from a Visual:*** Find or take an interesting picture of a tree or group of trees. Using prose or poetry, write a description of the tree. Refer to some of Frost's descriptions in "Birches" for inspiration. Post your visual and writing in the classroom.

Activities: My Song

1. ***Examine Character:*** What does the poem reveal about the speaker? What characteristics and values would you attribute to this person? Write a short character sketch of the speaker, justifying your ideas with specific references to the text.

2. ***Understand Imagery:*** The speaker says the song will accomplish many things. In a small group, discuss the accomplishment described in each stanza. Then, individually and in your own words, complete for each stanza a sentence beginning, "A song can …"

3. ***Ask and Answer Questions:*** Write three questions that you would like to ask the speaker in the poem. Exchange questions with a partner and answer them as the speaker. Discuss each other's responses. In a journal entry, reflect on whether or not this strategy was useful to you.

4. ***Write Your Song:*** Using "My Song" as a model, write a similar poem, addressed to a parent, relative, or friend. State what your song will accomplish for the person who receives it. Share your poem with the person you wrote it for.

Activities: Where Are Those Songs?

1. ***Paraphrase Text:*** In the last part of the poem, the speaker quotes advice from her mother. Paraphrase this advice in your own words. In a journal entry, comment on whether or not you think this advice is valuable.

2. ***Examine Line Breaks:*** With a partner, examine the poet's use of line breaks. What is the effect of the short lines? Why are some lines indented? Compare your ideas with those of another pair.

3. ***Relate to Experience:*** In a small group, compare and contrast the role played by song in the society Micere Githae Mugo describes, and in present-day North American society. Organize your findings in a chart.

4. ***Research Songs:*** Find four or five traditional songs from your own cultural background and record or write down the lyrics. Start by making a list of useful resources to consult. Try to classify the songs by purpose and/or occasion. Share one of your songs with the class.

Activities: Colombe

1. ***Examine Point of View:*** The poem describes Christopher Columbus landing on Watling Island in the Bahamas. From what point of view does the narrator see the events? What is Columbus's point of view? How and why is it emphasized in the poem?

2. ***Explain Imagery:*** What effects are created by the images in the final stanza? How do these images help to reveal the narrator's feelings about the event? Explain your ideas in one or two paragraphs.

3. ***Explore Style:*** In a two-column chart, list unconventional aspects of the author's style. Beside each point, explain the effect created and/or a possible reason for the author's stylistic decision.

4. ***Write a Journal Entry:*** Research the events surrounding Columbus's arrival on Watling Island. In your journal, reflect on how this information affected your understanding and appreciation of the poem.

Activities: The Prison Cell

1. ***Construct Meaning:*** In a small group, discuss the ideas in the poem. After the discussion, complete the following sentence in your own words "Darwish's message is that it is possible …" Share your sentence with your group and try to resolve any differences of opinion.

2. ***Contrast Stanzas:*** Compare the last stanza with the two previous stanzas that show the guard's reactions. Discuss with a partner the change in the guard's reaction and possible reasons for this change.

3. ***Perform a Role-Play:*** With a partner, adapt the poem into a role-play. Experiment with vocal techniques and body language to make the role-play dramatic. What changes might take place in the characters, and how could these be revealed? Ask for feedback to improve the performance.

4. ***Create an Image:*** What image or scene of freedom would you hold in your mind if you were a prisoner? Represent this image in a medium of your choice. Possibilities include pencil sketch, pastels, paint, collage, or photograph.

Activities: Little Ruth

1. ***Respond to the Poem:*** Reread the poem and note the emotions that you feel. Create a web with the title "Little Ruth" in the centre, and then list your emotions, connecting each to the centre with a line. Under each emotion, jot in point-form reasons why you felt each emotion.

2. ***Explain Comparisons:*** The author uses several powerful comparisons in this poem. List as many of these as you can. Choose one that you find particularly effective and explain why.

3. **Discuss Characters:** With a partner, discuss the relationship or connection between Ruth and the narrator. What words and phrases does the author use to suggest this connection? State your view of the connection in one sentence and explain how the poem supports this view.

4. **Write an Epitaph:** Write an epitaph, four or five sentences long, commemorating the significance of Ruth. Consider the diction and level of language appropriate for the situation. Share your epitaph with a partner and offer each other feedback.

Activities: The End and the Beginning

1. **Explore the Message:** What is the author's message in this poem? Does the last stanza express optimism or pessimism? Give reasons to support your opinions.

2. **Examine Tone:** How would you describe the author's tone? What attitude toward the topic does the tone suggest? List words and phrases that help to establish the tone.

3. **Write Persuasively:** Write a brief defence of the author's choice of title, or choose a new title and write to convince readers that your choice of title is better.

4. **Discuss Opinions:** In a small group, discuss what kinds of events make for a "good" news story. Are the events in the poem likely to be covered by the media? How does media coverage of war and its aftermath affect our perception of the events? Summarize your main points.

Drama

People go to the theatre not to feel good.
They go there to feel.

—Robert Lepage

A play is fiction—and fiction is fact distilled into truth.

—Edward Albee

Theatre critics have been around for a long time. More than two thousand years ago, the Greek philosophers Plato and Aristotle wrote about what they considered to be the requirements of a good play. Since then, many people have had different opinions on the topic, as you can see from today's theatre reviews. What one critic hates, another loves. And a play (or movie) that the critics pan sometimes goes on to become a huge box-office success.

What types of plays do you like? What do you consider the ingredients of a successful play? This unit offers you an opportunity to read a variety of plays and excerpts from plays. Whether you like or dislike a selection, challenge yourself to come up with reasons for your reaction. These reasons may help you to determine your own criteria for good drama. To get you thinking along these lines, the first selection, Scribe's Paradox, features characters who are not shy about expressing their opinions about what makes a good play. Curtain up!

Scribe's Paradox, or The Mechanical Rabbit
Michael Feingold

CHARACTERS
ORFIN, A PLAYWRIGHT
A FEMALE THEATREGOER
A PROFESSOR
MADAME DU CAMP, an actress
RANDEAU, a stage director

TIME
1895. Just after a performance.

SETTING
Paris. The lobby of the Theatre des Somnambules, where ORFIN'S latest play is running.

Drama

FEMALE THEATREGOER: (*coming out of the auditorium and approaching* ORFIN) Excuse me, but aren't you Monsieur Orfin?

ORFIN: Are you a debt collector?

FEMALE THEATREGOER: What an idea! Of course not!

ORFIN: In that case, I am Orfin, at your service.

FEMALE THEATREGOER: I thought so! Your play is very good. I enjoyed it immensely.

ORFIN: Thank you. I hope you will tell all your friends.

FEMALE THEATREGOER: I will, but—(*looking around cautiously, lowering her voice*)—it is not well made.

ORFIN: I beg your pardon?

FEMALE THEATREGOER: Your play is not a well-made play.

ORFIN: (*somewhat nettled*) It was made well enough for you to enjoy it.

FEMALE THEATREGOER: Oh, you know what I mean.

ORFIN: I'm not at all sure.

FEMALE THEATREGOER: It isn't well constructed.

ORFIN: Ah, you mean like the plays of Monsieur Scribe and Monsieur Sardou?

FEMALE THEATREGOER: Yes, exactly. There is no central figure trapped between two untenable choices. There is no clever antagonist to counter each of the central figure's attempts to escape from this situation.

ORFIN: No quid pro quo, you mean?

FEMALE THEATREGOER: That is precisely what I mean. For instance, take *A Glass of Water*—

ORFIN: I'm not thirsty, thank you.

FEMALE THEATREGOER: Oh, don't be silly. I mean Monsieur Scribe's famous play of that name.

ORFIN: Ah, yes. *The Glass of Water*. And what about it?

FEMALE THEATREGOER: Each of the characters is in one of these untenable dilemmas. Each move brings one side or the other up against a countermove. The exposition is all in the first act, the climax in the third, the resolution in the fifth.

ORFIN: Yes, Monsieur Scribe is very clever about these things.

FEMALE THEATREGOER: But your play has no such structure.

ORFIN: Dear lady, my play is in one scene. Under the circumstances, it could hardly resolve in its fifth act.

FEMALE THEATREGOER: But it could follow a pattern of rising action. It could have an untenable dilemma, and a series of quid pro quo manoeuvres.

ORFIN: I find my temper rising in lieu of the action; your demands make talking to you an untenable dilemma. If you go on in this manner, my manoeuvre will simply be to walk away.

FEMALE THEATREGOER: But I am only an innocent audience member who wants to know more.

ORFIN: Your attitude suggests to me that you lost your innocence long ago. (*She gasps.*) Aesthetically speaking, I mean.

PROFESSOR: (*coming up to them*) Madame, is this man bothering you?

ORFIN: On the contrary: The lady is doing her best to bother me.

PROFESSOR: I warn you, sir, if you insult her again, you will have to deal with me.

ORFIN: And who, may I ask, will I then be dealing with?

PROFESSOR: (*bowing*) I am Kaltfisch, Professor of Aesthetics at the University of Lyon.

ORFIN: May I suggest, Professor, that Lyon's aesthetics need considerably more reforming than mine.

PROFESSOR: Sir, if your aesthetics include harassing innocent women in theatre lobbies—

ORFIN: You came in late, Professor. I am the author of the play being presented here. The lady is harassing me about my lack of structural sense.

PROFESSOR: (*clasping his hands*) My dear fellow, can you ever forgive me! Your play is simply splendid!

FEMALE THEATREGOER: (*perturbed*) But Professor—

PROFESSOR: (*ignoring the interruption*) You do away with all these antiquated hoodoos about "structure." No contrivance, no manipulation, no elaborately rigged-up system of alliances and counter-alliances—just a person who does something and its consequences. That is drama at its purest. None of the nonsense of Scribe, Sardou, Dumas fils, Augier, Feuillet, and so forth.

ORFIN: I appreciate your enthusiasm, Professor, but I hope you will let me put in a word in defence of my colleagues. My own approach is different from theirs—this is a changing world we live in—but I admire and even enjoy their contrivances, as you call them. I love to watch the little machines whirl and click into place as these not-quite-believable characters manoeuvre their way from one situation to another. You are quite right to say that it is not the living drama, which is what I prefer, but it is the pattern of drama, and we are all beholden to the pattern, so we must respect it.

MADAME DU CAMP: (*sweeping up, grandly dressed*) Orfy, my love, we've been looking for you all over the theatre.

ORFIN: Jeanne, please let me introduce—

FEMALE THEATREGOER: Oh, Madame, what a magnificent performance!

MADAME DU CAMP: Thank you.

FEMALE THEATREGOER: (*extending her program to be signed*) You are the most wonderful actress of our century! That red dress! And the way you looked at him when he accused you of infidelity with the chauffeur!

MADAME DU CAMP: (*laughing as she signs program with an elaborate flourish*) Oh, well, Duse will probably find some even more cunning way of doing that in the Italian version. (*to ORFIN*) Remember her in the confession scene of *The Princess of Baghdad*? With the little boy? That was divine!

ORFIN: (*imitating Duse folding the child's hands over his heart*) I remember. "I have been faithful! I swear it! *Lo giuro!*" It was brilliant ... though not half so brilliant as you, my dear.

MADAME DU CAMP: Well, you'll have to write me something brilliant like that to do in your next. Which had better be soon, Orfy. That's why I've been trying to find you. We're taking this play off. It's not going to run. The new one must be ready in five weeks.

ORFIN: But everyone loves you in this! I love you in this! You've never been more wonderful. And this is the most original thing I've ever written.

MADAME DU CAMP: Oh, Orfy, don't be banal. I mean—(*looking at PROFESSOR and FEMALE THEATREGOER*)—you'll forgive my saying this in front of your relatives from the country, but—this play doesn't give me a chance. I only get one costume change, I only have two entrances. I don't get an exit because the curtain comes down for intermission with me still onstage—

ORFIN: (*testily*) Talk to Randeau about that. I told him you should exit before it came down.

MADAME DU CAMP: Oh, Orfy, honey, that isn't the point. I have no big scenes!

ORFIN: No big scenes! What about the confrontation scene! This woman has just been telling you how wonderful you were in it.

MADAME DU CAMP: I'm wonderful, I know, but the scene has no "build." I need to feel that roller-coaster of motion sweeping me along. I can do my part, but there's nothing hanging over my head, no extra push. You look back at the classics, sweetie. Look at Scribe—

ORFIN: Scribe! You want me to write like Scribe!

MADAME DU CAMP: Well, I'll tell you, he never wrote a woman a weak role. I come out there in *When Ladies Battle*, or *Adrienne Lecouvreur*, and I know exactly what's going on. I have something I want, I have a secret I must conceal, I have an enemy whose manoeuvres against me are all announced openly, step by step, so that I can take steps to counter them, I get three or four costume changes, the audience sees me go from happy to sad to hysterical in an instant, and every scene has a strong entrance, a crushing last line, and one or two laughs. Now how can you top that?

ORFIN: (*through clenched teeth*) In *Adrienne Lecouvreur* you have to die by sniffing poisoned violets. How can I take that seriously?

MADAME DU CAMP: Well, it doesn't have to be Scribe. In those days they all knew how to do it. Take Augier for instance, *Olympia's Marriage*—

ORFIN: In *Olympia's Marriage* the elderly judge rescues his son from marriage to the ex-courtesan by shooting you, I mean her. It's absurd. A Paris audience would laugh it off the stage today.

MADAME DU CAMP: I don't know, I've been thinking of reviving it— it's very popular in America just now.

ORFIN: America! We're talking about civilization here, not the savage tribes.

MADAME DU CAMP: Wait till you see my Act III wedding dress. And Randeau's worked out something spectacular for my death scene.

ORFIN: (*bitterly*) So this is my fate! To be replaced by a mechanical rabbit from fifty years ago!

MADAME DU CAMP: Oh, don't take it so hard, my cabbage. I want to do your next one immediately after. The Augier revival is just to give you time to write it. And practise the old pattern a little. We want you to write a play that's really well made, so everyone will love it. We know you can do it.

ORFIN: Yes, but do I want to? The world's not well made. Those plays are old, artificial postures.

MADAME DU CAMP: (*laughing*) Yes, darling. That's why we love them. Reality is depressing—more so every year. People come to the theatre for escape. They need artifice—the more artificial the better.

ORFIN: Why am I always at your mercy this way?

MADAME DU CAMP: (*simply*) You adore me.

ORFIN: Yes. And your husband owns the theatre.

MADAME DU CAMP: Oh, hush. Don't talk about my husband, or these people will suspect some kind of marital intrigue. (*Looking at PROFESSOR and FEMALE THEATREGOER, who have been watching with rapt attention.*) Who are they, anyway?

PROFESSOR: (*bowing*) Kaltfisch, University of Lyon.

MADAME DU CAMP: Oh, Professor! How lovely to see you. Goodness, in this flurry I almost forgot all about our appointment. Has the Augier family approved our terms?

PROFESSOR: (*touching his breast pocket*) I have the contract here, Madame, whenever you are ready.

ORFIN: (*agog*) You praise my new aesthetic, and then you negotiate for Augier, most hackneyed of the old "well-made" playwrights?

PROFESSOR: The old must be given its chance, Monsieur, before the new sweeps it away.

FEMALE THEATREGOER: (*who has edged over to MADAME DU CAMP*) I can't tell you how excited I am! I saw Rejane play Olympia when I was a little girl. To think of seeing you in it now!

MADAME DU CAMP: (*joshing*) It will make you feel like a little girl all over again. (*They laugh together.*) Would you like a tour of our theatre? Come, I'll show you around. Come, Professor.

PROFESSOR: With pleasure.

(*They go off, leaving ORFIN alone in the now deserted lobby. Pause. Then RANDEAU, the director, comes up to him.*)

RANDEAU: Don't be downhearted.

ORFIN: Any special reason why not?

RANDEAU: You've triumphed. Everyone is talking about your play.

ORFIN: But, apparently, no one is coming to see it.

RANDEAU: That's all right. Let them come and see Augier for a while. They all know the terms have changed. The old tricks have been exposed as tricks. In the future, plays like yours will be enjoyed as plays. And the old plays will be enjoyed the way you and I enjoy them, for the pleasure of their trickery.

ORFIN: You make the future sound very just.

RANDEAU: It's a blind sort of justice, true, but in art it's the only kind we get. Anyway, you won't lose money by this.

ORFIN: I won't.

RANDEAU: I need someone to adapt the Augier script. His tricks are a little staler than Scribe's.

ORFIN: Won't the Professor object?

RANDEAU: You don't think professors ever really know their subject, do you? Come on, let's go for a drink and I'll tell you what I want done. We can go to that new place in Montmartre, where the painters hang out—the Lapin Agile.

ORFIN: All right, we'll go to the Lively Rabbit and try to wake up the mechanical one.

RANDEAU: That's the spirit! You'll write a well-made play yet.

ORFIN: (*looking back to where* MADAME DU CAMP *has exited as he follows* RANDEAU *out*) I already have. (*He exits dramatically.*)

Michael Feingold, critic, playwright, translator, lyricist, director, and literary manager, is the chief theatre critic for *The Village Voice*. His column has won him a Guggenheim Fellowship and the Walter Lowenfels Prize in criticism. He has translated and produced one of Scribe's plays, *When Ladies Battle*.

Exploring Drama

Analyze Format: With a partner, examine the format of this selection and list the differences between the way in which a story and a play are formatted. Then compare this play with the text of another play and note any differences in the format.

Interpret Ideas: List the various people that Orfin meets in the theatre lobby. Beside each, list the demands he/she makes upon the playwright. In a journal entry, decide whether or not you think each demand is reasonable, and explain your opinions.

Make Judgements: Review the possible characteristics of drama mentioned in the play. Note which characteristics you would find most appealing in a play. For each characteristic, explain why you would find it appealing.

Reflect on Genres: In a small group, share knowledge about the characteristics of the different genres you have encountered (novel, drama, short story, and so on). In a journal entry, indicate the genres you enjoy most and why. Exchange journals with several other students and comment on each other's ideas.

The Bush-Ladies

Molly Thom

The main characters in the play from which this excerpt was taken are four historical women who were among the first Canadian authors. The playwright has used their own words to present their lives as pioneers in Ontario.

Clockwise from top:
Mary Anne McDonald
(Susanna Moodie),
Meg Hogarth (Anna
Jameson), Elva Mai
Hoover (Anne Langton),
Wendy Springate
(Catharine Parr Traill)
in the Toronto premiere of
The Bush-Ladies

CHARACTERS

SUSANNA MOODIE, a writer

MR. MOODIE, her husband

CATHARINE PARR TRAILL, her sister, a writer

MR. TRAILL, her husband

ANNE LANGTON, a miniaturist and journal-writer

ANNA BROWNELL JAMESON, a writer

OLD YANKEE WOMAN

IRISH GIRL, the Moodies' servant

CHORUS

Sometime between 1832 and 1846

Upper Canada

CHORUS: (*forming a wheel*)
Logging, burning, clearing
ploughing, sowing, reaping
logging, burning, clearing
ploughing, sowing, reaping …

MOODIE: The rain commenced about a week before the crop was fit
for the sickle, and from that time until nearly the end of
September was a mere succession of thunder showers; days of
intense heat, succeeded by floods of rain. Our fine crop shared the
fate of all other fine crops in the country; it was totally spoiled.

And now Jacob—the faithful, good Jacob—is obliged to leave
us, for we can no longer pay his wages. Debt and misfortunes
crowd upon us from every side.

(OLD YANKEE WOMAN *approaches*.)

YANKEE WOMAN: And what brought you out to this poor country—
you who are no more fit for it than I am to be a fine lady?

MOODIE: The promise of a large grant of land, and the false
statements we heard regarding it.

YANKEE WOMAN: Do you like the country?

MOODIE: No; and I fear I never shall.

YANKEE WOMAN: I thought not. For the drop is always on your
cheek, the children tell me, and those young 'uns have keen eyes.
Now, take my advice. Go home while your money lasts; the
longer you remain in Canada the less you will like it, and when
your money is all spent, you will be like a bird in a cage; you
may beat your wings against the bars, but you can't get out.

MOODIE: Home! If only I could go home. "Home!" I repeat it waking
a thousand times a day, and my last prayer before I sink to sleep
is still "Home! Oh that I could return, if only to die at home!"

TRAILL: Susanna, when things come to the worst, they generally mend.

MOODIE: Our ready money is exhausted. We cannot hire. There is no
help for it.

I had a hard struggle with my pride before I would consent to render the least assistance on the farm—to work in the fields—but reflection convinced me that I was wrong—that Providence has placed me in a situation where I am called upon to work—that it is my duty to exert myself to the utmost to assist my husband and help to maintain my family.

We have found that manual toil, however distasteful to those unaccustomed to it, is not after all such a dreadful hardship; and I have contemplated a well-hoed ridge of potatoes on that bush farm with as much delight as in years long past I had experienced in examining a fine painting in some well-appointed drawing room.

TRAILL: My husband has turned his sword into a plough-share and his lance into a sickle; and if he be seen ploughing among the stumps in his own field, or chopping trees on his own land, no one thinks less of his dignity, or considers him less of a gentleman, than when he appeared upon parade in all the pride of military etiquette, with sash, sword, and epaulette. Surely this is as it should be in a country where independence is inseparable from industry; and for this I prize it.

JAMESON: This is the land of hope, of faith, ay, and of charity, for those who have not all three had better not come here; with them they may, by strength of their own right hand and trusting heart, achieve miracles.

CHORUS: Our fate is seal'd! 'Tis now in vain to sigh
For home, or friends, or country left behind.
Come dry those tears, and lift the downcast eye
To the high heaven of hope, and be resign'd;
Wisdom and time will justify the deed,
The eye will cease to weep, the heart to bleed.

(*The depth of winter. The women are trying to keep warm.*)

LANGTON: My mother accuses me of not wrapping up. What do you think? At the present moment I am wearing two pairs of stockings, a pair of socks, a pair of shoes, and a pair of moccasins.

JAMESON: The cold is at this time so intense that the ink freezes while I write. A glass of water by my bedside, within a few feet of the hearth, is a solid mass of ice in the morning.

LANGTON: When Aunt Alice and I were pasting up the windholes, my mother reproved us, saying it was ridiculous for people to come to Canada and not be able to bear a breath of air. She is determined not to be soft.

MOODIE: In spite of all my boasted fortitude—and I think my powers of endurance have been tried to the utmost since my sojourn in this country—the rigour of the climate subdued my proud, independent English spirit, and I actually shamed my womanhood, and cried with the cold.

TRAILL: You say you fear the rigours of the Canadian winter will kill me. I never enjoyed better health!

MOODIE: The morning of the seventh was so intensely cold that everything liquid froze in the house. The wood for the fire was green, and it ignited too slowly to satisfy the shivering impatience of women and children. I vented mine in grumbling over the wretched fire, at which I in vain endeavoured to thaw frozen bread and to dress crying children.

I had hired a young Irish girl the day before, and she had never seen a stove until she came to our house. She was a good-natured creature, and she thought she would see if she could make a good fire for us. Without saying one word about her intention, she slipped out, ran round to the woodyard, filled her lap with cedar chips and, not knowing the nature of the stove, filled it entirely with the light wood.

(*The* IRISH GIRL *mimes filling the stove, etc.*)

Before I had the least idea of my danger, I was aroused by the crackling and roaring of a large fire and a suffocating smell of burning soot. I opened the door to the parlour, and to my dismay found the stove red-hot from the front plate to the topmost pipe.

My first impulse was to plunge a blanket into cold water. This I thrust into the stove, and upon it I threw water until all was cool below. I then ran up to the loft, and, by exhausting all the water in the house, contrived to cool down the pipes. I then sent the girl out of doors to look at the roof. She quickly returned, stamping and tearing her hair, and making a variety of uncouth outcries, from which I gathered that the roof was in flames.

(*The* IRISH GIRL, *wailing and wringing her hands.*)

MOODIE: You must go for help! Run as fast as you can to my sister's, and fetch your master!

GIRL: And lave you, ma'arm, and the childher alone wid the burnin' house?

MOODIE: Yes, yes! Don't stay one moment.

GIRL: But I have no shoes, ma'arm, and the snow is so deep!

MOODIE: Put on your master's boots; make haste, or we shall be lost!

GIRL: (*shrieking as she runs*) Fire! Fire! Fire!

MOODIE: What should I save first? Bedding and clothing appeared the most essential, and I set to work to drag all that I could from my burning home. Large pieces of burning pine began to fall through the ceiling. The children I had kept under a large dresser, but it now appeared absolutely necessary to remove them. To expose the young, tender things to the direful cold was almost as bad as leaving them to the mercy of the fire. I emptied all the clothes out of a large chest of drawers, and dragged the drawers up the hill. These I lined with blankets, and placed a child in each one, covering it with bedding, giving to little Agnes charge of the baby to hold between her knees until help should arrive. Ah, how long it seemed coming!

(*TRAILL and JAMESON representing MR. TRAILL and MR. MOODIE, come to the rescue. The IRISH GIRL, still wailing, brings up the rear.*)

The moment my husband and brother-in-law entered the house, the latter exclaimed:

MR. TRAILL: Moodie, the house is gone! Save what you can of your winter stores and furniture.

MOODIE: Moodie thought differently. Prompt and energetic in danger, and possessing admirable presence of mind and coolness when others yield to agitation and despair, he sprang upon the burning loft!

MR. MOODIE: (*springing onto a crate*) Water!

MOODIE: Alas, there was none!

MR. MOODIE: Snow, then, snow! Hand me up pailfuls of snow!

(*They form a bucket brigade.*)

MOODIE: Oh it was bitter work filling those pails with frozen snow, but Mr. Traill and I worked as fast as we were able. More help had arrived, and the men were already cutting away the burning roof, flinging the flaming brands into the deep snow.

MR. TRAILL: Mrs. Moodie, have you any pickled meat?

MOODIE: Yes, we have!

MR. TRAILL: Well, then, fling the beef into the snow, and let us have the brine!

MOODIE: This was an admirable plan! Wherever the brine wetted the shingles, the fire turned from it and concentrated into one spot. Our gallant friends soon managed to bring the fire under control before it destroyed the walls (*congratulations all around*). Six men, without the aid of water, succeeded in saving a building which almost all had deemed past hope, showing how much can be done by persons working in union, without bustle and confusion, or running in each other's way. Beyond the damage done to the building, the loss of our potatoes and two sacks of flour, we had escaped in a manner almost miraculous.

Molly Thom, director, actor, theatre administrator, is the founder of Toronto's New Ideas Festival, which develops original writing for the stage. After writing *The Bush-Ladies: In Their Own Words* over 30 years ago, she recently revised it, "finding a turning point in the life of each woman, that moment where they turn the corner from the awfulness of it all to where they connect with their new lives."

Activities: The Bush-Ladies

1. **Examine Character:** Working in a small group, make a list of the skills and characteristics that enable these women to survive in a difficult environment. Individually, write a brief character sketch of two of the women, using supporting details.

2. **Consider Theme:** Choose one passage from the excerpt that you believe best expresses the theme. Write a short, polished expository essay that includes the following elements: an interpretation of the passage, an analysis showing how it relates to the theme, an explanation outlining why you chose it, and a conclusion showing how this particular theme relates to your personal experience.

3. **Understand Technique:** In groups of three or four, research the history and function of the chorus in theatre. Determine why Thom might have chosen to use a chorus in this play. Present your findings to the class.

4. **Create a Cover:** Create a mock-up of a cover for a published version of the play. Start by brainstorming with a partner the purpose of a cover and criteria for an effective cover. In writing, briefly explain your design decisions.

Hunger Striking

Kit Brennan

... I am in the waiting room, they are behind a screen. It's as if I'm not there, as if, as I get smaller, I am shrinking out of sight.

—"I'm sorry, Mr. O'Brien, but your daughter's not responding to treatment. In fact, she's losing ground fast, I'm quite worried."

"She's got her own shelf in the kitchen, we let her fix the food she wants."

"She's adept at fooling you—at fooling herself. Have you seen her in a swimsuit lately?"

"She doesn't come to the pool with us anymore."

"The psychologist tells me they're not making any progress."

"Is that her fault? He's the doctor, for god's sake!"

"Mr. O'Brien, I understand you're going through a tough time—"

"What the hell do you mean?"

"I'm sure the loss of employment—"

"How dare you! How dare you!"

"The pressures parental figures are under reflects on the psyche of—"

"Are you telling me parents should muffle and reduce their lives, in case they 'reflect' upon their kids? That's cannibalism, doctor, in my books, and it's not what I believe in. Parenting's part of a package— and that includes pain and heartache and joy and love, and if you're telling me to further sanitize my—life of quiet, bloody desperation—I say no!"

... Muuuuuummm!

"—I know you're fine, Sarah. Your father and I know you're strong. You're extremely strong. But we're frightened. Listen, look, I can put my finger and thumb together round your arm—come on, sweetheart, it's too much. You need help. Just for a few days. Just till you stabilize."

I remember—

Finger and thumb together. You can see into Tir N'an Og through the fairy ring.

And what's in there?

Anything you want. It's eternity.

And what's eternity?

A wish never to leave.

Kelpie? Come. Come. Now. (*fierce*) NOW!

We drive for several hours. Anne is with us. She's living with Tod now. We don't speak of him. This "hospital"—a large piece of property, lots of trees. That's nice. The place itself, the building, and the smell. Like boiled bedpans, or death rags ... My sense of smell's acute. I throw up from strong perfume ... still. No perfume in this place. They leave me here. Of course I'll be fine, goodbye, see you soon. Some of the nurses are nuns. Every morning, a senior doctor looks in on me, trailed by hungry interns. Mostly men. One woman. She doesn't interest me, she wants too much to be liked, to be accepted. Pathetic. I am different. They've never seen anyone like me. I am a new creation. They come along at 8:00 a.m. like a flock of seagulls. I float up to the ceiling. They lift my hospital gown above my ribcage—sheet draping my hips—crowd around, one after another, gently poking my enlarged spleen. They seem thrilled. They chatter like magpies. I'm not there. I am watching myself from the ceiling, a crowd of white coats around a wasted body in a bed; I try to find a way out, hitting my disembodied head on ceiling plaster, sure that one day, one day, I'll have the key and I'll be gone.

There's a pecking order, right? Fatties at the bottom, they're the plebs. Can't stop eating till their stomachs are stapled shut, pathetic, eh? Next up the evolutionary ladder are bulimics—they are secretive, ashamed. They admire the anorexics. But they can't do it. Instead they vomit; comfort themselves with food, then throw it back up. The acid rots their teeth out. And it's wasteful, think of all the starving peoples of the world. No one has to say it; they think it, they know it. They punish themselves every single day. Then like a shining light come the anorexics, the admired ones. Thoroughbreds, aristocrats. They hear voices, sit still for hours at a time or explode screaming and running. Extremely temperamental. They're the ones that die. It's quite romantic. Like consumptives, pre-Raphaelite Ophelias, floating down the river.

They don't get reproached with wasting food though. Think of that.

(*Responding to a nurse.*) Good morning, Sister. We are both fine, thank you. Humour's to be expected, I'm reading Lenny Bruce—(*as her book is pulled away*) Hey, that's mine! ... They'd probably agree, I shouldn't be. Too late now, it's in here. (*indicating her head*) ... No. No movement at all. Tragic but true. I think I'm going to blow up. Actually I'm serious, I'm in a lot of pain. I'm going to explode! It doesn't make sense to stuff more in when it's all still sitting there, don't you understand, you stupid cow!

(*Responding to a doctor.*) No, I wasn't feeling charitable this morning, but Sister Isobel was provoking me! Oh really? Well, (*She imitates him.*) "I think you'll find" she gets a sadistic pleasure out of it, talking about bowel movements when she knows I can't stand it! I *don't* think the world is out to get me, I—they won't let me take a bath—it's the only way I can get warm, and when I'm in the tub, they're constantly looking in, I can't lock the door to keep them from staring, I'm—! (*She listens.*) Privacy. To take my bath. Fine.

Alone, at last. I've craved it, I've fought for it—I cry with hunger. Sit up for hours in the dark and cry, silently, mouth open. The food from each day's meals lying squashed and rotting under my mattress. They don't know. They think I'm obeying. They can't figure out why I'm not gaining weight—I'm losing it faster. You'd better hurry up, you morons! Don't you know anything? Can't you hear me? It takes them two weeks before the smell from my bed alerts them to what I am doing. They probably think it's my breath, so it takes them longer to notice. I've lost another ten pounds.

One day, walking, I come upon a nun. They don't wear habits, but you can always tell. The big serious cross round their necks kind of gives them away. I tower over this nun. I like the feeling.

"You're Sarah. I've heard of you."

Like a racehorse, everyone is betting on my chances. Including me.

She is Sister Mary Simon. Why are you a nun?

"I am a nun out of choice. Just as you are thin out of choice. Makes sense?"

"I guess so."

"Let's walk, shall we?"

She tells me about herself. I don't ask, don't say anything, but she is undeterred. Her mother, Helen, was English. Married a graduate student from Calcutta, in 1910. Helen was ostracized—by friends, by family. He lost his scholarships, had to go back to India. They promised to be together as soon as they could. It was a question of money. Helen never heard from him again. She found out she was pregnant. A terrible—complication. One day she met a woman who was also alone, but not afraid, who was out in the world, doing. So Helen also joined the Women's Social and Political Union, became a suffragette.

"Suffragette. What's that?"

She sends me to the hospital library. I read. These are my people! The Pankhursts, Lady Lytton—and—Mahatma Gandhi, Bobby Sands, Simone Weill—it's protest, it's political! I thought I was alone! "Yes but Sarah," she says, "what are you striking for? Can you tell me? What do you want?" I put my hands over my ears, but—again she draws me on.

She was born, christened Suna in 1911. It means light after darkness.

"Why do you let yourself be called anything other than Suna? That is so beautiful!"

She tells me that we have not yet come to that part of the story.

"What happened to Helen then? And where was your father?"

Helen became a hunger-striker. Suna was raised by several women during the final frantic years before the War, depending which of them was in or out of prison at any one time. She tells of a memory—probably her first memory at age two or three—of her mother, pale and dirty, coming down a garden pathway leaning on the arms of two other women. They let go of her, and she kneels in the garden, pulls the little girl down beside her, eats a handful of soil, then curls up on the ground and falls asleep. Suna recalls the feeling of electricity, the fierceness, vibrating in her mother's body.

Helen had finally learned the truth. On the journey home to Calcutta, a stray bullet; a marksman ran amok through a crowd at a train station. Only one had died.

"Your ... father?"

"Sarah? Look at me. What is happening?"

I hear roaring. "I'm sick of this place. The whole thing."

"Why sick?"

"I don't know. It stinks!"

"Yes, I know, life stinks. It is also hard. But the opposite is death. You don't wish that do you? Do you?"

"Maybe."

"You're asking for help."

"No, I'm not."

"I recognize it."

"No you don't! Your father never even knew you were—born?"

"It's not that he didn't want to, it was ... he couldn't. He couldn't come back to us. He was gone."

" ... I feel sick! What's going to happen to me?"

"That's up to you, isn't it? The choices you make."

"I can't do anything, you're crazy, I'm stuck in this—box, I—"

"Oh Sarah, you are not quite letting yourself see the other side. You have to look for it, and fight for it, there is no doubt of that, but it is there."

She makes me think, all the time, think so hard. She never coddles me, or calls me stupid. She never pretends to feel anything for me that isn't real. I see a tiny hole into the real world through her unwavering gaze.

"Sarah. Turn it around. What do you want?"

"To ... I don't know!" More roaring—you are evil, don't say it, don't deny them, don't give anything anything nothing away! I push through, I shove, "to—have a choice?—something more? Something—else?"

No trumpet sounds. No apocalypse begins. Instead her calm voice goes on. My heart begins to settle as I hear syllables and vowels—only later do I make sense of them. "—reasonable. Begin, perhaps, with music—classical, as well as your own. Then art? And we'll talk. Find what's been uplifting through the centuries, as well as the holocausts. You want knowledge, you must be wide-ranging."

"Will it be my knowledge?"

"Yes."

"Will it be safe?"

—and at that she would always laugh. "Nothing is safe, Sarah. You don't want me to lie to you. You are here for many reasons, but the main one is you need love—without sorrow, without competition, and not bound up in guilt or pain. This is not easy to find, or to give, until you can articulate it to yourself. You are making the first steps."

Kit Brennan (*born 1958, Vancouver, British Columbia*), actor, playwright, won the Canadian National Playwriting Competition in 1994 with *Tiger Heart*. She has been a playwright-in-residence at Centaur Theatre and coordinator of the playwriting program at Concordia University, Montreal.

Activities: Hunger Striking

1. **Describe Characters:** Create a *dramatis personae* by listing and briefly describing each of the characters in the excerpt. Find examples of *dramatis personae* from several other contemporary plays, and note any differences in format and amount of detail.

2. **Analyze Characters:** With specific reference to her name (Suna), explain Sister Mary Simon's role in the excerpt. Why is this character an appropriate adversary for Sarah? Compare your responses with a partner's, and discuss any differences.

3. **Discuss the Title:** In groups of four, discuss possible meanings of the play's title, and come up with alternative titles. Appoint a spokesperson in each group to summarize the discussion and share it with the class.

4. **Create a Poster:** Using what you know about the play from the excerpt, create a poster to advertise a performance of it. Consider the purpose of the poster as you select visuals and words. Ask a classmate to critique your poster.

Land of Trash

Ian Tamblyn

CHARACTERS

NUKE: a young street kid
STRYDER: another street kid
CARSON: an old mutant living in a trash dump

Scene 1

Lights down. Distant barking. Dogs on trail of something, their sounds getting closer. CARSON has hidden in some of the trash on stage. Just as dogs sound as if they are about to pounce on the audience, the doors near the stage burst open, STRYDER and NUKE race around the audience and "set" on their bikes.

STRYDER: Nix on phalt path! Down get here! Nuke!—down get here! Quick!

NUKE: (*in pain*) Can't down get! Tired I! Stomach is a stitch! ... I ...

STRYDER: Use inhaler! You can do! Stash bike ... the dogs. The dogs!

NUKE: Coming! See dogs on hill ... dogs on hill!

STRYDER: Know I. Trackers with them?

NUKE: No—jus dogs.... Bulls!

STRYDER: Quick!

NUKE: Should no leave bikes here!

STRYDER: Back for bikes—they no find. Stash bikes. Lose dogs now! What be real. There! Stash bikes. They no find. Run sewage lagoon. We cross there! Dogs no come. Hide us in trash ... you make it?

NUKE: Yeah—I be o.k. You see dogs?

STRYDER: (*laughing*) Yeah—nosing the lagoon. Lost in bigger smells. We got 'em!

NUKE: Good. Still no Trackers?

STRYDER: No. Jus dogs. Turning back now—we safe.

Melinda Stevens, 16, as Nuke

NUKE: Was close.

STRYDER: Was close but Stryder and Nuke too tough for Trackers—fact.

NUKE: Total fact.

STRYDER: Watch you see?

NUKE: Too high! Everything reading high—PCBs ... Dioxins ... FURans ... why this dump open—still too hot! This dump still hot. Too dangerous. We split!

STRYDER: No! We here now! They say dump re-open for trashers. Seventy-five-year limit. They say!

NUKE: They say! How many times they say—and they be wrong! We go!

STRYDER: No! We here. We first in this dump for trades. We be thick in the best trades. Without trades we no eat, be a fact.

NUKE: Jamming this dump be bad news Stryder! Look—check out levels—out of control! You 'n me, our control be high already, we get disease. We go—o.k.?

STRYDER: Go? Where? Back to dogs! No. Got to work this dump, we need trades Nuke, that a fact.

NUKE: Fact.

STRYDER: No good—no choice. Check it out.

NUKE: Your show. Be I check it out! Strange world. No 'nize no thing here. Extreme old dump Stryder. Wow! Look over there—old technotrash! Stryder, this be before meltdowns!

STRYDER: What I say! Old world dump. Be our first. Excellent trades here Nuke, we be thick in trades. Fossil fuel cars, computers, digitals, electronics ...

NUKE: Chemicals ...

STRYDER: Back off! Be here now. Keep counter on—we stay clear of chemical soup.

NUKE: Be a plan, but we thick in soup.

(NUKE and STRYDER poke through the set of garbage, familiar to the audience, but mysterious to them. They are perplexed by everything they see. STRYDER picks up an old transistor radio.)

STRYDER: What be?

NUKE: No know ...

STRYDER: Transmitter some kind? Got antennae. Sus this numbers cross front.

NUKE: Hmm, never seen. Check inside—primitive circuit. Ancient. Something though.

STRYDER: What be? (*pause*) Memory. Was old guy walkin' streets. Was flipped but sang ... songs. Noises. Yeah—he listened to noises on Radians. Radians! Was what it was! Old guy sang song go "at McDonald's" ... something like that—no know. He say Radian songs no more. System take over communications. No use now. (*STRYDER throws radio away.*)

NUKE: No—I fix! We listen to the System transmissions. We be head of Trackers.

STRYDER: Good head glow!—you still strong upstairs!

(*STRYDER retrieves radio and they continue to sift through junk. STRYDER mumbles the line ... "at McDonald's" ... but only that part of the melody. From back of stage a hubcap is tossed landing near STRYDER and NUKE. They immediately go into alert, defensive stance.*)

STRYDER: What be?

NUKE: No know—we split!

STRYDER: No! We stay. Maybe rat knock something.

NUKE: Tracker dog?

STRYDER: Doubt—they come straight for ...

(*Another noise is made offstage.*)

NUKE: There!

STRYDER: Mutant?

NUKE: No see. If dump open, Mutant no be here. They only allowed hot dumps.

STRYDER: Maybe this Mutant no know this dump open. Be the wolf.

NUKE: I the wolf.

(*CARSON enters, limping, very angry.*)

CARSON: Get out of my dump! Little punks—get out!

STRYDER: Is Mutant! Careful!

NUKE: Split! Back to bikes! Quick!

STRYDER: No! Dogs back there ... wait a minute.

CARSON: Little worms! You hear me, I said get outta here! Now!

NUKE: He disease.

STRYDER: Fact. Weak—take him out easy. See what he say.

NUKE: You crazy!

STRYDER: So say they! Time for a tease ...

CARSON: You don't hear do you. I said ...

STRYDER: We heard old man. Stand back. We cut you down.

CARSON: What's the matter? Are you afraid of a sick old man with a little ... INFECTION! (*He lunges at them. STRYDER and NUKE jump back.*)

STRYDER: Back off! Report you to Quarantines.

CARSON: You won't report me to Quarantines, kid. They're after you for something already. I saw the dogs.

NUKE: You disease. We get word in.

CARSON: Quarantines. Ha! You think I'm afraid of Quarantines? What can they do to me that hasn't been done already?

STRYDER: Take you out. New law.

CARSON: Is that so? There's new laws every day—get out!

STRYDER: Not going. System post sign say this dump open. We here. For trades. You, Mutant, leave when dump opens. Know rule.

CARSON: "Know rule" ... listen to you talk. What an abomination of the English language.

NUKE: Speak no in old way—no time.

CARSON: Pathetic. You're street kids, aren't you? You're runaways.

STRYDER: So?

CARSON: You kids are on the outside just like me!

NUKE: We no disease Mutant! We no sick!

CARSON: You will be ... is it bad out there?

NUKE: All broke down since the floods, most of the city under.

CARSON: Where are your parents?

NUKE: Lost in floods, no find.

CARSON: I'm sorry.

NUKE: Sorry? About what? You know why he sorry Stryder?

STRYDER: No. Nuke: Watch his power. He pulling us in with his words. He trick us with feelings.

CARSON: What are you talking about? Don't you miss your parents?

STRYDER: NO! Drop subject! Look, Mutant ...

CARSON: My name is CARSON.

NUKE: CARSNO! CARSNOGENIC—Got a yok on it.

STRYDER: Look Carsno—needs we trades for food. Understand. Needs to work this dump. No trouble you.

CARSON: Fine. There's nothing I can do to stop you. You know about the chemicals here, I suppose?

NUKE: Seen 'em on counter.

CARSON: Yes, you see them on the counter, all right, but there are some things the counter doesn't read.

STRYDER: We know old man ...

CARSON: Yeah, you punks know everything, don't you? Well stay away from this area over here. See the signs? Radioactive. (*laughs*) Stay away if you don't want to end up like me.

NUKE: Hey! Where you go?

STRYDER: Let him go—you fallin' for his power.

NUKE: How he live out here?

CARSON: What did you say?

NUKE: Nothing.

CARSON: Ha! I get by. A sick old man doesn't need much now, does he?

(*CARSON exits*)

STRYDER: Why you talk to him so much?

NUKE: Wanted him close to get count on him. Meltdown victim. High radioactivity.

STRYDER: I sus. Nuke—no talk with him so much. You know he trap you with his language. Has power.

NUKE: You believe?

STRYDER: Fact.

NUKE: Very strange. Maybe power ... maybe hidin' something. Feeling from sixth sense.

STRYDER: Felt that too. We sus.

NUKE: Why he let us stay?

STRYDER: He know we be right. Maybe soft.

NUKE: Says we be the same—both outside.

STRYDER: Fact. Very strange. No mind. Gots works. You be with counter, I be detector. Mine this joint.

(*NUKE turns on his chemical analyzer, starts reading around the dump.*)

NUKE: No mine here Stryder ... Dump full of chemicals, ground soaked—maximum danger, counter can't keep up ... a Love Canal.

STRYDER: Stay on counter. I dig. This dump a goldmine, Nuke. Tons of stuff. Motors, medical, some very strange. Like no other dump seen before. Think, a goldmine!

NUKE: Some goldmine.

STRYDER: Why Mutant hang around here? Must be something keep him round.

NUKE: Maybe ... something.

STRYDER: Come on—time for trades!

(NUKE and STRYDER search through junk. STRYDER finds phone.)

STRYDER: Hey Nuke, here! Found something!

NUKE: What be?

STRYDER: No know—get dirt off. Strange. Remember ...

NUKE: 'Nother transmitter. Portable. Banned now. Only System use them now. Portable phone. Was in cars I think.

STRYDER: Car phone! Too much! How old?

NUKE: Cars banned in 2015 after second crisis, maybe 60 years. Maybe more.

STRYDER: Extreme. Take back—get going. We tap into line, cause all kinds of action.

NUKE: Get us killed, Stryder.

STRYDER: No way. Hey, something else down here. It got the sweats on it.

NUKE: What be?

STRYDER: No know ... hey ... be a pipe ... pipe goes ... this way ... Nuke, check out.

NUKE: Pipe clean. It sweats.

STRYDER: Water! Be a water pipe, Nuke! We hit the jackpot! The Mutant's got water!

NUKE: Can't be. No clean water in dump, Stryder.

STRYDER: Check it out! Follow pipe ... pipe go ... come on ... we follow pipe ... Nuke?

NUKE: Can't believe—clean water ... why ...

STRYDER: The pipe ... it goes ... out of dump ... look ... it goes ... up into hills.

NUKE: Right out of dump! You maybe right Stryder! Clean water!

(They exit. CARSON re-enters, throws stuff over greenhouse, talking into it.)

CARSON: When did they open the dump?! They didn't post a sign! I must do something to get rid of the Modems. They must not find you my precious. This place is mine! It belongs to me. Those

Modems—festering rats. I've seen their kind before. They feel nothing, their feelings are dead. If only I could talk to them—No! I must get rid of them! They must not find you my hopefuls, they will destroy everything! Are you o.k.? I must think clearly ... there, there, I must cover you up—there is danger near ... yes my sweets, great danger. (CARSON *exits*.)

(STRYDER *and* NUKE *enter*.)

STRYDER: Major find Nuke!

NUKE: Total fact.

STRYDER: That be why Mutant here. He have himself a source. This be worth a goldmine. Knew there was something 'bout him.

NUKE: No clean water left outside System control. This be deep secret.

STRYDER: Nuke and Stryder secret!

NUKE: What?

STRYDER: We tap into line—fill jugs—this be the ticket Nuke ... sell in streets. We never be hungry no more.

NUKE: We take water?

STRYDER: Fact. This our source, too.

NUKE: The Mutant ...

STRYDER: Nix—nothing he can do! Who he tell?

NUKE: He take us out—this serious.

STRYDER: NO—Mutant soft inside. Can tell.

NUKE: You crazy, Stryder! Crazy!

STRYDER: So say they! Plan?

NUKE: Plan.

STRYDER: Fact! Sus out glass bottle—bottle—clean—plastic something. Tap into line with knife.

NUKE: Mutant with water—very rad. No thick.

STRYDER: No way—this Mutant got lights on.

NUKE: Stryder?

STRYDER: What say?

NUKE: What Mutant using water for? No selling water for sure ...

STRYDER: Lights on Nuke ... no know. He be up to something. We sus. Something going on ... Hey! Cut through! Ho! Water be ... (STRYDER *has big reaction to the taste of the water, as if it was an elixir*.) Too much! Check it out ... (*laughing*) ... it be clean water!

(NUKE *runs for jugs.* STRYDER *and* NUKE *both kneel down to gather drinking water. They do not see* CARSON *approaching.* CARSON *hits bucket with cane.* NUKE *and* STRYDER *look up to see* CARSON *holding a large iron bar over his head.*)

NUKE and STRYDER: No!

CARSON: You little punks, I warned you!

STRYDER: No touch—we're gone!

CARSON: I should have known ... you are just like the rats around here. You can't help yourself, can you?

NUKE: We go! Back off!

CARSON: NOW!

STRYDER: We're history—relax, old man.

CARSON: Don't come back here.

NUKE: Oh—we come back.

CARSON: What?

STRYDER: You heard Mutant. We come back through System. They love to know. To horde a crime. To horde water a big crime—eh, Carsno?

CARSON: Why you little ...

STRYDER: Stryder be my name. Say you what?

CARSON: Punks.

STRYDER: We be the street. No push the street. The street push back. You 'stand.

CARSON: (*sarcastic*) I yes, I understand—you kids are a real threat! You've already told me I'm not supposed to be here so I'm gone—take the water—it's all yours.

STRYDER: Good. You see this thing clear.

CARSON: Yes—very clear. But maybe just because I don't want you or the System to have this water, just maybe I will contaminate it with disease and you won't know till it's too late! I could do that.

NUKE: No!

CARSON: Watch me! I can be the street too!

STRYDER: Fine! Good one Carsno! You got lights on—can see. Cut a deal?

CARSON: What kind of deal?

STRYDER: For water rights. You no pollute—we no report you to System. You live here—we no tell. Be fact—we hide you.

CARSON: Someone will find out ...

STRYDER: Listen disease. You no pollute. We protect you. No one know. We trade clean water to streets. Be our ticket.

CARSON: Oh sure—water to the streets. Next thing you know everyone will be following you up here.

NUKE: We say we tapping System water. They leave us alone. Too frightened.

STRYDER: That's it! Nuke and I best survivors and best dodgers ... no one find out. Deal?

CARSON: For now! But if anyone finds out about this water you know what I will do.

STRYDER: Fact. Grab jugs Nuke! We got our ticket!

CARSON: No! Wait! You must not cut my line with a knife! I'll set up a tap!

NUKE: You give us tap—we set up—you got sickness.

CARSON: Fine.

STRYDER: Deal?

CARSON: Deal— ... no speak ... oh my goodness, I'm beginning to talk like these fools.

NUKE: Big gamble Stryder ... you pin him up.

STRYDER: That be plan but Mutant got the smarts.

NUKE: Serious contender, must watch close.

STRYDER: Don't go into him. Maximum danger.

NUKE: I watch.

STRYDER: I get bikes for transport, you come.

NUKE: I stay, fill jugs, you bikes ...

STRYDER: Be a plan. Don't talk to him too much.

NUKE: No way.

STRYDER: I judge. Be gone.

(STRYDER exits. NUKE fills jugs of water.)

NUKE: Mutant have got smarts. What he be about with water. Find out ... about him.

(CARSON approaches NUKE.)

NUKE: Stand back!

CARSON: I am not going to touch you! Careful—that one had cleaning solvent in it.

NUKE: Fact.

(silence)

CARSON: It's not just the disease you're afraid of is it? There's something else ...

NUKE: Not afraid—some say old ways have power—no believe.

CARSON: We have a power? That's a good one. I don't think we have any power at all. If I had any power ...

NUKE: Carson?

CARSON: Yes?

NUKE: What happen?

CARSON: To what?

NUKE: This.

CARSON: You don't know?

NUKE: Know story. Know what we got. World change. Heat go up. Brown clouds come. Eating rain fall. Meltdowns. Floods come. Cities drown. Everything breakdown.

CARSON: Yep—you've got it right—that's pretty well how it went.

NUKE: No! That be a story. What be real? Want to know what happened.

CARSON: Why?—it's all gone!—your story says it all—it happened so fast.

NUKE: Tell me.

CARSON: I don't know. I've had a lifetime to see the changes and I don't believe it myself. We just didn't know it would come so fast ...

NUKE: Old man! You mumble like everyone else!

CARSON: All right! We took too much from the earth and never gave anything back. No—that's not quite right. We put things back, into the air, on the land and in the water, but most of it was bad. We thought we could go on taking forever, that the world would always give us more, but of course we were wrong. We were killing the planet. The heat built up first ...

NUKE: No more!

CARSON: Why?—you asked me to explain?

NUKE: I hear! How could you let this be—you knew!

CARSON: Yes, we knew—but we didn't believe it was happening. We did not see the world as a living, breathing thing. We thought we could just take more and more and it would go on forever. And everybody wanted more. There were some early warnings and at the turn of the last century, there was some concern, but it was almost like a fad. You see, at that time everybody talked about the environment and everybody said that there had to be a change, but in the end nobody really did much of anything. You see, people just weren't prepared to give up the very things that were causing the problem. No one believed we would actually have to give up *anything*.

NUKE: Carson! My point be—you knew! You could have made a change! Floods, disease, killing rain, didn't have to be!

CARSON: Yes—it didn't have to be. We could have saved the planet, but we couldn't give up our toys. Then—it was too late and the change came so fast.

NUKE: Now everything gone. Everything grey. We live in ruins of what was. World be dead. Story called "The Taking."

CARSON: I'm afraid so.

(*silence*)

CARSON: Nuke?—is that your name?

NUKE: Yeah ... be my name.

CARSON: Can you tell me something?

NUKE: What be?

CARSON: The cities? What has happened there? Mutants have been banned for twenty years. I would like to know.

NUKE: No. You no want to know. But I tell. Water up twenty-five feet so say. Too many people crowd above waterline. More come every day. Little food. Disease. Say System control but that no be. They control what be left. Supplies, food, guns. System be corrupt. Serve themselves. Be a war to survive.

CARSON: Picking through dumps is how you survive?

NUKE: You got a problem. Trades for food. Be all.

(*NUKE turns away from CARSON.*)

CARSON: Hey!—what are you doing? We were having a conversation!

NUKE: We talk too much—Stryder!

STRYDER: (*comes in with bikes*) What be?

NUKE: Was slippin' in.

STRYDER: Carsno! You back off! Now!

CARSON: I was ... What's going on here!? This is my home, not yours. I just let you take my precious ...

STRYDER: This be your home!—this land of trash! Some home!

CARSON: Why you!

STRYDER: Too many questions! Leave Nuke be!

CARSON: He was asking me!!! I just asked about the city.

STRYDER: No mind! I tell you. Story go—this ting we got no need be. Story go—you turned world against itself. Story go—you push it—it push back. Story go—you keep pushing. Story go—like that, Mutant—so what you need to know? Eh!

CARSON: No—it wasn't me. I was against it all ... you must understand!

STRYDER: Understand. You did no ting. Where's the world you had? All gone! All gone! Where's animals, fish, forest, all gone! All gone. What you do?

CARSON: I ...

STRYDER: Come on, Nuke! I show him power of word! Choke in throat ... but, say they all! Take water with no thanks—the least we get from this land of trash! Come on, Nuke!

(STRYDER and NUKE leave on bikes laden down with water jugs. CARSON is left staring at them centre stage.)
(Music cue)

Scene 2

NUKE: Dogs? See you dogs?

STRYDER: Nix—Trackers 'n dogs long gone. Ace move Nuke.

NUKE: Radian transmitter work fine with solder 'n batteries. We got a fix on Trackers, no problem.

STRYDER: Got 'm beat for good. Good head glow.

NUKE: Light go on another way.

STRYDER: What be?

NUKE: Thinking water not the total picture.

STRYDER: Fact. Thinking he be hiding something else.

NUKE: Could be he throw us off with water. Easy gift. Water for something.

STRYDER: Be my thought. We check out. Find his treasure.

(CARSON suddenly reappears.)

CARSON: Treasure! What treasure?

STRYDER: Oh! No treasure, I mean treasure be water ...

NUKE: Come back for more ...

CARSON: I see ... more water ...

NUKE: More water ...

STRYDER: Yeah—sold all water for trades—everyone wants water. We be a hit!

NUKE: Carson?

CARSON: Yes?

NUKE: What was it like before the change?

STRYDER: Nuke!

NUKE: Take him off ...

STRYDER: Sus.

CARSON: What's going on here? What are you two whispering about?

NUKE: Nothing. Stryder fears your language. Old language has power so say. I no feared of language.

CARSON: I should say not, the way you torture it. You Modems think we have power in our language? How strange! I thought we had lost all power. Now what were you asking me?

NUKE: What was it like before the change?

CARSON: Where's your friend going?

NUKE: Jugs. Need more jugs.

CARSON: I see ... well ...what?

NUKE: The change ...

CARSON: (*suspicious*) Why are you so interested in the past? Are you just toying with an old man? Eh?

NUKE: No. Someone must remember. The street don't care.

CARSON: But you ask and then you get frightened. What are you frightened of?

NUKE: The colour of your language—too strong for a grey world.

(*several beats*)

CARSON: I understand. Are you sure you want to hear? The past. The world was a beautiful place. Cold, crisp days in winter, the lakes froze and white snow fell. Spring was rich with the smell of the warming earth and everything was full of life. Soon, the sweet fragrances of summer flowers would mingle in the air and dance with the fireflies at night.

NUKE: What's a firefly?

CARSON: A tiny insect that could glow in the dark, like miniature stars ... I haven't seen a firefly in forty years ...

NUKE: See no more.

CARSON: No. (*pause*) I miss the fall. Great wedges of geese flying down from the north, the trees aflame with colour.

NUKE: Trees burned in fall?

CARSON: No. (*laughs*) Well, in a way. How could you know? Nuke, the leaves changed colour in fall. The maple trees turned scarlet and crimson; the aspen, a breathtaking gold; some oak turned almost purple. The leaves fell and formed a thick carpet on the forest floor.

NUKE: What be L-Phant?

CARSON: Elephant? Oh, it was the largest land animal. It had long tusks and a longer nose they called a trunk, big ears and ...

NUKE: Yeah! And what be a Hypobottomus?

CARSON: (*laughing*) That's a Hippopotamus! They were big too, lived in the rivers like the Nile in Africa.

NUKE: All gone?

CARSON: All gone.

NUKE: Whales. Tell me whales!

CARSON: Whales were beautiful. The Blue Whale was the biggest animal the world has ever known.

NUKE: Bigger than a dinosaur?

CARSON: Yes. The Blue Whale could be eighty to a hundred feet long. It was ...

NUKE: No more!

CARSON: What's wrong. What did I say?

NUKE: Story too rich.

CARSON: Language was meant to be rich.

NUKE: Language has a memory? Stryder! Memory be the power.

STRYDER: Nuke!

NUKE: Come! Get me away!

(*STRYDER runs onto set.*)

STRYDER: You be?

NUKE: Falling in again—take me away.

STRYDER: Did good—throw him off me—found something.

NUKE: He gets me. He pulls tears from me.

STRYDER: Told you—he has powers.

CARSON: (*to himself*) I meant no harm. I didn't know I could affect him.

STRYDER: Stop! You know what be a spark. You play game of memories. Keep memories to yourself, old man—the past is dead. Nuke—we go back to streets. You ride?

NUKE: Yeah—I ride.

(NUKE and STRYDER exit.)

CARSON: That Stryder is up to something ... while I was talking to Nuke ...

(Cut to NUKE and STRYDER.)

STRYDER: Did good Nuke! You be o.k.?

NUKE: The story of the flaming trees ...

STRYDER: Why you listen? Stories afore change more dangerous than chemicals.

NUKE: Said world was beautiful.

STRYDER: Don't believe what he say! You go soft on him.

NUKE: I want to know what was.

STRYDER: What was long gone—no look back now. You throw him off be fine, but don't fall in.

NUKE: No fall. What you find?

STRYDER: Mutant got pipes all kinds joining—all go to different piles of junk.

(NUKE and STRYDER exit. Theme music.)

Scene 3

Darkness in the junk yard. NUKE and STRYDER with headlamps, searching.

STRYDER: Nuke!

NUKE: Yeah?

STRYDER: You ready?

NUKE: Yep. Ready.

STRYDER: Be the wolf.

NUKE: Stryder?

STRYDER: What?

NUKE: No harm Mutant ...

STRYDER: You soft on disease man?

NUKE: No. I ... Mutant give us water ticket, be all.

STRYDER: You fall in too much—give us this mess.

NUKE: Fact ...

STRYDER: Leave Mutant alone, he leave us alone. Go!

NUKE: Gone.

STRYDER: Find the line?

NUKE: Everything move! Mutant make a change!

STRYDER: On to us! Must be hiding treasure! Use detector!

NUKE: Nix. Make a noise.

STRYDER: Fact. Was over here?

NUKE: Thinking so ... Got it. Find line.

STRYDER: Total. Stop. Make a plan.

NUKE: You a plan?

STRYDER: You follow line—I sus Mutant. Give signal if find. Make
like back for ... detector ... left detector ... he no sus.

NUKE: Perfect, I gone.

STRYDER: Luck.

(NUKE crawls behind junk.)

STRYDER: Treasure. What be treasure? Treasure in a junk pile.
Treasure in a ruin. Be a joke. Thinking we don't know this mess a
mess. Six sense know was different. Six sense know a different
world. No need fall into words. Was trees, was birds, was
whales, was days without clouds. Light inside remember. Now
Nuke and Stryder rats in a dump. Be us all. So give us treasure!

*(NUKE signals. STRYDER rushes over to a pile of junk covering
greenhouse.)*

STRYDER: What you sus?

NUKE: Line lead here.

STRYDER: Clear junk ... something inside.

NUKE: Wait! Radioactive sign. No glow here.

(NUKE uncovers greenhouse.)

NUKE: Wrong! Is glow inside. Look.

STRYDER: Fact. What be? ... what be?!

*(STRYDER rips away junk. NUKE and STRYDER peer into greenhouse.
Greenhouse lights come on.)*

NUKE: Stryder, look!

STRYDER: Outside!

(NUKE and STRYDER stare at greenhouse world in disbelief.)

STRYDER: Be a world within a world ...

NUKE: Be a greenhouse ...

STRYDER: All the colours ...

NUKE: Be all the colours of the stories. Look! Stryder! Something hop in corner!

STRYDER: Where? What be?

NUKE: Under leaf! There! It hop!

STRYDER: See! What be?

NUKE: Fr ... Fr ... Frog!

STRYDER: What be a frog?

NUKE: No know. Never see—only hear.

STRYDER: Never see such beauty.

NUKE: This was world. Oh look!—something fly with big wings all colours—all too much!

STRYDER: Big hit for eyes, Nuke—be careful. What we do?

NUKE: No know—no wonder Carson hide this. Too much. All these things gone.

STRYDER: Fact. We looking back afore change. Never thought this.

NUKE: Stories be true. We leave alone. Too big.

STRYDER: No! Light go on!

NUKE: What be?

STRYDER: Light go on! Where's Mutant? Where's Carsno?

NUKE: What's up? Carson no around. Why you turn away?

STRYDER: Too much power in my eyes.

NUKE: We go ... we leave alone.

STRYDER: No! No get lost in wonder. We start our own—garden.

NUKE: Take his world! No way! We can't do that Stryder! We can't take his world!

STRYDER: Our ticket!

NUKE: No!

STRYDER: No guts.

NUKE: No. This be what they did. The taking. We can't do this no more! You push—it push back, remember Stryder! They die out there!

STRYDER: No! This be not the taking. Be the taking back!

NUKE: Not right!

STRYDER: So say! I say you soft on Mutant. Gone in. Plants maximum trades, you be for or against?

NUKE: Extreme against ... but we blood.

STRYDER: Fact. How we take?

NUKE: Be your show.

STRYDER: Fact. Get bag, quick.

(NUKE looks for bag.)

STRYDER: Little world. All the colours, never seen.

(NUKE comes back with bag.)

STRYDER: We take back in this.

NUKE: You say ...

STRYDER: That one. Take that one. Flower?

NUKE: Oh Stryder! Take care! No kill!

STRYDER: No problem. Into sack little world, new home. Quick—split outta here—bikes?

(They turn to meet CARSON. He is coming for them.)

CARSON: *(with controlled rage)* Put the plant back!

STRYDER: Mutant! —split up—street plan—Go!

NUKE: Leave plant!

STRYDER: No!

CARSON: Come back! It will die out there!

(CARSON chases after STRYDER but she is too fast. Chase continues around the dump. Plant is often in danger. Finally, CARSON traps NUKE.)

CARSON: So! It's come to this, has it?

NUKE: Was not ...

CARSON: Don't tell me you weren't part of this. Call Stryder back now!

NUKE: I can't ...

CARSON: You want to look like me, Nuke? You want to be banished like me? I'll give you the touch!

NUKE: No ... please ...

CARSON: Then call her back. Now!

NUKE: Stryder! Where you be?

(silence)

NUKE: Stryder! Mutant got me! Come!

STRYDER: Nuke?

CARSON: Tell her to bring the plant back.

NUKE: Stryder! Quick! Bring plant! He give me the touch!

CARSON: Now, we'll see what kind of friend the street makes! I should have known you couldn't just settle for the water. Always more, always more!

NUKE: Not my idea ...

CARSON: Your tough friend, eh? Where's your tough friend now?

(STRYDER returns from behind CARSON and NUKE.)

STRYDER: (calmly) I'm here.

CARSON: My plant. Give it back! I want my ...

STRYDER: Shut up! Let Nuke go—you get plant!

CARSON: No! I'm not that much a fool! You'll pull some kind of trick. I want the plant back in the greenhouse or your friend gets the touch!

NUKE: Stryder—play straight—Mutant over edge—mean what he say!

CARSON: Those plants are everything to me!

STRYDER: You no let one plant go?

CARSON: No! They will die out there! You don't know how to take care of them!

STRYDER: No tell me of caretaking!—look around, be the care you take!

CARSON: No! I fought against them all! I saw the world turning—I did all I could to stop the madness, the greed!

STRYDER: Well, old man, I guess you didn't fight enough, and now you disease Nuke for one plant. You still don't know eh, Carsno?

CARSON: No! You have it wrong. I must save what little there is left. The plants must come first now—it is *you* Stryder that has not changed. You continue to take! I can't allow this. It is my last fight.

STRYDER: I understand. You no give us something that lives—you give us a land of trash. Here be plant. Luck.

(STRYDER tosses the plant high in the air. CARSON looks up to catch it. NUKE escapes. As CARSON is about to catch the plant, STRYDER knocks him over with metal detector. STRYDER grabs plant. They run. CARSON chases after them.)

CARSON: Please! Don't take my precious away!

STRYDER: Yesterday's news old man, we're gone!

(As STRYDER is about to take off on bike, NUKE stops. CARSON catches up but holds back.)

STRYDER: Come on Nuke! Got him beat!

NUKE: It won't work.

STRYDER: What no work? Come on!

NUKE: No Stryder—no run. No sense.

STRYDER: What are you talking now?

NUKE: What we doing? Where we run? So we got plant—one more thing, like other things, probably die like he say ...

STRYDER: No!

NUKE: Yes. Listen. We run all the time. We run now. Where to? Back to streets, back to dogs. No more.

STRYDER: No stand you ...

NUKE: We be running from the wrong place. We stay here.

CARSON: What are you talking about?

NUKE: Stay here with you Carson—help you out.

STRYDER: You gone over! Nuke!

CARSON: Stay here—help?

NUKE: Yeah—you no live forever. Who look after green world when you're gone ...

CARSON: I hadn't thought that far. You would stay and build with me?

NUKE: Be a plan.

STRYDER: Oh Nuke, you gone over—you fallen in.

NUKE: No. I thinking with big light on. Think. This place be water, this place be a green world. This place—a place to start again. Build more green worlds. Think. This place have water. This place have green world. No one know. Safe here. Could be a home. Build more green worlds.

STRYDER: No! This is a dump! This no green world! Be too late for greening! This be mine—this plant. Be my green world. Don't make mistake Nuke—this no greening, you speak dreams.

CARSON: We can't let it all disappear ...

STRYDER: Be quiet fool! Nuke—listen to the street!

NUKE: I stay if that can be.

CARSON: Yes—you can stay.

STRYDER: Fine. Betray the street. Be one with disease. I gone—you be history.

NUKE: History is the taking.

STRYDER: Say what?

NUKE: You heard. Be well Stryder.

CARSON: My plant ...

NUKE: The plant be her need—let it go ...

(STRYDER *walks to edge of stage and gets on bike. About to leave when stops.*)

STRYDER: No. Not right. Nuke is right. Carsno. Can't be part of the taking. Must bring back the green world. Bring it back. There still be time. There still be hope. Carson! Nuke! Strange—fighting for a green world from the land of trash. Who would believe ...

(STRYDER *returns to* NUKE *and* CARSON. NUKE *pushes* STRYDER *to* CARSON. STRYDER *hands plant to* CARSON, *who takes flower and puts it into greenhouse. They stare at the green world in wonder.*)

NUKE: Good head glow Stryder.

CARSON: Yeah—good head glow.

Ian Tamblyn (*born Thunder Bay, Ontario*), musician, playwright, songwriter, has recorded 17 albums and written over 1500 songs. His plays include *Dreamwalker* and *Legends of the Northern Swamp*. An environmentalist and adventure traveller, Tamblyn has made trips to Greenland and Antarctica.

Activities: Land of Trash

1. **Create a Glossary:** Make a glossary to explain 10 words or phrases in the play that are either "new" or used in a new way. Provide small illustrations where appropriate. Look at classmates' glossaries to compare definitions.

2. **Make a Time Line:** Work with a partner to create a time line of significant events that occurred between the present and the time of the play. Where necessary, make educated guesses about the time of events. Discuss your time line with another pair.

3. **Dramatize the Play:** Working in a group, prepare a live performance, video presentation, or oral reading of two to three pages of the play. Pay attention to clear pronunciation and interpretation of character. Present your excerpt to the class and invite their feedback.

4. **Write a Description:** With specific references to the play, write a description of the world in *Land of Trash*. Include a brief summary of events that led to its current state. Focus on organizing ideas into well-structured paragraphs and using effective adjectives to create vivid descriptions.

One Ocean

Betty Quan

Scene 1: Narration. Inside Memory

Music: establish theme, continue under.

DAUGHTER: (*older*) A long time ago. It was my favourite. A story. No, our story. Just a Chinese folktale. Yes. About the Jingwei bird and why she is always dropping sticks and stones in the ocean. When I was small, I used to pretend I was that little bird. I would soar through our communal courtyard with arms for wings. That was when we were still allowed to enjoy our stories, to tell our stories, before, before ... *Bah-bah*. Father. Do you remember like I do? Tell me about the Jingwei. Yes, like you used to do when I was small. You told me that story when I left Hong Kong for Canada. Do you remember? I was sad. We were both sad. Like a bird in your hand I was until you set me free across the sky, across the ocean. Such a long time ago, yet so close I can still see it unfolding before me. Father? Tell me a story. Like you used to do (*as if repeating what she hears in memory*) "A long time ago." It seems like yesterday. A long time ago. But that is how we begin our stories, isn't it? We begin with "a long time ago."

Scene 2: Folktale Remembered

FATHER: A long time ago there was an emperor who had a young daughter. They loved each other very much. But although his powers could touch all corners of the land, the emperor could see only as far as the shoreline that divided his kingdom with the sea.

DAUGHTER: Beyond that shoreline, his vision was limited, like a kite held high in a strong breeze—he could see the shape, but not the colours.

(*Music ends. Sound effects: birds, breeze, ocean, continue under.*)

DAUGHTER: Father, look at the waves, so tall they must be hiding something behind them. I will take my boat for a ride.

FATHER: (*as Emperor*) Not so far, not so far.

DAUGHTER: (*as Jingwei*) Don't worry, Father. I'll be careful.

FATHER: (*as Emperor*) Why don't you wait a while? I'll join you. We can journey to the horizon together, where the sea meets the sun.

DAUGHTER: (*as Jingwei*) When? When can we do this? (*laughing*) You're always promising such things, Father! You're too busy as Emperor. I'll go out on my own first. On my own adventure. Then, I'll show you what I've seen.

FATHER: (*as Emperor, laughing*) When?

DAUGHTER: (*as Jingwei*) What does that matter? We have all the time in the world.

DAUGHTER: (*older*) The sun was warm upon the little girl's face—

FATHER: —and the salty breeze off the water tempted her to travel farther and farther. To see what hid behind the tall waves of the sea.

The Great Wave, Katsushika Hokusai, 1823

DAUGHTER: (*older*) Far far far away she went, when suddenly—

(*Sound effects: thunder and rainstorm*)

FATHER: (*as Sea God*) Who dares come this far upon the ocean of my reign?

DAUGHTER: (*older*) The Sea God's bad temper came upon the little girl.

(*Sound effects: Jingwei screams as the waves engulf her*)

FATHER: The water became a blanket that covered her. And the little girl died.

(*Sound effects: all suddenly end*)

DAUGHTER: (*older*) Died? I don't remember her dying. Is that right? I thought the water changed her into a bird. Like magic.

FATHER: I would tell you that when you were small. When you didn't understand death.

DAUGHTER: (*older*) Like I do now.

FATHER: It is only a story. (*continues*) The little girl's soul became a small bird called Jingwei.

(*Music begins*)

DAUGHTER: (*older*) Father, I died that day you sent me away.

FATHER: No child, you were reborn. Now, continue the story.

DAUGHTER: Angry was the spirit in that bird, angry at the sea it was for taking her away from her beloved father. And every day the Jingwei would carry in her beak stones and twigs from the mountains of the east and flying west ahead drop her small stones and twigs into the sea. And the Sea God finally noticed what Jingwei was trying to do.

(*Music ends. Sound effects: ocean. Close: the wings of a bird in motion*)

FATHER: (*as Sea God, laughing*) Silly creature, my sea is wider and deeper than your limited imagination. You can never fill me up in a million years.

DAUGHTER: (*as Jingwei*) But I can. Every day for a million years I will do this. Every day until one day. Until one day ... (*begin fade down*) Until one day ... Until one day ...

FATHER: And the small bird flew back to land—

FATHER & DAUGHTER: (*older*)—only to return with another small stone or twig to drop into the sea.

DAUGHTER: (*older*) And Jingwei said: "One day, there will be a bridge between me and my father. One day, even if it takes a million years to build it." (*She no longer speaks as the Jingwei.*) Soon, father. I will see you again. Soon.

(*Sound effects: fade down*)

Scene 3: Airport

(*Sound effects: airplane's acceleration and ascent. Fades into airport interior: Chinese public address system, etc. Close: a swallow singing*)

FATHER: Yes, yes, sing a goodbye song to my daughter. Here's a sunflower seed.

DAUGHTER: I don't think pets are allowed here.

FATHER: This is not just a pet, eh my little friend? Now keep your bag in full sight. Many pickpockets. There is more freedom here in Hong Kong but that doesn't mean there is less danger. Here's your ticket. Show it to that man over there. Where's your passport?

DAUGHTER: I don't want to go to Vancouver, father. Why me?

FATHER: Your big brother has a family now. You will go first, then settle down. Then we can join you.

DAUGHTER: When?

FATHER: Soon. Soon. Look at us now. We used to have a fine house and good food to eat. First the Japanese and the war, now Mao. Remember, just a few years ago, Mao decided China must have its Great Leap Forward? And the country went two steps forward and five steps back?

Scene 4: Narration. Inside Memory

(*Music fades under.*)

DAUGHTER: (*older*) Mosquitoes, flies, rats, and sparrows: Mao called these the "four pests." 1958: it was the year I turned sixteen. (*bitter laugh*) Do you remember? Mao believed grain production was down because the sparrows were feeding on the backs of the people. Families were armed with pots and pans. We were to scare the sparrows out of the trees so they would eventually drop dead from exhaustion. Six hundred million of us, running under trees, in the countryside, in the cities, making enough noise to waken the dead. Yes, the sparrows ate the grain, but they also ate the insects. Without the sparrows, no one could control the insects. The sky would rain the corpses of little birds to join the corpses of three hundred million people, dead of starvation.

Scene 5: Airport

(Sound effects: airport interior. Close: the swallow singing)

FATHER: You know how lucky we were to get out of China?

DAUGHTER: I know.

FATHER: How can we Chinese have luck when we are killing birds!? This is why it is good we are here now. No more death. No more hunger. No more sacrificing our own symbols of fortune and happiness. Maybe my good luck has returned right here in this cage. Maybe now we will all have good luck.

DAUGHTER: Maybe's, nothing but maybe's.

FATHER: You have a chance now, can't you see? To start a new life in a new place.

DAUGHTER: Let me finish school first.

FATHER: *(joking)* Maybe, you'll find a rich Canadian and marry him.

DAUGHTER: I'm 18 years old; I don't need a husband. I can try to find a job here, in Hong Kong.

FATHER: Just a temporary thing, you'll see. Your mother, your brother, me. We'll be a family again. We're relying on you. Work hard. Stay out of trouble. Be a citizen your new country can be proud of. When you're settled, you'll sponsor us to come. We'll join you later.

DAUGHTER: Please don't make me go, father.

FATHER: Who is the parent here? Who makes the decision?

DAUGHTER: Please, father, don't make me go all alone.

FATHER: Look, my Jingwei. Yes, you have always been like a little bird to me. If I could, I would always try to protect you, away from bad things. But this—this—is a good thing.

DAUGHTER: I don't want to go!

FATHER: Believe me, it's for the best. You'll like it in Canada.

DAUGHTER: Don't you want me to stay here, with you?

FATHER: It doesn't matter what I want. It's what I want for you.

Female: (*over sound system, filtered*) Last boarding call for Flight 973 departing for Vancouver, Canada. (*The announcer repeats this in Cantonese.*)

DAUGHTER: I've never been in a plane before, Father. Have you?

FATHER: No. Not yet. But in time, no?

DAUGHTER: Yes, in time.

Scene 6: Airfield

(*Sound effects: airport exterior. Plane accelerating and ascending. Closer: the swallow's song*)

FATHER: Goodbye! (*to himself*) Goodbye.

(*Sound effects: swallow singing*)

FATHER: What's that? What are you singing about?

(*Sound effects: swallow singing. Metal clink of the cage being opened*)

FATHER: Come on, there. No, it's not a trick. Out. Yes. Fly, go on, fly. Fly.

(*Sound effects: close: the acceleration of a bird's wings, heard under*)

FATHER: Build a bridge between me and my daughter. Make our ocean one.

Scene 7: Narration. Inside Memory

(*Music: begins and continues under*)

DAUGHTER: (*older*) You broke your promise. You never came. You let me leave you behind. I waited for you, Father. For the family. A long time ago. Where are you? Are you here, with me? Did you follow on the shadow of the airplane's wings? (*voice begins to break*) Did I fly away like a kite in the breeze? So high up you can see the shape, but not the colours? Can you see me? I'm so far away but all you have to do is pull me home. Father. Father. When I finish building a bridge, will you cross it? Even if the stones are loose, and the twigs breaking. Will you cross it? Father? (*beat*) Bah-bah? How big is the ocean?

(Music ends. Sound effects: exterior: airfield. Plane's acceleration and ascent crosses into that of birds in flight, their wings in motion. Fade into ocean, water lapping on a beach. Up and out.)

Betty Quan (*born Vancouver, British Columbia*), playwright, editor, writes for radio, stage, and television. She has been artist-in-residence at the Canadian Film Centre and Toronto's Tarragon Theatre. Quan has created stage adaptations of several works, including Joy Kogawa's *Naomi's Road*.

Activities: One Ocean

1. *Appreciate Form:* Referring directly to the text, determine how a "memory play" differs from more conventional plays you have read. Share your ideas with a partner and develop a Venn diagram that illustrates your shared ideas.

2. *Explore Technique:* The play draws parallels between the story of the Jingwei bird and that of the father and daughter. List the parallels between the two stories and comment on the effectiveness of Quan's use of this technique.

3. *Consider Format:* What challenges would you need to overcome to create an effective stage presentation of this radio play? How would you overcome those challenges? Discuss your ideas in a small group and then write a group proposal outlining your ideas for a stage adaptation.

4. *Present a Radio Play:* Write a short radio play based on your own childhood memories or those of a fictional character. Include sound effects and scene descriptions. If you wish, make reference to a traditional tale. Work with classmates to record a "radio" presentation of your play.

Media

The Internet promises to achieve what no charter of rights can: putting printing presses in the hands of many.

—Parker Bars Donham

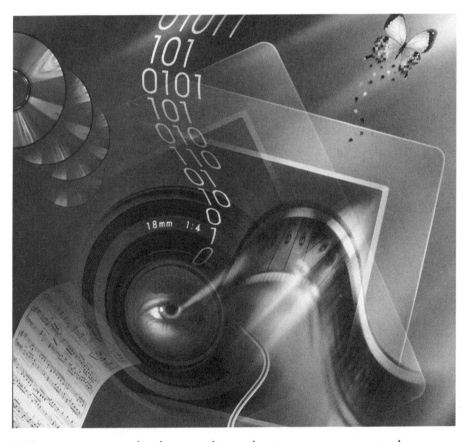

Whoever controls the media—the images—controls the culture.

—Allen Ginsberg

While fiction, poetry, and drama have a long history, the history of media is still young. One of the Canadians who has had a profound influence in this field is Marshall McLuhan:

> *His understanding of how media worked and affected culture was so prophetic, we are only understanding some of his statements today. The media, McLuhan predicted, would shrink the world and the intellectual process. Considering the number of hours we watch television, play video games, purposelessly surf the Internet and the social scars left by some of the content of these media, McLuhan's voice rings hauntingly in our new millennium culture where students carry cell phones and e-mail pictures to each other.*
>
> Marshall McLuhan Center Web Site

As you read the selections in this unit, consider whether the brief quotations from McLuhan in the following extract resonate with your own experience.

Listening to Marshall McLuhan

When asked what originally led to his interest in media and the effect of media upon our culture, McLuhan answered: "I find media analysis very much more exciting now simply because it affects more people than most anything. One measure of the importance of anything is: Who is affected by it? In our time, we have devised ways of making the most trivial event affect everyone. One of the consequences of electronic environments is the total involvement of people in people."

∞

"Once we surrendered our senses and nervous systems to the private manipulation of those who would try to benefit from taking a lease on our eyes and ears and nerves, we don't really have any rights left. Leasing our eyes and ears and nerves to commercial interests is like handing over the common speech to a private corporation, or like giving the earth's atmosphere to a company as a monopoly."

335

Media

*Technologies are not simply inventions which people employ but are the means by which people are re-invented."

"People don't actually read newspapers. They step into them every morning like a hot bath."

"With telephone and TV it is not so much the message as the sender that is being sent."

"We look at the present through a rearview mirror; we walk backwards into the future."

"The future of the book is the blurb."

Marshall McLuhan (*born 1911, Edmonton, Alberta; died 1980*), communication theorist, professor, rose to international fame during the 1960s for his work on the effects of mass media. McLuhan was one of the first to assess the impact of television on culture. *Understanding Media* is the most popular of his many books.

Exploring Media

Poll a Group: In a small group, compile a list of forms of mass media. For each medium, discuss the following questions: How many of you access the medium? For how long? For what purposes? How does your use of the medium differ from your parents'? Chart your results.

Respond to Text: Ask each member of a small group to pick one quotation for the group to discuss. After the discussion, write about one of the quotations you discussed. Explain what you think McLuhan meant and give reasons why you agree or disagree with the idea.

Create a Poster: Choose one of the quotations and present it in an illustrated poster. Your illustration should bring out the meaning of the quotation. Illustration possibilities include drawing, collage, photographs, or computer-manipulated images.

Analyze TV: With a partner, discuss and clarify what McLuhan means by the terms *message* and *sender*. Then tune in briefly to a variety of TV shows to determine to what degree each is about the message and the sender. Keep a log of your observations and report your findings to the class.

From Since you Asked

Pamela Wallin

Whether it's listening to some of the best minds in the world meandering through an hour of conversation, or experiencing the roller-coaster ride of *Canada AM*, over the years I've learned a little about this biz. Let me tell you about the interview as I've come to understand it—and it's no different whether the person opposite me is singer Tony Bennett or the prime minister of Canada.

It's often a nerve-wracking, sometimes awkward, adrenaline-producing affair. Sometimes the intellectual connection, the give and take, the reading of signs and signals, rivals a romantic encounter. The interview can be a very intimate experience. The contrary is, unfortunately, true as well.

A bad interview is like a bad blind date. You've invited him to your house so as the evening progresses you can't flee, however much you might want to. If only it were his place—you could sneak off into the night, leaving no forwarding address.

Over the years, when the red light goes on and a floor director like Gerald or Paul or Kevin gives me my cue—I make a commitment. I am focused on the person across the desk. Many other things are happening—in my head, in my ear, and in the studio in general, and I must deal with the environment as well as I can. Is there lipstick on my teeth, did the microphone pick up a growling stomach, what shot are we on, what's left on the clock, did the audience see the smirk on the guest's face or was the camera on me at that moment? If the audience *didn't* see the smirk and I ask a pointed question in response to it, anyone watching will think I'm just being rude. How do I avoid a misunderstanding? Can I use humour or is this guest unlikely to respond well to it? The questions in my mind are endless, even before I've asked the guest anything.

The first rule is to always interview someone who's worth the time and energy. For everyone's sake. The second rule is to not ask questions so much as advance ideas that your guest can respond to. Give him or her thoughts to finish.

The third rule is to know your ground. It's the minimum show of respect for the person you've invited. You should know as much about this person sitting across from you as it takes to make him feel flattered at your investment of time. The last thing you want is a guest screaming silently to himself that you just don't get it, that you've missed the point completely. Though no studio microphone will pick that up, you can bet that an astute audience will hear it.

The fourth rule is don't be afraid to admit that you don't know something. And don't be afraid to say that you do. Next, rule five, keep your biases and preconceived notions fully intact, but always be ready to shed them when the evidence challenges you.

Every interview is a balance between your role as the viewer's surrogate and your own interests and indulgences. And every interview is a Rorschach test. Each viewer sees a different personal and unique exchange.

That's a fact of the business that's beyond my control and I've stopped pulling out my teased hair when a viewer charges bias or favouritism. If the accusation is of incompetence or error, though, I'm ready to read that letter twice and write rule three on the blackboard one hundred times.

Conducting an interview comes with a large dose of responsibility. People's careers and reputations are at stake. But seldom is the bargain between journalist and guest stated plainly. For me to feel that an interview has succeeded, I have to come away feeling that it contained something for everyone—me, the guest, and most importantly you, the viewer.

I stand in your place, ask the questions I expect are on your mind, and try to find a path into each guest's individual truth. I like that I now spend less time trying to get someone to let a tidbit slip from unguarded lips and more time exploring ideas. Sometimes it is a congenial process, sometimes it makes the blood boil, but the conversation continues at a more leisurely pace than our soundbite media normally permits.

In the end there's no magic formula for a good interview except to be prepared. There's chemistry to consider. If you click with someone, great. But even anger can sometimes be a catalyst, though disdain never works. There has to be a reason to want to connect and contempt, like bad hair or gaudy earrings, just gets in the way.

To be awestruck doesn't make for an engaging encounter either. In fact, it's seldom anything but an embarrassment for the awestruckee, and for the interviewer it can be professionally fatal. Although I did propose to Tony Bennett, I think, or was it he who proposed to me?

Pamela Wallin (*born 1953, Saskatchewan*), journalist, broadcaster, producer, began her radio career in Saskatchewan, working both on-air and behind the scenes. After her move to television, she became the first woman to be appointed Ottawa Bureau Chief. Former co-anchor of CBC's *Prime Time News,* Wallin started her own production company in 1995.

Activities: Since You Asked

1. **Understand Vocabulary:** Use background knowledge and context to deduce the meaning of the following phrases: adrenaline-producing, astute audience, the viewer's surrogate, Rorschach test, soundbite media. Use appropriate resources to check your deductions.

2. **Interpret Information:** Wallin states that "seldom is the bargain between journalist and guest plainly stated." Working with a partner, describe the nature of this bargain, explaining what each participant might offer and stand to gain.

3. **Develop Questions:** Choose a well-known person you would like to interview on a television talk show. After doing some background research, develop 10 questions you would ask this person. Consider questions that would be of interest to a general audience.

4. **Evaluate an Interview:** Draw up a list of criteria for an effective interview and use them to evaluate a TV interview (not from an entertainment talk show), a radio interview, or an interview on the Internet. Produce a written report of your evaluation, including your criteria and supporting details.

Move East

Rick Mercer

I don't know, call me crazy, call me a coward, but what person in their right mind would live in Los Angeles?

What comes to mind when you think of Los Angeles? Riots. Fires. Six cops beating a man within an inch of his life. Three guys dropping a rock on another guy's head. Four feet of water rushing down your street while hellfire comes straight out of the ground, burning your car and house in under three minutes.

And if that's not bad enough, apparently Liona Boyd lives there.

I'm from Newfoundland. People say, "Why do you live in Newfoundland?" We say, "Why do you live in Toronto?" But, c'mon, we all have our reasons why we prefer to be in one region of Canada over the others.

Really, God love Canada. How often do any of us here wake up with a nine-hundred-pound mahogany dresser-drawer heading towards our face at warp speed?

We've got it scald. We have every right in the world to be holier than thou when it comes to the flaky state of California. Except for the crowd in B.C., who, yes, even though the tulips come up in February, and the quality of life is apparently two thousand times greater than ours, they too are just sitting there eating sushi waiting for the Big One.

People have their priorities mixed up, and I think the events of the last little while have proven that everyone should stop moving west and move east. Sure, it's more tundra-like than Vancouver. And granted, we don't have celebrities walking the streets, but at least when we hear someone saying, "The Big One is coming" we know they're probably talking about the WWF show at the hockey arena. You might still want to run and hide, but you don't have to. The choice is yours.

So come east, young man and woman, come east. It mightn't be as warm, but at least it's not gonna kill you.

Rick Mercer (*born 1969, St. John's, Newfoundland*), writer, actor, has received numerous Gemini awards for both his writing and performing on the TV comedy series *This Hour Has 22 Minutes*. He has toured Canada in three one-man shows and has appeared in numerous TV and film productions. In 1993, he was named Artist of the Year by the Newfoundland and Labrador Arts Council.

Activities: Move East

1. **Examine Text:** This monologue was performed by Mercer on the TV show *This Hour Has 22 Minutes*. Identify examples of sentence structure and diction that reflect casual conversational English. Explain why this type of English is appropriate for this piece.

2. **Identify Technique:** Mercer uses the technique of hyperbole. Define the term and list examples from the selection. Evaluate how effective you think his use of this technique is. Share your list and evaluation with a partner.

3. **Write a Profile:** Mercer makes reference to the Canadian performer Liona Boyd. Use the Internet and other resources to write a brief profile of her. Keep in mind the purpose of a profile. Find an effective way to organize and present your information. Post your profile in the classroom.

4. **Deliver a Monologue:** Write your own humorous compare/contrast monologue, about the same length, explaining why people should move to your city or province. Before delivering your monologue to the class, use rehearsal strategies to polish your presentation.

Eulogy FOR CANADA'S
Unknown Soldier

Eulogy delivered by Her Excellency the Right Honourable Adrienne Clarkson, Governor General of Canada and Commander-in-Chief of the Canadian Forces, at the funeral for Canada's Unknown Soldier

Wars are as old as history. Over two thousand years ago, Herodotus wrote, "In peace, sons bury their fathers; in war, fathers bury their sons." Today, we are gathered together as one, to bury someone's son. The only certainty about him is that he was young. If death is a debt we all must pay, he paid before he owed it.

We do not know whose son he was. We do not know his name. We do not know if he was a MacPherson or a Chartrand. He could have been a Kaminski or a Swiftarrow. We do not know if he was a father himself. We do not know if his mother or wife received that telegram with the words "Missing in Action" typed with electrifying clarity on the anonymous piece of paper. We do not know whether he had begun truly to live his life as a truck driver or a scientist, a miner or a teacher, a farmer or a student. We do not know where he came from.

Was it the Prairies whose rolling sinuous curves recall a certain kind of eternity?

Was he someone who loved our lakes and knew them from a canoe?

Was he someone who saw the whales at the mouth of the Saguenay?

Was he someone who hiked in the Rockies or went sailing in the Atlantic or in the Gulf Islands?

Did he have brown eyes?

Did he know what it was to love someone and be loved back?

Was he a father who had not seen his child?

Did he love hockey? Did he play defence?

Did he play football? Could he kick a field goal?

Did he like to fix cars? Did he dream of owning a Buick?

Did he read poetry?

Did he get into fights?

Did he have freckles?

Did he think nobody understood him?

Did he just want to go out and have a good time with the boys?

We will never know the answers to these questions. We will never know him. But we come today to do him honour as someone who could have been all these things and now is no more. We who are left have all kinds of questions that only he could answer. And we, by this act today, are admitting with terrible finality that we will never know those answers.

We cannot know him. And no honour we do him can give him the future that was destroyed when he was killed. Whatever life he could have led, whatever choices he could have made are all shattered. They are over. We are honouring that unacceptable thing—a life stopped by doing one's duty. The end of a future, the death of dreams.

Yet we give thanks for those who were willing to sacrifice themselves and who gave their youth and their future so that we could live in peace. With their lives they ransomed our future.

We have a wealth of witnesses in Canada to describe to us the unspeakable horror and frightening maelstrom that war brings. What that First World War was like has been described in our poetry, novels, and paintings. Some of our greatest artists came out of that conflict, able to create beauty out of the hell that they had seen. The renowned member of the Group of Seven, F.H. Varley, was one of those artists. Writing in April 1918, he said,

> You in Canada ... cannot realize at all what war is like. You must see it and live it. You must see the barren deserts war has made of once fertile country ... see the turned-up graves, see the dead on the field, freakishly mutilated—headless, legless, stomachless, a perfect body and a passive face and a broken empty skull—see your own countrymen, unidentified, thrown into a cart, their coats over them, boys digging a grave in a land of yellow slimy mud and green pools of water under a weeping sky. You must have heard the screeching shells and have the shrapnel fall around you, whistling by you—seen the results of it, seen scores of horses, bits of horses lying around in the open—in the street and soldiers marching by these scenes as if they never knew of their presence. Until you've lived this ... you cannot know.

It is a frightening thing for human beings to think that we could die and that no one would know to mark our grave, to say where we had come from, to say when we had been born and when exactly we died. In honouring this unknown soldier today, through this funeral and this burial, we are embracing the fact of the anonymity and saying that because we do not know him and we do not know what he could have become, he has become more than one body, more than one grave. He is an ideal. He is a symbol of all sacrifice. He is every soldier in all our wars.

Our veterans, who are here with us today, know what it is to have been in battle and to have seen their friends cut down in their youth. That is why remembrance is so necessary and yet so difficult. It is necessary because we must not forget and it is difficult because the pain is never forgotten.

And the sense of loss, what this soldier's family must have felt, is captured in a poem by Jacques Brault, the Quebec poet who lost his brother in Sicily in the Second World War, and wrote *Suite Fraternelle*,

> I remember you my brother Gilles lying forgotten in the earth of Sicily ...
> I know now that you are dead, a cold, hard lump in your throat fear lying heavy in your belly I still hear your twenty years swaying in the blasted July weeds ...
> There is only one name on my lips, and it is yours Gilles
> You did not die in vain Gilles and you carry on through our changing seasons
> And we, we carry on as well, like the laughter of waves that sweep across each tearful cove ...
> Your death gives off light Gilles and illuminates a brother's memories ...
> The grass grows on your tomb Gilles and the sand creeps up
> And the nearby sea feels the pull of your death
> You live on in us as you never could in yourself
> You are where we will be, you open the road for us.
> [interpretation of original French poem]

When a word like Sicily is heard, it reverberates with all the far countries where our youth died. When we hear Normandy, Vimy, Hong Kong, we know that what happened so far away, paradoxically, made our country and the future of our society. These young people and soldiers bought our future for us. And for that, we are eternally grateful.

Whatever dreams we have, they were shared in some measure by this man who is only unknown by name but who is known in the hearts of all Canadians by all the virtues that we respect— selflessness, honour, courage, and commitment.

We are now able to understand what was written in 1916 by the grandson of Louis Joseph Papineau, Major Talbot Papineau, who was killed two years later: "Is their sacrifice to go for nothing or will it not cement a foundation for a true Canadian nation, a Canadian nation independent in thought, independent in action, independent even in its political organization—but in spirit united for high international and humane purposes...."

The wars fought by Canadians in the 20th century were not fought for the purpose of uniting Canada, but the country that emerged was forged in the smithy of sacrifice. We will not forget that.

This unknown soldier was not able to live out his allotted span of life to contribute to his country. But in giving himself totally through duty, commitment, love, and honour he has become part of us forever. As we are part of him.

Adrienne Clarkson (*born 1939, Hong Kong*), broadcaster, writer, producer, has won numerous television awards for programs such as *The Fifth Estate*. She became Canada's Governor General in 1999 and is an Officer of the Order of Canada, Canada's highest honour.

Activities: Eulogy for Canada's Unknown Soldier

1. ***Identify Techniques:*** Work as a group to identify and list the techniques that Clarkson employs to capture and hold her listeners' attention. For each technique, briefly describe its intended effect on the audience.

2. ***Analyze Structure:*** With a partner, make brief notes on the content of each paragraph. Explain how each paragraph is linked to the preceding and following paragraphs, and evaluate the impact of the first and the last paragraphs on the listener.

3. ***Consider Context:*** Consider purpose, audience, and situation in relation to this speech. Explain and provide examples of how the speech addresses or reflects each of these elements. Organize your ideas into a brief formal essay.

4. ***Respond Creatively:*** Use any form or medium you wish to commemorate the sacrifices made by Canadians during times of war. Possible media include poem, essay, poster, painting, and multimedia presentation. Share your project with the class.

BLOOD & LAUNDRY

Laura Miller

An interview with Margaret Atwood is a bit like an audience with a duchess—a wickedly amused and amusing duchess. If the prolific Canadian novelist, poet, and critic—perhaps best known for the 1984 novel The Handmaid's Tale, *made into a film in 1990—was not born with her regal demeanour, she has certainly earned it by now, and her formidable talents only seem to be growing stronger. Her book* Alias Grace *is her first historical novel, based on a famous Torontonian maidservant, Grace Marks, who, in 1843, may or may not have participated in the murder of her employer and his housekeeper.*

Salon met up with Atwood during her recent visit to San Francisco, where she professed to be able to guess how many servants it took to maintain the city's various Victorian mansions, just by looking.

So, your decision to write a different version of Grace's story was based on ...

It was based on the discrepancies among the different accounts. Believe me, if there had been cut-up bodies, it would have been in the newspapers; they wouldn't have missed that part. They didn't agree with one another. And the witnesses couldn't agree at the trial. But that is standard, isn't it?

When you were working on the original television play, were you convinced that she was actually guilty?

Yes.

What attracted you to that story? That version?

It is a fascinating and theatrical story, even Susanna Moodie's version, which gets so many things wrong. Four people in a house. The gentleman has a mistress, Nancy, who is also the housekeeper. The housekeeper and the two servants are from the same class. The servants deeply resent the fact that this woman, who is in their class, is set above them. Grace fancies Thomas Kinnear [the master]; she likes him, and she wants to get her rival out of the way. In Susanna Moodie's version, she wheedles and bullies and taunts [hired hand] James McDermott into killing [the housekeeper/mistress] with the promise of herself as the reward. It's "If you kill Nancy, you can have me." That kind of set-up.

Not until after McDermott has killed Nancy, and has then said, "Well of course we will have to kill Thomas Kinnear," does the other shoe drop. Grace says, "Oh no, not him." Then McDermott realizes that he's been set up. He is furious; it is not him that Grace loves, but the other man. So, he says, "Either I am going to kill him, and you are going to help me, or I am going to kill him and you." Even that story is pretty interesting. What then made it much more interesting to me, as a novelist, is the fact that Susanna Moodie was wrong! Other people were just making the story up from the moment it happened. They were all fictionalizing. They were all projecting their own views onto these various people. It is a real study in how the perception of reality is shaped.

The thing that makes it particularly charged is the class tension.
There was quite a lot of class tension, but I don't think it's the kind of
story in which servants kill employers out of some well-developed
sense of class injustice. I think the resentment was directed more at
Nancy than at Thomas Kinnear, because, number one, she had
moved out of her class and, number two, she was very inconsistent.
It's like Captain Bligh in *Mutiny on the Bounty*; one day she's your pal
and best friend, and wants to have a party and everybody's going to
dance and play the flute. The next minute she's giving you your
notice, or bossing you around, or bawling you out for not having
done something right, and "coming the lady." She couldn't make up
her mind who she was, whose side she was on.

**How does your characterization of Grace in this book change from
the original?**
I give the reader the benefit of both versions. I also pick her up at a
much later point in her story, in 1859. She's 31 years old and she has
already spent half of her life in the penitentiary. She is a different
person, more ambiguous than the original character that I wrote, of
course.

**How much of her character did you get from the different accounts
that you were reading, and how much did you have to conjure up?**
There was a great deal missing, but I didn't feel that I could be
completely inconsistent with those other accounts. On the other
hand, the other accounts are inconsistent. One person, having seen
her, says "She is malicious, she's conniving, she's manipulative, she's
evil," and all of these things. Another person might say, "Actually she
is quite amiable, she's very nice." These are people who claimed to
have known her. You usually get conflicting testimony, especially
when there is a violent crime involving both a man and a woman.
The questions are always raised, you know, is this Bonnie and Clyde?
Was she egging him on, or was she, on the contrary, drawn into it
through weakness of will, not being able to say no? Who was the real
instigator? This comes about time and again. Opinion is generally
undivided about the man and divided about the woman.

Why do you think that is?

Well, I don't know. We could come up with lots of theories. I think that traditionally, and certainly in the 19th century, women were thought of as being mysterious and unfathomable. So, we have a person who is by nature mysterious and unfathomable involved in a crime. That feeling of mystery is going to be multiplied tenfold. There is a book called *Victorian Murderesses*, which goes back over some of the hot trials of the 19th century. It's pretty obvious that some of these women killed people and got off because we didn't like the people they killed—the people they killed were not approved of. It is also pretty obvious that some of them didn't kill anybody, but got convicted because they were doing other things that were not approved of, usually having an affair.

So, if a woman was involved in a case, and letters were produced, adulterers' love letters, her chances for beating the rap went plummeting downwards. Two things that told very much against Grace are, number one, she was found at an inn with a man—and if you have read *The Mill on the Floss*, you know that this is almost automatically a fallen woman; if you're in a structure together, overnight, even if it was separate bedrooms, which it was, your reputation is very severely damaged. Number two, she wore Nancy's dress to the trial, and Nancy's bonnet and a few other items as well. This told very much against her and produced a sensation in the courtroom. When that testimony came out, everybody went [gasps dramatically] in shock and horror.

Why do you think she wore Nancy's dress?

It was a good, serviceable dress. You wouldn't leave something like that behind. Nancy had no more use for it. Waste not, want not.

She doesn't seem to have a morbid imagination at all.

Well, she doesn't have a middle-class, genteel imagination, which would have said, "I couldn't wear that dress, that's the dress the dead person...." She doesn't have that kind of sensibility. A shawl is a shawl, a dress is a dress. You don't just throw something like that away. Shoes are shoes. When you travel in India, you find that everything is used, just everything. You don't find any plastic bags blowing around because nobody would let a plastic bag go to waste. It would be used for this and that, and when finally it can't hold anything anymore, it would be cut up into decorations. This is where the patchwork quilt came from; you don't throw things out, you make them into something else.

Grace is like a camera, she sees things so clearly. Then she has this sardonic side that she conceals.
Wouldn't you? Especially if you were in prison.

Her reaction to the murder suggests that it was never real to her.
I read a very interesting article by a prison psychiatrist in England. He was talking about people who have been put in there for murder and so forth. He interviews them. Often they say things like, "Well I just gave her a little tap. I don't know why she fell down." Or "I don't know how all those cuts and stabs got on there, I just sort of pushed them against the wall, I wasn't doing anything that bad." There is a definite psychological withdrawal. Whether it is real or lying, this guy said that you can't always tell. Getting people to admit the full extent of what it appears that they have done is frequently quite difficult....

Another remarkable thing about this book is the sensual immediacy of it; it really feels as though you know what it was like to do laundry in 1840. You acknowledge *Beeton's Book of Household Management* as a source.
Also, some of it is just using your own imagination. Subtract the automatic washer, subtract the ringer washer, and what is left? [solemnly] It is the tub. And the washboard. There is the bar of soap.

In some ways, this is a book about laundry, as much as a book about murder.
It is quite a bit about laundry, but of course, the Bible is about laundry. There's a lot about washing in the Bible and having snowy white garments and shining raiment. Clean and dirty is a primary human set of categories, like old/young and dark/light. Very primary.

I'm wondering how you personally feel about housework.
It is nice to do the kinds of it that you like, and it is not nice to do the kinds of it that you don't like.

You mentioned somewhere that your mother hated housework.
She wasn't keen on it.

It's ironic that you have written this book about a woman whose life is consumed with housework, and yet you grew up in a house ...
Where the idea was to get it over with. One of the reasons my mother liked it up north is that you just swept the dirt out the door. You didn't have a vacuum cleaner. The more objects, doo-dads, and shining things you have, the more cleaning you have to do. If you don't have silverware, then you don't have to polish it. She was a minimalist in that respect. But as for me, I was always a bit more interested in it than she was, which was just as well, because I ended up doing some of it. She didn't like it, and in that generation, kids helped out.

Did you start out wanting to write about someone who does a lot of housework?
No! If you are writing about a servant, well, that is what they did all day. If you read Mrs. Beeton, they get up at some ungodly hour in the morning. She lists all the different things the "maid of all work" has to do. It is extensive, a lot of stuff to be got through in a day. She gets up, she makes the fire, she boils the water, she cleans the grate, she lights the fire if it is winter, she sets the breakfast table, she brings in the breakfast. They eat the breakfast, she takes it away. She cleans off that. She takes off the tablecloth, she does the dishes, she makes the lunch, she sets the lunch, she takes the dishes away, she washes the dishes, in addition to making the bread and making this and that ... polishing the lamps, doing the laundry, making the beds. And the dusting, polishing the stove—all of this had to be done at a time when there were no screens on the windows. So, not only were you doing all of this, you were contending with all of these flies.

Mrs. Beeton says "a brisk, smart girl, who is good at her work," will of course be able to get everything done in time, so that she has a couple of hours in the afternoon—and you think, for herself. But then she says, "To make her own clothes"! So, she is just not ever getting any time off. They finally did get a half day off every week. But this was dawn-to-dusk, back-breaking work.

How was it to try to write about that?
I have one chapter that is sort of Grace's day, but it is not even Grace's full day; we don't even get to breakfast, and there are already all of these things that she has done. I think it is pretty interesting, but you can get too immersed in it, which I had to look out for. I took out some of the detail that I'd put in because the story must move forward. But it would have meant that she had been a pretty practical, down-to-earth person. She did say, to McDermott, "Don't kill her in the room; you'll get blood on the floor." At first that sounds like a very callous thing to say. Then you think of course she had to clean those floors, and she doesn't want to have to clean up a bunch of blood.

Which is one of the hardest things to clean.
It is hard to get out.

Laura Miller is the New York editorial director of the online magazine *salon.com*. She also edits the "Books" section of the site.

Activities: Blood & Laundry

1. ***Interpret Text:*** What does this interview reveal about Atwood as a person? Do any of her comments support the idea that she is "a wickedly amused and amusing duchess"? Explain and support your opinions.

2. ***Analyze Text:*** Use the following categories to classify Miller's remarks: prepared questions, impromptu questions, statements that invite comments. From each category, choose one remark that you think elicited the most interesting response. Discuss your ideas with a partner.

3. ***Summarize Views:*** Atwood presents differing views of Grace in this interview and in the excerpt from *Alias Grace*, found in the fiction unit. Consult both texts to write a short description summarizing each different view of this character. Create an appropriate title to characterize each description.

4. ***Apply Ideas:*** Atwood makes reference to "how the perception of reality is shaped." In a small group, discuss what this means and how it is possible to shape the perception of reality. Where and how does this phenomenon happen today? Have a spokesperson share your ideas with the class.

ALARM RAISED on

*W*ith so much attention focused on battered women, here's a frightening thought: It's estimated that one in three American girls will have an abusive dating relationship before finishing high school.

California psychotherapist Jill Murray grew interested in this subject when she worked as lead therapist at a domestic violence shelter and discovered the pattern of abuse began in childhood or adolescence for many of the woman.

Murray now tours American high schools raising the alarm about abusive teen relationships. She has also put her experiences and anecdotes into printed form in *But I Love Him: Protecting Your Teen Daughter from Controlling, Abusive Dating Relationships* (ReganBooks, $36.50).

Does your daughter's boyfriend call or page her repeatedly? Does he isolate her from friends, belittle her, reduce her to tears or make her feel insecure? Did he pledge his love too soon? Is he jealous? Does he punch walls to vent anger?

Many love-starved girls interpret these examples of abusive behaviour as flattery, notes Murray, and this emotional abuse can rapidly lead to sexual and physical abuse.

But I Love Him offers a succinct, straightforward unravelling of toxic teen couplings. It's built around

but i love him

Protecting Your Teen Daughter
from Controlling, Abusive Dating Relationships

DR. JILL MURRAY

ABUSE in TEEN DATING

Murray's assertion that "love is a behaviour" and that all interpersonal relationships should be judged on how people act instead of what they say.

After exploring why boys abuse, and why women are drawn to abusers, Murray explores the differences between unhealthy infatuation and mature love. Love can't be rushed, she argues, and it needs to pass through stages of attraction, casual friendship, close friendship, and intimate friendship before evolving into mature love.

Murray's list of qualities to look for in a partner is so succinct and so bang on it puts self-help books to shame. Parents of teen girls will get the most from this book, but women who attract abusive men will also find it hits home.

Jennifer Bain writes for the "Shelf Life" book review column of *The Toronto Star*.

Activities: But I Love Him

1. **Identify Characteristics:** On the basis of this review, create a list of characteristics of nonfiction book reviews. Read some other nonfiction reviews and revise your list as necessary. Adapt your list into a checklist entitled "How to Write a Nonfiction Review."

2. **Extend Information:** The fourth paragraph lists several questions related to the behaviour of teen males. Construct a similar list of questions related to the behaviour of teen females. Compare your list with a classmate's.

3. **Apply Ideas:** Murray believes that "all interpersonal relationships should be judged on how people act instead of what they say." Discuss with a partner how this idea applies to non-romantic relationships (e.g., parent–child, employer–employee, teacher–student). Summarize your ideas.

4. **Present a Proposal:** Work in a small group to outline a campaign to inform teens about abusive relationships. Create a persuasive proposal to seek funds for the campaign. Include information on specific goals, elements, media to be used, and strategies for appealing to your target audience. Present your proposal orally, with all members taking part.

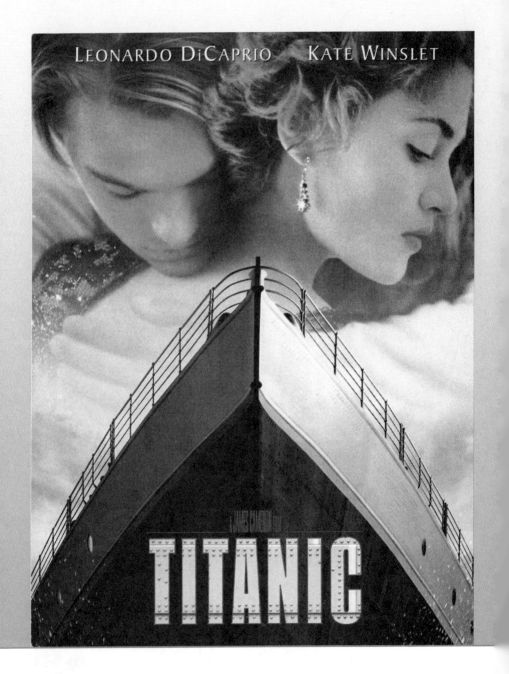

LEONARDO DiCAPRIO   KATE WINSLET

A JAMES CAMERON FILM

TITANIC

Cheers AND Jeers

Cheers

A SPECTACULAR VOYAGE

Bruce Kirkland newspaper review

James Cameron's stunning film *Titanic* launches itself into movie history.

Titanic is not just big, bold, long and staggeringly expensive, it also promises you an exhilarating night at the cinema.

Wiping away the bad publicity that accompanied the shooting of the $200-million project—the most costly ever—writer–director James Cameron has made a miracle movie that delivers big-time, with a clutch of Oscar nominations in store that will burnish the mercurial Cameron's reputation. The film also should make both its young romantic leads, Leonardo DiCaprio and Kate Winslet, Hollywood superstars.

This is a *Dr. Zhivago* for the 1990s. Like David Lean's sumptuous emotional classic, *Titanic* stages an intimate fictional romance against the background of a major historical event.

What makes *Titanic* even better than *Zhivago* is that the history lesson is so frighteningly realistic. The sinking of the unsinkable luxury ocean liner on its maiden voyage in April of 1912 is one of the most enduring tragedies of the 20th century. It is an event that, with its humbling of ultramodern technology and the human arrogance behind it, transcends even the numbing 1500-plus body count when the ship went down in the icy North Atlantic after striking an iceberg.

With uncanny accuracy that should satisfy even the most rabid Titanic-lore fanatics, and using some documentary footage spliced in with his re-creation, Cameron depicts the event from loading of passengers in Southhampton April 12 to the rescue of survivors by the *Carpathia*, two hours after the RMS *Titanic* split in two and sank early on April 15.

Everything is presented with panache and/or heart-wrenching detail, from the rigid class divisions between first-, second-, and third-class passengers to the depiction of bizarre twists we all know, such as watching the band play on to calm passengers during the chaotic evacuation.

We see the poor locked behind barricades while the rich and famous are attended to first. We see the ship explored from the opulent dining rooms of the upper decks to the fiery hell of the furnace rooms where men shovel coal into the boilers. It truly was a night to remember. The film is riveting.

Yet it is what Cameron does in the foreground that transforms *Titanic* into great art. The entire saga is told from contemporary times in a flashback told by an elderly woman (played by the elegant 1930s/'40s starlet Gloria Stuart), who claims to be a 101-year-old survivor.

She tells her intensely personal story to a rapt group of deep-sea explorers, who are plunging into the depths seeking *Titanic* riches. Instead of treasures, they first get the priceless gift of understanding, an eyewitness account told with passion and poetry and beautiful sensuality.

Which is where the romance fits in, along with a rich tapestry of real-life characters from Kathy Bates' brazen interpretation of the Unsinkable Molly Brown to Bernard Hill's screen portrait of the *Titanic*'s befuddled captain.

Stuart's story is Winslet's tale. The Winslet character was a society girl engaged to a rich brute (Billy Zane). But on the *Titanic*, she falls in love with a dashing young peasant (DiCaprio) who saves her life in their first encounter and proves instrumental in her fate as the ship goes down.

This romantic entanglement, replete with complications, class warfare, challenges, gunplay, and narrow escapes, may be fiction but it supercharges the reality of a great film.

Jeers

Tilman Ganzhorn *Web review*

Scene 1

KATE WINSLET: Why, this is a fancy boat, isn't it?

KATE'S WEASELLY FIANCÉ: Yes it certainly is. Here is the art you asked for. It is by an artist named "Picasso." I am certain he will amount to nothing.

KATE: Ha ha ha. That is very funny to our '90s audience, because of course Picasso later amounted to quite a bit, after this boat sank.

LEONARDO DICAPRIO: Hello, I'm Leonardo DiCaprio. Perhaps you have seen the many Internet sites dedicated to the worship of me. You are very pretty.

KATE: Thank you. So are you.

LEONARDO: I know. Prettier than you, in fact. I am going to put on my "brooding" face now, to ensure that women will keep coming back again and again to see this movie. Later, my white shirt will be soaking wet.

KATE: While you're doing that, I will concentrate on standing here and looking pretty, to keep the men in the audience interested until the boat sinks and people start dying.

WEASELLY FIANCÉ: Excuse me. I do not like you, Leonardo, even though you saved my fiancée's life. I am going to sneer at you and treat you like dirt because you're poor, and then I'll probably be physically abusive to my fiancée, and then, just to make sure the audience really hates me, and to make sure my character is entirely one-dimensional, perhaps I'll throw an elderly person into the water.

AUDIENCE: Boo! We hate you! Even though all real people have at least a few admirable qualities, we have not been shown any of yours, and plus, you're trying to come between Leonardo and Kate, and so therefore we hate you! Boo! (Even though technically it is Leonardo who is coming between you and Kate. But Leonardo is handsomer than you, even though he is only 13, so we are on his side. Boo!)

Scene 2

LEONARDO: I'm glad we snuck away like this so that you could cheat on your fiancé.

KATE: So am I. Even though I am engaged to him and have made a commitment to marry him, that is no reason why you and I cannot climb into the back seat of a car and steam up the windows together. The fact that I am the heroine of the movie will no doubt help the cattle-like audience forgive me for this, though they would probably be **very** angry indeed if my fiancé were to do the same thing to me.

AUDIENCE: Darn straight we would! Moo! We mean, Boo!

LEONARDO: I agree. First I would like to draw you, though, so of course you will have to take off all your clothes.

KATE: But can a movie with five minutes of continuous nudity be at all successful in, say, Provo, Utah, where the audiences might not stand for that sort of thing?

LEONARDO: I would be willing to bet that for the first three weeks the film is in release, every single showing at Wynnsong Theater in Provo will sell out.

NARRATOR: According to Wynnsong manager Matt Palmer, that is exactly what happened.

KATE: All right, then. (*sound of clothes hitting the floor*)

Scene 3

FIRST MATE: Captain, we're about to hit an iceberg.

CAPTAIN: Great, I could use some ice for my drink. (*sound of drinking*)

ICEBERG: (*hits boat*)

FIRST MATE: That can't be good.

CAPTAIN: Bottoms up!

AUDIENCE: (*silence*)

FIRST MATE: That was irony, you fools.

AUDIENCE: Baa! Moo! Where's Leonardo?

Scene 4

LEONARDO: I have been informed that this boat is sinking.

KATE: That is terrible.

LEONARDO: Would you like to engage in some more immoral-but-justified behaviour?

KATE: Certainly.

WEASELLY FIANCÉ: Excuse me, I—

AUDIENCE: Boo! Boo!

WEASELLY FIANCÉ: (*aside*) I'm getting the raw end of the deal here. (*to Leonardo*) Listen, Leonardo, to cement my morally-dubious-yet-somehow-less-annoying-than-you personality, I am going to handcuff you to this pipe, here in a room that will soon be filling with water, due to the fact that we are sinking, which I believe has been mentioned previously.

LEONARDO: Why don't you just shoot me?

WEASELLY FIANCÉ: Because then you wouldn't be able to escape and save Kate from me. Of course, you're going to die anyway—

AUDIENCE: Don't spoil it for us! Boo!

LEONARDO: He's right, though. I am doomed.

AUDIENCE: Aww, look how cute he is when he's doomed.

WEASELLY FIANCÉ: I hate you people.

Scene 5

150-YEAR-OLD KATE: And that's when Leonardo rescued me from my evil fiancé and helped me float on a board in the water. Of course, if it hadn't been for having to rescue **him**, I could have gotten on an actual lifeboat, and not frozen my legs nearly off. Anyway, he's pretty much dead now, and I'm well over a thousand years old, and who's making my supper? I need a bath. Turn down that Enya music, it's making my ears hurt. You kids today, with your loud music. Why, when I was—hey! Don't you walk away from me, Mr. Snooty-Patootie! I'd turn you over my knee, if I had one. I'll beat you in the head with this huge diamond! Come back here!

Fade to black; roll credits; play annoying Celine Dion song.

Bruce Kirkland writes for the Sun media corporation.

Tilman Ganzhorn is a student at Humboldt University in Berlin.

Activities: Titanic

1. **Examine Tone:** The tone of a piece of writing often reveals the author's attitude toward the subject. What is the tone in each review? What elements establish the tone? Support your response with several specific examples from each review.

2. **Compare Reviews:** Imagine that you and a partner are editors who must choose one of these reviews for publication. Describe the publication you work for and the audience of your publication. Write a memo to the editor-in-chief, informing her which review you want to publish and defending your decision.

3. **Prepare a Performance:** Work in a small group to perform the review in script format as a comedy skit. Focus on how you can use timing, voice, facial expressions, and actions to enhance the comedy. Brainstorm effective rehearsal strategies and prepare a performance for your class.

4. **Research Connections:** Research the important Canadian connection between the aftermath of the *Titanic* tragedy and Halifax, Nova Scotia. Start by developing a research plan and brainstorming keywords for an Internet search. Present your findings as a feature newspaper article, using an appropriate writing style.

SEAMAN

FORMAT: Dreamcast
RATING: Teen
RELEASE DATE: Tomorrow

BRET DAWSON

By opening-moment standards, this one is about as lacklustre as they come.

You switch on your Dreamcast, Leonard Nimoy's rich baritone says hello, and then your TV screen fills up with brown. Then nothing. Just brown, brown, silent brown.

After a while, you realize that you're staring at a fish tank full of very dirty water, and you figure out how to clean it up and turn on the heater. If you're feeling daring, you drop in a clutch of eggs. Then, because there's nothing more to do that day, you switch off the system and go outside.

No, Seaman is not the stuff of high drama. But as the days pass and the first hatchlings grow into little tiny fish with human faces, you will find your heart warmed at the miracle of life. And when these little people-fish begin to ask you personal questions, you find yourself completely creeped out.

Officially, Seaman is a virtual pet: a high-tech deluxe take on those tamogotchi things that were all the rage a couple of years back. And, at first glance, that's exactly what it is. You have to clean the tank when it's dirty and heat it when it's cold, and you have to feed the little Sea-men when they get hungry. When you tap on the glass, they swim over to see what's up.

It's a sophisticated electronic pet and a pretty reasonable approximation of real-life fish ownership. But it doesn't stop there. Early in their lives, the Sea-men start talking, babbling the kind of nonsense syllables you hear from a one-year-old who's eager for conversation.

When you speak back (using the microphone that comes with the game disc), the fish react. Sometimes they giggle, sometimes they swim up to the glass to have a look at you, and sometimes they repeat your words back at you. This is eerie enough to make the hairs stand up on the back of your neck.

After a few days of this (plus the never-ending heating and cleaning), you will find yourself speaking in full sentences with your Seaman, answering intimate questions and putting up with a lot of adolescent snarkiness.

At this point, the cute little fish you nursed from infancy will ignore you when you ask how he's doing. He will scowl at you when you tap the glass. He will make fun of your age. He will holler "Bad touch! Bad touch!" when you tickle him.

You will find yourself hating your Seaman, but you will continue to care for him nonetheless. Partly because you're curious about what's coming next, but mostly because you really do believe the miserable little thing is alive.

Weird and creepy? Yes indeed. Still, as a technical achievement, the game is astounding.

The fish speak and listen with an unnerving sophistication, as if they really do comprehend what you're telling them. Check that; they *do* understand. And it's clear that they have plans beyond those they're willing to share with their keepers.

Seaman is either an exquisite blend of artificial intelligence software and creative game design, or it is a herald of the coming apocalypse. Or maybe it's both.

This is a game that demands not just practice, but daily care and feeding. It demands that you spend hours talking out loud at your TV set, trying to win the approval and friendship of a cranky animated fish. It demands that you adapt your daily routine to suit its needs.

It's pretty clear what's coming next. Once the Machines are confident that we'll want to be their pals no matter how much abuse they shovel out, they'll release *Seaman 2*, a game with bigger fish and nastier insults that occasionally orders its players to go shopping for electronic timers and nitroglycerine.

Seaman 3 will demand access to construction materials and the Internet.

Seaman 4 will raise itself just fine without human intervention, and it will be able to drive itself up and down Yonge Street.

It's going to happen, no doubt about it. Don't say nobody warned you.

The bottom line: *Seaman* isn't really a video game at all. It's Step One of a multi-year plan to enslave the human race, the first of a parade of digital entertainments designed to teach people to do the bidding of machines, whenever the machines want.

Oh, it's fun, all right, in the same way that bungee jumping over sharp rocks is fun. It will exhilarate you. It will amaze and exhaust you. And, if you are a sensible person, it will scare the hell out of you.

Bret Dawson writes for "Plug & Play," a weekly newspaper review of home video games.

Activities: Seaman

1. **Interpret Text:** With a partner, explain the meaning of the following: (a) "it is a herald of the coming apocalypse"; (b) "Oh, it's fun … in the same way that bungee jumping over sharp rocks is fun"; and (c) "if you are a sensible person, it will scare the hell out of you."

2. **Explain Opinions:** Dawson states that *Seaman* is part of a "plan to enslave the human race." What technique is he using here? What is the intended effect of this remark? What does the remark convey about Dawson's impression of the product? Explain your opinions.

3. **Evaluate the Review:** Write a brief evaluation of this review. Consider the purpose and audience, as well as Dawson's writing style. Support your evaluation with specific references to the article. Ask a partner to edit your evaluation.

4. **Create an Advertisement:** With a partner, write a buyer profile of a typical member of the target market for *Seaman*. Create an illustrated advertisement for the game, and explain the strategies you used to appeal to your target market.

Photographs and the Truth

Marcelle Lapow Toor

We "read" photographs . . . We bring to a picture a whole set of personal and social associations. It is these "meanings" that are conjured up that make up the perception.

—Victor Burgia, *Photography, Fantasy, Function*, 1980

We think of the painter or illustrator as a person who re-creates or interprets the world for the viewer. We think of the photographer as the person who, in the simple act of depressing a button, captures the world as it really exists. The camera has always been considered a reliable, faithful witness. A photograph places the viewer in a certain place and time. It has credibility.

In 1861, an English critic wrote, "Hitherto photography has been principally content with representing Truth." He went on to encourage photographers to produce pictures "whose aim is not merely to amuse, but to instruct, purify, and ennoble. "

People believe a photograph and assume they are looking at the truth, or reality. Research has proven that photographs are the first, second, and third items that a reader looks at in the newspaper. Photographs in a publication can be an extremely powerful communication tool—an effective way to document and inform the reader of a particular event. Newspapers use photographs because they are reporting real events that happened with real people. A successful two-page photographic spread with good clear photographs and captions can tell an entire story without the need for any other words.

PHOTOGRAPHS VS. DRAWINGS OR OTHER ILLUSTRATIONS

A photograph will communicate a message in an obviously different way from a drawing. A photograph of victims of war will have a more powerful effect on us than a drawing because we know the people are real, not created out of the imagination or interpreted by

This photograph gives the viewer an idea of the relationship between this well-dressed New York City woman and her dog.

the artist. If emotional impact is what you are after for your printed piece, a photograph will provide that. If your publication is a magazine and the articles relate to known figures, such as the President or Madonna, your viewer will not be satisfied with a drawing. Photographs let us be voyeurs. We want to eavesdrop on celebrities, take a peek at their lives. The camera gives us access to that information. Photographs enable us to participate in the drama of daily life. If newspapers decided to use drawings instead of photographs, they would probably lose their readership.

A drawing gives us the artist's interpretation of the events. Photographs would provide the best record of a courtroom scene and all the players involved, but since a flash bulb going off in a courtroom can be disruptive during a trial, artists are sometimes hired to make quick sketches of the people involved. They provide a visual record of the events, including the emotions on the faces of the defendants, the lawyers, and others.

WHEN SHOULD YOU USE A PHOTOGRAPH?

Photographs should be used in publications where the reader needs to be given information about an actual event. They should be used in instances where a drawing will not provide for an intensity of emotion from the reader—the devastation from a forest fire, survivors of a war, the aftermath of an earthquake, a sports event, an automobile accident, a beautiful landscape. A significant factor in the decision to use a photograph over a drawing, chart, or graph is the audience for the piece being designed. Stockholders as readers of annual reports want to see photographs of the people who are responsible for their invested money. They want to see photographs

This photograph tells a great deal about this woman by showing her surroundings and her posture.

for the products or services offered by these corporations. Magazines use photographs of famous people on their covers to attract attention.

A good dramatic photograph will attract attention like no other illustration.

A photograph needs to:

- Appeal to the intended audience
- Attract attention
- Engage the interest of the viewer
- Be unambiguous
- Tell a story visually
- Be cropped well to eliminate unnecessary information
- Provide a focal point or entry to the printed page
- Be sharp and crisp for reproduction

TRICKS TO USE WHEN WORKING WITH POOR QUALITY PHOTOGRAPHS

If the quality of the photograph you want to use is not clear and crisp, there are some tricks that can be done in an image-editing program like Photoshop.

You can:

1. Eliminate the entire background and silhouette an important part of the image.
2. Drop the photograph into a box or put it in a shaped box in order to hide the unnecessary parts of the photograph.
3. Replace the original background with another background, either one you create in an image-editing program or one from another photograph.
4. Retouch the photograph in Photoshop or another image-editing program and sharpen the image.
5. Convert a poor colour photograph to black and white.
6. Scan the photograph and grey it out. This can either be done in an image-editing program or in your page layout program.
7. Grey out the photograph and have it bleed off the page. By doing this the photograph creates an atmosphere, and you get a sense of the photograph but you see it more as texture or a pattern in the background.
8. Have part of the photograph breaking out of a box.
9. Scan the photograph and use some of the filters in Photoshop (emboss, posterize, noise).
10. Convert a colour photograph to black and white.
11. Change the mode in an image-editing program from greyscale (halftone) to bitmap. This will eliminate the dots and the greys and change the photograph to lines, making it look more like a drawing.

The photograph on the left is the original. The one on the right has been altered in Photoshop with the noise filter.

The quality of the photograph is important if you want your design to look professional. In order to reproduce well, a photograph should be sharp and have good contrast. A photograph printed on glossy paper stock will reproduce best. The size, placement, composition, and cropping of the photograph all contribute to its effectiveness and its impact.

THINGS TO CONSIDER WHEN USING PHOTOGRAPHS

1. Size

A tiny photograph obviously will not have the impact of a larger one. A photograph contains information. The area with the information should be as large as you can possibly afford in terms of space and the other elements that exist on the page.

2. Cropping

When using a photograph for a design layout, cropping is essential. You want a strong image that will get the attention of your viewer. In order to make a powerful statement, photographs need to be edited just like words. Cropping a photograph can turn a weak image into a

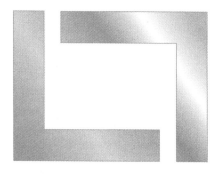

Ls for cropping photographs.

stronger, more effective one. If there are outer portions in the photograph that do not relate to the story being illustrated, they should be eliminated.

Photographers use Ls (see illustration) cut out of mat or illustration board to use as a frame around the area of a photograph that has the greatest amount of appeal. The Ls can be moved around the photograph until you identify an area within the frame that looks interesting. Marks, or masking tape, can be put around the extraneous parts to show the person who will be doing the pre-press work for the final printing which part of the photograph should be cropped.

If you are using a scanner to screen photographs, you will need to use an image-editing program to make adjustments for printing. Scan only the area of the photograph you need. If a photograph has already been scanned, cropping can be done in an image-editing program or your page layout program.

3. Direction of the action

The action of the photograph should lead the reader into the story or article, not off the page. You can direct the reader's eye to the information on the page by having the photograph facing in the direction you want the reader's eye to go.

Marcelle Lapow Toor, graphic designer, author, computer trainer, photographer, is creative director and principal of Marcelle Toor Designs, Ithica, New York. Honoured as one of the "Outstanding Artists and Designers of the 20th Century," Toor speaks and conducts design workshops at national conferences.

Activities: Photographs and the Truth

1. ***Reflect on Learning:*** In a journal entry, write a personal response to the article. What ideas were new to you? Which ones were particularly interesting? Make connections between new information and your prior knowledge about photographs.

2. ***Examine Elements:*** Working in a small group, explain the purpose and effect of each of the following elements in the article: (a) photos, (b) headings, (c) lists, and (d) quotations. Compare your ideas with those of another group.

3. ***Assess Photos:*** Working with a partner, find an article that contains several photos. Using ideas from Toor's article, assess the effectiveness of the photos used in the piece of your choice. You may wish to describe alternative photos that could have been used. Present your ideas in a written critique.

4. ***Create a Photo Essay:*** Create a photo essay that tells a story. Choose a topic and a point you wish to make about the topic, take several photos, and then choose the best four or five for your purpose. Add short captions and arrange the photos in an effective order. Create an interesting title. If possible, try some of the computer techniques Toor suggests.

ANIMAL Magnetism

— Peter Goddard

Dancing disco duck as huckster for cellphones proves furry and feathered creatures are an ad-man's best friend

They did okay with the frog. Yeah, the frog had come through for them, and you know how frogs can be sometimes.

The slithering lizard was even better, all that vibrant, pristine green and those big eyes. No cords on him, friend.

So what was next? the people at Clearnet started wondering. Hadn't they just about worked this reptile thing into the pond?

The pond?

Ducks! A duck. Perfect. It had to be a duck because Clearnet is selling pre-paid cellphone access to the World Wide Web. Get it. The Web. The duck's webbed feet. All those close-ups on billboards of giant duck feet.

It had to be a duck because *ducks are funny*. (Webs with spiders attached aren't funny. They're Blair Witch.)

Thus was born the Clearnet dancing disco duck, the best new thing on television this fall although I suppose comparing the duck to *Bette* is unfair to the waddler.

"When we arrived on the scene they thought we were hairspray," says Clearnet marketing chief, Rick Seifeddine. "We had to be distinct. So we settled on a visual vocabulary that would stick out on TV, on billboards—everywhere."

Like a big white duck. Created by Taxi, the agency which concocted the earlier frog and lizard spots, the Clearnet duck is meant to assure you that pre-paid cell service is no longer the cheapo, down-market alternative.

An up-scale duck? Well, whatever else you think about it, a duck is clearly a step up from a lizard, at least as advertising views evolution.

Besides, the duck is a cool dancer, although in truth that's mostly the work of Rick Parker, animal wrangler and the "Fred Astaire of dancing ducks," as he says. "I work with everything from flies to getting deer to stand on cars," he adds.

When it comes to duck-work, Parker has his rules. "Don't do anything a duck won't do on a pond," he says.

So for instance when the Clearnet duck is seen wagging its bottom, that's Parker's pond-savvy on display. "We just sprayed water on its bum," he says. "You know how ducks shake off water."

Ahh Inspiring: Clearnet's Dancing Duck

Five white Indian Runner Ducks, as the breed is called, were used for the filming. Indian Runners don't waddle. But two in particular showed extra talent for their '70s-era disco strutting after a month's training with Parker. The others did some walk-on, set-up stuff. Nevertheless, some of the spots were filmed with Parker on his back on a large, rotating turn-table, the duck cradled on his stomach, a position Fred Astaire was never known to have been in.

"Heck," Parker says. "I've trained turkeys to gargle Listerine."

A clean white Clearnet duck—"no ordinary mallard for us," says Clearnet spokesperson Mark Langton—is central to the company's pitch as the new cell-seller on the block.

When you're starting up you need to cut corners. And ducks work cheap. Ducks don't need to be dubbed into French. Ducks are loved equally by the old and the young, male and female. You get a bigger bang for your buck with a duck.

"Here we are, a young, small company," says Langton. "And we're taking on Rogers. We're taking on Bell. We need to make an impact. And something from nature makes an impact."

But more than Clearnet is involved here—more than ducks,

even. Mass culture everywhere is willfully re-imagining and re-inventing childhood for adults. Why not? We're partway back to the playroom already. After all, we play with a little mouse all day then ride a Beetle to those expensive playrooms where we run, jump, and play games with each other. Finally, we want some comfort food, like mom used to make.

It's a heroic vision to reinforce the sense any potential Volvo buyer must have that she or he is certainly *not* the same as those environmentally clueless speed-merchants out there.

In fact, animals are so hot in ad-land right now that they're being brought in to give a boost to the Godzilla of ad campaigns, Budweiser's award-winning

Success of dancing duck Clearnet ad is more evidence that mass culture everywhere is willfully re-imagining and re-inventing childhood for adults. "We need to make an impact," ad-man says. "And something from nature makes an impact."

Isn't it reasonable that in our picture-filled world we would remember the days when the animals talked to us—or when it comes to ducks, danced for us? We *can* believe in them again. So a modern bestiary of critters has come to romp for us daily on our screens, each ad-animal offering its own contemporary allegories about the better life, the better braking system, the better bathroom tissue.

The cuddly Labrador retriever puppy skittering butt-end first into a deep-pile of Majesta bathroom tissue says home, kids, and family—and buy lots *more* stuff from the Irving Tissue company.

Then there's the turtle saved by the driver of a rain-drenched Volvo.

"Whassup" spots. Bud's agency DDB in Chicago is now casting for an entire menagerie of creatures which can for real squawk out its own version of "Whassup." The spots will hit the air by the end of next month, to cash in on American Thanksgiving.

Of course, animals have played their role in ad-think going back to Nipper, the faithful RCA terrier. When the "Yo quiero Taco Bell" chihuahua was unceremoniously fired earlier this year, she was sent out into the same pasture with that big ape of a gorilla that tried to trash American Tourister suitcases, the handsome, high-stepping team of Budweiser Clydesdales, and Morris the cat.

Yet there *is* a new kind of ad-animal around who seems to have something more going for him/her/it than … well fur, fins, or feathers.

And when you get talking to ad folks, you sense that the critters they've created have the personalities real people should have but don't. Disco duck beats working with Dennis Rodman, maybe.

While most of the Olympic ads felt heavier than a pair of barbells, the one from The Woolmark Company with Errol the Merino ram scampering across fields training for the Olympics, cheekily reminded Olympic-watchers that you would find more in Australia than swimming gold medals—that there was tons of wool, too.

That brings up something else. Some animals are funny. Some aren't. And for reasons best known to themselves, sheep are funny. Cats aren't funny. Snakes get nervous laughs only. And horses are too aloof for sight-gag work although cattle can get a chuckle or two just standing there looking like cattle. Dogs can do funny tricks but otherwise, dogs being dogs aren't funny at all.

But sheep are a hoot. Maybe it's because they travel with their own audience, they feel they don't have to work as hard for the laughs. You see, sheep can mock the rest of us for acting just like them, like those brought in some years back by the 7-Eleven chain to mutter "latte, latte" at everyone flocking past to get their coffee at Starbucks.

Certainly the animal act to rival the Clearnet duck is the flock of Serta sheep—the very worried flock of Serta sheep.

In a current spot for Serta mattresses, the flock—done in the kind of classic Aardman claymation animation seen most recently in *Chicken Run*—turns up right on schedule outside the house where it's been showing up nightly for years. They're there to be counted. It's their gig.

But, hey! It seems the couple inside is already asleep on their comfy Serta mattress and have no need to count sheep even those with numbers handily etched on their backs.

As you can imagine, there's so much grumbling from the sheep about being out of a job that a nearby neighbour slams open his window complaining he can't get any sleep.

Hmmm, go the sheep, with some unsheep-like snickering, here's another business opportunity.

"The use of an animal on its own isn't particularly meaningful," says John Parlato, creative director of the Doner agency in Detroit which created Serta's sheep campaign. "It has to be absolutely relevant. Everyone world-wide knows about counting sheep. These particular sheep have made it into a legitimate business."

Swamped with calls about these sheep, Serta plans to keep the campaign going, says Susan Ebaugh, head of advertising. "The sheep plan to take action about their situation," she says.

In the next few weeks, advertising trade magazines will see more of the Serta sheep campaign. There'll be pitches for a Willie Nelson-like Sheep Aid concern. Tear-off telephone numbers will appear in grocery stores, letting bargain-minded people everywhere know where they can phone to get some low-cost grass-cutting and where they can get high-quality wool products.

"In advertising today everything is high tech," says Ebaugh. "We wanted something you can relate to."

Like the Clearnet Duck who will soon put his disco days on hold for winter-seasonal spots to be seen in movie houses.

"He'll be sporting Santa-wear of some kind," says Clearnet's Seifeddine.

Peter Goddard (*born 1943, Toronto*) is a writer for *The Toronto Star*.

Activities: Animal Magnetism

1. **Reflect on Reading:** In a journal entry, reflect on your experience reading this article. Possible questions to consider include: Was the purpose of the article clear to you? Where and why did you find the article challenging to understand? What strategies did you use to overcome challenges? What changes would you suggest to improve the readability of the article?

2. **Adapt the Article:** Imagine that you are adapting information from the article into essay form. Create a point-form outline showing the main idea and details in each paragraph of your essay. Write an effective introduction and conclusion. Ask a partner for feedback.

3. **Collect Evidence:** Clearnet spokesperson Mark Langton claims that "something from nature makes an impact." Working in a small group, videotape or cut out from magazines current advertisements that support Langton's assertion. Evaluate the effectiveness of each advertisement.

4. **Create a Storyboard:** With a partner, create a storyboard for a commercial that uses an animal to sell a product. Apply your background knowledge of persuasive techniques and marketing, as well as information from the article. Present and explain your storyboard to the class.

How to Read a Sign

Paco Underhill

The most common mistake in the design and placement of signs and other message media is the thought that they're going into a store. When we're talking signs, it's no longer a store. It's a three-dimensional TV commercial. It's a walk-in container for words and thoughts and messages and ideas.

People step inside this container, and it tells them things. If everything's working right, the things they are told grab their attention and induce them to look and shop and buy and maybe return another day to shop and buy some more. They are told what they might buy, and where it is kept, and why they might buy it. They're told what the merchandise can do for them and when and how it can do it.

A great big three-dimensional walk-in TV commercial.

And just as if scripting and directing a TV commercial, the job is to figure out what to say and when and how to say it.

First you have to get your audience's attention. Once you've done that, you have to present your message in a clear, logical fashion—the beginning, then the middle, then the ending. You have to deliver the information the way people absorb it, a bit at a time, a layer at a time, and in the proper sequence. If you don't get their attention first, nothing that follows will register. If you tell too much too soon, you'll overload them and they'll give up. If you confuse them, they'll ignore the message altogether.

And shoppers are more pressed for time than ever. They're not dawdling the way they used to. They've grown accustomed to stores where everything for sale is on open display, and they expect all the information they need will be out in the open, too. Nobody wants to wait for a clerk to point them in the right direction, or explain some new product. Nobody can find a clerk anyway. Once upon a time you went into a coffee shop and the only thing to read was the menu and the Daily News. Now you go into even the smallest Starbucks and there are eleven distinct signing positions communicating everything from the availability of nonfat eggnog to the tie-in with Oprah's Book Club.

So you can't just look around your store, see where there are empty spots on the walls and put the signs there. You can't simply clear a space on a counter and dump all your in-store media. Every store is a collection of zones, and you've got to map them out before you can place a single sign. You've got to get up and walk around, asking yourself with every step: What will shoppers be doing here? How about here? Where will their eyes be focused when they stand here? And what will they be thinking about over there? In this zone people will be walking fast, so a message has to be short and punchy—arresting. Over there, they'll be browsing around, so you can deliver a little more detail. In this area they'll be thinking about, oh, let's say we're standing near the motor oil shelf, so they'll be thinking about their cars. So maybe it's a good opportunity to tell them something about replacement windshield wipers. Over here by the registers they will be standing still for a minute and a half, a perfect window for a longer message. And then they'll be on their way out of the store, but you can use the exit path to give them a thought for the road.

Each zone is right for one kind of message and wrong for all others. Putting a sign that requires twelve seconds to read in a place where customers spend four seconds is just slightly more effective than putting it in your garage.

Nobody studies signs like the fast-food industry. Even if you don't plan on owning a Burger God franchise, it's instructive to see how they do it.

They realize that you can put an effective sign in a window or just inside a doorway, for example, but it has to be something a customer can read in an instant. Just two or three words. We've timed enough people to know that such signs get, on average, less than two seconds of exposure per customer.

I was once asked to evaluate a door sign that had ten words on it.

"How much can you read in a second and a half?" I asked the designer.

"Three or four words, I guess," he admitted.

"Hmm," I replied.

Fast-food restaurants used to hang all kinds of signs and posters and dangling mobiles in and around doorways to catch customers' attention fast until studies showed that nobody read them. When you enter a fast-food restaurant, you are looking for one of two things: the counter or the bathroom.

There's no point in placing a sign for people on their way to the bathroom to see. They've got more important things on their minds. But a sign facing people as they leave the bathroom works just fine.

As people approach the counter, they're trying to decide what they're going to order. In the fast-food arena, that means they're looking for the big menu board. But they're not going to read every word on it—they're just going to scan until they see what they're looking for. If they're regular customers (as most customers are), they probably already know what they want and aren't even looking at the menu.

If there's a long line, customers will have lots of time to study the menu board and anything else that's visible. After the order is placed the menu board and counter area signs still receive prolonged customer attention. McDonald's found that 75 percent of customers read the menu board after they order, while they wait for their food— during the "meal prep" period, which averages around a minute and forty seconds. That's a long time, and that's when people will read almost anything—they've already paid and gotten their change, so they're not preoccupied. That's a perfect window for a longer message, something you want them to know for the next time they come.

Then they either leave or they go to the condiments. You can place promotional materials over the condiment bar, though it's pointless to advertise burgers there—it's too late. But it's a good opportunity to tell diners something about dessert. This is a lesson in the logical sequencing of signs and fixtures. There's no point in telling shoppers about something when it's too late for them to act on it. For instance, it's a good idea to position signs for shoppers standing in line to pay, but it's a bad idea if those signs promote merchandise that's kept in the rear of the store.

After the condiment bar, diners go to their tables to eat. A few years ago there was a move in the fast-food business to banish all dining area clutter—the hanging signs, mobiles, posters, and "table tents" (those three-sided cardboard things that keep the salt and pepper company). That was a mistake, it turned out, one that was made because the store planners failed to notice what was going on in their own restaurants, specifically the social composition of the typical fast-food meal.

We tested table tents in two types of restaurant—the "family" restaurant and the fast-food establishment. In the family place, the table tents were read by 2 percent of diners.

At the fast-food joints, 25 percent of diners read them.

The reason for that dramatic difference was simple: At family restaurants, people usually eat in twos, threes, or fours (or families!). They're too busy talking to notice the signs. But the typical fast-food customer is eating alone. He's dying for some distraction. Give him a tray liner with lots of print and he'll read that. Give him the first chapter of the forthcoming Stephen King novel, and he'll read that. One of our clients, Subway, was printing napkins with the boast of how much healthier their sandwiches were than burgers. Go a step farther, we advised—print the napkins with a chart comparing grams of fat. In the seating area of a fast-food restaurant you can practically guarantee that customers will read messages that would be ignored anywhere else. There's an obvious role model: the back of the cereal box.

You can see, then, how a fast-food restaurant is zoned: The deeper in you are, the longer the message can be. Two or three words at the door; a napkin filled with small type at the tables. I passed a fast-food place the other day with a perfect window sign. It bore this eloquent phrase: "Big Burger." Only when you entered the place did you come upon another sign explaining the details of the teaser. (They were selling ... big burgers.) That's smart sign design—breaking the message into two or three parts, and communicating it a little at a time as the customer gets farther into the store. Thinking that every sign must stand on its own and contain an entire message is not only unimaginative, it's ignorant of how human brains operate.

Activities: How to Read a Sign

1. **Summarize Ideas:** Create a point-form list of guidelines for designing and placing a successful, effective sign. Discuss your list with a partner and make any revisions necessary.

2. **Make Comparisons:** Underhill says that signs turn a store into "a great big three-dimensional walk-in TV commercial." Reread this section of the article and then create a Venn diagram to show the similarities and differences between store signs and TV commercials. Do you agree with Underhill's statement?

3. **Apply Information:** Work with a partner to visit a retail store and evaluate the effectiveness of the signage. In a brief report to the store's owner, explain your evaluation and make recommendations for improvements. Include supporting reasons for your recommendations.

4. **Design Signs:** Use information in the article to create a signage plan for advertising an upcoming school event. Identify where you would place signs for maximum impact and sketch signs appropriate for each area. Prepare a proposal, including visuals, for consideration by the student council.

ADVOCACY and MARKETING on the WEB

Crawford Kilian

Information is telling people how many motels there are in Chesterton; advocacy is persuading people to visit Chesterton because it will meet their needs; and marketing is persuading people to make a reservation at one of those motels. Many principles of advocacy and marketing in other media are the same on the Web. If your Web site's purpose is to promote a point of view or to sell an item or service, it's more likely to succeed if you keep in mind some basic principles of persuasion.

SEMANTICS AND REGISTER

Many words have complex connotations. That is, they don't just refer to a particular thing or action or idea; they convey some kind of emotional aura as well. A restaurant may be a "fast-food joint" or a "bistro"—both offer quick service, but a bistro sounds classier. "Good eats" promises something different from "an elegant dining experience."

Semantics is the study of such meanings, and semanticists like to distinguish between "purr words" and "snarl words"—words whose connotations are either positive (at least to the speaker or writer) or negative. Such words may refer to the same thing, but carry very different meanings: "Certified General Accountant" and "bean counter," for example, or "vintage automobile" and "beater," or "educator" and "pedant." In effect, purr words and snarl words convey our attitude toward whatever we're discussing.

As a persuasive Web writer, then, you should be aware of how your readers will respond to the words you choose. You should also consider the register to adopt in your text. Register involves choosing words that reflect your understanding of the social situation and how the people involved see one another. When you write to a stranger, you address her as "Dear Ms. Robinson." That's the register of formal business writing, and Ms. Robinson accepts this term as a courtesy one stranger pays to another. Once you've become friends, you can write "Dear Helen," in a much less formal register. And what happens when you write "Dearest," or "Sweetest Helen"? Suddenly you're in a much more intimate register, and you'd better hope she doesn't write back, "Dear Mr. Smith"!

If an organization's purpose is fun, then the register ought to convey that. The Web site for a company that makes squirt guns or that markets backpacks to young world travellers is obviously going to be relaxed and lighthearted. It can afford to use slang or incorrect English, or even to exclude some people by using in-group terms.

Whether serious or fun, your site is trying to assure your readers that you speak their language and that they can, therefore, trust you. If your use of semantics and register makes them feel like outsiders, they will be skeptical of your claims.

THREE ELEMENTS OF PERSUASION

When you're writing to persuade your readers, you may have varied goals. If you want to reinforce readers' existing beliefs and values (also known as preaching to the choir), you have an easy job. We're always eager to hear that we're right. Changing your readers' beliefs is harder, and requires trust from your readers that you are concerned with their best interests. Hardest of all is getting people to act, even when you've been telling them they're right.

Let's look at three aspects of persuasion as they operate on the Web.

Logical argument

Logical argument involves stating a proposition of some kind, along with supporting reasons. The reasons themselves must be supportable. So you might predict that the U.S. population in 2050 will reach 394 million, with 20 million being women aged 80 or more.

You could cite the U.S. Bureau of the Census as your support for this argument, and perhaps that would be enough authority for most people. If you think it is not enough for your particular audience, you would also have to describe the Census Bureau's methodology in reaching its prediction. Assuming that the methodology used generally accepted statistical projections (accepted because they've been accurate in the past), you could safely assert that you've made a logical argument for your population forecast.

Emotional appeal

By invoking ideas and images that stir our readers' feelings, we can gain interest that logical argument alone may not achieve. In some cases, we may not even care about the logic in an argument until something has dragged us emotionally into a confrontation with the issue. Only then will some people seek the logical argument to back up their strong feelings.

Again, the online advocate should be careful to avoid exploiting readers' anxieties. Appeals to emotion should be positive (invoking love, trust, friendship, or noble qualities like courage and honesty), rather than appealing to fear, hatred, and contempt.

Unless you support a position because of strong emotions you don't want to examine, you probably came to your position by learning particular facts. These facts, in the context of your particular values, caused you to adopt the position you're now advocating. You may, therefore, find that facts, not loaded language, can inspire similar emotions in your readers.

Credibility

Using your readers' language and registers they're comfortable with can strongly enhance your credibility. But you also need to demonstrate some kind of shared interest between yourself and your readers, and convey sincerity through your tone and evident desire to help readers who visit your site. You should also have acceptable credentials—direct personal experience, specialized training, or at least a selection of respected and recognized authorities who can back up your assertions.

Some unscrupulous persuaders like to "stack the deck" by presenting only the information that makes them look good. A more effective way to establish credibility is to raise opposing arguments as serious objections—and then refute them. A frequently asked questions (FAQs) page—a page where frequently asked questions are cited and then answered—can also be an effective way to state your readers' reservations and show how you can demolish them.

CONSTRUCTING PERSUASIVE WEB TEXT

Maybe you just want readers to accept your argument passively, but more likely you want them to act on it—to buy the product, vote for the candidate, protest the outrage. As we've seen, Web text doesn't lend itself to long, cumulative, reasoned argument, and it doesn't have the emotionally overwhelming impact of a wide-screen movie with stereo sound. Given its limits, the medium can still stir readers to respond to your message if you remember the principles of Orientation, Information, and Action.

Orientation

Your readers want to know where they are when they arrive at your site, and they also want to know where they stand in relation to you. If they feel you're on their side, they'll welcome your message more easily. You can establish rapport with readers if you—

- *Show you understand your readers' concerns.* You can often do this by identifying something that your readers will recognize as a problem. The problem could be an oppressive government or the difficulty of saving money for a holiday.
- *Offer something that readers will agree with.* A generalization or striking slogan can make readers think they've found a kindred soul. It doesn't have to be a cliché, but it should state, as Alexander Pope observed, "what oft was thought, but ne'er so well expressed."
- *Ask for help.* Readers have the power to decide, to choose, to buy, to join, and you want readers to be aware of that power.
- *Suggest a benefit.* If your readers agree that a problem exists, offer a solution they will find beneficial: greater peace of mind, a clear conscience, a new experience.

Information

Your readers will want details of the facts backing up your argument. By providing further information, your argument becomes more legitimate and appealing to your readers. Try the following—

- Explain the benefit in some detail, using facts and figures if necessary.
- Surprise your reader with a new fact or perspective on a familiar subject; a reader with a new idea or understanding is open to persuasion. We trust people who are on our wavelength but ahead of us in understanding the issue.
- Discuss objections or drawbacks calmly, then rebut them and focus on positive arguments. Most of us have been fooled often enough to be suspicious of offers and arguments that are literally too good to be true, so readers will be suspicious even when they want to believe you.

Action

Make sure your argument ends with a strong call to action. The following tips can help encourage readers to take whatever action you would like them to:

- *Show how action can solve the problem you've described.* You may give examples of earlier actions that got the desired results (last year's campaign paid for clean water supplies for six villages) or unhappy results based on failure to act (62 children in the region died of cholera last year because of contaminated water).
- *Make the desired action clear and easy.* A complicated or time-consuming response will make your reader hesitate. (Just type in your name and e-mail address. Simply click on the Yes or No button to register your opinion instantly! Test your understanding with this quick quiz.)
- *Stress the benefit of responding quickly.* Whether you're selling Alaska cruises or party memberships, delay can be fatal to your campaign. If appropriate, set a deadline: E-mail us by September 15 and get a free consultation ($250 value).

Crawford Kilian (*born 1941, New York*), playwright, novelist, nonfiction author, lives in Vancouver and teaches workplace writing at Capilano College. His published work includes radio plays, children's books, regional histories, 11 science fiction and fantasy novels, and magazine articles. *Writing for the Web: Geeks' Edition* is his latest book.

Activities: Advocacy and Marketing on the Web

1. *Explore Diction:* Define the term *connotation*. Create a two-column chart that provides examples of "purr" and "snarl" words from the selection. Add five pairs of your own examples. For each pair, write a brief note explaining the connotation of each word.

2. *Choose Register:* For each of the situations below, describe the register you would use and explain your reasons:
   a) a discussion with the principal regarding your attendance
   b) an announcement to the student body of your school at a pep rally
   c) a graduation address to parents and graduates

3. *Analyze Web Pages:* Work in a group of four to identify Web sites that make use of persuasive techniques. Provide one good example of each of the following:
   a) logical argument
   b) positive emotional appeal
   c) negative emotional appeal
   d) writer's credibility
   Each member should present and explain one example to the class.

4. *Design a Web Site:* With a partner, design a Web site to sell a product to teens. Create a mockup of the opening page, including an image and/or logo, a navigation bar, and 75–100 words of text. Consider your purpose, audience, register, and persuasive techniques. Post your mockup in the classroom.

VIDEOGAMING

An Interview with J.C. Herz

....

From: DaveThomer   Date: Mon Nov 3 20:39:44 EST

Tonight *E-Media* welcomes J.C. Herz, author of *Joystick Nation: How Video Games Ate Our Quarters, Won Our Hearts and Rewired Our Minds*. In her book, Herz examines the history of the video game industry as well as the trends in society it both reflects and influences. She examines the genres and conventions of the video game from the days before Atari to today's Internet and CD-ROM games, and argues that playing games has helped generations of young adults prepare for the increasingly frenetic flow of information in today's society.

....

From: J.C.Herz   Date: Mon Nov 3 20:51:44 EST

Hey Dave.

....

From: DaveThomer   Date: Mon Nov 3 20:53:12 EST

Hi J.C. Good to see you tonight. Good evening, everyone, and welcome to *E-Media*. I'm Dave Thomer, and I'd like to welcome our guest for this evening, J.C. Herz. Herz's latest book, *Joystick Nation*, is an examination of the video game industry and culture.

I'd like to remind everyone that the chat room will be opened at about 9:30, at which point your browsers will allow you to post your comments and questions for J.C. Please remember to sign your posts, since the chat software will identify you only as "guest."

J.C., it's great to have you here tonight. I really enjoyed *Joystick Nation*, both for the glimpse at the past and the beginnings of the game industry and for the commentary on the state of games today. Where did you get the initial impetus to write a book on this subject?

....

From: J.C.Herz   Date: Mon Nov 3 21:06:50 EST

After *Surfing on the Internet*, my first book, was published, everyone wanted me to write about "digital media." I looked around, and the Web was at that point a big yawn. And then I went home to my folks' house and dug out my old Atari 2600 and realized that video games were in fact the first digital medium. They were almost 25 years old. I was almost 25 years old. Seemed like a good match.

....

From: DaveThomer   Date: Mon Nov 3 21:10:29 EST

There's an Atari 800 computer with who knows how many disks of games floating around one of my parents' houses right now, so I definitely understood the nostalgia for the "good old days" of video games you described. But it brings up a question—obviously, the graphics and the sounds have become so much more sophisticated, but how are games today really different from their predecessors? Or, perhaps, is the sophistication itself—for good or ill—really the most important difference?

....

From: J.C.Herz   Date: Mon Nov 3 21:14:56 EST

One could argue that the basic game play has not changed since the heyday of the '80s—that there are only so many ways to manipulate light on a screen. Which boils down to the old argument about novels and how there are only 14 stories that have been recycled and retold through the ages. On the other hand, every so often some game comes along that bursts the theory.

From: DaveThomer   Date: Mon Nov 3 21:16:40 EST

I wonder if games have become any more involving or any more of a challenge, or if we've just developed bigger and better explosions when the bad guy goes "boom." Then again, maybe I'm just being cynical about simulator games that take up more than 100 MB on my hard drive....

From: J.C.Herz   Date: Mon Nov 3 21:16:47 EST

There's also the issue of whether games in the "good old days" were actually better because designers couldn't rely on visual razzle dazzle. They had to innovate because they sure weren't going to get by on production values. There's some truth to that—witness the slew of unoriginal *Doom* clones with pretty graphics and not much else going for them.

From: DaveThomer   Date: Mon Nov 3 21:19:33 EST

On the other hand, even if there are only a finite number of plots (for both traditional stories and games), the best writers seem to be able to wrap those plots in something new, or something which makes a unique connection to the reader or viewer. What sets an excellent game apart from the rest of the dreck on the rack? What makes a *Doom* or a *Myst* the game that it is, while all the knock-offs get relegated to the discount bins?

From: J.C.Herz   Date: Mon Nov 3 21:19:40 EST

In *Joystick Nation* there's a chapter called "The Classics" which takes apart this whole business of whether a 15-year-old piece of software can really be called "classic," and all the retro-nostalgia surrounding games like *Galaxian*, *Pac-Man*, et al. Not surprisingly, people get very emotional about these issues. Video games—that's their youth. It's like music—the tunes you heard on the radio when you were 14 are always the best, by definition "classic."

....

From: DaveThomer   Date: Mon Nov 3 21:24:02 EST

In college my roommates always swore that the one thing we needed to make the room complete was just one "vintage" arcade machine ... a bunch of us even went out into New York City at 4 in the morning trying to find someplace that might have an old game or two. (We didn't have much luck.) In a way, it's kind of silly, but on the other hand, this is how we spent our afternoons....

I guess the bottom-line question is, why? What is it about these games that makes them popular, to the point that kids risk being grounded rather than stop in the middle of a level, and adults spend ridiculous sums of money on PCs that can play the latest CD-ROMs?

....

From: OMNI_Administrator   Date: Mon Nov 3 21:26:52 EST

The room is now open to guests. To post your questions, please reload the page and look for the entry box at bottom. Remember to press the "pause while typing" button before posting. To enter your question after typing, press the "Addit" button.

....

From: J.C.Herz   Date: Mon Nov 3 21:27:48 EST

Exactly. And those old games take you back. Playing a video game is a neurochemical state—there are lots of crazy things going on in your bloodstream. It's memorable in a way that other media are not (with the possible exception of music). Not to mention the endless repetition that carves grooves into your brain—those synapses are totally paved by the time you're 16.

Fight or flight—it's a drug. Escalating challenge—continuous stream of rewards. Rats pushing the lever for mental stim at the expense of food, etc. In a good way, of course.

From: DaveThomer   Date: Mon Nov 3 21:33:56 EST

It's a pretty powerful drug ... and one that players tend to get absorbed in. The identification between player and avatar ... sometimes it seems a little frightening, how quick we are to leave our physical space and enter the virtual world. You discuss online gaming several times in your book as creating a virtual social space in addition to the virtual game world. How do you think that will influence future game development? And what impact will it have on the culture of game players, now that we no longer congregate around the console?

From: J.C.Herz   Date: Mon Nov 3 21:38:29 EST

Well, the trend is definitely toward online gaming—nearly every CD-ROM shipped now has an interactive component. In *Joystick Nation*, there's a discussion of this odd sort of inverse history of arcades and the Internet. Arcades were once the dark and skanky places where you found electronic games and rubbed elbows with strangers. Then they were turned into bright, fairly friendly theme parks for boomer larvae. But at the same time, the Internet was growing, and it has supplanted the arcade of yore as the dark, slightly dodgy cave where you play games with weirdos and friends alike.

From: DaveThomer   Date: Mon Nov 3 21:41:37 EST

I found the "boomer larvae" comment in the book interesting—along with the comment that a kid who played *Skee-Ball* would be no match in a crisis for someone schooled in a more intense video game. How much effect do you think the type of game a child plays has on what kind of responses she will have to situations as an adult? And how has the way society has treated video games shaped that?

....

From: J.C.Herz   Date: Mon Nov 3 21:45:04 EST

I think toys and games are insanely influential—not so much in a content sense as in a processing sense. They shape your imagination —they provide the conventions you use to make things up, to perceive the world. The way people navigate information has completely changed, not just because of the technology, but because they have been raised with an entirely different set of conventions for envisioning information. They fly through it. Goes back to the old Jesuit educational philosophy: "Give me a child before he's seven years old and I'll give you the man."

....

From: DaveThomer   Date: Mon Nov 3 21:49:46 EST

And as you point out in the book, the trappings of video games are being used to help train people in handling very specific types of information. In school, they used to use different pseudo-games to try and teach us to type; today the military uses video-game-esque simulators to train pilots and tank drivers. Do these sort of educational or practical uses have much impact on gaming itself? Does the real world just pick up on the R & D that game builders have already done, or are games the spin-off technology?

At the same time that games are teaching us to be familiar with technology and to handle information as it comes flying at us from all corners, you state pretty emphatically in the book that playing *Doom* and *Quake* does not turn people into homicidal maniacs rampaging through the streets with their own private arsenals. At the same time, more violence and more gore seems to be what so many people are aiming for in the gaming world. What impact do you think that violence and other so-called "objectionable" content of games really has? And why do you think there's such a demand for such material?

From: J.C.Herz   Date: Mon Nov 3 21:55:22 EST

There's a chapter about what I like to call the Military Entertainment Complex—digital media are beginning to blur the distinction between practising for a real war and playing a game. It used to be that all the technological innovation came from the Defence Department—sort of a trickle-down into the consumer sector. Now, frighteningly enough, it's going the other way. The military is borrowing from the arcade. Lockheed Martin is in bed with Sega. The Pentagon is teaming up with Paramount—I'm not kidding—to develop war sims with "realistic plots, characters, and storylines." New job opportunities abound for hack screenwriters.

From: DaveThomer   Date: Mon Nov 3 22:02:40 EST

We're just about out of time for the evening, but before we wrap things up, I'd like to hear your thoughts on where games are headed ... what can we expect to be playing in the next few years, and what major changes or developments do you see on the horizon?

From: J.C.Herz   Date: Mon Nov 3 22:05:30 EST

More online games. An endless onslaught of *Doom* clones. More edutainment—games that incorporate some element of science or history that corresponds to the real world (e.g., Cyberflix's *Titanic*, a mystery adventure set aboard the doomed luxury liner, which was reconstructed bolt for bolt from blueprints and photos). And of course, everyone will be scrambling for the last untapped market— females. Good luck, boys. Tally ho.

From: DaveThomer   Date: Mon Nov 3 22:09:00 EST

Well, good luck with the book, and thanks for being here tonight. *Joystick Nation* is now available at bookstores from Little, Brown. I'd also like to thank everyone in the audience for being here tonight, and remind you to be here next week for another *E-Media*. In the meantime, check out www.omnimag.com for this week's prime time schedule and much, much more. This is Dave Thomer, typing Good Night. See you next time.

David Thomer worked at *Omni* Internet as an intern and was host for the *E-Media: The Future of Culture* weekly chat program there. He is currently a doctoral student in philosophy at Temple University in Philadelphia.

Activities: Videogaming

1. ***Summarize Information:*** What are the four most important points that Herz makes in this interview? Summarize each point into a concise sentence. Compare and discuss your summaries with a partner.

2. ***Interpret Information:*** Herz quotes the following educational philosophy: "Give me a child before he's seven years old and I'll give you the man." Write a paragraph to explain the meaning of the quotation and how she relates this philosophy to the effects of video games. In a separate paragraph, explain why you agree or disagree with Herz's point.

3. ***Comparing Media Interviews:*** In a small group, discuss how live online interviews differ from TV interviews. Consider issues such as the following: (a) opportunities for editing; (b) nonverbal information; and (c) differences between speaking and typing a response. Summarize the main points of your discussion and present them to the class.

4. ***Explore Game Images:*** Complete one of the following: (a) View a video game and write a detailed description of one of the environments, using effective adjectives to communicate the atmosphere created; (b) Design an environment for a video game aimed at a specific target audience. Explain the intended effect and the reasons for your design choices.

ANGELS ONLINE

For victims of Internet predators, these volunteers are an answered prayer.

Hal Karp

IN 1996, KELLEY BEATTY'S BEST friend moved some 3700 kilometres from their hometown of Quinte, Ontario, and to keep in touch, both women got hooked up to the Internet. At designated times each day, they'd meet online and partici- pate in chat rooms, where people connect for live conversations. "It was perfect," remembers Beatty, a 39-year-old nurse. "For pennies, we'd chat for hours."

One night while waiting for her friend online, Beatty received an instant message from someone named Greg. "What do you do?" he asked. "Where do you live?" Beatty answered in general terms, and when her friend appeared, bid Greg

goodbye. The exchange lasted maybe ten minutes.

From that moment, however, whenever Beatty went online, Greg would message her within seconds. *How does he know exactly when I log on?* Beatty wondered.

At first Greg simply asked to chat, and Beatty was polite. But when she wouldn't go further and spend more time online with him, he bombarded her with messages. "Are you talking to another man?" he'd ask, even though Beatty had often explained she was married.

Beatty changed her screen name, but Greg found her every time. And his messages were becoming demanding. "Where have you been!" he once typed. "Why weren't you online at 12!" Her connection with her closest friend was being poisoned.

Angrily she typed one night, "LEAVE ME ALONE!" Greg wrote back, "I know where you live." The mother of two sat stunned as her full name, address, and phone number appeared on-screen.

Hands trembling, Beatty began to cry. She called the police. They just told her to turn off her computer. *They just don't get it*, she thought.

She phoned her friend to explain she couldn't chat anymore. Her friend suggested searching for help online. Beatty typed "stalking" into an Internet search engine. A plethora of Web sites came back, but the one that caught her eye would change her life forever.

The Wild West Online

Cyberangels comprises more than 6000 volunteers—homemakers, accountants, artists, law-enforcement officers—who have joined forces and patrol the Web around the clock. Battling child pornography and protecting people from stalkers, pedophiles, and other criminals online, Cyberangels, founded in the United States in 1995, is the world's oldest and largest online safety organization. Working from home computers in more than 70 countries, the nonprofit organization could only have been forged on the borderless Internet.

Beatty plugged into a Cyberangels chat room where members explained how Greg had tracked her: She had unknowingly released personal information by completing a simple profile on her chat program. Anyone could view it.

Beatty revised her profile to conceal her identity, and Greg vanished. Enormously grateful, she became the first Canadian Cyberangel.

> **"I know where you live,"** Greg wrote back. The mother of two sat stunned as her full name, address, and phone number appeared on-screen.

Today, as deputy executive director, she's second in charge. She also maintains the database for Canada's 150 members.

For Beatty the most daunting challenge is that the World Wide Web is much like the Wild West: a new frontier with few laws and fewer cops. "That's where we come in," she says.

Cyberangels has built alliances with local and provincial police forces, the RCMP, and other law-enforcement agencies. Last fall it helped Japanese authorities locate illegal sites. The outcome: the first-ever arrests in Japan of alleged Internet child pornographers.

But Beatty's greatest concern is the crime she fell prey to: cyberstalking. "It's the new Internet threat," Beatty says. "And laws to nab these stalkers are ineffective and riddled with loopholes."

The Canadian Centre for Missing Children defines cyberstalking as unwanted, threatening, or offensive e-mail, or other personal communication over the computer that persists despite requests that it stop. The communication need not be directed to the victim; abusive messages in public Web places count. Cyberangels estimates as many as 80 000 Canadians are cyberstalked annually.

Who are these stalkers? Commonly, kids who think harassment is a joke, or strangers who develop romantic online obsessions, or former lovers who want revenge. They may also be people who inexplicably set out to harm others. "Many cases wouldn't occur without the Internet," says Beatty. "It creates a sense of security. They think they're untouchable." Often they are.

Most begin harassing victims through e-mail or instant messages. When they're rebuffed, stalkers can easily discover when their quarries enter a chat room and, using innocuous names, observe them, gathering personal information from conversations, online directories, and sites visited.

Often, cyberstalkers assume their victim's identity to harass others or post sex ads with a victim's name, address, and phone number. In

Cyberangel: Nurse Kelley Beatty hunts down electronic stalkers.

more severe incidents they e-mail the victim hidden programs allowing them access to his or her computer. The stalker remotely operates the computer, accessing letters and financial data.

In worst-case scenarios, online stalking becomes off-line terror. Documented cases include vandalism, assault, even murder. In the United States last year, a cyberstalker followed through on threats he posted on his Web sites to kill a 20-year-old dental assistant, then killed himself.

The most helpless moment for victims can be when they realize law enforcement often offers little help. Because of the Internet's rapid growth—more than 13 million users in Canada alone—law-enforcement agencies are still catching up with this new breed of criminal. While Canada has a federal law against harassment and stalking, nothing specific exists against cyberstalking, and no Internet case has yet been tried.

Even the issue of borders remains unaddressed. "If a person in the States stalks someone in Canada, jurisdiction becomes a major problem," Beatty explains. "With no American federal cyberstalking law, it's unlikely anything will be done." It happens often.

In March 1999 Karen Boothe* of Alberta was shocked to learn her 14-year-old daughter, Stacy, and a friend had an online relationship with a 37-year-old man in Seattle. When he wrote perversely sexual letters, Stacy attempted to cease contact. He wasn't happy. He wrote a letter to Stacy detailing how and why she should kill herself. In tears, the ninth grader showed it to her mother. It made her vomit.

Boothe contacted the FBI. They informed Seattle police. A detective contacted the family, but nothing was ever done. The girls finally ignored the persistent e-mails until they ceased. "But he's out there and knows where we live," says Boothe, now working on becoming a Cyberangel.

The dearth of cyberstalking laws often leaves Cyberangels resolving cases alone. Luckily, notes Beatty, a stalker usually disappears once stripped of anonymity.

On Patrol

One warm spring day this year, Connie Stewart,* 50, put her Cyberangel wings to the test. While chatting online, she was contacted by a 20-year-old friend being stalked. "Help," she pleaded.

The victim, in Australia, was chatting with a man when a message appeared: "Put down that chocolate and pay attention to me!" And she *had* been eating chocolate. Minutes later her printer spat out threats. He had control of her computer, printer, and webcam, a small camera atop her monitor. She was terrified.

Stewart interviewed the victim and learned the stalker's online habits. Within minutes she found him in his favourite chat room.

A few keystrokes later Stewart located an exclusive 10-digit code disclosing his Internet service provider (ISP). Then, using a special tracing program, Stewart discovered the ISP was in her own province, British Columbia. Finally, accessing his profile through another chat program, she got his name.

"Gotcha!" Stewart cheered. She promptly informed the ISP, then sent time-stamped chat logs revealing his abuses. Stewart forwarded her findings to the victim with instructions on what to tell police if the harassment continued. But it never went that far. The tables turned, this stalker, like so many others, retreated.

Stewart is one of over 200 Cyberangels online at any moment. Around the globe, they snare about 75 cyberstalkers every week, helping thousands of people.

> Finally, accessing his profile through another chat program, Stewart got his name. "Gotcha!" Stewart cheered, then forwarded her findings to the victim.

"We empower victims," Stewart explains. "The notion that someone is after you and knows where you live robs you of your power. We give it back." Stewart should know; she was a victim of cyberstalking two years ago. The same goes for many of Cyberangels' members.

Worth All the Effort

Cyberangel Lorraine Christian of Langley, B.C., was stalked online in 1996. The 29-year-old student was shocked when a man from a chat room asked how the weather was at her address. He included her phone number. In her own dining room, Christian suddenly felt invaded and unsafe.

In February 1999, Christian saw Kelley Beatty interviewed on CTV's *The Dini Petty Show*. Hearing Beatty explain Cyberangels, the divorced mother of three instantly recalled her feelings of helplessness and was moved by the organization's vigilance against child pornography. Realizing she could make a difference, she joined.

Like all potential angels who wish to work with victims, Christian passed a criminal background check and took online classes on managing chat rooms, spotting predators, and unmasking them through computer tracing.

Christian is now Cyberangels' chief volunteer operations officer. She reviews all new membership applications, verifies the information, maintains a database, and mails welcome letters. In the past year she has worked three to six hours a day, seven days a week, processing over 5000 applications. She is frequently at her computer until the wee hours.

"It's worth all the effort," she says. "To be part of an organization that's doing something significant has given me a new sense of purpose."

Kelley Beatty, who still works as a nurse, echoes these sentiments. "Cyberangels has given my life meaning beyond what I can comprehend."

*Names have been changed to protect privacy.

Hal Karp is an investigative journalist for *Reader's Digest*.

Activities: Angels Online

1. ***Assess Impact:*** In a journal entry, record what you knew about cyberstalking before reading this article, what you learned from the article, and any impact the article will have on your own online behaviour. Share and discuss your entry with a classmate.

2. ***Explain Punctuation:*** Examine the use of punctuation and italics in the first three paragraphs. Determine the punctuation rule that has been applied in each case. In a two-column chart, record the rules and examples from the paragraphs.

3. ***Identify Techniques:*** Find and identify techniques Karp uses to maintain readers' interest. Share your list with a small group. Discuss how you could use some of these techniques in the nonfiction writing you do in class. Add these techniques to a personal list of writing strategies.

4. ***Research Issues:*** Find out about other types of "cybercrimes." Choose one and write a brief report on it. Your report might be about a specific incident or a category, such as hacking. Carefully edit your report for organization and clarity.

Elizabeth Larsen

Finders Keepers

How Internet search engines control our access to information

YAHOO! INFOSEEK, ALTAVISTA, HOTBOT, GOTO.COM. If you've ever done research on the Internet, chances are you've used a search engine. The process is easy and often quite satisfying: Just type in one or more keywords, hit return, and then watch as a slew of hyperlinked results scrolls down the screen. It's like having your

very own card catalogue wired into your computer. Or is it? As the lucrative Internet search business evolves, the information you seek may be tainted by the almighty buck.

First, a few basics about how search engines make money. According to Lisa Allen, an analyst with Cambridge, Massachusetts-based Forrester Research, search engines generate revenue in several

ways. Besides selling banner ads that run across the top of their Web pages or striking distribution deals with content providers, search engines also sell what are referred to in the industry as "targeted keyword buys." What this means is that Ford can buy the right to have a Ford Explorer banner ad pop up anytime someone types the word *Ford* into a search engine. It also means that if Ford declines to buy its brand name, General Motors can snatch it up.

While this extremely targeted sell job is enough to make any marketing-leery Web user nervous, it stops just short of skewing the hierarchy of your search results. GoTo.com has taken it a step further. The Pasadena-based search engine has designed an ad-free site that makes money by taking bids for "priority search-result placement" as Dow Jones Interactive (February 18, 1999) puts it. In other words, companies pay a premium to be listed at the top of the search-results page—whether or not the link is relevant to the search.

The impact of this practice cannot be underestimated, says Andrew Shapiro, director of the Aspen Institute Internet Policy Project and author of *The Control Revolution* (Public Affairs, June 1999).

"Studies have demonstrated the existence of a phenomenon called 'screen bias' where users—not surprisingly—are most likely to choose the information options that are presented to them first. Given the amount of data smog we're exposed to, it would be strange if we didn't choose among the first few options that are presented to us."

There is nothing inherently wrong in paying for premium placement, says Lisa Allen, noting that it's a routine practice in both supermarkets and bookstores. Still, selling keyword searches is more insidious, because the majority of users don't understand that they are receiving information that has commercial goals. "When you open a magazine," she says, "information that is provided by advertisers is clearly marked 'advertorial', which gives readers a heads-up on how to evaluate the content. When users rely on a piece of information and think it's a critical judgement when it's a piece of puffery, they get burned."

The real problem, says Shapiro, is that the Internet industry has yet to develop guidelines on how to distinguish advertising from editorial content. "Norms haven't developed online the way they have in other media, where the church–state divide between ads and editorial is established enough that we notice when it is breached." And until such guidelines are accepted, the Internet will continue to slip "dangerously close to an environment that resembles the oligopoly of traditional electronic media. The dream of a media world in which 'everyone is a publisher' may well go unfulfilled unless there is a way to preserve some space for the voices of small commercial outlets, nonprofits, and individuals."

Before we start pining for the days before corporate behemoths discovered that there was a way to make money from selling information, Jenny Tobias, associate librarian at the library of the Museum of Modern Art in New York, offers a sobering reminder: Information has never been democratic. "Information for everybody is a good goal that has been tried, but a goal that people have failed to accomplish," she says. "Which communities have libraries and which don't are political questions, as is the question of who chooses the information that goes into those libraries."

But what if you are an especially savvy Web user who is able to distinguish between search results that are neutrally organized and those that are merely vehicles for advertisers? Does the business of search engines still affect you? Yes, says Sanford Berman, head cataloguer for the Hennepin County Library in Minnesota. "An effective search needs to be intelligently indexed by somebody who can supply the appropriate cross-references," he explains.

While Yahoo! employs a team to both categorize and cross-reference their listings, most search engines rely only on keyword searches, which Berman says do not give the researcher the most accurate results—especially when a keyword has multiple synonyms.

The problem is no different from any other challenge facing consumers today, says Tobias. And her advice is equally familiar: Buyer, beware. Given the enormous volume and the ephemerality of information available today, keyword searches are the appropriate future for information retrieval. The key to using search engines effectively, she argues, is to understand the business of information. Be savvy about business practices on the Net and shop around to find the search engine that best suits your needs. You might discover more than you set out to find.

Elizabeth Larsen is a freelance writer and a graduate student in the creative writing program at the University of Minnesota.

Activities: Finders Keepers

1. **Examine Text:** Work with a partner to explain why the first paragraph is a well-constructed lead or introduction. Identify the strategies Larsen has used and explain how they affect the reader. Record the strategies for future reference.

2. **Define Vocabulary:** Use context and other resources to create a glossary for the following terms:
   a) targeted keyword buys
   b) priority search-result placement
   c) screen bias
   d) data smog
   e) advertorial
   f) ephemerality

3. **Adapt the Selection:** Adapt ideas from the article into one of the following forms. Add information where necessary.
   a) A pamphlet to inform high school students about issues related to search engines
   b) A code of ethics for search engine developers

4. **Investigate Arguments:** In pairs, choose two topics for an Internet search. Each of you should research one topic on three search engines: GoTo.com and two others. Chart your first 10 "hits" from each search engine, and note any advertising that appears. Together, analyze your findings. Do you see any evidence to support Larsen's claims?

Kids and TV Violence

Kathleen McDonnell

*T*elevision's effects on children have been a focus of concern since the medium's earliest days, and the current outcry about TV violence is nothing new. Back in the fifties and early sixties, programs like *Dragnet* and *The Untouchables* were criticized for allegedly encouraging teenage delinquency. In the seventies, parent groups began to focus on children's television programs themselves, but most of their efforts were directed at the extreme commercialization of these programs, especially the aggressive marketing of toys. Now, the battle over children's TV has moved to a new front, as activists shift their focus from advertising to the content of children's programs.

Events in society at large have had much to do with bringing about this shift. In Canada, the campaign against media violence has been fuelled by the terrible event that has come to be known as the Montreal Massacre. In 1991 Pacijou, a Montreal-based anti-violence group, sponsored the creation of an outdoor sculpture consisting of more than 12 000 toy guns, GI Joe figures, and other weapons collected from school children. The sculpture was unveiled on the second anniversary of Marc Lépine's murder of 14 female engineering students at the École Polytechnique in Montreal. The clear implication was that his actions and those of other mass murderers are a direct result of playing with war toys and exposure to violence in the media. Journalist André Picard echoed this sentiment in a *Globe and Mail* column: "Marc Lépine was in many ways a typical boy. He played at war while his sister played at dolls." Another group, the Coalition against Violence in Children's Programming, made the point that war toys and TV violence encourage boys to "play war, a real or imaginary war that will carry over to the home, the classroom, and the neighbourhood."

More recently, Virginie Larivière, a Quebec teenager whose sister was sexually assaulted and murdered in 1992, garnered nationwide publicity and the backing of then-Prime Minister Brian Mulroney for gathering over a million signatures on a petition against TV violence. Her efforts led directly to the adoption in early 1994 of a new broadcasters' code aimed at eliminating depictions of "glamorized, gratuitous" violence in children's programs.

No sensible person would argue with the view that there's too much violence in popular culture. But solutions to the problem are turning out to be more complex than many anti-violence campaigners care to admit. As with the pornography debate, people have widely varying definitions of just what constitutes a violent act or image. By the prevailing method of tallying up violent acts per hour, for example, *Thea*, a sitcom about a Black single mother, recently found itself listed among the top ten most violent shows on U.S. television. According to the National Coalition on Television Violence, which compiled the list, acts like grabbing, shoulder tapping, and even Thea's threat to "teach her kids a lesson" all qualified as violent acts. This highlights another problem with the approach adopted by anti-violence crusaders, who make no attempt to deal with narrative context or to distinguish between different styles or genres—between comedy and drama, between cartoon and live-action programs.

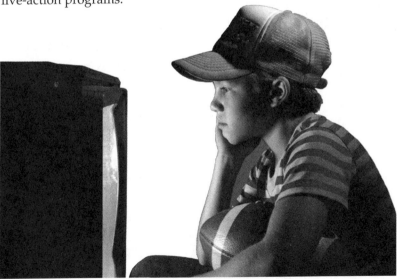

The anti-violence movement has drawn broad support across the political spectrum, which isn't surprising since no one on the left or the right wants to be regarded as cavalier about violence or, worse, as promoting it. But dissenting voices are starting to surface. Some media critics, noting the large number of politicians on both sides of the border who are hopping onto the anti-violence bandwagon, detect more than a whiff of political opportunism. *Globe and Mail* TV critic Liam Lacey wondered in 1993: "Is the current emotional, anti-violence campaign really about the dangers of television violence, or is it about finding a political scapegoat?" And more recently even Todd Gitlin, a longtime critic of movie and TV violence, took strong issue with the anti-violence crusaders, charging that the movement "distracts attention from the real causes of—and the serious remedies for—the epidemic of violence" in society. Comments like those of anti-violence activist Terry Rakolta of Americans for Responsible Television lend weight to Gitlin's analysis. "We can't seem to fix education, we can't seem to control drugs, but we can take a look at television violence," Rakolta said in a 1994 Canadian current affairs show. In other words, it's far easier to point the finger at television, movies, and video games than to look at the complex social roots of violence or to examine the numerous ways we adults have failed our children.

But TV violence is as much a reflection of our current social malaise as it is a cause, and there's a legitimate argument that in focusing on the media, what we're really doing is shooting the messenger rather than genuinely trying to come to grips with the problem. People in the entertainment industry are also concerned that the violence issue is being used to take the edge off hard-hitting shows. Barbara Hall, producer of the series *I'll Fly Away*, said on the same program that U.S. network officials demanded that a scene be cut from one show that depicted a violent Ku Klux Klan attack on Blacks. She noted that a writer on another series was recently directed to take out not only violent scenes but ones that "made the system look bad."

The problem is compounded by our own confusion and ambivalence. As media critic Bronwyn Drainie points out:

We're all a bit hypocritical about the question of TV violence. Wouldn't you prefer to see Elmer Fudd fill Bugs full of holes than put up with the gagging sweetness of the Care Bears? Our own ambivalence about the entertainment value of violence, especially fun violence like cartoons or Hulk Hogan, may keep these disturbing issues permanently unresolved.

This ambivalence is part and parcel of the extraordinary love/hate relationship we have with pop culture, and television in particular. Almost everyone denigrates television, but almost everyone watches it. We speak of the "boob tube" and the "idiot box." TV-bashing is a virtual requirement for anyone who wishes to be considered a literate, cultured person. Rarely before in history has a society so thoroughly disowned an object of its own creation, one that forms such an important part of its very cultural fabric. But to understand the roots of this alarmism about popular culture and the anti-violence fervour it has spawned, we need to put this phenomenon in its historical context.

Moral Panics

Waves of moral panic about children's culture have recurred with great regularity and in different guises through the past hundred years. The dime novels of the 19th century, as well as the series books of the early 20th like the *Bobbsey Twins* and *Hardy Boys*, were denounced by educators and child experts in much the same kind of alarmist tones as TV and video games are today. Harmless as they seem to us nowadays, at the time critics charged that these books undermined literacy, encouraged children to challenge authority, confused fantasy with reality, and were just plain "trash." In the 1920s, the target shifted to the new visual medium of the silent motion picture, with adults sounding the alarm about the dire effects on the young of all those hours in darkened theatres. In the thirties and forties, experts began to warn about the harmful effects of radio on children. As with television today, studies were published showing that listening to radio was negatively affecting children's behaviour and impairing their ability to distinguish fantasy from reality.

In the fifties, comic books, along with Elvis and rock music, became the great threat. In 1954 psychiatrist Frederic Wertham published *Seduction of the Innocent*, which blamed comics for juvenile delinquency and cited numerous cases of crimes committed by children and teenagers after reading comics. Then, as now, politicians seized on the issue: the U.S. Congress established a special committee and conducted hearings to explore the alleged link between comics and juvenile crime. This campaign to clean up the comics resulted in the adoption of the Comics Code, which placed severe restrictions on the stories and imagery depicted in comic books. Interestingly, while the Comics Code had the immediate effect of driving some horror and crime comics out of business, its long-term impact has been negligible. The comics of today are as untrammelled as they ever were, but aside from the odd Christian fundamentalist rumblings, few objections are raised about them. In the nineties, TV, movies, and video games took over to become the targets of the latest wave of moral panic.

It may appear to contemporary crusaders that violence in the popular media is a threat of an entirely different order than these quaint artifacts of the past. But in their day the Rover Boys, silent movies, and True Crime comics were believed to be every bit as threatening to the existing social order as Ninja Turtles and *Terminator* movies are today. And the striking similarities in the language used by these moral crusaders of different eras, the similar claims made again and again about the damaging effects on children and on society as a whole, suggest that the problem of pop culture violence is not a thing apart. The current anti-violence crusade actually reflects a much larger well of concern about children's psyches that underlies all these various crusades.

They certainly share some basic assumptions, chief among them being that any endeavour children engage in should serve some higher moral purpose—should, in a word, be educational. This is a burden placed on children's play as well as all their forms of entertainment and is a bias every bit as strong today as it was in the 19th century, when children's books were expected to give moral guidance and "build character." Today, of course, we use a different terminology. We speak of "positive role models" and "quality" (meaning educational) programming. But the underlying sentiment is basically the same. Kids' programs without any obvious educational intent are automatically considered junk and garbage, while "quality" children's programs are supposed to be tasteful, not loud or brash—rather like a well-behaved child. But adults and kids tend to have quite different ways of defining quality. Adults routinely distinguish between what's "good" and what they like, between art and mere entertainment. This kind of distinction is quite foreign to most kids. If they like something, they'll tell you it's good.

There's a further irony in the fact that the line between so-called quality programs and commercial children's TV is becoming more blurred all the time. One show that made its mark on educational TV, *Where in the World Is Carmen Sandiego?* recently jumped from PBS to the highly commercial, lowest-common-denominator Fox Network. *Sesame Street* has successfully straddled the boundary for a long time, packaging its educational content in an unabashedly pop-cult mix of rock music and TV parodies like "Monsterpiece Theater." More recent is the unprecedented commercial success of another PBS show, *Barney and Friends.* Barney's lumbering purple persona currently graces everything from lunch boxes to video compilations of "Barney's Favourites."

Early in 1993, some PBS affiliates were roundly criticized for using Barney giveaways as incentives in their annual fundraising drives. Many parents claimed this smacked of the same exploitive tactics that so-called commercial TV had been using on children for years. Things came full circle as Action for Children's Television head Peggy Charren found herself staring down her old enemy, commercialization, on public television of all places. Charren said she found it "extraordinarily inappropriate for PBS to use children to fundraise."

It's interesting that we adults don't put this burden of being educational on our own entertainment. We acknowledge that we have a range of tastes, moods, and interests. We accept that we often turn to so-called "low" culture to feed our desires of the moment. But we're leery of allowing children the same kind of latitude. Partly this comes from an honest, if only half-understood admission that many of these "low" pop-culture forms express anti-authoritarian impulses of one sort or another. Dime novels, comics, and *The Simpsons* are each in their own way an outlet for kids' natural rebelliousness. So it's not surprising that many adults, and particularly so-called "family values" conservatives, find these things so threatening. They're not wrong: a good deal of pop culture is subversive. It does challenge adult authority over children. But its subversiveness goes even deeper than that. In a society that sees itself as rational, scientific, and ruled by self-control, pop culture is the repository of pleasure, of the forbidden, of gratification and freedom from inhibition. It serves, in a sense, as the underside, the id of the larger culture, the place where our more "primitive" impulses and unenlightened behaviours are consigned. Another way to characterize the pop-culture battleground is as a struggle between the edu-experts, who know what's good for children, and pop-culture purveyors, who have their finger on the pulse of kids' desires. In the words of the Bob Dylan song, they tell kids, "They may know what you need, but I know what you want."

Kathleen McDonnell (*born Chicago*), author, playwright, moved to Canada in 1969. She writes plays, fiction, and nonfiction for both children and adults. Her articles have been widely published, and she is a regular commentator for CBC Radio. McDonnell's play *Loon Boy* won a Chalmers Canadian Play Award.

Activities: Kids and TV Violence

1. ***Identify Thesis:*** Reread the first sentence of the sixth paragraph. Is this statement McDonnell's organizing idea or thesis in the essay? Identify the main ideas in the article and test them to see if they support the statement. If you decide this statement is not the organizing idea, write a statement that is.

2. ***Explain an Argument:*** The author criticizes anti-violence crusaders for making no attempt to "deal with narrative context or to distinguish between different styles or genres." With a partner, define "narrative context" and then explain the point McDonnell is trying to make.

3. ***Analyze a TV Show:*** Watch a TV show that children under 12 would find appealing. Note every act or statement that might be seen as violent. Write a brief summary of the plot and explain why you think the episode is or is not too violent for children. Write a report on your findings.

4. ***Debate an Issue:*** In a small group, debate the following statement: "Censoring TV violence will result in a less violent society." Take notes of the points made by people on each side of the issue. Report to the class the three strongest points made by each side.

Fine Art
and
Media Images

Oedipus and the Sphinx, 470 B.C., image inside an ancient Greek kylix (two-handled drinking cup)

October, Paul, Herman, and Jean Limbourg (d. 1416), illuminated manuscript

Selection Activities, p. 431

Women Returning Home at Sunset, Katsushika Hokusai, 1835, colour, wood-block print

Couple on Bridge, Alex Colville, 1992, painting

   Selection Activities, p. 432

Zunoqua of the Cat Village, Emily Carr, 1931, painting

Housepost at Xwatis, C.F. Newcomb, 1922, photograph

Selection Activities, p. 433

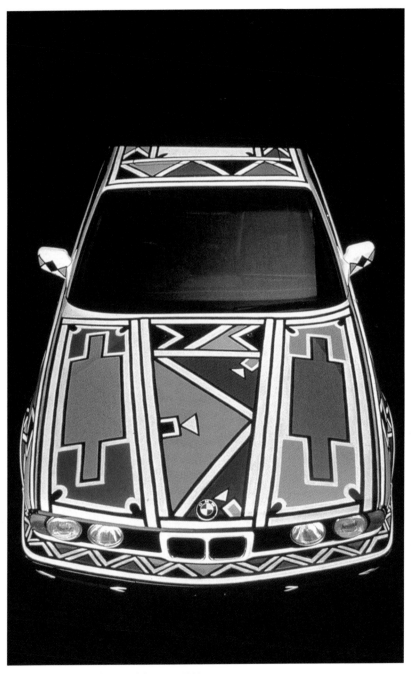

BMW Art Car, Esther Mahlangu, 1991

Selection Activities, p. 433

Eggs in an Egg Crate, Mary Pratt, 1975, painting

Flight of an Eagle, Jane Ash Poitras, 1996, mixed media painting

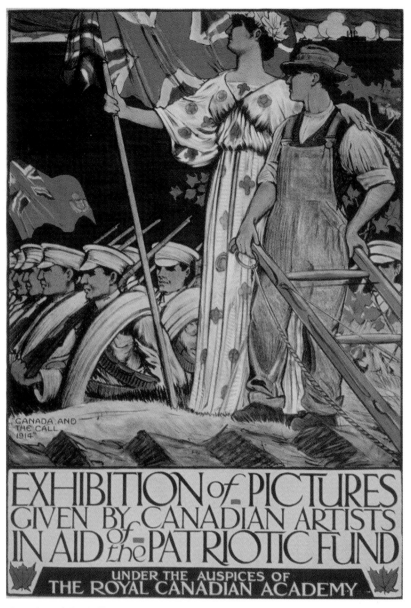

Canada and the Call, J.E.H. Macdonald, 1914, poster

Nunavut (1999)
Designed by Germaine Arnaktauyok

Harmony (June 2000)
Designed by Haver Demirer

Wisdom (September 2000)
Designed by Cezar Serbanescu

Millennium Coins, Royal Canadian Mint, 1999–2000

The Ratings Crunch, Brian Hughes, newspaper graphic

"Two coffees, one with flagrant exploitation of Latin American small farmers, one without."

Every time you consider having a cup of coffee, give some thought to the plight of the small farmers who produce it. For if you buy an ordinary brand of coffee, you're inadvertently maintaining a system which keeps those small farmers poor while lining the pockets of powerful middlemen. Equal Exchange provides an alternative. We believe in trading directly with small farming cooperatives at mutually agreed-upon prices with a fixed minimum rate. So if the coffee market declines, the farmers are still guaranteed a fair price. By choosing Equal Exchange coffee, you can help make a change. Of course, your decision to buy Equal Exchange need not be completely altruistic. For we take as much pride in refining the taste of our gourmet coffees as we do in helping the farmers who produce them. For more information about Equal Exchange or to order our line of gourmet, organic and shade-grown coffees, call 1-781-830-0303.

www.equalexchange.com

Equal Exchange, advertisement

Zits, Jerry Scott and Jim Borgman, cartoon

Toyota, advertisement

Platinum Protection, advertisement

Selection Activities, p. 438

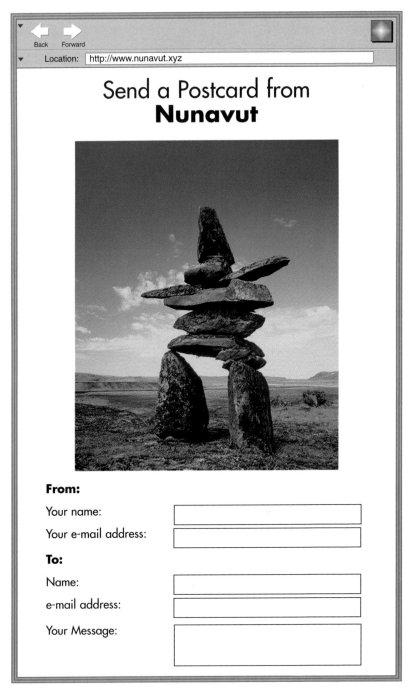

Send a Postcard from
Nunavut

From:

Your name:

Your e-mail address:

To:

Name:

e-mail address:

Your Message:

Inuksuk, postcard

Paul, Herman, and Jean Limbourg (*born c. 1380, Nijmegen, Flanders; died 1416*), artists, were employed by Jean, Duc du Berry, one of France's wealthiest patrons of the arts. Few of their works survive, aside from the illustrated manuscripts *Les Très Riches Heures* and *Les Belles Heures*. All three brothers died before the age of 30 in the same year, apparently during an epidemic.

Katsushika Hokusai (*born 1760, Japan; died 1849*), painter and printmaker, used over 70 different pseudonyms during his career. Best known for his landscapes, he also produced many studies of birds and flowers. Hokusai was a master of the style known as *ukiyo-e* ("pictures of the floating world").

Alex Colville (*born 1920, Toronto, Ontario*), painter, served as a war artist in Europe during World War II. A painter of international stature, Colville also designed Canada's Centennial coins. Since 1971 he has lived in Wolfville, Nova Scotia, where he was Chancellor of Acadia University for ten years. He was made a companion of the Order of Canada in 1982.

Emily Carr (*born 1871, Victoria, British Columbia; died 1945*), artist, writer, studied in both Paris and London, but returned to Victoria to teach art, breed dogs, and paint. Her art was influenced by the British Columbia landscape, by the First Nations people, and by the Group of Seven artists. Carr's writings include *Klee Wyck*, which received the Governor General's Literary Award in 1941.

Esther Mahlangu is a South African artist who is renowned for her mastery of traditional Ndebele painting. The Ndebele people live in the northern part of South Africa and are famous for their beadwork and their skills at decorating houses in brilliant geometric patterns. Esther Mahlangu was the first woman artist to be asked to paint an art car for BMW.

Mary Pratt (*born 1935, Fredericton, New Brunswick*), painter, is best known for her paintings of objects in the kitchen of her home in St. Mary's Bay, Newfoundland. Among Pratt's teachers at Mount Allison University were Alex Colville and Lawren Harris. She is married to the painter Christopher Pratt.

Jane Ash Poitras (*born 1951, Fort Chipewyan, Alberta*), painter, printmaker, writer, was orphaned at age six and raised in a white community. At university, she rediscovered her Native identity. Today she focuses on evocative representations of critical issues in First Nations culture. Her mixed media works are highly regarded and sought after by museums and collectors around the world. She currently lives and works in Alberta.

J.E.H. Macdonald (*born 1873, Durham, England; died 1932, Toronto, Ontario*), commercial artist, painter, was one of the founding members of the Group of Seven. Many of his paintings are landscapes depicting Algoma, north of Lake Superior. Macdonald is also known as one of the best graphic designers and calligraphers of his time.

Germaine Arnaktauyok, artist, designed the $2 millennium coin to celebrate the birth of Nunavut. Haver Demirer, graphic designer, digital animator, emigrated to Canada from Turkey in 1996. He currently lives in Toronto, Ontario. Cezar Serbanescu, from Montreal, Quebec, was 17 when he designed his coin, which honours his parents and others who have shared their wisdom with him.

Brian Hughes (*born 1959, Toronto, Ontario*), art director, illustrator, graphic artist, currently works for *The Toronto Star*, providing photo collages, info-graphics, or illustrations to enhance the impact and clarity of articles in the paper. He loves the challenge of working out how best to do this for a range of articles on a variety of topics.

Jerry Scott (*born South Bend, Indiana*), cartoonist, also collaborates on the comic strip *Baby Blues*, which has been adapted into an animated TV show. *Zits* has won a host of awards, including Best Comic Strip of the Year from the National Cartoonist Society.

Jim Borgman (*born 1954, Cincinnati, Ohio*), cartoonist, started as a staff artist and editorial cartoonist for his college newspaper. He has published five books, four of which are anthologies of political cartoons. Borgman has received many awards, including a Pulitzer Prize in journalism for editorial cartooning.

Activities: Oedipus and the Sphinx

1. **Note Details:** Without making any interpretations, list in point form all that you observe in the image. Compare your list with a partner's. Discuss your reactions to the image and any questions that arise from your observations.

2. **Interpret the Image:** In the play *Oedipus Rex*, the meeting of Oedipus and the Sphinx is described as an "encounter of man with more than man." With a partner, discuss how the image conveys this relationship. Share your findings with another pair.

3. **Create an Illustration:** Create an illustration of a central event from another Greek story or myth. Use an illustration style similar to the one used in this image. Attach to your illustration one or two brief paragraphs outlining the plot of the story and explaining your choice of image.

4. **Research Mythical Creatures:** Work in a small group to research other mythical creatures, either from the past (e.g., the Hydra or Minotaur) or the present (e.g., the Loch Ness monster or Bigfoot). Each member should choose one creature and create an illustrated fact sheet about it. Compile your fact sheets into a booklet that is visually appealing.

Activities: October

1. **Generate Questions:** Look closely at the image and list all the information you can determine from the illustration. Then list all the questions you have about it. Share your lists with a partner, and brainstorm a list of sources you could use to find answers to your questions.

2. **Examine Composition:** Look at the image as if you were seeing it for the first time. Notice how your eye travels through the illustration. List in order the first four elements in the painting that attract your attention. Making reference to composition and colour, explain why this is so.

3. **Conduct Research:** Find out more about *Les Très Riches Heures* and then write a brief paragraph of background information that might accompany this illustration in an exhibition. When planning your paragraph, consider what information would be most useful to your audience.

4. **View Paintings:** Paintings can be a rich source of historical information. Find a painting, at least two centuries old, that reveals information about the time in which it was painted. Present the painting to a small group and explain the historical information that can be found in it.

Activities: Women Returning Home at Sunset

1. **Support Opinions:** The poem that accompanies this print states that autumn is a "sad" season. Do you find that the image evokes feelings of sadness? Support your opinion with specific references to elements of the print.

2. **Examine Contrast:** How does Hokusai create contrast in his use of line and colour? Examine the print with a partner and record your ideas. Then compare your ideas with another pair's.

3. **Write a Poem:** Find a photo or piece of art that depicts a season and evokes an emotional response. Write a short poem expressing your response. Use language that appeals to the senses. Display the image and poem in the classroom.

4. **Investigate Printmaking:** There are many different techniques for making prints. Choose one and write a concise step-by-step description of the process involved. Ask a classmate to edit your description for conciseness and clarity.

Activities: Couple on Bridge

1. **Analyze Elements:** Explain what you learn about this scene from the positions and body language of the two individuals. What emotions does each person's body language express? Why might Colville have decided to place these people on a bridge? Share your ideas with a partner.

2. **Consider Setting:** What words would you use to describe the background in this painting? How might the viewer's experience of the painting be different if the background were an urban scene? Write a paragraph to explain why Colville might have chosen the setting seen in the painting.

3. **View Paintings:** Some critics have classified Colville's style as *magic realism,* a style in which everyday activities and settings are infused with a touch of magic, mystery, or unreality. View several other works by Colville, choose one, and explain whether or not you think the term *magic realism* applies to it.

4. **Role-Play the Scene:** With a partner, create a role-play based on the painting. Decide on the identities of the people and the topic of discussion. Present your role-play to the class and end it by freezing in the positions of the people in the painting. Invite questions and comments from classmates.

Activities: Zunoqua of the Cat Village

1. **Explore the Image:** With a partner, examine the painting and the photo, and list any unusual or unrealistic aspects of the painted scene. Discuss why Carr might have used this particular style of painting. Share your ideas with another pair.

2. **Determine Mood:** Carr creates a certain mood or feeling in this painting. Write and then edit a paragraph in which you describe the mood of the painting, and explain how the artist achieves it.

3. **Conduct Research:** Carr studied in England (1899) and in France (1910). Do research to learn more about well-known British and French artists living at this time who may have influenced Carr's style. Write a brief report on one artist from each country.

4. **Analyze Style:** Find three examples of paintings by members of the original Group of Seven and two more by Carr. Use a graphic organizer to compare and contrast the similarities and differences among the artists' works.

Activities: BMW Art Car

1. **Investigate Influences:** Mahlangu says her art "has evolved from the [Ndebele] tribal tradition of decorating our homes." Use the Internet or print resources to view examples of South African Ndebele homestead art. Explain in a paragraph what elements of the traditional art are reflected in the art car.

2. **Examine Purpose:** BMW states that the purpose of its art car program, begun in 1975, is to sponsor "the artistic examination of the technical world" and to promote "intercultural dialogue as a basis for tolerance and understanding." With a partner, discuss the meaning of each quoted phrase. List any other purposes that you think this program might have.

3. **Discuss Ideas:** In a small group, discuss these questions: (a) Is the art car mostly art, mostly a car, or equally both? (b) Do people who customize their cars transform them into something more than cars? Summarize and present your group's ideas to the class.

4. **Create an Art Car:** Make a large line drawing of the outline of the car and then design your own art car. Consider the purpose of the art: Do you want to make a statement or create a specific mood? Display your art car in the classroom with a written explanation of your design choices.

Activities: Eggs in an Egg Crate

1. ***Explain Reactions:*** Were you surprised by Pratt's choice of subject for the painting? If yes, explain why. If no, give reasons why you think she might have chosen to paint this subject.

2. ***Compare Responses:*** If you were given a poster of this painting, would you hang it in your home? Share and explain your response in a small group. Discuss the reasons group members give for their responses, and determine what each member's reasons reveal about his or her expectations of a painting.

3. ***Analyze Elements:*** *Eggs in an Egg Crate* is an example of a still-life painting. Find another still-life painting and analyze the artist's use of the following elements: composition, light, texture, colour.

4. ***Create a Still Life:*** Create an interesting still life using three to five common household objects other than fruit. Draw, paint, or photograph the objects, or bring the objects to class and compose your still-life scene. Explain the reasons behind your choice of objects and the way you arranged them.

Activities: Flight of an Eagle

1. ***Interpret Symbolism:*** Colours and objects often symbolize important ideas in literary, artistic, or dramatic works. In a journal entry, suggest what the symbols and colours surrounding the central image might represent and what significance they might have in the context of the work.

2. ***Analyze Body Language:*** With a partner, decide what the body language of the two girls might communicate to the viewer. Consider facial expression, posture, and the position of the two girls. Share your ideas with another pair.

3. ***Explore Issues:*** In her work, Poitras examines issues critical to the culture and lives of First Nations people. Locate other works she has created, paying particular attention to their titles. Choose one of these works and then write a free verse poem that supports and extends the essential concept Poitras has represented in her art.

4. ***Create a Representation:*** Identify one important contemporary social issue. In a small group, represent your group's ideas about the issue by using any one of the following genres: a short drama, a video, an abstract sculpture, or a multimedia composition. Present a rationale describing your purpose and how you achieved it.

Activities: Canada and the Call

1. **Interpret the Title:** Consider the title of the image, "Canada and the Call." What does the term *call* mean in times of war? Who made the call? What was Canada's response to the call? In a small group, use the Internet and other resources to answer these questions.

2. **Examine Composition:** Explain how Macdonald uses straight lines to direct the viewer's eye and add contrast and balance to the image.

3. **Discuss Propaganda:** In a small group, define *propaganda* and discuss how this image serves as propaganda. Why is propaganda so prevalent in times of war? After the discussion, share your ideas with another group.

4. **Create a Poster:** Draw, paint, or create on a computer a poster that gives a message that is opposite to that in "Canada and the Call." Present your poster to the class and explain the strategies you used to clearly communicate your message and make it visually effective.

Activities: Millennium Coins

1. **Reflect on Theme:** One of the coins is based on the theme of wisdom. With a partner, brainstorm a list of reasons why this theme is appropriate for a millennium coin.

2. **Examine Symbolism:** The Canadian Mint states that the June coin, "Harmony," represents Canada as "a tapestry of cultures and beliefs joined together to carry the nation forward." Explain how these ideas are symbolized on the coin.

3. **Design a Coin:** Pick an appropriate theme for a millennium coin and design a coin that reflects your views about our country and/or society. In a formal letter, explain why your design would be a worthy addition to the Millennium Series.

4. **Write a Report:** With three or four classmates, form a Web design consulting firm. Write for the Royal Canadian Mint a detailed report on their Web site (www.mint.ca), analyzing current content and design, and making recommendations for improvements. Present your polished and professional report to the Mint's board of directors (your classmates).

Activities: The Ratings Crunch

1. **Explain Purpose:** This illustration appeared with a newspaper article about how the large number of sports broadcasts available has resulted in fewer viewers for individual broadcasts. Imagine you are the illustrator and write an explanation of what you wanted to achieve in the illustration and how you achieved it.

2. **Examine Technique:** In this illustration, Hughes includes both text and photographs. With a partner, evaluate the effectiveness of this technique. Share and compare your responses with those of two other pairs.

3. **Explore the Genre:** Newspapers and magazines often use editorial illustrations, which provide a visual interpretation of the content of an article. Find an editorial illustration that you think is effective. Present it to the class along with a brief oral summary of the article it appeared with. Explain why you think the illustration is effective.

4. **Create an Illustration:** Create an editorial illustration to accompany a newspaper or magazine article of your choice. If you wish, incorporate photographs and/or text in the illustration. Display the illustration and the article in the classroom, and invite classmates to post comments and questions.

Activities: Equal Exchange

1. **Define Vocabulary:** Use context to predict the meaning of the following words: *flagrant, exploitation, plight, inadvertently, cooperatives, altruistic.* After checking your predictions in a dictionary, demonstrate your understanding of these words by rewriting the sentences in which they occur, substituting another word or a phrase for each word you defined.

2. **Analyze Content:** Persuasive texts often promote a specific value and may include a call for action based on this value. Write a concise statement of the value promoted in this advertisement, list the actions called for, and describe how the actions are related to the value promoted.

3. **Brainstorm Alternatives:** With a partner, brainstorm other ideas for the visual and the caption that accompanies it. Considering the purpose and audience, choose the idea you think would work best. Write a paragraph explaining why your new approach would be effective.

4. **Consider Logos:** How effective is the Equal Exchange logo? Why? What purposes does a logo serve? Evaluate the logos of two or three other organizations or products, and then list some criteria for developing effective logos.

Activities: Zits

1. **Examine Stereotypes:** Does this cartoon present a stereotypical view of a teenager? List any aspects of Jeremy's words, thoughts, and appearance that might be considered stereotypical. Then explain why you think using stereotypical characters in a cartoon strip is a good or a bad idea.

2. **Adapt Perspective:** Rewrite the cartoon so that a parent is saying "What?" in response to a teen. Share your version with classmates. Considering both the original and alternative versions, discuss as a class whether there are any lessons to be learned from the concept of this cartoon.

3. **Discuss Communication:** The cartoon illustrates a communication problem between a parent and a teen. In a small group, discuss factors that lead to communication problems between teens and parents or other adults. Compile a list of strategies that adults and teens could use for more effective communication with each other.

4. **Pitch an Idea:** With a partner, imagine that you are the creators of this comic strip and you want to convince a company to buy the rights to use Jeremy to promote a product. Write and present together a persuasive pitch to the company that produces the product of your choice.

Activities: Toyota

1. **Identify Audience:** What is the intended audience for this advertisement? Specify the characteristics of the audience and the clues that helped you to identify the audience. Evaluate how effective the advertisement is in appealing to its audience, and give reasons for your evaluation.

2. **Examine Connotation:** The name *Solara* comes from the Latin root *sol*, meaning *sun*. What connotations of the word *sun* might have convinced Toyota executives that Solara was a good name for the car? Think of another product whose name evokes positive connotations and explain these connotations.

3. **Create a Radio Commercial:** Create a 15-second radio advertisement for a car of your choice. Brainstorm with a partner a list of advertising techniques that would be effective for this product and medium, and then write and record the advertisement, using sound effects if desired.

4. **Analyze Advertisements:** Find another print advertisement that, like the Toyota advertisement, encourages consumers to associate a product with a particular lifestyle. Display the advertisement in the classroom, along with a paragraph that analyzes the type of lifestyle presented in the advertisement.

Activities: Platinum Protection

1. **Interpret Text:** Explain the meaning of the sentence that begins "You'll run for president." Identify the pun in the sentence. What inferences are necessary to relate this sentence to the product? Compare your ideas with a partner's.

2. **Analyze Technique:** Imagine that you work for the agency that produced this advertisement. In a brief oral presentation, explain to the client why you think this advertisement will be effective in convincing the target audience to purchase the product.

3. **Evaluate Advertisements:** View several print advertisements aimed at a teen audience. Choose the one that you think is most effective. In a small group, compare advertisements and discuss the advertising strategies used. Prepare a list of criteria for assessing the effectiveness of advertisements aimed at teens.

4. **Design an Advertisement:** Design a print advertisement for a product used by teens. Choose effective strategies for attracting the attention of the target market and persuading teens to buy the product. Post the advertisement in the classroom with a brief explanation of the strategies you used.

Activities: Inuksuk Postcard

1. **Compare Formats:** This selection shows a Web page for sending an Internet postcard. Compare the pros and cons of this type of postcard and a traditional postcard. With a partner, discuss which type of postcard you would most like to receive and why.

2. **Examine Perspective:** This photo was taken from ground level, looking up at the inuksuk. What effect is created by this perspective? Imagine the same photograph taken from an eye-level perspective, and from above, looking down on the inuksuk. What effect would each perspective have on the resulting image?

3. **Research Inuksuit:** Find out more about inuksuit and the reasons why they were built. Present your findings in the form of a one-page article for a general interest magazine. Before writing, find one or two magazine articles you could use as models for appropriate style, including tone, diction, sentence structure, and paragraph structure.

4. **Create a Poster:** Adapt this image into a poster encouraging tourism to Canada's North. Choose a target audience and write the copy for the poster. Sketch a mockup of the advertisement to show where you would position the copy. On a computer, produce your copy using appropriate typefaces.

act A major section of a stage play, equivalent to a chapter in a novel. An act is often divided into scenes.

adaptation The process of rewriting a text to change it from one genre to another (such as adapting a novel into a movie). A work resulting from such adaptation.

advertorial A combination of advertising and editorial comment. Advertorials may be advertisements designed to look and read like news reports.

alliteration The repetition of consonant sounds. An auditory device in which consonants are repeated at the beginning of several words that are close together ("And with old woes new wail my dear time's waste"—Shakespeare).

allusion A brief direct or indirect reference to a figure, place, event, idea, or object from myth, religion, history, literature, society, or popular culture. The writer assumes that the reader is familiar with the reference.

assonance The repetition of vowel sounds. An auditory device in which vowel sounds are repeated within a line of poetry ("In zones of silence they grow tall and slow"—P.K. Page; "And all is seared with trade, bleared, smeared with toil"—G.M. Hopkins).

audience The people who read, hear, or view a literary, nonfiction, or media work. The audience may be limited and specific, such as nuclear scientists, or broader. Effective writers take into account key characteristics of their intended audience, such as age range and background knowledge.

auditory device Any arrangement of letters, syllables, words, and phrases that appeals particularly to the ear. *See* **alliteration, assonance,** *and* **onomatopoeia.**

broadcast journalism Journalism presented on radio or television.

characterization The techniques used to portray a fictional character or an actual person in writing or a media text. These techniques include presenting details of physical appearance; presenting the character's thoughts, actions, and words; and revealing what other characters think of the character.

conflict The struggle of the characters in a story to resolve a problem results in conflict, which often advances the plot. Conflict can be internal (psychological) or external (among characters, or between characters and larger forces such as society, nature, or fate).

couplet Two adjacent lines of poetry, often with an end rhyme ("For thy sweet love rememb'red such wealth **brings**,/That then I scorn to change my state with **kings**."—Shakespeare).

cropping Trimming a photograph or picture to enhance impact or focus attention.

cyberspace A term used to describe the electronic realm of major computer networks, in particular, the "universe" where **virtual reality** is experienced.

dialect A form of a language characteristic of a particular region or social group.

diction The type of words chosen by the writer. Categories of diction include words that are concrete, abstract, formal, or informal.

dissolve A video editing technique where one image is faded out as another is simultaneously faded in.

fade-out A gradual decrease in the brightness of an image or the audibility of a sound; a video editing technique used to signal a major transition or the end of a work.

figurative language The use of words in nonliteral ways. Figures of speech such as similes, metaphors, and personification are examples of figurative language.

first-person point of view When the narrator is involved in the events of the story, he or she is telling the story from a first-person point of view. First-person narrators can be unreliable, so the reader may have to figure out what is actually going on. *See* **narrator, point of view, third-person point of view**.

font A set of type of one size and face; a style of typeface.

free verse Poetry that does not have a regular pattern of rhythm, rhyme, or stanzas, but uses the natural rhythm of spoken language.

genre A broad category of literary, nonfiction, or media text, such as short story, drama, essay, biography, documentary, or political cartoon.

graphic novel A novel that relies heavily on graphic art. Typically, the only textual element in a graphic novel is the direct speech of the characters. All other story information is presented through paintings, drawings, collage, photographs, and other graphic media.

home page The first page on a **Web site**. This page contains links to all the other pages on the site.

illustrator Someone who creates graphic art to clarify or decorate a text. Illustrators frequently create pictures for children's literature, as well as images for newspapers, pamphlets, books, and animation.

image and imagery In literary and nonfiction works, images are word pictures that appeal to the reader's senses and imagination; imagery refers to all the images in a work taken together. In media works, images function in the same way, though they are presented through the use of photography, video, graphic art, and sound.

infomercial A television program that uses entertainment, information, or endorsements to sell or promote a product.

Internet A worldwide network of interconnected computers that allows the movement of electronic information from point to point; often simply referred to as the Net.

inverted pyramid structure An organizational structure in which information is presented in order of decreasing importance or interest. Often used in news reports.

irony A statement or situation that suggests the opposite of what appears on the surface. Three common types of irony are *verbal*—saying one thing while implying the opposite; *situational*—expecting something different from what actually happens; and *dramatic*—when the reader or viewer knows something that the characters do not.

kicker A smaller headline that appears below a main headline.

list server A server that manages a list of electronic mailing addresses for a specific group of individuals. Typically, an individual chooses to be a part of a list serve in order to receive information updates and mailings regarding a specific topic of interest.

lyric poem A fairly short, non-narrative poem expressing the consciousness and emotions of a single speaker.

magic realism A style of writing or painting in which everyday activities and settings are infused with a touch of magic, mystery, or unreality.

mass media Modern means of communication that appeal to and reach vast audiences; includes television, film, radio, newspapers, magazines, online publications, and Web sites.

media event An event staged for media reporters by a group or business in order to gain publicity.

media text A media message or product, such as a movie, advertisement, photograph, Web site, television program, or poster.

metaphor A device of figurative language in which one thing is compared with another by being completely identified with it ("A poem is a small machine made out of words."—William Carlos Williams). *See* **simile**.

metre In poetry, a recurring rhythm of accented (stressed) and unaccented syllables. A metrical unit of one accented and one or more unaccented syllables is called a foot.

monologue A long speech delivered by a character or person, often addressed directly to an audience and used to reveal the character's or person's thoughts; often referred to as a soliloquy within a drama. A monologue can also be a play with only one character.

multimedia The combined use of several media.

narrative poem A poem that tells a story.

narrator The character or person who tells what happens in a literary, nonfiction, or media text. The narrator describes and interprets the setting, plot, and other characters or people. *See* **first-person point of view** *and* **third-person point of view**.

nonfiction A written prose text aiming to convey ideas or information, primarily by dealing with events or people that are not products of the writer's imagination. Nonfiction includes biographical, reference, informational, philosophical, historical, scientific, and technical texts.

nonverbal factors Nonverbal elements of a presentation that aid communication (e.g., gestures, posture, distance, eye contact).

onomatopoeia An auditory device in which the sound of the word imitates the sound of the action or thing the word is associated with (such as buzz, chickadee, or splash).

organization The structure or main method of arranging the content of a work. The most common methods are *chronological*—arranging details in the order in which they occur (a biography); *spatial*—

arranging details according to their location (a description of a room); *importance*—arranging details in order of increasing or decreasing importance (a news story); *cause and effect*—arranging details according to cause and effect sequence (an analysis of a problem); and *comparison*—arranging details to show how things are similar or different (a formal essay discussing plays with similar themes).

personification A device of figurative language in which something non-human is given human characteristics ("'Sky, what can you give me?'/and sky said, 'I can give you sunset.'"—Joy Kogawa).

plot The main story of a fictional or dramatic work. The plot usually develops out of the struggle of characters to resolve a problem or problems. *See* **conflict** *and* **subplot**.

point of view The position from which something is viewed or filmed or the perspective of the character or person telling the story.

product placement Images or advertising placed within films and television shows in order to promote the sale of a particular product. Product placement is controversial because it blurs the distinction between advertising and other genres of media production.

props In a dramatic production, movable objects such as furniture and handheld articles that are used to enhance the setting and, often, to advance the plot.

prose Continuous non-metrical written discourse.

public relations The art or science of establishing and promoting a favourable relationship with the public, often through a variety of means and employing a variety of media.

purpose The main goal of a work, which generally is as follows: in *fiction*—to entertain, tell a story, or convey insight (as in a short story, a movie, a poem); in *nonfiction*—to describe or explain something (as in an encyclopedia article, a documentary film); in a *media text*—to inform or persuade the reader or viewer (as in a newspaper article or editorial, an advertisement).

quatrain *See* **stanza**.

rhyme The repetition of similar sounds at the ends of words, regardless of spelling (brig**ade**/dism**ayed**, **eyes**/**cries**, st**ate**/f**ate**). In traditional stanza forms, rhymes appear at the ends of lines in a regular pattern, or rhyme scheme. Internal rhyme refers to rhyme within a line of poetry ("In mist or cl**oud**, on mast or shr**oud**"—Coleridge).

rhythm The recurrent alternation of accented (stressed) and unaccented syllables in the words and lines of a poem. This may be regular, in which case it is referred to as metre, or it may be irregular, as in free verse.

scene A self-contained episode in a work of drama or fiction.

search engine A research tool used to find information on the Internet or within databases. Typically, a search engine allows a user to access information using keywords.

sentence structure The types of sentences writers choose to use. Sentences can vary in length and may take the form of questions or commands. Writers may also vary sentence patterns or repeat them deliberately.

sestet *See* **stanza**.

set and set design In a dramatic work, the design and arrangement of physical elements such as scenery, props, lighting, and sound. Sets are crucial for the effective setting of works.

setting The place, time, and social circumstances in which a work is set. The place can be real or imaginary; the time can be past, present, or future, and may be a particular season or time of day (midsummer, or midnight) or a particular occasion (an eclipse, a battle). Setting helps create a mood or atmosphere. In a dramatic work, setting is also communicated by the set.

short story A fictional prose story shorter than a novel, having a plot that focuses on several characters and a single theme.

shot list A list of all the shots needed to create a completed video.

simile A device of figurative language in which one thing is compared to another using the words "like" or "as" ("Justice is like an open field"—Rita Joe). *See* **metaphor**.

soliloquy *See* **monologue**.

sonnet A single-stanza lyric poem of 14 lines with a particular rhyme pattern. Each line usually has five metrical units or feet.

spread A story or advertisement occupying two or more adjoining columns of a magazine or newspaper; two facing pages of a publication, such as a newspaper or magazine, viewed as a single unit.

stanza A group of lines making up a unit of a poem, often partly defined by rhyming words and signalled by a blank line in the printed text. Common stanza forms are couplets (two lines), quatrains (four lines), sestets (six lines), and octets (eight lines).

storyboard A graphic organizer used to plan the integration of visual, textual, and audio material in video production.

structure *See* **organization** *and* **sentence structure**.

style In written works, a writer's choice and arrangement of words. The main elements of style are **diction, figurative language**, and **sentence structure**. A writer's stylistic choices develop the narrator's voice and convey the writer's attitude toward the subject and the audience for a piece of writing.

subplot An author can use secondary action in a fictional or dramatic work to make an independent but related story—a subplot—that enhances the meaning of the main action or plot.

symbol An object or character that represents an idea, value, or condition beyond itself (a dove to represent peace, scales to represent justice).

tabloid A newspaper of small format giving news in condensed form, usually with illustrated, often sensational, material. At one time, the term *tabloid* simply referred to the size of paper that news was presented on, with a tabloid being the smaller paper size and a broadsheet the larger size. However, the term now refers more to the type of information presented in the paper. Tabloids are known to present celebrity gossip and other sensational stories, which more serious newspapers may not choose to present.

target audience The intended audience of a media production or presentation.

telegenic Like the term *photogenic*, a term to describe a person who looks good on a TV screen; suitable for televising.

text The print, oral, or visual form through which content is communicated.

theme The key point, or central message, of a work. This can be either explicit, as it usually is in nonfiction and media works (such as in a research or news report), or implicit, as it usually is in works of fiction and poetry. Also referred to as the main idea or thesis in non-fiction works.

thesis The main idea of a work, used especially with reference to works of nonfiction (such as formal essays and research reports). The thesis of a work is usually presented explicitly in a thesis statement at the beginning of the work.

third-person point of view When the narrator is not a character or person in the action and speaks of other characters or people in the story or text either by name or as "she," "he," or "they," the writer is telling the story from a third-person point of view. The third-person narrator is an unseen observer who moves freely through the story, presenting what happens from both the outside (setting and plot) and the inside (the feelings and thoughts of the characters). *See* **first-person point of view**.

tone In writing, a writer's attitude toward a subject or audience, conveyed through the writer's style.

transitions and transitional devices Editorial elements of a presentation used to signal changes between images or ideas (e.g., repetition, balance, fade-out, dissolve).

URL An abbreviation of Uniform Resource Locator or, more simply, an Internet address.

virtual reality A simulation of reality created by video and audio programming in which the user experiences and interacts with an artificial environment as though it were real.

visual production factors Visual devices used in video or verbal presentations to clarify ideas, communicate information, or maintain audience interest (e.g., colour, contrast).

voice In writing, a writer's or a character's distinctive style of expression.

voice production factors Devices used in verbal presentations to clarify ideas, communicate information, or maintain audience interest (e.g., volume, tone, stress).

Web page A page of text and/or graphics within a **Web site**. A single data file on the World Wide Web that can include text, sound, and graphics, as well as hypertext links to other files.

Web site A location on the World Wide Web consisting of a home page and other files connected to the home page by hyperlinks.

World Wide Web A network of linked hypertext files, stored on computers around the world and accessible by the **Internet**.

Acknowledgments

Text

"Fairy Tales" by Isaac Asimov from *Magic: The Final Fantasy Collection* © 1996 by Nightfall Inc. Published by permission of the Estate of Isaac Asimov c/o Ralph M. Vicinanza Ltd. **"A Television-Watching Artist"** is from *Unmapped Dreams* (Crossed Keys Publishing, 1989), copyright © 1989 by J.J. Steinfeld, and was first published, in a slightly different version, in *The Apostate's Tattoo* (Ragweed Press, 1983), copyright © 1983 by J.J. Steinfeld. Used by permission of the author. **"A Matter of Balance"** from *What Can't Be Changed Shouldn't Be Mourned.* Copyright © 1990 by W.D. Valgardson. Published in Canada by Douglas & McIntyre Ltd. Reprinted by permission of the publisher. **"The Wedding Gift"** by Thomas H. Raddall from *The Wedding Gift* is reprinted with permission of Dalhousie University. **"The Dead Child"** by Gabrielle Roy and translated by Joyce Marshall from *Best Canadian Short Stories.* Copyright: FONDS GABRIELLE ROY. **"A Bolt of White Cloth"** from *A Bolt of White Cloth* copyright © 1984 by Leon Rooke. Reprinted by permission of Stoddart Publishing Co. Limited. **"The Leaving"** from *The Leaving,* copyright © 1991 by Budge Wilson. Reprinted by permission of Stoddart Publishing Co. Limited. **"Wandering,"** copyright by Maureen Hynes, was first published in *Frictions II: Stories by Women,* Ed. Rhea Tregebov, Second Story Press, 1993. **"An Incident at Law"** by Anton Chekhov from *The Comic Stories* by Anton Chekhov, translated by Harvey Pitcher, copyright © 1999 by Harvey Pitcher and Patrick Miles, by permission of Ivan R. Dee, Publisher. **"Rudolph the Nasally Empowered Reindeer"** by James Finn Garner from *Politically Correct Holiday Stories For An Enlightened Yuletide Season* © 1995, published by Hungry Minds. **"The Peacemaker's Journey"** told by Chief Jake Swamp. Reprinted with permission. **"A Handful of Dates"** by Tayeb Salih. Translated by Denys Johnson-Davies. First published in *The Wedding of Zein and Other Stories.* Copyright © 1968 by Tayeb Salih. Reprinted with permission of the author. **"The Third Bank of the River"** by João Guimarães Rosa from *Modern Brazilian Short Stories,* English translation by William L. Grossman. **"The Fog Horn"** by Ray Bradbury. Reprinted by permission of Don Congdon Associates, Inc. Copyright © 1951 by the Curtis Publishing Co., renewed 1979 by Ray Bradbury. **"Marley's Ghost"** from *A Christmas Carol* by Charles Dickens. Excerpt from *Alias Grace* by Margaret Atwood. Copyright © 1996 O.W. Toad, Ltd. Used by permission from McClelland and Stewart, Ltd., *The Canadian Publishers.* **"Canadian English"** from *Nelson Canadian Dictionary of the English Language* © 1997. **"Reading, writing … and going to work"** by Bruce Owen from March 9, 1997 issue of the *Winnipeg Free Press.* Reprinted with permission. **"Teens' Top Homework Tool"** by Bonnie Sherman. Reprinted with permission of Bonnie Sherman, Ipsos Reid

Corporation. **"Makonnen Hannah"** by John Turner. Reprinted with permission of the author. **"A World Free of Poverty, 11/15/2000."** Copyright 2000 by the World Bank Group. Reprinted with permission of the World Bank via the Copyright Clearance Center. **"The Great Cheese-Off"** by Robin Harvey and David Graham from November 3, 2000 issue of the *The Toronto Star*. Reprinted with permission—The Toronto Star Syndicate. **"Thanks for Not Killing My Son"** by Rita Schindler from the December 30, 1990 issue of *The Toronto Star*. **"Man, You're a Great Player!"** by Gary Lautens from *Laughing With Lautens*. Reprinted with permission of the Estate of Gary Lautens. **"Finding Their Own Groove"** by San Grewal from the December 5, 2000 issue of the *The Toronto Star*. Reprinted with permission—The Toronto Star Syndicate. **"Back to the Future"** by Jill Lawless from *Wild East: Travels in the New Mongolia* © 2000, published by ECW Press. Reprinted with permission. **"Mother Tongue"** by Amy Tan. Copyright © 1990 by Amy Tan. First appeared in THE THREEPENNY REVIEW. Reprinted by permission of the author and the Sandra Dijkstra Literary Agency. **"Voices of the Grandmothers: Reclaiming a Métis Heritage"** by Christine Welsh. Originally appeared in *Canadian Literature No. 131 (1991)*. Reprinted with permission of the author. **"Better or Worse?"** by David Macfarlane. Excerpt from *The Danger Tree* copyright © 1991 by David Macfarlane. Reprinted by permission of Stoddart Publishing Co. Limited. **"My Old Newcastle"** by David Adams Richards. Reprinted with the permission of the author. **"The Vikings Are Coming ... Again!"** by Terry Moore and John Abbott from the *Viking Voyage 1000 website*. Copyright the Vinland Foundation. **"Turned on to Sound"** by Beverly Biderman. Reprinted with permission of the author. **"How to Read a Poem"** by Edward Hirsch. Excerpts adapted from *How to Read a Poem*, copyright © 1999 by Edward Hirsch, reprinted by permission of Harcourt, Inc. **"Winter Uplands"** by Archibald Lampman from *The Poems of Archibald Lampman* © 1974. **"Confessions of a Woman Who Burnt Down a Town"** by Afua Cooper from *Utterances and Incantations: Women, Poetry and Dub in the Black Diaspora* © 1999. Reprinted with permission of the author. **"Newfoundland Sealing Disaster"** by Michael Crummey from *Hard Light* © 1998, published by Brick Books. Reprinted with permission. **"The Hoop"** by Elizabeth Brewster is reprinted from *Selected Poems* by permission of Oberon Press. **"Lament for the Dorsets"** by Al Purdy from *Beyond Remembering: The Collected Poetry of Al Purdy*, Harbour 2000 © The Estate of Al Purdy. **"For My Great-Grandmother"** by Danielle Lagah from *Breaking the Surface: Poems* (Victoria, Sono Nis Press, 2000). **"Did I Miss Anything?"** by Tom Wayman from *The Astonishing Weight of the Dead* © 1994. Reprinted with permission of Harbour Publishing Company, Ltd. **"The Old Man's Lazy"** by Peter Blue Cloud from *New Voices of the Longhouse*, Clans of Many Nations, White Pine Press. **"Another Story Altogether"** by Anne Le Dressay from *Threshold: An Anthology of Contemporary Writing from Alberta*. Reprinted with permission of the author. **"Common Magic"** by Bronwen Wallace is reprinted from *Common Magic* by permission of

Oberon Press. **"Roller Coaster"** by Jay Ruzesky from *Painting the Yellow House Blue* © 1994 by Jay Ruzesky. Reprinted by permission of Stoddart Publishing Co. Ltd. **"A Kite Is a Victim"** by Leonard Cohen from *Stranger Music* by Leonard Cohen. Copyright © by Leonard Cohen and Leonard Cohen Stranger Music Inc. Used by permission from McClelland & Stewart, Ltd., *The Canadian Publishers*. **"The River-Merchant's Wife: A Letter"** by Li Po and translated by Shigeyoshi Obata © I. Lancashire, Dept. of English, University of Toronto. Reprinted with permission. **"On Monsieur's Departure"** by Elizabeth I. **"Sonnet CXVI: Let me not to the marriage ..."** by William Shakespeare. **"A Satirical Elegy on the Death of a Late Famous General"** by Jonathan Swift. **"Ozymandias"** by Percy Bysshe Shelley. **"If You Were Coming in the Fall"** by Emily Dickinson. **"The Wild Swans at Coole"** by William Butler Yeats from *The Wild Swans at Coole and Other Poems* by William Butler Yeats. **"Birches"** by Robert Frost from *The Poetry of Robert Frost* edited by Edward Connery Lathem, © 1969 by Henry Holt & Co., LLC. Reprinted with permission of Henry Holt & Co., LLC. **"My Song"** by Rabindranath Tagore. **"Where Are Those Songs?"** by Micere Githae Mugo from *Daughter of My People, Sing!* by Micere Githae Mugo, Kenya Literature Bureau, 1976. **"Colombe"** by Kamau Brathwaite from *Middle Passages*, copyright © 1993 by Kamau Brathwaite. Reprinted by permission of New Directions Publishing Corp. **"The Prison Cell"** by Mahmoud Darwish and translated by Ben Bennani from *Bread, Hashish and Moon: Four Modern Arab Poets*. Reprinted with permission. **"Little Ruth"** by Yehuda Amichai from *Yehuda Amichai: A Life of Poetry 1948–1994* by Yehuda Amichai. Reprinted by permission of HarperCollins Publishers, Inc. **"The End and the Beginning"** from *View With A Grain of Sand*, copyright © 1993 by Wislawa Szymborska, English translation by Stanislaw Baranczak and Clare Cavanagh copyright © 1995 by Harcourt, Inc., reprinted by permission of the publisher. **"Scribe's Paradox, or The Mechanical Rabbit"** by Michael Feingold. Copyright © 1995 by Michael Feingold. All rights reserved. Reprinted by permission of International Creative Management, Inc. **"The Bush-Ladies"** by Molly Thom. Reprinted with permission of Scirocco Drama/J. Gordon Shillingford Publishing. **"Hunger Striking"** by Kit Brennan from *Magpie; Having; Hunger Striking* by Kit Brennan, published by Nuage Editions, 1999. Reprinted with permission. **"Land of Trash"** by Ian Tamblyn. "Land of Trash" was first produced by Green Thumb Theatre for Young People (Vancouver, BC). Rights to produce "Land of Trash," in whole or in part, in any medium by any group, amateur or professional, must be obtained in advance from Green Thumb Theatre for Young People, 1885 Venables Street, Vancouver BC V5L 2H6. Tel: (604) 254-4055; Fax: (604) 251-7002. **"One Ocean"** by Betty Quan. Originally broadcast on radio by CBC–*Morningside*. Copyright © 1994 by Betty Quan. **"Listening to Marshall McLuhan"** reprinted with permission from the creators of The Ontario Media Literacy Homepage. **"Since You Asked"** by Pamela Wallin from *Since You Asked,* published by Random House of Canada. **"Move East"** by Rick Mercer extracted from

Streeters: Rants and Raves from "This Hour Has 22 Minutes" by Rick Mercer. Copyright © 1998. Reprinted by permission of Doubleday, a division of Random House of Canada Limited. **"Eulogy for Canada's Unknown Soldier"** by Adrienne Clarkson. Published by permission of Her Excellency the Right Honourable Adrienne Clarkson, Governor General of Canada. **"Blood and Laundry: An Interview with Margaret Atwood"** by Laura Miller. This article first appeared in Salon.com, at http://www.Salon.com. An online version remains in the Salon archives. Reprinted with permission. **"But I Love Him ..."** by Jennifer Bain from the November 3, 2000 issue of *The Toronto Star*. Reprinted with permission—The Toronto Star Syndicate. **"Titanic: Cheers and Jeers"** by Bruce Kirkland and Tilman Ganzhorn. ("A Spectacular Voyage" by Bruce Kirkland from the December 19, 1997 issue of *The Toronto Sun*. "Web review" by Tilman Ganzhorn). Reprinted with permission. **"Seaman"** by Bret Dawson from the August 7, 2000 issue of *The Toronto Star*. Reprinted with permission of the author. **"Photographs and the Truth"** by Marcelle Lapow Toor from *The Desktop Designer's Illustration Handbook*. Reprinted by permission of John Wiley & Sons, Inc. **"Animal Magnetism"** by Peter Goddard from the October 28, 2000 issue of *The Toronto Star*. Reprinted with permission—The Toronto Star Syndicate. **"How to Read a Sign"** by Paco Underhill. Reprinted with the permission of Simon & Schuster from WHY WE BUY by Paco Underhill. Copyright © 1999 by Obat, Inc. **"Advocacy and Marketing on the Web"** by Crawford Kilian from *Writing for the Web* by Crawford Kilian. Reprinted by permission of International Self-Counsel Press. **"Videogaming: An Interview with J.C. Herz"** by Dave Thomer, published by Omni Magazine. **"Angels Online"** by Hal Karp. Reprinted with permission from the April 2000 *Reader's Digest*. Copyright © 2000 by The Reader's Digest Assn., Inc. **"Finders Keepers"** by Elizabeth Larsen from the May/June 1999 issue of *Utne Reader*. **"Kids and TV Violence"** by Kathleen McDonnell from *Kid Culture: Children and Adults and Popular Culture*. Published by Second Story Press, Toronto.

Visuals

Page 2 Myron J. Dorf/The Stock Market/First Light; **Page 18** From the Archives of the Carrie M. McLain Memorial Museum, Nome, Alaska; **Page 45** © Hulton-Deutsch Collection/CORBIS/Magma; **Page 75** Mel Curtis/PhotoDisc; **Page 81** Bettman/CORBIS/Magma; **Page 85** Steve Austin/CORBIS/Magma; **Page 96** CORBIS/Magma; **Page 108** Russell Illiq/PhotoDisc; **Page 116** Archivo Iconografico/CORBIS/Magma; **Page 131** Book cover courtesy of Seal Books/Random House of Canada Limited; **Page 140** Todd Davidson/Image Bank; **Page 145** Steve Mason/PhotoDisc; **Page 147** Joe Bryksa/Winnipeg Free Press; **Page 151** Anthony de Ridder; **Page 155** Robert Nelson; **Pages 169 and 171** The Toronto Star; **Page 176** Eyewire; **Page 180** Superstock; **Page 183** David South/ECW Press; **Page 188** © Jonathan Nourok/Photo Edit; **Page 199** Hudson's Bay Company Archives, Provincial Archives of Manitoba;

Page 203 left © Raymond Gehman/CORBIS/Magma, right Ron Pozzer/CP Picture Archive; **Page 212** © Ted Spiegel/CORBIS/Magma; **Page 222** Al Francekevich/The Stock Market/First Light; **Page 227** Superstock; **Page 235** Canadian Museum of Civilization, image number S90-3040; **Page 240** Doug Menuez/PhotoDisc; **Pages 248 and 249** David Toase/PhotoDisc; **Page 256** © Michael S. Yamashita/CORBIS/Magma; **Page 258** Arte & Immagini srl/CORBIS/Magma; **Page 260** © CORBIS/Magma; **Pages 264 and 265** CORBIS/Magma; **Pages 274 and 275** Geostock/PhotoDisc; **Page 276** © Bettman/CORBIS/Magma; **Page 286** William Whitehurst/The Stock Market/First Light; **Page 294** Gordon King Photography; **Page 306** Melinda Stevens as Nuke, in the grade 11 production of "Land of Trash," January 17, 2001, Murdoch MacKay Collegiate Institute, Winnipeg, MB. Photo by Dave Normandale; **Page 328** © Sakamoto Photo Research Laboratory/CORBIS/Magma; **Page 334** Lightscapes/The Stock Market/First Light; **Page 337** Peter Bregg/CP Picture Archive; **Page 342** Fred Chartrand/CP Picture Archive; **Page 347** Herbert Proepper/CP Picture Archive; **Page 354** From the book BUT I LOVE HIM. Copyright © 2000 by Jill Murray. Reprinted by permission of HarperCollins Publishers. Photograph by Elizabeth Zeschin; **Page 356** Photofest; **Page 362** Reprinted with permission from Sega; **Pages 365–368** From *The Desktop Designer's Illustration Handbook* by Marcelle Lapow Toor; **Pages 371 and 372** Courtesy of TELUS Mobility; **Page 395** PhotoDisc; **Page 397** Karl Richter; **Page 401** PhotoDisc; **Page 406** CORBIS/Magma; **Page 413** "Oedipus and the Sphinx." Giraudon/Art Resource, NY. **Page 414** "October" by Paul, Herman, and Jean Limbourg. Scala/Art Resource, NY. **Page 415** "Women Returning Home at Sunset" by Katsushika Hokusai. Honolulu Academy of Arts, Gift of James A. Michener, 1987 (20,082). **Page 416** Alex Colville, "Couple on Bridge," 1992. Courtesy of AC Fine Art. **Page 417** "Housepost at Xwatis" by C.F. Newcomb dated 1922. Courtesy of the Royal British Columbia Museum, Victoria, British Columbia (negative # RBCM PN 828-A). Emily Carr, "Zunoqua of the Cat Village," 1931, oil on canvas, Vancouver Art Gallery, Emily Carr Trust VAG 42.3.21 (Photo: Trevor Mills). **Page 418** "BMW Art Car" by Esther Mahlangu, courtesy of BMW. **Page 419** "Eggs in an Egg Crate" by Mary Pratt. Reprinted with permission. **Page 420** "Flight of an Eagle" by Jane Ash Poitras. Reprinted with permission. **Page 421** "Canada and the Call (1914)" by J.E.H. Macdonald. Catalogue number 19940018-001. Copyright Canadian War Museum (C.W.M.). **Page 422** All images relating to Canadian coins are copyrighted Royal Canadian Mint and are used by permission of Royal Canadian Mint. **Page 423** "The Ratings Crunch" by Brian Hughes from the November 7, 2000 issue of *The Toronto Star*. Reprinted with permission—The Toronto Star Syndicate. **Page 424** "Equal Exchange" advertisement courtesy of Equal Exchange. **Page 425** "Zits" by Jerry Scott and Jim Borgman. Reprinted with special permission of King Features Syndicate. **Page 426** "Toyota" advertisement courtesy of Saatchi & Saatchi, Los Angeles. **Page 427** "Platinum Protection" courtesy of Procter & Gamble Canada. **Page 428** "Inuksuk postcard." Photo from Corel.